MERRION
HISTORY OF THE
CRICKET CLUB (1892-2010)

MERRION

HISTORY OF THE
CRICKET CLUB (1892-2010)

ALAN LITTLE
& DANNY PARKINSON

Saltwater

Dedicated to the memory of Rollie Shortt, Cecil Little, Jack O'Donnell.

First published 2011

Saltwater Publishing Ltd
119 Lower Baggot Street
Dublin 2, Ireland
www.saltwater.ie

British Library Cataloguing in Publication Data.
A catalogue record for this book is available from the British Library.
ISBN 978-1-908366-02-3

Printed and bound in the UK by the MPG Books Group, Bodmin and King's Lynn
Typesetting and origination by Megan Sheer
Cover design by www.sinedesign.net.

CONTENTS

APPENDICES

'ON BEING GIVEN OUT LEG BEFORE WICKET WHEN PLAYING FOR DENMARK AGAINST A NEIGHBOURING STATE.'

Hamlet: 'I'm out, Polonius.'
Polonius (batting at the other end): 'I fear so, sire.
Or so the umpire doth declaim.'
Hamlet: 'Then I must go; yet 'tis a monstrous thing
That all this great and most momentous issue
Should hang upon a churlish umpire's nod.
(Enters pavilion)
How now, my lords. The ball hath bias on it,
And if my leg hath been in front, as 'twas not,
Would not have hit the sticks, no, not by yards.
It did not pitch straight; it was rising high.
Besides, the man was bowling round the wicket.
Yea, I could summon up a thousand reasons,
Which being pondered on, conspire to show
The verdict of yon purblind idiot false.
Well, well, the thing's an allegory.
How accident doth await on carefulness
And all precaution used. I took "one leg",
I wisely questioned if my toes were clear,
And all for this! ... Oh, Sirs, the pity of it!
I was fairly set as an oak tree
In the sylvan glade. The ball to me appeared
As large as the full harvest moon,
Sailing above the straw-stack. I had meant
To score a hundred, when that echoing yell,
Both from bowler and the wicket-keeper
(A prearranged duet of knavery)
Checked me in mid-success and cut me down.
What weak-kneed umpire could resist that roar?
There's not a doubt on it; I was bustled out.
Give me a pipe; I'll drown my grief in smoke.
This cricket is a passing beastly game.'

Attributed to Patrick Henry Pearse Waldron.

INTRODUCTION

This is the story of how a small and relatively unsuccessful Junior cricket club, born of the British Civil Service in Ireland, grew into one of the largest clubs on the island, capable of winning the Irish Senior Cup in 2010. Rarely could a sports club have suffered so many slings and arrows of outrageous fortune: from its difficult early years through to Senior status in 1926; from the glorious double in 1940 to the subsequent twenty successful years; from the barren decades of the '60s, '70s and '80s, when its 1st XI won nothing, to the threatened return to Junior status in 1994, which was averted thanks to the support of good friends like Pembroke; to the final years of recovery, growth and success, due chiefly to the efforts of a few determined individuals, a legend who became a coach, one exceptional professional and a prolific cricketing dynasty.

In the absence of hard data for the early years up to 1925, the research for this book depended largely on reports in the *Freeman's Journal*, *The Irish Times*, *Sunday Independent*, *The Irish Field* and John Lawrence's *Handbook Of Cricket In Ireland, 1865-1881*. Reference was also made to *Thom's Directory* to confirm the identity of certain Land Commission players. Although much of the Junior cricket played in those days went unreported in detail, most of the fixtures were documented, giving us the nucleus of each season's span.

The origin myths about Merrion Cricket Club are dealt with in Chapter 1. The true foundation date of the club is 1906, although our clear ancestors, the Land Commission Cricket Club, started playing in 1892. Chapter 2 details all reported games played by the Land Commission Club between 1892-1900 and the twenty years of Merrion as a Junior club (1906-1925), when they played home games at Dolphin's Barn in 1906 and 1907, before moving to Anglesea Road in 1908. Chapters 3 and 4 focus on the development of the Senior side from 1926-2010, and summarise the achievements of the Junior teams. These Junior results are necessarily incomplete in some years, as not all cricket matches were reported in newspapers. The *Club Notes* sections include all available minutes of meetings from January-December for each year. Unfortunately, the minutes of club meetings were not available prior to 1945, although some financial details were. Minutes for meetings from 1964-1973 also appear to have gone missing. The history of women's cricket in Merrion is summarised in a separate chapter. The book contains all the trophy-winning team photographs that could be found, including Senior teams that won or were runners-up in competitions and winning Junior sides. Other teams are depicted in collages. Full scorebook details are provided only for all Senior men's trophy-winning games.

All men's statistics are included in the Appendices, and are based upon the Leinster Senior Leagues (both short and long) and the Leinster Senior Cup, from the beginning of 1926 until 30 September 2010. The Irish Senior Cup, Beckett Cup and 20/20 competitions are not included, nor are they a part of any fixture count. Friendlies obviously don't count either, although the

1930/31 'club games', when the Senior League was in abeyance, are included. Players get no points for a 'no result' fixture. For most of the tables, professionals are excluded. They have their own tables. The Merrion profiles are driven by these statistics, except for those players who helped to start the club and to bring it to Senior status, such as Bill Rumney and Fred Fryer. Also included are all internationals, 1sts captains, certain exceptional performers such as Jimmy McAlinden and Gerry Doyle (all 10 wickets in Junior matches), outstanding servants such as Tom Quinn and John Heavey Snr, who held office for over five years, one groundsman, one scorer, one coach, one gatekeeper, Merrion's best woman cricketer and the only Junior captain to bring home more than five trophies. Our apologies go to the many unnamed stalwarts who did not score 1,000 runs, take 100 wickets, catch more than 50 batsmen in the outfield or

Standing: Rollie Short, Cecil Little. Sitting: Jack O'Donnell.

catch/stump 25 batsmen for Merrion men's 1sts in Leinster Senior cricket over the years, and others who have given their unrecognised service to the club. We know who you are.

Our grateful acknowledgements and thanks go to the staff of the National Library, the National Archives and the National Photographic Archives. The list of people who helped us with the source material and their memories of cricket and Merrion is long, and includes: Derek Scott, Anthony Morrissey, Gerard Siggins, Eddie Lewis, John Heavey Jnr, Denis McKenna, Jack McConnell, Gerry Byrne, Peter Geoffroy, Paddy Waldron Junior, Mark Rutledge, Brendan Curley, Gerry Doyle, Michael Sharpe, Mary Sharpe, Dermot Soraghan, Vinny Holloway, Paul Warren, Pat Kehely, Niall Morrissey, Tom McGeady, Adam O'Keeffe, Angus Hancock, Robert Quinn, Tommy McAlinden Jnr, Rodney Bernstein, Niall Tempany, Barry Little, Rosalinde McCartan, Eleanor O'Donnell, Gerry Duffy, Angus Fleming, Jim Joyce, Oliver Rye, Noel Hayden, Derek Hayden, Michael Boyle, Chandra Aramalla, Gary Morris, Mark Forbes, Des Murray, Liam Casey, Eddie Bohane, Jimmy O'Clerigh, Alex Burns, Paddy Willis, Norman Reeves, Stewart Kenny, Stephen King, Kevin Allwright, Jim Walsh, Andy Irvine, Kevin O'Herlihy, Isobel Joyce, Damian Joyce, Dominick Joyce, Gus Joyce, Ray Clarke, Simon Hederman, Will Houston, Damian Poder, Kade Beasley, Jeff Short, Tikitsh Patel, John Anderson, Derek Kilpatrick, Peter Hayes, Fergus O'Flynn, John O'Hagan, Anne Keogh, Andrew Nixon, Robbie Stanton, Ken McDonald, Peter McWilliam, and Michael O'Doherty.

1

ORIGIN MYTHS

1.1. THE FIRST MERRION CRICKET CLUB: 1864

'What's in a name? that which we call a rose
by any other name would smell as sweet'

Shakespeare (or Marlowe, Bacon, Jonson…?)

The name Merrion, in the context of nineteenth-century Dublin City, could mean several things: a street, a road, a square, a district, a hall, a cricket club – or indeed … *several* clubs. The earliest record of Merrion as a cricket club occurs in Anthony Morrissey and Colm Magee's fine history of the Civil Service Cricket Club, *First Class Service*, wherein it is stated that, 'J. Doran scored the Club's first fifty, with 62 against Merrion on June 18th 1864'.

Apart from the regular duels of Phoenix v. Leinster, Dublin University v. the Curragh Brigade, the Durham Light Infantry v. the 13th Hussars (where a military band might attend), the garrison sport of cricket was a casual affair in those days of British rule, with a variable number of players per side, often moving from team to team. Many of the smaller clubs played their friendly games – there were no league structures then – on rough pitches in the Nine Acres of the Phoenix Park, as did the first Merrion.

According to the *Freeman's Journal*, in the year that overarm bowling became legal, Merrion played fourteen games, winning five, losing eight, and drawing one. Most games were of two innings, between the hours of 12p.m. and 7p.m., but if the 2nd innings had not finished by the designated time, the match was won on the 1st innings. If the 1st innings was not concluded by both sides, a draw in favour of the higher score was the result. Winning the toss was vital. That meant you might get to bat twice, and your opponents only once. But it was a double-edged sword. An innings could be a short affair, due to the appalling state of the pitch (which would probably have been prepared with a scythe), and a two-digit total was not unusual, with Ernest Extras often top-scoring:

Opponent	Result	Mer. 1st	Opp. 1st	Mer. 2nd	Opp. 2nd	Best Batting: Runs	Best Bowling: Wickets
Civil Service	Lost	50	73		76/9	J. Edge: 20	C. Minchin: 13
Civil Service ~	Lost	25	157	52/6		S. Williams: 30*	C. Minchin: 8
12th Regiment	Lost	48	72		60/9	S. Williams: 13	C. Minchin: 9
Mr Barlow's XI	Won	52	52	37	26	J. Edge: 16	S. Williams: 12
Leinster 2nds	Lost	37	95	84	27/2	C. Minchin: 26	S. Williams: 10

Leinster 1sts	Lost	83	78	52	61	A. Meldon: 32	Minchin/Williams: 8 each
Roebuck	Lost	84	114			B. Sharp: 15	S. Williams: 5
Roebuck	Lost	29	75	16/5	75	E. Extras: 17	J. Warren: 10
Bray	Won	107	85		66/5	G. Hanlon: 20	J. Warren: 5
Ormonde	Won	124	55			J. Crawley: 35	Minchin/Warren: 4 each
Ormonde	Drawn	144	55/7			T. Kennedy: 26	J. Warren: 4
Sandycove	Lost	57	102	73	14/1	A. Meldon: 27	C. Minchin: 7
Sandycove	Won	68	66	51	36	C. Minchin: 44	C. Minchin: 10
Civil Service	Won	76	21	16/3	79	J. Caffrey: 18	C. Minchin: 8

Although it is tempting to suggest that this Merrion team was the precursor of our present club, there is no evidence to support such a notion, bar the name. The team disbanded and its better players went to other clubs the following year – Crawley and Williams to Leinster, and Minchin to Malahide – where they were to remain for years to come. The unfortunately named Edge brothers vanished altogether.

NB Other teams playing at this time: Rutland, Emerald, Portobello, Powerscourt.

1.2. MERRION WANDERERS: 1873-1875

The next record of a team called Merrion playing cricket was reported in John Lawrence's *Handbook Of Cricket In Ireland, 1865-1881*. Merrion Wanderers played fifteen away games over a three-year period, winning six, losing eight, and drawing one. These games took place during the months of August and September, suggesting a casual vacation side. The team was organised by Beresford B. MacMahon, Baronet of the United Kingdom, whose family owned thirty-two acres of prime Dublin South property, including the Bloomfield estate in the district of Merrion, which was purchased in 1960 by Elm Park Golf Club. The highlight of the Wanderers' brief innings was undoubtedly the battle against Charles Stuart Parnell's XI on 5 September 1874 at Avondale:

Opponent	Result	MW 1st	Opp. 1st	MW 2nd	Opp. 2nd	Best Batting: Runs	Best Bowling: Wickets
Academic Institute	Won						
Camolin	Won	129	32		57/7	S. Dickson Smith: 51	
Rathfarnham	Won	136	103			G. Rae: 45	V. Rae: 5
Charleville	Lost						
Malahide	Won						
Rathmines School	Lost	36	36	19	24	M. Egan: 15	
Navan	Lost	107	168			J. Frazer: 44	
Pembroke	Won	90	74		30/2	S. Chatterton: 37	
Kingstown School	Lost	49	118			L. MacMahon: 10	
Mr Parnell's XI	Lost	22	45	38/4	65	Revd J.C. Creed: 7	
Meath	Won	79	76			L. MacMahon: 27*	
Navan	Lost						
H. Plunkett's XI	Lost						
St Columba's Coll.	Drawn					J. Frazer: 86	
Malahide	Lost						

A suggestion had been made that the Merrion Wanderers team constituted members of the Church Temporalities Commission, a precursor of the Land Commission, whose offices were also at 24 Upper Merrion Street, but there is little hard evidence to support this. None of the team are listed in *Thom's Directory* as working for the Temporalities Commission during those years. None of the players reappear in the Land Commission team seventeen years later. Anyway, Merrion Wanderers disbanded after 1875, with players like the aptly named Revd J.C. Creed moving to Lansdowne, and thence to Phoenix, where he was still to be found, thirty years later, nurdling away.

NB Other teams playing at this time: Stoics, Nondescripts, Eblana, Esoterics.

1.3. CHURCH TEMPORALITIES OFFICE: 1876

One short record in *The Irish Times* showed a Church Temporalities XI playing Dublin University 2nds in the College Park on 24 June 1876. It was a rather one-sided match, with the visiting side enjoying quite a long day in the field:

Opponent	Result	CTO 1st	Opp. 1st	CTO 2nd	Opp. 2nd	Best Batting: Runs	Best Bowling: Wickets
DU 2nds	Drawn	25/4	387			J. Dean: 14	

This match might be regarded as a slender link in the chain to the Land Commission Cricket Team, sixteen years later, and thence to the present club, but for the obvious lack of continuity.

NB Other teams playing at this time: Mountpleasant, Arbutus, Emeriti, Mountmerrion.

1.4. THE SECOND MERRION CRICKET CLUB: 1881-1884

Another deceptive Merrion cropped up in 1881, playing two games against a Catholic University High School 2nds. This same team played one game in 1882 against Irishtown. There was also note of the following fixture: Drumcondra 2nds v. Merrion 2nds, Nine Acres, Phoenix Park on 22 May 1884:

Opponent	Result	Mer. 1st	Opp. 1st	Mer. 2nd	Opp. 2nd	Best Batting: Runs	Best Bowling: Wickets
CUS 2nds	Lost	29	58	45	19/1	B. Sinclair: 18	B. Sinclair: 3
CUS 2nds	Lost	35	62	47	25/5	H. Owens: 16	E. Skyne: 4
Irishtown	Lost	15	116	20		J. Dudgeon: 10*	W. Ritchie: 3

As none of these players' names correlated with the Merrion Wanderers or Land Commission teams (1sts or 2nds), or were listed in *Thom's Directory* as working for the Land Commission, it was assumed that this occasional side had been named after the district and bore no relationship to the present club. Another rose by any other name.

NB Other teams playing at this time: Garville, Annesley, Shamrock, Inchicore.

1.5. MERRION SQUARE: 1900-1901

The final *non sequitur* in the history of Merrion Cricket Club was Merrion Square. On 4 August 1900, they played a game against a Mr C. Allen's XI – the same day the Land Commission played Richmond Asylum. Seven friendly away games were recorded in 1900 and 1901, before Merrion Square also fell off the radar:

Opponent	Result	Mrs. 1st	Opp. 1st	Mrs. 2nd	Opp. 2nd	Best Batting: Runs	Best Bowling: Wickets
Mr C. Allen's XI	Won	42	30	33	40		C. Donovan: 10
Sandymount 3rds	Lost	10	38				
Sandymount 3rds	Won	62	19	14/0	52		
Newtown	Won	134	60			C. Donovan: 41	C. Donovan: 6
DU Long Vacation	Lost	70	135			C. Donovan: 16	W. Coffey: 6
Belgrave	Won	32	27				
Rathmines CBB	Lost	19	72				

It has been suggested that the Land Commission *became* Merrion Square after it was forced to disband in 1900, but this is far from the truth. The team didn't reform immediately under a different name and at a different location. Many of the Commission players went to other clubs, including one or two to Merrion Square, which already existed, probably made up of members from other government departments based in that location. And as none of the names correlated with subsequent Merrion names (1sts or 2nds), it was assumed that, again, this casual team had nothing to do with the history of the present club, bar the name.

NB Other teams playing at this time: Calaroga, Rapperes, Videsians, Grangecon.

The Land Commission offices, 24 Upper Merrion Street.

2

THE EARLY YEARS

2.1. THE LAND COMMISSION: 1892-1900

When the Church of Ireland was disestablished by an Act of Parliament in 1869, it was the largest landlord in Ireland, with about 11,000 tenants on 900 different estates. On disestablishment, its property was transferred to the Commissioners of Church Temporalities in Ireland, previously known as the Ecclesiastical Commissioners, who were based at 24 Upper Merrion Street. (This was the former home of Arthur Wellesley, 1st Duke of Wellington, who had once proudly declaimed, 'My successes in the Army are owing in great measure to the manly sports of Great Britain, and one sport above all – cricket.') The duties of the Church Temporalities Commission (Appendix A) continued throughout the 1870s, until the Irish Land Commission was formed in 1881 in response to the 1879 Land War and the demands of Michael Davitt and the Wicklow cricketer Charles Stewart Parnell for fairer rents through the Land League. The Temporalities Commission was then dissolved, and the new Land Commission assumed its remaining functions, inheriting some of its clerical staff and its headquarters.

Although the foundation date of Merrion Cricket Club has been believed for many years to be 1879, coinciding with the formation of the Land Commission, the two-year gap and the absence of any reported Land Commission cricket fixtures between 1879 and 1891 (during which the annual Foxrock Cricket Club end-of-season Married v. Singles match received the full attention of the press) suggest a different story. We must wait until 1892, the year the Land Commission Department was organised on a permanent basis, and the Land Registry was created to provide a system of compulsory registration of land titles, before the modest beginnings of Land Commission cricket are reported, encouraged by the newly appointed Judicial Commissioner, Judge Thomas Edmond Bewley.

As many of the better cricketers in this single department of the British Civil Service would have opted to play for 'Civil Service', it took a while for the Land Commission to make its mark in Irish cricket. The team was created from junior clerical staff – second-division and third-class clerks – and played mainly friendly cricket against the 2nds and 3rds of stronger clubs, before winning the Leinster Junior Cup in 1897, 1899, 1900. (Years later, this knockout competition – 'Junior Cup, Leinster Branch, Irish Cricket Union' – was renamed as the 'Intermediate Cup'.) Their home ground was on the back pitch of the old rugby union ground at Lansdowne Road, which had originally been created as a multi-sports venue – the Irish Champion Athletic Club – incorporating athletics, croquet, archery, tennis, soccer, rugby and cricket. A steady upward graph through the 1890s would describe their progress, which ended in 1900 with close games against Phoenix and Civil Service, the strongest teams of their day.

The best cricketer to play for the Land Commission was Frances Henry Browning, although he only played a couple of times against Phoenix, in 1893 and 1894. Obviously he was guesting to even out the sides, as he went on to play most of his cricket for Phoenix and Civil Service and captain the Gentlemen Of Ireland many times. His sad demise is recorded in *First Class Service*:

> *In his later years Browning became a member of the Irish Volunteer Defence Corps, a benign Home Guard style organisation for men who were over the military age. The Corps wore Khaki and the King's Insignia, 'G.R.', thus becoming locally known as the 'Gorgeous Wrecks'. The 'Wrecks' were returning from a route march on Easter Monday, 1916, and as they trudged back over Mount Street Bridge, unaware of the Rising that had taken place, nearby Rebels opened fire on them. Poor Browning was hit in the volley of shots and died from his wounds two days later, aged forty eight.*

However, the true mainstays of this team during 1892-1900 (part of the 'golden age of cricket') were four young locals: all-rounders J.A. Swaine (Record Dept. attendant); A.P. Ross (third-class clerk); W.E. Callan (third-class clerk) and W.A. Robinson (abstractor, data collector). Their first game, against the vulgarly named Cursis Stream – the Dublin and Lucan tramway – was reported in *The Irish Times* of Monday 4 July 1892, 'Played by permission on the Lucan ground on Saturday and resulted in a win for Cursis Stream by 20 runs, chiefly owing to the bowling of Luckhurst who secured 10 wickets for 25 runs.'

NB The fixtures below represent matches detailed in *The Irish Times* and *Freeman's Journal*. Other games were noted as fixtures, but the results were not reported. Unless otherwise stated, the games were all friendlies, or 'club games' as they were called then. Seconds' fixtures are denoted in the opponent column by an asterisk (*).

1892: LAND COMMISSION CRICKET BEGINS

Junior: fixtures 4, reported 4, won 2, lost 2. It is a slow start:

Opponent	Result	LC 1st	Opp. 1st	LC 2nd	Opp. 2nd	Best Batting: Runs	Best Bowling: Wickets
Cursis Stream	Lost	64	84				
Leinster 2nds	Lost	27	220/9	46		M. White: 17	W.A. Robinson: 5
GS & WR	Won	97	63			C. Rooke: 32	J.A. Swaine: 5
Corrig Long Vacation	Won	66	35		35	W.A. Robinson: 27	A.E. White: 10

1893: F.H. BROWNING GUESTS FOR LAND COMMISSION

Junior: fixtures 18, reported 13, won 7, lost 5, drawn 1. But getting better. M. White scores a century against Leinster 3rds. A.P. Ross scores 63 against Monkstown. B. McDonnell takes 8 wickets against the Munster & Leinster Bank. F.H. Browning takes 7 wickets against Phoenix:

Opponent	Result	LC 1st	Opp. 1st	LC 2nd	Opp. 2nd	Best Batting: Runs	Best Bowling: Wickets
Wanderers	Lost	55	144			M. White: 14	W.A. Robinson: 7
Phoenix	Lost	83	191			F.H. Browning: 26	F.H. Browning: 7
Cursis Stream	Won	183/6	100			M. Ball: 43	A.E. White: 4

Clontarf	Lost	40	99	19/3		A.P. Ross: 28	A.P. Ross: 6
Cursis Stream	Won	73	52	65		E.J. Gilligan: 22	Robinson/Swaine: 4 each
Monkstown	Won	125/2	104			A.P. Ross: 63	
GS & WR	Won	62	47	39/7		J.A. Swaine: 28	J.A. Swaine: 6
Munster/Leinster Bank	Won	146	36		23/3	M. White: 61*	B. McDonnell: 8
North Strand	Won	72	34	33/5		G.A. Leech: 19	
Leinster 3rds	Won	184	170		48/1	M. White: 111	J.A. Swaine: 4
Pembroke 2nds	Lost	30	70			W.A. Robinson: 6	W.A. Robinson: 7
Clontarf	Lost	37	60	48/7		M. White: 37	A.E. White: 4
Dolphin	Drawn	98/6	66/6			G.A. Leech: 40	

1894: A YEAR OF GROWTH

Junior: fixtures 24, reported 16, won 5, lost 9, drawn 2. First mention of a Land Commission 2nds fixture, against Dublin County Boy's Brigade. A.P. Ross represents the Land Commission on the Leinster Branch of the Irish Cricket Union. F.H. Browning scores a century against Phoenix. M. White scores 74 against Vincent's Hospital. W.A. Robinson emerges as a bowling force, with 51 wickets:

Opponent	Result	LC 1st	Opp. 1st	LC 2nd	Opp. 2nd	Best Batting: Runs	Best Bowling: Wickets
Phoenix	Won	192/3	104			F.H. Browning: 115	W.A. Robinson: 4
Dundrum	Lost	68	119			W.B. Stewart: 18	F. O'Carroll. 6
Valuation Office	Won	58	34	44/8	51/4	W.A. Robinson: 27	J.A. Swaine: 8
Pembroke 2nds	Drawn	126/8	74/7			W. Searer: 32*	F. O'Carroll: 5
Ordnance Survey	Lost	27	110	22/8		R. Esmonde: 14	W.A. Robinson: 5
Leinster 2nds	Won	76	54	134		A.P. Ross: 47	F. O'Carroll: 8
St Columba's Coll.	Drawn	97/8	72/5			H.E. Marchant: 28	W.A. Robinson: 2
Chapelizod	Won	94	70			H.E. Marchant: 25	W.A. Robinson: 5
North Strand 1sts	Lost	28	123			W.A. Robinson: 18	Latimer: 3
Vincent's Hospital	Won	145	83			M. White: 74	W.A. Robinson: 6
North Strand 1sts	Lost	25	58			W.A. Robinson: 9	
Co. Wicklow	Lost	70	151			W.A. Robinson: 8	W.A. Robinson: 6
GS & WR	Lost	41	102			C.V. Rooke: 10	W.A. Robinson: 4
Ballyarthur	Lost	54	59	72	103	M. White: 40	W.A. Robinson: 8
Leinster 2nds	Lost	33	144	96		C.V. Rooke: 42	W.A. Robinson: 4
Clontarf	Lost	29	54		48/7	C.V. Rooke: 10	W.A. Robinson: 7

1895: JUNIOR CUP RUNNERS-UP

Junior: fixtures 39, reported 24, won 12, lost 11, drawn 1. Season starts badly, but improves. Robinson takes 93 wickets. A.P. Ross scores 93 runs against Phoenix. The Leinster Junior Cup is inaugurated. Land Commission lose the Junior Cup final to Athy:

Opponent	Result	LC 1st	Opp. 1st	LC 2nd	Opp. 2nd	Best Batting: Runs	Best Bowling: Wickets
Phoenix	Lost	193	212/3			A.P. Ross: 93	
Civil Service	Lost	78	82			J.H. Brennan: 18	W.A. Robinson: 7
GS & WR 2nds*	Lost	42	68	43	26/1	G. Searight: 16	

Opponent	Result					Best Batting: Runs	Best Bowling: Wickets
GS & WR	Lost	54	88			J. Maher: 18	J.A. Swaine: 3
Sandymount	Won	90	43		62/8	S. Lawrenson: 13*	W.A. Robinson: 9
Dollymount*	Lost	44	79			G. McAlister: 15*	E.J. Gilligan: 4
Co. Wicklow	Lost	41	170			F. Crosbie: 8	W.A. Robinson: 6
St Columba's Coll.	Lost	66	105			C.V. Rooke: 27	W.A. Robinson: 5
Clontarf	Lost	38	64		71/1	W. Callan: 10	Callan/Robinson: 5 each
Workingmen	Won	149/6	28			F.W. Taylor: 45	W. Callan: 4
Leinster 2nds	Won	77	76	62/2	83/9	C.V. Rooke: 42	W.A. Robinson: 10
St Columba's Coll.	Won	73	45		83/7	W. Callan: 14	W.A. Robinson: 7
Pembroke 2nds	Won	59	47	45/7		A.G. Lewis: 27*	Swaine/Robinson: 5 each
Corrig School P&P	Won	127	52			S. Lawrenson: 30	W.A. Robinson: 7
Ballyarthur	Won	80	47	56/2		J.H. Brennan: 49	W. Callan: 5
Wicklow CC	Won	23	18	42	11	J.H. Brennan: 17	Callan/Robinson: 9 each
Co. Westmeath (C)	Won	36	21	38	40	W.A. Robinson: 19	W.A. Robinson: 14
Four Courts*	Won	77	61	24/5		J. Maher: 44*	Connor/Maher: 4 each
Corrig Long Vacation	Lost	73	111/8			J.A. Swaine: 23	Swaine/Maher: 2 each
Sandymount (C)	Won	90	54	79	67	J.A. Swaine: 36	
Knapton*	Lost	64	68			J. Annesley: 18	S. Robinson: 4
Leinster 2nds	Drawn	99/9	168/9			A.P. Ross: 35	W. Callan: 3
Athy	Lost	43	65	62	41/1	W. Callan: 26	W.A. Robinson: 5
Junior Cup final							
Co. Wicklow	Won	83/9	81			J.A. Swaine: 37	W. Callan: 5

1896: ROBINSON, ROSS, CALLAN PLAY FOR LEINSTER

Junior: fixtures 37, reported 16, won 5, lost 7, drawn 3, tied 1. A.P. Ross, W. Callan, W.A. Robinson are selected to play for Leinster against Ulster in what is heralded as a 'Junior International Match'. The Land Commission lose the semi-final of the Leinster Junior Cup to Athy. Robinson takes 54 wickets:

Opponent	Result	LC 1st	Opp. 1st	LC 2nd	Opp. 2nd	Best Batting: Runs	Best Bowling: Wickets
Sandymount	Won	96	55			W.A. Robinson: 38*	W.A. Robinson: 4
Co. Wicklow	Won	79	36			A.P. Ross: 22	S. Lawrenson: 5
Civil Service	Drawn	66/6	158			A.P. Ross: 15	W.A. Robinson: 4
Dundrum	Lost	64	137/8			A.P. Ross: 16	Robinson/Callan: 3 each
Dollymount*	Lost	38	72		58		
Knapton	Drawn	119	77/5			S. Lawrenson: 48	W.A. Robinson: 5
DU 2nds	Won	90	18			J. Johnston: 28	W.A. Robinson: 5
Clontarf	Drawn	123/7	63/6			C.V. Rooke: 32	W.A. Robinson: 4
Athy (C)	Lost	81	161	128	51/0	C.V. Rooke: 41	W.A. Robinson: 7
DU Long Vacation	Won	66	26			J.H. Brennan: 20	
Athboy	Lost	73	85/4			W. Callan: 26	W.S. Browne: 2
Athy	Lost	98	118			W.A. Robinson: 19	W.A. Robinson: 8
Sandymount	Lost	27	64		56/5	J. Maher: 12	W. Callan: 8
Clontarf	Won	83	43			S. Lawrenson: 31	Callan/Robinson: 4 each
Leinster 2nds	Tied	54	54	69/4		C.V. Rooke: 32	W.A. Robinson: 6
Civil Service	Lost	62	116/9			C.V. Rooke: 25	W.A. Robinson: 4

1897: JUNIOR CUP WINNERS

Junior: fixtures 30, reported 11, won 2, lost 7, drawn 2. Although they lose most games, the Land Commission start playing against the 1st XIs of stronger sides such as Clontarf and Phoenix. Ross scores centuries against Phoenix and Civil Service. Land Commission 1st XI win Leinster Junior Cup for the first time, beating Knapton by 106 runs, with Swaine top-scoring on 45 and Robinson taking 15 wickets in the match:

Opponent	Result	LC 1st	Opp. 1st	LC 2nd	Opp. 2nd	Best Batting: Runs	Best Bowling: Wickets
Dundrum 2nds*	Lost	27	170/4			J. Douglas: 7	E.J. Gilligan: 2
Phoenix	Drawn	175	111/7			A.P. Ross: 115	W. Callan: 4
Civil Service	Drawn	212/9	250			A.P. Ross: 134*	W.A. Robinson: 5
Dundrum	Lost	62	255			W.S. Browne: 16	W.A. Robinson: 5
Knapton	Lost	39	84/9			C.V. Rooke: 11	W.A. Robinson: 6
Co. Meath	Lost	54	145	46/3		J.A. Swaine: 34	W.A. Robinson: 6
Clontarf	Lost	49	59			A.P. Ross: 25	S. Lawrenson: 5
Co. Wicklow	Lost	67	158/4			J.A. Swaine: 22	W.A. Robinson: 3
Sandymount (C)	Won	111	70			J. Maher: 41	Callan/Robinson: 5 each
A.J. Nicholl's XI*	Lost	38	54	43		C.J. Nolan: 29	C.J. Nolan: 5
Knapton	Won	159	105	98	46	J.A. Swaine: 49	W.A. Robinson: 15

Junior Cup final

LEINSTER JUNIOR CUP FINAL 1897, KNAPTON V. LAND COMMISSION

Land Commission

1st Innings			2nd Innings	
C.V. Rooke	b. Campbell	10	c. Martelli b. Grace	2
A.E. White	not out	9	c. Devoy b. Le Peton	2
J.A. Swaine	b. Grace	45	b. Exshaw	4
W. Connor	b. Grace	1	b. Exshaw	7
J.H. Brennan	c. Grace b. Exshaw	4	c. Martelli b. Campbell	25
A.P. Ross	b. Campbell	8	c. Martelli b. Exshaw	26
J. Maher	b. Exshaw	39	b. Grace	0
W. Callan	b. Campbell	28	b. Exshaw	2
W.A. Robinson	b. Campbell	4	b. Le Peton	28
S. Lawrenson	b. Le Peton	0	b. Exshaw	0
W. Redmond	b. Grace	5	not out	1
	Extras	6	Extras	1
	Total	**159**	**Total**	**98**

Knapton

1st Innings			2nd Innings	
R. Rice	b. Robinson	17	b. Callan	0
A. Martelli	b. Robinson	11	b. Robinson	0
E. Le Peton	b. Robinson	0	b. Robinson	8
W. Exshaw	b. Robinson	15	c. White b. Robinson	7

E. Grace	c. & b. Callan	24	b. Robinson	4
H. Campbell	b. Robinson	0	b. Robinson	8
H. Stokes	b. Robinson	1	c. Redmond b. Robinson	0
R. Exshaw	b. Robinson	17	c. Redmond b. Callan	14
M. Devoy	b. Robinson	8	c. Ross b. Robinson	3
J. Fellwood	l.b.w.b. Lawrenson	7	not out	2
C. Williams	not out	3	absent	
	Extras	2	Extras	0
	Total	**105**	**Total**	**46**

1898: ROBINSON SCORES 307 RUNS AND TAKES 56 WICKETS

Junior: fixtures 29, reported 11, won 3, lost 8. The Dublin and District Junior Cricket League is formed. The Land Commission do not participate. Their season starts well, but ends badly. Because the Commission cannot field teams, several games are cancelled. A.P. Ross scores 63 against County Meath. J. Maher makes 61 against Phoenix. Robinson totals 307 runs and 56 wickets in the season:

Opponent	Result	LC 1st	Opp. 1st	LC 2nd	Opp. 2nd	Best Batting: Runs	Best Bowling: Wickets
Co. Wicklow	Won	89	59	54/4		J.H. Brennan: 26	Gordon: 4
Leinster 2nds	Won	92	89	100/5		W.A. Robinson: 55	W.A. Robinson: 9
Belgrave*	Won	83	76				
Newtownbarry	Lost	51	96	57	13/0	W.A. Robinson: 29	Gordon: 5
Phoenix	Lost	157	160/6			J. Maher: 61	S. Scroope: 4
Athy	Lost	23	89	71			
Workingmen	Lost	50	89			Kennan: 20*	Callan/Robinson: 4 each
Ballyarthur	Lost	37	182			S. Lawrenson: 11	W. Callan: 7
Civil Service	Lost	72	103/5	46		J.H. Brennan: 32	Swaine/Robinson: 7 each
Phoenix	Lost	86	228			W.A. Robinson: 33	W.A. Robinson: 7
Co. Meath	Lost	116	172/6			A.P. Ross: 63	W.A. Robinson: 3

1899: JUNIOR CUP WINNERS

Junior: fixtures 20, reported 13, won 5, lost 6, drawn 2. 'Old Connaught Ladies v. Mr Weir's XI: Gentlemen will bowl and field left-handed, and bat with broomsticks' – *The Irish Times*. The men win. W. Callan takes 36 wickets. Land Commission gain an easy victory over Old St Mary's in the Leinster Junior Cup final, thanks to Ross's 84 runs and Callan's 8 wickets, but still don't play in the Dublin Junior League:

Opponent	Result	LC 1st	Opp. 1st	LC 2nd	Opp. 2nd	Best Batting: Runs	Best Bowling: Wickets
Phoenix	Lost	79	192/9			C.V. Rooke: 29	W.A. Robinson: 4
Leinster 2nds	Lost	47	148	50/2		J. Maher: 31	W. Callan: 5
St Columba's Coll.	Lost	78	108/6			J.A. Swaine: 26	W. Callan: 3
Dundrum	Won	107	78			J.A. Swaine: 27	T. Gregg: 9

Athy	Lost	26	190	35		G. Johnston: 16	J.A. Swaine: 4
St Columba's Coll.	Won	54	45			W. Callan: 16	W. Callan: 7
Leinster 2nds	Drawn	86/6	300/2			J.A. Swaine: 28	
Athy	Lost	53	82/3			C.V. Rooke: 17	W.A. Robinson: 2
Ballyarthur	Won	125	57		23	J.A. Swaine: 38	W. Callan: 13
Coollattin	Won	180	40				
Co. Wicklow	Drawn	54/3	125/7			J.A. Swaine: 23	Dawson: 3
Phoenix	Lost	48	148			C.V. Rooke: 16	W.A. Robinson: 3
Old St Mary's	Won	178	89	35/3	117	A.P. Ross: 84	W. Callan: 8

Junior Cup final

LEINSTER JUNIOR CUP FINAL 1899, OLD ST. MARY'S V. LAND COMMISSION

Old St Mary's

1st Innings			2nd Innings	
R.J. Molloy	run out	2	c. Swaine b. Callan	0
R.J. Kinahan	c. Taylor b. Gilligan	15	b. Dawson	0
D. O'Brien	run out	20	c. Callan b. Gilligan	8
A. Harrison	st. Rooke b. Swaine	18	c. Rooke b. Callan	0
J. Dodd	c. Taylor b. Gilligan	1	not out	15
L. Molloy	l.b.w. b. Callan	16	b. Dawson	43
E. Donovan	not out	3	b. Callan	6
D. O'Neill	b. Callan	0	run out	21
C. Moran	b. Swaine	2	b. Gilligan	15
E. Swaine	c. Waters b. Callan	0	c. Redmond b. Callan	3
W. Delany	b. Dawson	8	b. Callan	1
	Extras	4	Extras	5
	Total	89	Total	117

Land Commission

1st Innings			2nd Innings	
J.A. Swaine	b. L. Molloy	33		
A.P. Ross	c. Dodd b. L. Molloy	62	not out	22
C.V. Rooke	c. & b. L. Molloy	36	l.b.w. b. Harrison	2
J.H. Brennan	b. L. Molloy	4	not out	3
W. Callan	b. L. Molloy	16	l.b.w. b. Harrison	8
A.W. Waters	b. L. Molloy	0		
S. Lawrenson	l.b.w. b. L. Molloy	15	c. O'Neill b. Harrison	0
E.J. Gilligan	b. Dodd	7		
M. Dawson	b. L. Molloy	0		
F.W. Taylor	c. Harrison b. L. Molloy	1		
W. Redmond	not out	0		
	Extras	4	Extras	0
	Total	178	Total (for 3 wickets)	35

1900: JUNIOR CUP WINNERS; LAND COMMISSION CRICKET CLUB DISBANDS

Junior: fixtures 23, reported 19, won 7, lost 8, drawn 4. C.V. Rooke makes 62 not out against Dublin University 2nds. W. Callan scores 85 against Civil Service. Ross and Robinson play only a few games. When they do play, the Land Commission usually win. Land Commission come back after a disastrous start against Old St Mary's to win the Leinster Junior Cup for the third time in four years. Robinson takes 12 wickets and Ross scores 80 in the 2nd innings. It's their last game, as they are forced to disband at the end of the season:

Opponent	Result	LC 1st	Opp. 1st	LC 2nd	Opp. 2nd	Best Batting: Runs	Best Bowling: Wickets
Celbridge	Won	51/8	42			Ryan/Keough: 10	M. Dawson: 6
Phoenix	Lost	98	160				
DU 2nds	Lost	128	185/7			J. Maher: 54	E.J. Gilligan: 2
D'Olier*	Lost	31	58				
Leinster 2nds	Won	104	51				
Co. Wicklow	Drawn	73/7	175			G.V. Ryan: 28*	W. Callan: 3
Dundalk	Won	82	37	69/0	86	C.V. Rooke: 49	W. Callan: 10
Clontarf	Lost	32	94	20/5		J.A. Swaine: 14	W. Callan: 8
Sandymount	Lost	81	101/9			J.A. Swaine: 32	E.J. Gilligan: 6
4th Rifle Brigade	Lost	50	52/7			R.F. Ratigan: 15	E.J. Gilligan: 4
DU 2nds	Drawn	117/2	142			C.V. Rooke: 62*	M. Dawson: 7
DU Long Vacation	Won	109	67			J. Maher: 28	E.J. Gilligan: 6
Dundalk	Lost	37	48			W. Redmond: 15*	W. Callan: 5
Richmond Asylum	Lost	58	152			J. Maher: 20	J.A. Swaine: 5
Phoenix	Drawn	112/8	154/5			J.A. Swaine: 50*	M. Dawson: 3
Civil Service	Won	132	114			W. Callan: 85	E.J. Gilligan: 8
Beaumont (C)	Won	265	96		34		
Old St Mary's	Drawn	43/5	70			W. Callan: 16	W. Callan: 7
Old St Mary's	Won	62	161	272	105	A.P. Ross: 102	W.A. Robinson: 12

Junior Cup final

LEINSTER JUNIOR CUP FINAL 1900, OLD ST MARY'S V. LAND COMMISSION

Land Commission

1st Innings			2nd Innings	
J.A. Swaine	c. Molloy b. Baldwin	11	run out	27
J.H. Brennan	b. Harrison	1	b. Dodd	30
A.P. Ross	c. Moran b. Harrison	22	c. & b. Baldwin	80
J. Maher	l.b.w. b. Harrison	4	l.b.w. O'Brien	41
W. Callan	c. & b. Harrison	4	b. Dodd	20
C.V. Rooke	c. J. Dowling b. Harrison	1	b. Baldwin	28
W.A. Robinson	l.b.w. b. Harrison	12	run out	16
G.V. Ryan	b. Baldwin	1	l.b.w. b. Dodd	2
E.J. Gilligan	run out	1	c. Kinahan b. Harrison	1
E. Kearney	b. Baldwin	0	b. Dodd	1
M. Dawson	not out	0	not out	0
	Extras	5	Extras	26
	Total	**62**	**Total**	**272**

Old St Mary's

1st Innings			2nd Innings	
D. O'Brien	l.b.w. b. Robinson	6	c. Kearney b. Robinson	2
R.J. Kinahan	c. Robinson b. Callan	0	b. Robinson	18
E. Donovan	b. Robinson	3	b. Robinson	0
J. Baldwin	c. Ross b. Callan	37	c. Ryan b. Callan	12
E. O'Shea	c. Swaine b. Gilligan	30	not out	49
A. Harrison	b. Dawson	9	b. Robinson	0
R.J. Molloy	b. Robinson	9	c. & b. Robinson	1
J. Dodd	l.b.w. b. Robinson	28	b. Callan	8
C. Moran	c. Ryan b. Robinson	7	b. Callan	0
W. Dowling	not out	14	b. Callan	2
J. Dowling	b. Robinson	8	b. Robinson	0
	Extras	10	Extras	13
	Total	**161**	**Total**	**105**

After Judge Bewley retired, his replacement as Judicial Commissioner, the Honorable Mr Justice Meredith raised objections about the Land Commission lending its name to such a foreign and fantastic sport, and the cricket team was forced to disband at the end of 1900. In disgust, Callan and Ross arranged separate representative games, under their own names, against Phoenix at the end of the season. In 1901, John Swaine went to Leinster, where he played mainly for the 2nd and 3rd teams for several years. Walter Callan played regularly for Civil Service, Phoenix and the King's County (Offaly) over the next decade. Arthur Ross, the Land Commission's best batsman, appeared occasionally for Phoenix. William Robinson, by far the best bowler to play for the Land Commission, could not be traced. Of these four Land Commission stars, only John Aloysius Swaine would return to assist in the foundation of the third, and present, Merrion Cricket Club in 1906.

NB Other teams playing between 1892 and 1900: Primrose, Bog Of Allen, Free&Easy, Excelsior.

2.2. THE THIRD MERRION CRICKET CLUB: 1906-1913

There were no reports of cricket matches being played by any team with the name Merrion in its title between 1902 and 1905. The first report of a cricket match being played by the present Merrion Cricket Club was on Saturday 5 May 1906. The writer states, 'This match, which was to have been played as a league match on Saturday, was, owing to a late start, played as a friendly instead, and resulted in a win for Malahide by 25 runs and 9 wickets.' So began the story of Merrion cricket, born of enthusiastic parents from the old Land Commission Club and bolstered by members of other government departments in the Upper Merrion Street area, such as the Board of Public Works, the Church Property Department and the Department of Agriculture and Technical Instruction.

This first match was played on Merrion's home ground at Mulally Fields, Dolphin's Barn, behind the site of the former Imperial Tobacco Company, where they were to remain until the move to Anglesea Road in 1908. In those days, the Land Commission was under the auspices of Dublin City, so the players brought with them the old club colours of gold, maroon and lincoln green, and the city coat of arms, part of which features the three castles with the burning towers, symbolising the power of its citizens to defend the city against all attackers. This apt image of Merrion's struggles over the years that followed has remained a constant crest on the club cricket equipment to this day.

The Land Commission had grown in size since 1892, when 121 clerks had been assigned by the British Treasury. Now the clerks numbered 372, principally by the addition of junior second division clerks and abstractors, and the offices had stretched to include numbers 23-26 Upper Merrion Street. According to Hansard of 1 May 1907, questions were raised in the House of Commons as to why so many junior clerks and abstractors were employed by the Irish Land Commission, and whether the many different classes of clerk could be amalgamated. Fortunately for Merrion, the Chief Secretary to the Lord Lieutenant blustered his way through some evasive reply, and this pool of junior employees could continue to form the nucleus of the newly named club.

Of the twenty-six players who participated in the 1906 season, seventeen worked in the Land Commission. Of those seventeen, only J.A. Swaine, E.J. Gilligan, E.V. Kearney and J.H. Brennan had played for the Land Commission cricket team six years earlier. These four players were the founders of the modern Merrion Cricket Club, with John Aloysius Swaine as its main architect. Swaine was the guiding spirit behind both the Land Commission team and its successor, Merrion. Although he wasn't as good a cricketer as Ross, Callan or Robinson, he had played almost all the earlier games, and was responsible for purchasing the lease on Anglesea Road in 1908.

Merrion's early years as a Junior club were not successful. The 1sts and 2nds struggled in the Junior and Minor Leagues; on occasional years they opted out of the league structure altogether, possibly due to a lack of organisation within the club. No competitions were won during this period. All the following games were in the Junior or Minor Leagues, unless noted as friendlies.

1906: MERRION CRICKET CLUB BEGINS

Junior: fixtures 33, reported 21, won 7, lost 12, drawn 2. J.A. Swaine represents Merrion at the AGM of the Leinster Junior League in the Grosvenor Hotel on 7 April. The Junior League is split on merit into two divisions, each of which is further split into two tables – A and B. Merrion 1sts are in Division 1B, while Merrion 2nds are in Division 2B, but neither team wins anything. Another slow start. M. Martin and A.W. Ball emerge as possible stars of the new Merrion:

Opponent	Result	Mer. 1st	Opp. 1st	Mer. 2nd	Opp. 2nd	Best Batting: Runs	Best Bowling: Wickets
Malahide (F)	Lost	47	72/1			F.C. Gorman: 12	A.W. Ball: 1
CU 2nds (F)*	Lost	37	190/9			J. Jones: 12	J. Jones: 3
Workingmen	Won	41	33	33/4		J.A. Swaine: 13	E.J. Gilligan: 5
Croydon	Lost	24	30/2			A.W. Ball: 8	A.W. Ball: 1
Railway Union (F)	Drawn	32/4	56			E.A. Rooney: 26	E.A. Rooney: 5
Royal Vet. College (F)	Won	38	24	55/2	45	A.W. Ball: 38	M. Martin: 7
Dickeson*	Lost	62	90				
R & SPU	Drawn	33/4	93			E.B. Keating: 15	Martin/Brunt: 4 each
Malahide*	Lost	33	37/7				
Croydon	Won	96	43			Ball/Keating: 20 each	M. Martin: 5

Nat. Educ. Office (F)	Won	53/7	21		
Sandymount	Won	75	60	M. Daly: 19*	M. Martin: 6
Dollymount (F)	Won	73	67		
Workingmen	Lost	76	123	A.W. Ball: 35	Gilligan/Daly: 3 each
Malahide	Lost	74	76	A.W. Ball: 21	E.J. Gilligan: 5
GS & WR	Lost	15	54		
Malahide	Won	68/9	46	E.J. Gilligan: 18	E.J. Gilligan: 5
Leinster 2nds	Lost	64	113	M. Martin: 29	M. Martin: 6
Pembroke A (F)	Lost	26	92		
GS & WR	Lost				

PROFILE: JOHN SWAINE

Opening batsman and change bowler, whose best reported performances for the Land Commission were 50* in a drawn game against Phoenix in 1900 and 8 wickets against the Valuation Office in 1894. In 1910, at forty years of age, he played his last game of cricket for Merrion. He was working as an attendant in the Records Department of the Irish Land Commission at the time, with a status of assistant clerk/abstractor, although three years later he was transferred to the Irish National Health Insurance Commission. John had played all the Land Commission games, bowling and batting a bit, without actually being a star of the side. Newspaper reports suggest that he was heavily involved in the administrative side of the game, the equivalent of the Hon. Secretary of our time. After the Land Commission Cricket team folded in 1900, he joined Leinster and played mainly for the 2nds and 3rds there, although there is a record of him appearing once for the 1sts, probably in a tour game.

From 1903-1905, he disappears from reports of cricket in Dublin. During this period, he married Kathleen Kickham from Mullinahone in Tipperary, who was a niece of the famous Irish poet, novelist and Fenian activist Charles Joseph Kickham. Her nephew, in turn, was the 'manly Rody Kickham' referred to in A Portrait of the Artist as a Young Man by James Joyce (the other one): 'Rody Kickham was a decent fellow but Nasty Roche was a stink. Rody Kickham had greaves in his number and a hamper in the refectory.'

In 1906, John Aloysius Swaine, helped by Good, Cooper, Brennan, Kearney and Gilligan of the Land Commission, decided to start their own cricket club (possibly because they couldn't get regular games at an acceptable level in other clubs), based initially at Dolphin's Barn and subsequently at Anglesea Road. It was to be called Merrion, after the street where the Land Commission had its offices.

1907: MERRION WITHDRAW FROM LEAGUES

Junior: fixtures 24, reported 9, won 5, lost 3, drawn 1. Merrion is not mentioned in either the Junior or Minor League tables, suggesting a temporary withdrawal from league cricket by the club. During a limited season, they play only friendlies, winning most of them, including a close game against the Royal Hibernian Military School (RHMS), a strong cricketing force at that time. This facility at winning friendlies and losing league matches sets a trend that continues throughout the history of the club. Founder member E.J. Gilligan retires at the end of the season:

Opponent	Result	Mer. 1st	Opp. 1st	Mer. 2nd	Opp. 2nd	Best Batting: Runs	Best Bowling: Wickets
Civil Service 3rds (F)	Lost	13	147/2			R. Close: 7	P.J. Hayes: 1
Leinster 2nds (F)	Lost	47	136/5			M. Daly: 19	M. Martin: 3
St James's Gate (F)	Won	68	14				
Pembroke 2nds (F)	Won	54	44			W. Redmond: 18	J.J. Doody: 7
RHMS (F)	Won	60	57				
Dickeson (F)	Won	48	44				
Leinster 2nds (F)	Drawn	85/9					
Richmond Asylum (F)	Won	29	27				
Richmond Asylum (F)	Lost	78	211/7			A.W. Ball: 40	M. Martin: 6

1908: MERRION MOVE TO ANGLESEA ROAD

Junior: fixtures 26, reported 17, won 3, lost 14. MCC moves from Mulally Fields to Anglesea Road (Area A on the Anglesea Road diagram below). Swaine arranges a lease with the Ryan Estate, the owners of an uncultivated field – originally part of the old Simmonscourt Estate – between two elegant town houses, Dunluce and Hazeldene, beside the River Dodder. This river – famous as one of Samuel Beckett's 'infernal streams' in his first novel, *Dream of Fair to Middling Women* – is the largest tributary of the River Liffey and is known as a 'flashy' river

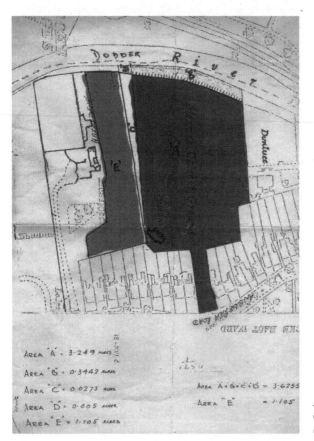

Anglesea Road. Location of Merrion Cricket Club's second home ground. (Note the different areas).

with a quick response to rainstorms, as its source is at a steep gradient in the Dublin mountains. The ground is separated from Hazeldene by a high-rise ditch with a stone wall on top, running from the corner of the present pavilion down to the river A small, galvanised shed costing £30 is purchased and positioned to the bottom right hand side of the current ground, in front of Dunluce House. A scythe is borrowed and they are ready to play.

To say that Merrion's first season at Anglesea Road is inauspicious is an insult to the word 'inauspicious'. In the Junior League, Merrion 1sts finish last, with a 100 per cent record – played 16, lost 16. No points. The club lowlight is a defeat for the 2nds by the Railway & Steam Packet Union (Railway Union) 2nds by 249 runs to 9. Only eight players turn up. Bradshaw stars with 4 not out, Jago gets 3 runs, and there are 2 extras. Founder member E.V. Kearney plays his final game for Merrion this season, before moving to Civil Service, possibly in disgust.

Of the forty-three players used this season, only fifteen work in the Land Commission. Despite the change of name and expanded pool of players, the team is still regarded by many as the Land Commission. The 'Cricket Chatter' column in *The Irish Field* of 1 August 1908 reports:

The Land Commission team is but a shadow of what it was some years ago, and unless a few enthusiastic members bestir themselves and others the club will soon become extinct. They have a nice little ground at Anglesea Road, near Donnybrook, which only needs some levelling and rolling to make it quite presentable.

Levelling?

Opponent	Result	Mer. 1st	Opp. 1st	Mer. 2nd	Opp. 2nd	Best Batting: Runs	Best Bowling: Wickets
Pembroke 3rds (F)*	Won	81	53			Murray: 39	E.F. Synott: 5
Pembroke 2nds	Lost	19	58			J.A. Swaine: 7	A.W. Ball: 4
Richmond Asylum	Lost	34	209			A.P. Hunter: 16	A.W. Ball: 4
Leinster 2nds	Lost	34	118				
Clontarf 2nds	Lost	76	142			E.V. Kearney: 33	E.V. Kearney: 4
R & SPU 2nds (F)*	Lost	27	67			Sayers: 6	Sayers: 4
R & SPU	Lost	20	23	22/8	22/1	A.S. Davidson: 6	A.W. Ball: 8
RIC (F)	Won	173	61			E.A. Rooney: 32	M. Martin: 5
Pembroke 2nds	Lost	62	181/6			E.V. Kearney: 15	A.P. Hunter: 2
Bray (F)	Won	49	23	14/0	39		
Catholic University	Lost	62	82				
Richmond Asylum	Lost	35	182/6			F.C. Gorman: 13	M.A. Hill: 3
Catholic University	Lost	76	98			R.J. Davidson: 15	M.A. Hill: 5
St James's Gate	Lost	19	23			F.S. Irvine: 7	E.F. Synott: 5
R & SPU 2nds (F)*	Lost	9	249			Bradshaw: 4*	Graham: 5
Leinster 2nds	Lost	19	150			W. Marlow: 3	Hill/Marlow: 4 each
R & SPU	Lost	53	160			A.P. Hunter: 23	A.W. Ball: 6

1909: MERRION WITHDRAW FROM LEAGUES AGAIN

Junior: fixtures 12, reported 8, won 7, lost 1. Apparently nobody does bestir themselves, as Merrion withdraw from all leagues again to lick their wounds. They play only friendlies and win most of those. A Merrion Associated Football Club plays soccer at Anglesea Road, and there are plans for a Merrion Rugby Club, with three teams, to move from Rutland

Avenue to Anglesea Road the following winter, where they will continue to play until 1921. All three sports involve members of the Land Commission. A few years later, the ground will be used to play soccer by Dublin United, Shelbourne, and Cafolla's, makers of ice cream, who are rumoured to have the biggest cornets in Dublin:

Opponent	Result	Mer. 1st	Opp. 1st	Mer. 2nd	Opp. 2nd	Best Batting: Runs	Best Bowling: Wickets
Dickeson (F)	Won	60	30				
Palmerstown (F)	Won	59	43			J. Ball: 19	M.A. Hill: 5
Palmerstown 2nds (F)	Won	153	73				
Dickeson (F)	Won	69	17			F.S. Irvine: 17*	M.A. Hill: 6
Bray (F)	Won	110/9	49				
Catholic University (F)	Won	90	44				
Drumcondra (F)	Won	35	19				
Leinster 3rds (F)	Lost	29	32				

1910: IRISH CRICKET UNION FORMED

Junior: fixtures 19, reported 12, won 3, lost 9. The Irish Cricket Union is formed. The Leinster Cricket Union is dissolved and the Leinster Branch of the Irish Cricket Union replaces it. It is a dangerous time of historical change in Ireland. *The Irish Times* reports, 'Shocking accident to a bell ringer at the Priory Church weekly practice. A lady bell-ringer was carried up to the ceiling of the belfry. She was removed to the vicarage in a precarious condition.' A recovery of sorts is underway, although Merrion 1sts fail to win Division B of the Junior League. J. Anstead scores 50 against Dickeson and F.S. Irvine takes 9 wickets against the same team. On 14 May, future president E.T. Cochrane makes his first appearance in Merrion colours, against Pembroke 2nds:

Opponent	Result	Mer. 1st	Opp. 1st	Mer. 2nd	Opp. 2nd	Best Batting: Runs	Best Bowling: Wickets
Pembroke 2nds	Won	65	59			Worrall: 18	W. Marlow: 5
Leinster 2nds	Lost	27	73			M. Hendrick: 12	W. Marlow: 5
Richmond Asylum	Lost	33	120			J.A. Swaine: 13*	
St James's Gate	Won	130	74			A.W. Ball: 34	Kirkpatrick: 4
Pembroke 2nds	Lost	44	149			H.C. Crawford: 12*	M.A. Hill: 4
Nat. Educ. Office (F)	Lost	31	43				
St James's Gate	Lost	21	57			M. Martin: 10*	F.S. Irvine: 4
Dickeson (F)	Won	120	27			J. Anstead: 50	
Jewish Athletic Ass.	Lost	61	102			F.S. Irvine: 14*	Ball/Irvine: 3 each
Richmond Asylum	Lost	80	148/7			F. Worrall: 17	M.A. Hill: 4
Leinster 2nds	Lost	36	252/5			H. Kelly: 11	M.A. Hill: 2
Dickeson (F)	Lost	23	63			V. Harkness: 8	F.S. Irvine: 9

1911: MERRION THIRD IN JUNIOR LEAGUE, DIVISION A

Junior: fixtures 26, reported 16, won 6, lost 7, drawn 3. Merrion have a tendency to win matches when batting first, and fall apart when batting last, suggesting a somewhat less than satisfactory level of fitness in their players. Merrion 1sts are more settled this year, and finish third in Division A of the Junior League, with 12 points, having played 12, won 4, lost 4, and drawn 4. Worrall, McConnell and Fitzpatrick score 50s, while Dix, Drummond and Irvine take most of the wickets. At one of their home games, an eleven-year-old boy, recently arrived in the big smoke from Boyle, Roscommon, gazes in gobsmacked wonder over a relative's back garden wall at the strange sight of plump, ghost-like figures loping around a field chasing a hard red ball while smoking cigarettes. His name? Cecil Little:

Opponent	Result	Mer. 1st	Opp. 1st	Mer. 2nd	Opp. 2nd	Best Batting: Runs	Best Bowling: Wickets
Leinster 2nds	Lost	69	227/4			F.S. Irvine: 43	J. Dix: 2
Richmond Asylum	Lost	55	192/4			F. Moore: 20	Irvine/Hill/Ball: 1 each
Irish Times (F)	Lost	31	141/6			F. Worrall: 13	D. Drummond: 5
Leinster 2nds	Lost	77	193/8			V. Harkness: 26	Kirkpatrick/Hill: 2 each
RHMS*	Lost	57	102/8				
CUS	Lost	38	84			F. Moore: 11	
RHMS (F)	Won	193	74			F. Moore: 44	J. Dix: 7
Municipal Office (F)	Won	104	50				
Pembroke 2nds	Won	126	79			J. McConnell: 37*	Dix/McConnell: 3 each
Pemb. Wand. (F)	Drawn	163/5	40/8			V. Harkness: 43	F.S. Irvine: 6
Carlisle*	Lost	34	54				
Richmond Asylum	Won	81	71			V. Harkness: 24	F.S. Irvine: 4
Dundrum Asylum (F)	Won	164	111			Graham: 47	
Pembroke 2nds	Drawn	222/4	138/6			J. Fitzpatrick: 68*	J. Dix: 4
CUS	Won	166	92			F. Worrall: 71	F.S. Irvine: 6
Co. Wicklow (F)	Drawn	109/2	110			J. McConnell: 77	D. Drummond: 4

1912: MERRION FOURTH IN JUNIOR LEAGUE, DIVISION A

Junior: fixtures 19, reported 13, won 4, lost 9. This year, twelve of the twenty players work in the Land Commission. J. Dix scores 45 runs, batting at number 11. F.S. Irvine takes 8 wickets against Railway Union. Despite some low scores, a decent all-round Junior team is emerging. *The Irish Field* calls the use of *Another* as a name, a 'stupid *nom-de bat*'. Merrion 1sts finish fourth in Division A of the Junior League, with 4 points, having played 7, won 2, lost 5:

Opponent	Result	Mer. 1st	Opp. 1st	Mer. 2nd	Opp. 2nd	Best Batting: Runs	Best Bowling: Wickets
Leinster 2nds	Lost	79	250/5			A. W. Ball: 21	J. Kelly: 3
Civil Service 2nds	Won	105	100			J. Dix: 45	J. Dix: 5
YMCA*	Won	64	38	37		A. Ellis: 30	F.S. Irvine: 7
Fairview (F)	Won	47	46				
Co. Wicklow (F)	Lost	130	164			E. T. Cochrane: 35	J. Dix: 4
Pemb. Wand.	Lost	16	88			J. Kirkpatrick: 6	Dix/Kirkpatrick: 4 each
Richmond Asylum	Lost	54	152/3			Worrall: 12	J. Dix: 2
YMCA*	Lost	30	74				
Clontarf 2nds	Won	93	32			F.S. Irvine: 24	J. Kirkpatrick: 5
Ordnance Survey	Lost	27	67			Another: 16	C. Campbell: 4
Pemb. Wand.	Lost	77	80			A. W. Ball: 28	J. Dix: 5
Richmond Asylum	Lost	23	82			F. Worrall: 6	Moore/Ball/Dix: 3 each
Railway Union	Lost	121	216			J. Dix: 32	F.S. Irvine: 8

1913: RELEGATION TO JUNIOR LEAGUE, DIVISION 2

Junior: fixtures 33, reported 27, won 4, lost 23. Of the forty players used this year, only thirteen are known to be employed in the Land Commission. J.A. Harrison scores 68 against Richmond Asylum. E.T. Cochrane scores 53 against Clontarf 2nds and 51 against Railway Union. S. Kirkpatrick takes 8 wickets against Richmond Asylum. It is a busy season, but success continues to elude the club. By now the Junior League has been split into two divisions, with promotion and relegation of one team between Divisions 1 and 2. Merrion 1sts are relegated, finishing 10/10, with 4 points, having played 18, won 2, lost 16. Merrion 2nds finish seventh in the Minor League, with 8 points, having played 14, won 4, lost 10. First appearance of Fred Fryer, a true stalwart of the future:

Opponent	Result	Mer. 1st	Opp. 1st	Mer. 2nd	Opp. 2nd	Best Batting: Runs	Best Bowling: Wickets
Clontarf 2nds	Lost	55	58/2			F.S. Irvine: 10	J. Dix: 2
Civil Service 2nds	Lost	66	103			C. Campbell: 22	A.W. Ball: 5
Pemb. Wand. 2nds*	Lost	21	119/9			E. Beatty: 6	
Leinster 2nds	Lost	42	57			J. Kirkpatrick: 12	
GS & WR	Lost	68	106			J. Kirkpatrick: 19	S. Kirkpatrick: 6
YMCA 2nds*	Won	67	35				
Richmond Asylum	Won	144	116			J.A. Harrison: 68	S. Kirkpatrick: 8
Railway Union	Lost	58	60/7			A.W. Ball: 18	S. Kirkpatrick: 4
Pemb. Wand. 2nds*	Lost	31	97			E. Beatty: 9*	F. Moore: 5
Pemb. Wand.	Lost	35	64			F.S. Irvine: 6	J. Kirkpatrick: 5
Sandymount 2nds*	Lost	21	48			F. Moore: 8	F. Moore: 7
Workingmen	Lost	21	86			J. Kirkpatrick: 7	S. Kirkpatrick: 3
YMCA 2nds*	Won	42	38			E. Beatty: 7	Marlow/Lea: 5 each
Clontarf 2nds	Lost	101	152/8			E.T. Cochrane: 53	J.G. Cooke: 4
Palmerstown	Lost	40	47/4			M. O'Sullivan: 10	Cooke/Irvine: 2 each
Civil Service 2nds	Lost	32	112/7			F.S. Irvine: 7	J.A. Harrison: 4
Pembroke 3rds*	Lost	108	182				
Leinster 2nds	Lost	81	202/7			A.W. Price: 32	S. Kirkpatrick: 2
Palmerstown 3rds*	Lost	35	106			V. Jeeves: 12	W. Marlow: 5
GS & WR	Lost	15	61/7	81/8		H. Ashton: 6	J.A. Harrison: 3
Clontarf 3rds*	Lost	26	143				
Richmond Asylum	Lost	63	125/3			J.G. Cooke: 20	J.A. Harrison: 2
Railway Union	Won	157	78			E.T. Cochrane: 51	J.G. Cooke: 5
Railway Union 2nds*	Lost	32	50				
Pemb. Wand.	Lost	53	84			F.S. Irvine: 22	D. Drummond: 4
Workingmen	Lost	112	117/1			J.A. Harrison: 38	D. Drummond: 1
Pemb. Wand.	Lost	129	133/6			R. Jago: 32	D. Drummond: 3

PROFILE

Other Junior cricketers of note: A.W. Ball, F.S. Irvine, V. Harkness, W. Marlow, M. Martin, M. Daly, J.G. Cooke, F. Moore, F. Worrall, C. Phillips, T. Kenny, J. Coughlan.

NB Other teams playing between 1906 and 1913: Dunleckney, Incogniti, Christendom, Myra.

2.3. THE GREAT WAR: 1914-1918

On 28 June 1914, Archduke Franz Ferdinand of Austria took a wrong turn in his motor car and was assassinated, an event that led to the First World War and the subsequent decimation of many Irish cricket teams. Yet it was mainly the Senior clubs such as Phoenix, Dublin University, the Garrison, Clontarf, etc., which were most affected. Some of these teams shut down altogether, while those that continued to play, like Leinster and Civil Service, performed unusually badly. The Junior League continued with either one or two divisions, and Merrion fielded teams in each division, although not always made up of eleven players. During this period, Merrion won Division 2 of the Junior League in 1914, and were runners-up in the Junior League in 1918.

But the club did not escape unscathed from the First World War. A tablet memorial to the thirty-one Land Commission employees who died in the Great War is located at No.24 Upper Merrion Street, accessible through the Merrion Hotel. Employees in other departments may also have been killed, but of these thirty-one, there are six names that appear in reports of cricket matches played by either the Land Commission or Merrion. Most of these men would have enlisted voluntarily, apart from Hill. He may have been conscripted at the end of the war, as they were running out of bodies at the front.

John Henry Brennan was the only founder member of Merrion Cricket Club to be killed in the Great War. Originally from Montreal in Canada, he was a second-class clerk and cashier in the Irish Land Commission who had been educated at St Columba's and Trinity Colleges, where he played cricket for both teams. He had started playing cricket for the Land Commission as early as 1895 and was a useful batsman, with a top score of 49 against Ballyarthur. He seems to have only played a single season with Merrion, in 1906, but was involved with the running of the club from the beginning. As early as 1902, he had obtained a commission in the special reserves of the 4th Battalion of the Royal Welsh Fusiliers. He was promoted to Captain in the 3rd Battalion in 1903. His obituary in *Irish Life* magazine states that he was very keen about his military service, obtaining 'special honours in a course at the Hythe School of Musketry'. He served with the Expeditionary Force in France and Flanders, and was killed in action near Zonnebeke, West Flanders, Belgium on 19 October 1914, while leading his men across an open plain. He was forty-five. There is a memorial to him at Ypres (Menin Gate).

David Drummond was a second-division clerk who was promoted to minor staff officer in the Irish Land Commission. He played for both Merrion 1sts and 2nds from 1909-1914, taking 5 wickets against *The Irish Times* in a friendly match in 1911. Originally from Perth in Scotland, he enlisted in September 1914 in the 1st Battalion, Royal Dublin Fusiliers, and rose to the rank of Sergeant. He saw service in the Near East with the 7th Battalion and met his death in Macedonia on the Struma Plain on 23 September 1916, during an offensive in the Bala and Zir district. Unmarried, he was buried in Struma Military Cemetery in Greece. He was thirty-three.

Irvine Johnston Smyth was a second-division clerk in the Irish Land Commission and a good all-round cricketer who scored a couple of 50s for Merrion 1sts and took 5 wickets against Sandymount 2nds in 1914, ending up with a total of 172 runs @ 10.81 and 57 wickets at 10.00 in that year. Originally from County Armagh, he was the son of a Methodist Minister, then based in County Cork. Irvine was educated at Belfast Academy and Methodist, Wesley and Trinity Colleges. He volunteered as soon as war broke out, signing up from TCD as a member of the 6th Black Watch and rising to the rank of 2nd Lieutenant in the 6th Battalion of the Royal Enniskillen Fusiliers. He served in the Gallipoli theatre of operations, where he was killed in action on 3 September 1915.

Above left: Captain John Henry Brennan, Land Commission cricketer and founder member of Merrion, who was killed at Flanders during the First World War.
Above centre: Second Lieutenant Irvine Johnston Smyth, Merrion cricketer, killed at Gallipolli during the First World War.
Above right: Sergeant David Drummond, Merrion cricketer, killed at Macedonia during the First World War.

Albert Victor Lea was a second-division clerk (Estates Branch) in the Irish Land Commission, who was a useful middle-order batsman, scoring a total of 139 runs @ 9.93 in 1914. He was probably more involved in the administrative side of Merrion cricket, acting as Hon. Secretary over several years. He placed advertisements in *The Irish Field* on many occasions, looking for Merrion fixtures. He was an Englishman, born in Burton-on-Trent, who had a family home in Edgeworthstown, County Longford. He enlisted in the 10th Battalion of the Royal Dublin Fusiliers and rose to the rank of Sergeant, before being killed in action on 13 November 1916. The location of his death is given as France and Flanders, suggesting that he may, like Hill, have been fatally wounded at Flanders and died in France.

Charles Anthony Victor Jeeves was a clerk in the Estates Commissioners' Department of the Irish Land Commission, who played occasionally for Merrion as a batsman. He was known as Victor Jeeves. From Worcestershire in England, he joined the 9th Battalion of the Royal Dublin Fusiliers, Devonshire Regiment, and was attached to the Liverpool Regiment temporarily as a 2nd Lieutenant when he was killed in action on 20 September 1917. He was thirty-seven. He was awarded the Military Medal for individual bravery on the field of battle.

Marshall Alfred Hill was a second-division clerk in the Irish Land Commission, who had been one of the best all-rounders for the club between 1907 and 1917, taking 41 wickets in that final season. Originally from Kerry, having enlisted as a private in the 1st Battalion of the Royal Dublin Fusiliers, he was an acting Lance Corporal when fatally wounded upon 'a fierier pitch in Flanders'. He died on 31 May 1918 and was buried at Aire Communal Cemetery in France.

'They shall not grow old as we that are left grow old:
Age shall not weary them, nor the years condemn'

1914: JUNIOR LEAGUE, DIVISION 2 WINNERS

Junior: fixtures 36, reported 25, won 16, lost 9. J. Anstead and A.P. Hunter move to Civil Service. Nevertheless, it is a good season for Merrion 1sts, who win Division 2 of the Junior League and are promoted back to Division 1. They gain 16 points, having played 10, won 8, lost 2. It is the first competition win for Merrion Cricket Club. The 2nds finish 4/6 in the Minor League, with 14 points, having played 14, won 7, lost 7. Yet a game against Clontarf 3rds is cancelled due to Merrion 2nds not turning up. Of the thirty-eight players used this season, only ten are known members of the Land Commission. First appearance of W. Rumney, future president of Merrion, and of a fourteen-year-old Cecil Little. On 13 June, Little makes 1 not out for Merrion 2nds against R & SPU. As he is a boarder in Kilkenny College at the time; it seems that the club has started coaching younger players with no links to the Land Commission and Upper Merrion Street. J. Smyth scores 50s against Leinster 3rds and Sandymount 2nds. Hill, Smyth and Fryer take the wickets:

Opponent	Result	Mer. 1st	Opp. 1st	Mer. 2nd	Opp. 2nd	Best Batting: Runs	Best Bowling: Wickets
Stewart Institution	Lost	103	126/7			O. James: 57	Spruce/Davidson: 3 each
RHMS	Won	127	108			O. Jones: 28	Spruce: 5
Pemb. Wand. 2nds*	Lost	17	144			Tyner: 6	Devaney: 4
Sandymount 2nds	Won	149	87			J. Smyth: 53	J. Smyth: 5
Palmerstown 3rds*	Won	42	38			T. Collins: 15	F. Fryer: 4
Carrickmines	Won	82	48				
Fairview*	Lost	29	42			T. Collins: 10*	J. Cooke: 5
Civil Service 3rds	Won	174/5	109				
R & SPU*	Won	148	88			F. Moore: 48	
GS & WR 2nds	Won	72	46				
Palmerstown 2nds	Lost	66	126/7				
Sackville Hall*	Lost	26	61				
Stewart Institution	Lost	68	106				
Palmerstown 3rds	Lost	52	113				
YMCA	Won	134	76			M. Gallaher: 40	J. Smyth: 8
Sandymount 3rds*	Won	28	18	28	22	T. Collins: 7	F. Fryer: 4
Sandymount 2nds	Won	74	21			F. Moore: 18*	M.A. Hill: 4
Pembroke 2nds	Won	136/6	54			M.A. Hill: 45	Smyth/Cooke: 3 each
Pemb. Wand. 2nds*	Lost	61	77			T. Collins: 23	F. Fryer: 7
Leinster 3rds	Won	138	100			J. Smyth: 53	M.A. Hill: 5
Sandymount 3rds*	Won	56	41				
YMCA 2nds*	Won	90	23			J. Archer: 25	F. Fryer: 5
Palmerstown 2nds	Won	90	29			W. Rumney: 44	Hill/Smyth: 3 each
Sackville Hall*	Lost	29	148/8				F. Fryer: 5
Pembroke 2nds	Won	131	117				

PROFILE: FRED FRYER

R–H middle-order batsman. R–A fast opening bowler. As well as helping the club to go Senior, topping the 1925 bowling averages with 46 wickets @ 5.52, Fred played sixteen games for the 1sts between 1926-1928, scoring 177 runs @ 11.80, with a top score of 36, and taking 51 wickets

@ 11.88, including 5 wickets in an innings on four occasions, and with best figures of 7/27 on debut against Civil Service. He may have taken the trail to England after that, looking for work.

1915: THE MERRION ALLOTMENTS

Junior: fixtures 28, reported 21, won 2, lost 19. Another dismal season. In the true sense of the word, Merrion are out of their league this year. The 1sts play in Division 1 of the Junior League and finish a bad last, with 2 points, having played 15, won 1, lost 14. Merrion 2nds also trudge along the bottom of Division 2, with 2 points, having played 13, won 1, lost 12. On 31 July, the 2nds are dismissed for 8 runs, possibly a record low score for a Merrion team, with eight of the batsmen failing to trouble the scorer. F.S. Irvine (Captain) and M.A. Hill are easily the best players in a season that sees the first appearance of future captain and president Jack (Geke) O'Donnell and of stalwart Frank Montgomery. O'Donnell takes all 8 wickets against R & SPU 2nds, while Irvine takes 9 wickets against Palmerstown. *The Irish Field* reports that for many clubs, members serving with the colours are to be granted honorary membership for the season. As did most of the Dublin clubs, Merrion makes its own contribution to the war effort by growing vegetables in allotments along the Dunluce side of the ground. How this affected the standard of cricket, or whether the cabbages and cauliflowers were even noticed by the players in the outfield, is unrecorded:

Opponent	Result	Mer. 1st	Opp. 1st	Mer. 2nd	Opp. 2nd	Best Batting: Runs	Best Bowling: Wickets
R & SPU	Lost	62	223/6			Dixon: 19	
Pemb. Wand.	Lost	49	93			Hobson: 13	M.A. Hill: 5
GS & WR	Won	168	125			M.A. Hill: 36	F.S. Irvine: 5
GS & WR 2nds*	Lost	24	71				
Leinster 2nds	Lost	169	240/6			J.I. Cooke: 32	M.A. Hill: 4
Pembroke 2nds	Lost	78	102			W. Rumney: 16	Croke: 5
Pemb. Wand. 2nds*	Won	41	37			W. O'Gara: 40	Devaney: 3
Palmerstown	Lost	59	157			McAteer: 22	
CYM*	Lost	69	232			H. Ryan: 39	O'Donnell: 5
Richmond Asylum	Lost	98	119/8			M.A. Hill: 46	M.A. Hill: 4
Civil Service 2nds	Lost	29	99/7			H. Ryan: 13*	W. Spruce: 4
GS&WR 2nds*	Lost	66	190			E. Cleary: 20	E. Cleary: 4
YMCA*	Lost	25	48				P. Devaney: 6
R & SPU	Lost	38	159			P. Devaney: 16	M.A. Hill: 5
R & SPU 2nds*	Lost	46	78			W. O'Gara: 12	J. O'Donnell: 8
Pemb. Wand.	Lost	40	119			P. Devaney: 16	F.S. Irvine: 7
CYM*	Lost	8	104/4			8 ducks	
Pemb. Wand. 2nds*	Lost	23	50				J. O'Donnell: 4
Pembroke 2nds	Lost	19	50				
Palmerstown	Lost	34	71			Spence: 16	F.S. Irvine: 9
Richmond Asylum	Lost	122	129/5			F.S. Irvine: 37	F.S. Irvine: 3

1916: THE EASTER RISING; JUNIOR LEAGUE, DIVISION B RUNNERS-UP

Junior: fixtures 12, reported 11, won 4, lost 6, drawn 1. Because of the Easter Rising, the season is shortened. The Junior League is split into two divisions of five teams each, with Merrion in Division B. A play-off is planned for 19 August. There is no Minor League. According to *The Irish Field*, 'The AGM of the Leinster Junior & Minor League was held in the Imperial Hotel on April 22nd. It was unanimously decided that no cup or caps be awarded to the team winning the Junior League title this season.'

F.H. Browning is not the only relevant victim of the rebellion. *The Irish Field* reports:

> *W.J. O'Gara, who played cricket and football for Merrion, met with a sad accident during the recent rebellion. While in bed one night a bullet came through the window, hitting him in the leg. Owing to not being able to be taken to hospital immediately, he lost a lot of blood, and his leg had to be amputated below the knee.*

But all is not necessarily lost. He might have been asked to play in the game between one-legged and one-armed veterans, organised in London after the war, which was won, weirdly, by the one-legged team. Years later, Cecil Little would tell the story of playing cricket in Anglesea Road towards the end of the Rising and noticing the flames of the GPO rising above the trees in Herbert Park, causing an early retreat to the nearest pub.

Of the twenty-one Merrion players this year, only four work in the Land Commission. Merrion play with just seven men against Sackville Hall. M.A. Hill, J.I. Cook and P. Devaney are the most effective performers. Hill scores 65 against Kingstown. P. McAteer scores 50 against R & SPU. Merrion finish second in Division B with 6 points, having played 9, won 3, lost 5, drawn 1:

Opponent	Result	Mer. 1st	Opp. 1st	Mer. 2nd	Opp. 2nd	Best Batting: Runs	Best Bowling: Wickets
Richmond Asylum	Lost	78	190/3			E. Buchanan: 26	M.A. Hill: 2
Pembroke 2nds	Lost	33	168			C. Mosberry: 9	J.I. Cook: 5
GS & WR	Won	170/6	118			J.I. Cook: 32	J.I. Cook: 5
R & SPU	Lost	103	220/1			P. McAteer: 54*	J.I. Cook: 1
GS & WR	Won	56/5	15			M.A. Hill: 24*	J.I. Cook: 5
Pemb. Wand.	Drawn	112/3	72/8			M.A. Hill: 41	P. Devaney: 5
Pemb. Wand.	Lost	21	50			M.A. Hill: 6	P. Devaney: 7
Richmond Asylum	Lost	102	122/4			A. Collins: 26	P. Devaney: 2
Pembroke 2nds	Won	76/7	56			J. O'Donnell: 24	J. O'Donnell: 5
Sackville Hall (F)	Lost	48	57			E.T. Cochrane: 20	T. Collins: 4
Kingstown (F)	Won	138	43			M.A. Hill: 65	M.A. Hill: 6

PROFILE: E.T. COCHRANE

R-H middle-order hard-hitting batsman. Wicket-keeper when Bill Rumney wasn't available. E.T. was captain of Merrion 1sts in that last year as a Junior club, 1925, under the pseudonym R.T. Jones. Subsequently he played only sixteen games for Merrion 1sts from 1926-1928, scoring 6 runs @ .66, and taking 8 catches and 4 stumpings. He continued to play many games for the Junior sides over the years and was club president in 1944.

1917: MERRION NINTH IN JUNIOR LEAGUE

Junior: fixtures 17, reported 17, won 3, lost 13, drawn 1. Of the thirty-five players used this year, only three are current or ex-employees of the Land Commission. The seesaw nature of Merrion's Junior cricket tenure continues with yet another abysmal season. There is only one Leinster Junior League division, with ten teams in it. Despite some close games, Merrion finish the season in ninth place, with 6 points, having played 17, won 3, lost 13, drawn 1. J. O'Donnell scores 65 not out against Richmond Asylum, the eventual league winners. M.A. Hill takes 41 wickets. Hill, O'Donnell and Phillips carry the rest of the team for most of the year:

Opponent	Result	Mer. 1st	Opp. 1st	Mer. 2nd	Opp. 2nd	Best Batting: Runs	Best Bowling: Wickets
Sackville Hall	Lost	18	57				Collins/Coughlan: 3 each
Pemb. Wand.	Lost	62	132/8			F. Jenkins: 27	Collins/Coughlan: 2 each
GS & WR	Lost	39	46			P. McAteer: 10	J. Coughlan: 7
YMCA	Lost	36	45			E.T. Cochrane: 12	J. O'Donnell: 6
Richmond Asylum	Lost	134	138/5			J. O'Donnell: 65*	
Pemb. Wand. 3rds*	Lost	16	53			E. Extras: 8	H.G. Cuthbert: 5
Leinster 2nds	Lost	84	140			E.T. Cochrane: 22	J. O'Donnell: 5
CYM	Lost	52	95/6			J. Spool: 12	M.A. Hill: 6
Pembroke	Lost	34	74			E.T. Cochrane: 15	M.A. Hill: 6
Civil Service 2nds	Lost	126	171			C. Phillips: 37	M.A. Hill: 4
Sackville Hall	Won	82	9			M.A. Hill: 24	M.A. Hill: 5
Pemb. Wand.	Lost	74	223			C. Phillips: 30	Little/Phillips: 3 each
YMCA	Won	108	71			C. Phillips: 47	M.A. Hill: 5
Richmond Asylum	Lost	61	155/6			J. O'Donnell: 19	M.A. Hill: 4
Leinster 2nds	Won	81/5	79			J. O'Donnell: 28*	M.A. Hill: 7
CYM	Lost	29	118/6			L. O'Connor: 13	Phillips/Little: 2 each
Civil Service 2nds	Lost	41	86/9			M.A. Hill: 23	M.A. Hill: 4

PROFILE: ROLLIE SHORTT

R-H batsman, the perfect number 11. R-A medium-pace bowler of sharp off-cutters. Could also swing the ball both ways. Educated at High School. Dentist. Later on, he often worked late and would practise in the dark with the gullible Brendan Curley and Gerry Doyle to fend off his phantom missiles. *Pick, Pack, Pock, Puck. Like drops of water in a fountain falling softly in the brimming bowl.* These were the days when Rollie was the only bowling machine that Merrion had. Every time he rattled one of their boxes, he'd mutter cheerfully, 'Sorry, old man.' He also played rugby, hockey and badminton.

Rollie gained one Irish cricket cap, in 1934, against the MCC, in which he gained a pair, and 3/66. He would have had many more if his physique had not ressembled that of an elephant with elephantisis. And he was a difficult man, who left Merrion in high dudgeon twice; once in 1922, to play for Pembroke, and once in 1949, to play for YMCA. Only Railway Union missed out, of Sandymount clubs.

Firsts captain in 1933, 1946. Played 270 Senior games, taking 701 wickets @ 13.69, with 5 wickets in an innings on 55 occasions. As he probably didn't have to bat that often, his run tally of 770 almost parallels his wickets. Passed his 1,000th competitive wicket for Merrion in 1948, and probably took another 200 over the following twelve years, having reluctantly gone down the ranks and captained the 2nds and 3rds for several years.

First Merrion player to 100, 200, 300, 400, 500, 600, 700 wickets. Hon. Treasurer during the 1930s. Rollie got married late in life, having been far too busy bowling for Merrion beforehand, to an enormous woman called Moss, which prompted Chris Mara to cajole him with the jibe, 'a rolling stone gathers no moss'. But all this excitement was far too much for the portly giant, and he died shortly afterwards.

1918: JUNIOR LEAGUE RUNNERS-UP

Junior: fixtures 20, reported 19, won 12, lost 6, drawn 1. This is the season that Merrion turns the corner in Junior cricket. Thanks to E.T. Cochrane (Captain) and J. O'Donnell (Vice-Captain and Secretary), the newly organised club is in contention to win the Junior League for the first time. However, they falter at the final hurdle against R & SPU, to give the Railway Union team the title by 1 point. Merrion finish 2/11, with 28 points, having played 20, won 14, lost 5, drawn 1. First appearance of future legend, Roland Henry (Rollie) Shortt. T. Kenny takes 65 wickets. C. Phillips makes 76 not out against Pembroke Wanderers and C. Little blasts 77 against CYM:

Opponent	Result	Mer. 1st	Opp. 1st	Mer. 2nd	Opp. 2nd	Best Batting: Runs	Best Bowling: Wickets
Richmond Asylum	Won	157	37			C. Phillips: 49	T. Kenny: 7
Pemb. Wand.	Won	193	57			C. Phillips: 76*	T. Kenny: 5
Richmond Asylum	Won	156	41			C. Phillips: 49	J. Coughlan: 6
Pembroke 2nds	Lost	22	156				J. Coughlan: 5
Leinster 2nds	Drawn	91/7	189/7			J. O'Donnell: 30*	T. Kenny: 3
CYM	Won	53	21			J. O'Donnell: 10	J. Coughlan: 6
GS & WR	Won	67	39			J. O'Donnell: 21	J. Coughlan: 6
University College	Lost	65	67			Nolan: 22*	T. Kenny: 6
Civil Service 2nds	Won	87	80			P. Kenny: 26	
R & SPU	Lost	64	183/8			T. Kenny: 19	T. Kenny: 7
Pemb. Wand.	Won	175	70			E.T. Cochrane: 47	R. Shortt: 4
Pembroke 2nds	Lost	46	70			T. Kenny: 16	T. Kenny: 8
Pemb. Wand. 2nds*	Lost	25	108			C. Little: 17	
Leinster 2nds	Won	95	86			Jones: 25	T. Kenny: 7
CYM	Won	147/9	45			C. Little: 77	T. Kenny: 6
GS & WR	Won	161	121			Redmond: 39	T. Kenny: 4
University College	Won	157	124			P. Kenny: 43	T. Kenny: 6
Civil Service 2nds	Won	58	43			Jones: 20	T. Kenny: 6
R & SPU	Lost	56	101			P. Kenny: 18	R. Shortt: 4

PROFILE: JACK O'DONNELL

R–H obdurate, defensive batsman. Occasional wicket-keeper and R–A seam bowler. *Geke* was educated at Blackrock College. A civil servant, he emigrated to America from 1923 to 1925 to join his brothers and make his fortune, and worked in a shoe shop in New York before returning to become a tobacconist in St Andrew's Street, and to lead Merrion into Senior cricket. Lived beside the Soraghan family in Anglesea Road, where his back garden housed an apple tree whose pink ladies encouraged at least one errant schoolboy into 'boxing the fox' and a life of crime. Also played rugby for Blackrock College and hockey for Pembroke Wanderers.

Played interprovincial cricket for Leinster and gained two Irish caps, in 1929 and 1930. Firsts captain on ten occasions and president in 1966, 1967. Captained the double-winning side in 1940. Played 222 Senior games, scoring 2,868 runs @ 16.20 and taking 70 catches. Hon. Secretary of Merrion for many years, and of the LCU for over twenty-five years. After a few scoops in the Red Bank Restaurant, the team's winter retreat, Geke's party piece was to sing 'On With The Motley' from *Pagliacci* on the steps of the old Irish Parliament building in College Green. '*Put on the costume…*' A Merrion titan and a strong captain and character, who suffered fools very heavily indeed, and who was the most wonderful servant to the club down the years.

NB Other teams playing between 1914 and 1918: Loughcrew, Ferns, Croom-Na-Boo, King Edward's Horse.

2.4. RECOVERY: 1919-1925

The Leinster League structure was reorganised after the war, with the introduction of a formal Senior League, an Intermediate League, and a Junior League. Most of the top teams, such as Civil Service, Pembroke and Leinster forsook their friendly battles to embrace competitive cricket in the Senior League. Phoenix also joined the party, after some deliberation. Other teams at this level included R & SPU, Trinity, University College (UCD) and the Royal Hibernian Military School. Clontarf joined in 1920, after their ground had recovered from growing vegetables during the war. County Kildare joined in 1921. But it would take another four years before the presentation of an actual Senior League Cup in 1923.

Merrion started this seven-year period in the Intermediate League, and finished it with promotion to the Senior League. The 2nds won the Junior League in 1920 and the 1sts were runners-up in the Intermediate League in 1923, and winners of that competition in 1924 and 1925. The political change created by the Anglo-Irish Treaty of December 1921, whereby the twenty-six counties became a self-governing dominion within the British Commonwealth, led to the departure of many English cricketers from the ruling bodies and a concomitant reduction in the standard of cricket played in Dublin. Teams such as the RHMS, University College (UCD) and County Kildare either vanished or were reduced in status, leaving a gap through which a successful Merrion Intermediate side could slip in 1926.

1919: THE WAR OF INDEPENDENCE; MERRION BECOMES AN OPEN CLUB

Junior: fixtures 29, reported 29, won 16, lost 12, drawn 1. The Anglo-Irish War of Independence starts in January, but does not affect a busy season of cricket. Merrion 1sts are in Division B of the newly formed Intermediate League. The 2nds are in the Junior League. For the first time, the club becomes open and accepts members from outside the Civil Service. J. O'Donnell is Secretary of the Junior Section within the executive committee of the Leinster Cricket Union (LCU), thereby commencing a period of service that will continue into the 1950s. The 1sts finish the season 4/7, with 14 points, having played 12, won 7, lost 5. J. O'Donnell scores 102 against Old Belvedere and C. Little scores 56 against YMCA. R. Shortt takes 51 wickets, while Kenny and Little complete a formidable bowling trio, who take 95 wickets between them:

Opponent	Result	Mer. 1st	Opp. 1st	Mer. 2nd	Opp. 2nd	Best Batting: Runs	Best Bowling: Wickets
Richmond Asylum (F)	Won	159	70			S. Nolan: 39	T. Kenny: 5
YMCA*	Lost	25	215			W.H. Long: 11	Mulligan: 2
R & SPU (F)	Lost	64	92			C. Little: 17	T. Kenny: 5
Old Belvedere*	Won	166/7	78			J. O'Donnell: 102*	F.S. Irvine: 6
Old Belvedere	Won	93	54			F.S. Irvine: 37	R. Shortt: 4
Avoca School*	Won	34	52	64	9		
Ordnance Survey*	Won	67	44			C. Little: 35	I. Healy: 7
Pembroke 2nds	Won	157	47			Stewart: 55	R. Shortt: 5
Civil Service 2nds	Lost	39	105	44	104	T. Kenny: 28	Kenny/Shortt: 6 each
CYM	Won	123	39			M. Abraham: 34*	R. Shortt: 7
Pemb. Wand. 2nds*	Lost	124	169/7			O'Donoghue: 33	I. Healy: 4
King's Hospital (F)	Drawn	96/6	122/6			C. Phillips: 28	F.S. Irvine: 3
Pemb. Wand. 2nds*	Lost	69	135			E. Beatty: 18	Collins/Little: 4 each
Pembroke 2nds*	Lost	99	129			F.S. Irvine: 29	T. Kenny: 5
CYM 2nds*	Won	95	50			E. Beatty: 40	P. Byrne: 5
YMCA	Won	147	141			C. Little: 56	R. Shortt: 8
King's Hosp. 2nds (F)*	Won	82	39			P. Byrne: 21	P. Byrne: 6
Old Belvedere 2nds*	Won	127	25			C. Little: 39	C. Little: 5
YMCA	Lost	62	163			C. Little: 13	C. Little: 5
Phoenix (F)	Lost	64	226/9			T. Kenny: 15	T. Kenny: 5
Ordnance Survey*	Lost	32	58			P. Byrne: 13	P. Byrne: 6
CYM	Lost	104	110			F.S. Irvine: 48	Irvine/Shortt: 5 each
CYM 2nds*	Won	49	43			Whitfield: 13	T. Collins: 8
Raheny (F)*	Won	71	45				
Civil Service 2nds	Won	82	47			T. Collins: 20	R. Shortt: 6
Leinster 3rds*	Lost	29	163/4	52		T. Collins: 24	McAllister: 2
Old Belvedere	Won	95	34			E.V. Jenkins: 37	C. Little: 6
Mr Stanley's XI (F)*	Won	107	52			C. Little: 47	R. Shortt: 6
Leinster 2nds	Lost	73	144/5			C. Little: 22	R. Shortt: 2

PROFILE: CECIL LITTLE

R-H wristy attacking batsman and R-A medium pace tweaker with a whiplash action. Fine close fielder. Could lash the ball over the wicket from boundary, underarm. Educated at Kilkenny College. Advertising representative and cricket and hockey coach in Masonic and St Columba's Schools. Used the pseudonym 'C.J. Fielder' when dodging work. Captained Leinster at interprovincial level. *Ces* declined an invitation to play for Ireland for reasons that are still unclear. Some say that it was due to business commitments; some argue that he might not have been able to afford it, as expenses in those days came out of the players' pockets; others claim that he preferred to go on one of the Merrion tours instead, and wasn't asked again. Yet his Palladian motto was, 'Have Bat, Will Travel' and he was known to cycle to places as far afield as Halverstown and Balrothery with his bat and pads strung across his shoulders, just to guest as one of their players.

Founder member of Pembroke Wanderers Hockey Club. Helped Merrion to Senior status in 1926 and played 260 Senior games between 1926 and 1958. Captained the 1sts in 1931 and 1937. Also played countless games for the 2nds, 3rds and 4ths, taking all 10 wickets for Merrion 2nds against YMCA in 1955. First Merrion batsman to 1,000, 2,000, 3,000, 4,000 runs. Scored

4,421 runs @ 22.10, including 4*100s and 20*50s. Took 516 wickets @ 15.30, including 29*5-wicket hauls. Took 88 catches and led the provincial all-rounder table in 1937 and 1940. He is third in the Merrion all-rounders' table and father to the brothers Barry and Alan. Like Walter Hammond, he regarded the hook shot as far too dangerous, but despite his nerves before batting, he was granted the title of 'Merrion's Bradman', by a Dublin sports writer. 'The Don' was a fixer of bats and bikes and a fellow of infinite jest with an impressive array of one-liners, such as, 'she was only the mortician's daughter, but anyone cadaver'. Get it?

1920: JUNIOR LEAGUE WINNERS

Junior: fixtures 23, reported 21, won 12, lost 9. The War of Independence continues and Merrion win another trophy. The 1sts finish 3/6 in Division B of the Intermediate League, with 10 points, having played 10, won 5, drawn or abandoned 2, lost 3. The 2nds tie for first place with Sandymount 2nds at the end of the season, and win a play-off, to win the Junior League. C. Little scores 50 for the 2nds against Ordnance Survey. Fryer, Little, Kenny and Shortt continue to share the wickets, with Little taking 7 for 29 in the play-off:

Opponent	Result	Mer. 1st	Opp. 1st	Mer. 2nd	Opp. 2nd	Best Batting: Runs	Best Bowling: Wickets
Carlisle*	Won	100	41			C. Little: 44	Healy/Little: 4 each
Leinster 3rds*	Lost	25	46			C. Moran: 8	J. Healy: 5
Leinster 2nds	Lost	35	111				
CYM	Won	135	11			E.W. Morris: 49	T. Kenny: 7
Nomads*	Won	81	27			Curtin: 17	Curtin: 5
Phoenix (F)	Lost	65	126	75	16/4	C. Phillips: 34	C. Little: 5
YMCA	Lost	79	122			W. Rumney: 22	T. Kenny: 6
Sandymount 2nds*	Lost	22	44	73	75	Chant: 22	F. Fryer: 11
Nomads (F)	Won	92	41			T. Kenny: 22	T. Kenny: 6
Ordnance Survey*	Won	114	36			C. Little: 50	F. Fryer: 8
CYM 2nds*	Lost	39	99	63	50	C. Moran: 22	D. Sheppard: 8
Pembroke 2nds	Won	97	40			F. Morris: 27	R. Shortt: 5
YMCA	Won	53	48			C. Phillips: 16	F. Fryer: 5
Ringsend United*	Won	112	15		49	D. Sheppard: 38	D. Sheppard: 10
Leinster 2nds	Lost	82	128			C. Little: 28	F. Fryer: 4
Richmond Asylum (F)	Lost	80	100			J. O'Donnell: 32	R. Shortt: 6
Ringsend United*	Lost	101	108			C. Moran: 43	R.D. Collins: 6
Mr Stanley's XI (F)	Won	99	27			C. Little: 33	F. Fryer: 8
CYM 2nds*	Won	125	48			W. McDonagh: 38	F. Fryer: 4
Ordnance Survey	Won	78	65			F. Fryer: 47	C. Little: 4
Sandymount 2nds	Won	90	79			F. Glanville: 31	C. Little: 7

Junior League Play-off*

LEINSTER JUNIOR LEAGUE PLAY-OFF 1920, SANDYMOUNT 2NDS V. MERRION 2NDS

Merrion 2nds			Sandymount 2nds		
J.A. Broderick	b. Taylor	1	R. Barnett	b. Little	5
W. McDonagh	b. Taylor	5	M. Maher	b. Little	9
F. Fryer	b. Darcus	0	A. Darcus	b. Little	4

R.D. Collins	b. Darcus	0	P. Byrne	c. Long b. Fryer	30
C. Little	c. Byrne b. Darcus	13	E. Head	run out	3
W. Rumney	c. O'Neill b. Darcus	10	J. Hussey	b. Little	1
F. Glanville	b. Taylor	31	A. Ducker	c. Broderick b. Little	0
D. Sheppard	b. Taylor	0	T. Hayden	run out	2
C. Moran	b. Taylor	8	J. Taylor	b. Little	0
W. Long	run out	5	H. Westrop	c. Fryer b. Little	10
P. Healy	not out	16	A. O'Neill	not out	1
	Extras	1		Extras	14
	Total	**90**		**Total**	**79**

1921: TWENTY-SIX-COUNTY DOMINION STATUS; INTERMEDIATE B LEAGUE RUNNERS-UP

Junior: fixtures 24, reported 22, won 14, lost 8. A short, rainy season, with mixed results. Merrion 1sts finish 2/6 in Division B of the Intermediate League, with 20 points, having played 10, won 7, lost 2, tied 1. The 2nds are 6/9 in the Junior League, with 15 points, having played 14, won 5, lost 9. There is a hint of a Merrion 3rds fixture this year, although no matches are reported.

In July, a truce is agreed and subsequent talks lead to partition and twenty-six-county dominion status for Southern Ireland. The popularity of cricket is affected by departing government officials, as well as the inroads being made by other sports, such as golf (ruining good walks) and lawn tennis. F. Glanville makes 33 out of a total score of 46 against Civil Service. Broderick, Rumney, Irvine and O'Donnell score 50s, while Fryer, Shortt and Sheppard share the wickets:

Opponent	Result	Mer. 1st	Opp. 1st	Mer. 2nd	Opp. 2nd	Best Batting: Runs	Best Bowling: Wickets
Civil Service 3rds*	Lost	46	109			F. Glanville: 33	D. Sheppard: 6
Epworth*	Won	75	29			E.W. Morris: 26*	F. Fryer: 6
DU 2nds*	Won	169	6				
Raheny*	Won	65	49			N.P. Healy: 21	M. Curtin: 5
YMCA	Won	160	71			W. Rumney: 38	F. Fryer: 5
Nomads*	Won	62	52			W. Long: 21	N.P. Healy: 8
Sandymount 2nds*	Lost	122	234/9			P. Broderick: 60	D. Sheppard: 3
Richmond Asylum	Won	152	41			F.S. Irvine: 55	R.H. Shortt: 6
Monkstown (F)	Won	115	83			J. O'Donnell: 36	F. Fryer: 5
Nomads*	Won	68	61			J. Bermingham: 11	N.P. Healy: 5
Sandymount	Won	118	69			F.S. Irvine: 41	Fryer/Shortt: 5 each
Clontarf 3rds (F)*	Won	155	58			J.A. Busher: 25	A. Aylward: 3
Leinster 2nds	Lost	122	175			J. O'Donnell: 61	O'Donnell: 4
YMCA 2nds	Lost	165	203			N.P. Healy: 37	D. Sheppard: 5
Sandymount	Lost	64	67			D. Sheppard: 17	R.H. Shortt: 7
Pembroke 2nds	Won	141	29			N.P. Healy: 26	R.H. Shortt: 5
Richmond Asylum	Lost	25	46	33			F. Fryer: 7
Sandymount 2nds*	Lost	52	75			C. Moran: 18	D. Sheppard: 6
Clontarf 2nds (F)	Won	76	56			W. Rumney: 35	R.H. Shortt: 6
Pemb. Wand.	Won	156/6	46			W. Rumney: 54	Sheppard/Fryer: 3 each
Civil Service 2nds	Won	203/6	64			W. Rumney: 64	R.H. Shortt: 4
Clontarf 2nds	Lost	43	48			E. Extras: 12	F. Fryer: 4

1922: CIVIL WAR

Junior: fixtures 15, reported 14, won 8, lost 4, drawn 2. An unsettled season, with bad weather and an inconvenient civil war erupting in the background. Sandymount win the Intermediate League. Merrion are depleted by the early departure of R.H. Shortt to Pembroke, the first of several huffy mood swings by the temperamental opening bowler. There is no sign of a 2nds team this year. Merrion start to play local schools. Michael Collins is assassinated, but cricket continues. J. O'Donnell (captain) and C. Little feature in a Leinster Junior interprovincial against Ulster, which Ulster win. C. Little gets a century against St Columba's College, as well as 68 against County Meath. Additionally there are 50s from J. O'Donnell, E.W. Morris, F. Fryer. Little, O'Donnell and Fryer also dominate the bowling:

Opponent	Result	Mer. 1st	Opp. 1st	Mer. 2nd	Opp. 2nd	Best Batting: Runs	Best Bowling: Wickets
Co. Meath	Won	165	31			C. Little: 68	R. Shortt: 5
YMCA	Won	83	37			J. O'Donnell: 29	F. Fryer: 4
CYM	Lost	56	82			C. Little: 12	Little/Healy: 2 each
YMCA	Won	182	89			J. O'Donnell: 60	C. Little: 7
St Columba's Coll. (F)	Drawn	248/3	125/6			C. Little: 101*	N.P. Healy: 3
High School (F)	Won	151	112			J. O'Donnell: 46	F. Fryer: 7
Sandymount	Lost	68	80			C. Little: 36	J. O'Donnell: 6
Leinster 2nds	Won	145	88			E.W. Morris: 53	J. O'Donnell: 4
Clontarf 2nds	Won	155	61			N.P. Healy: 45	F. Fryer: 6
Leinster 2nds	Lost	84	94			W. Rumney: 22	W. McDonagh: 6
Sandymount	Lost	72	81/9			R.T. Jones: 15	C. Little: 6
Hybla	Won	179/8	106			F. Fryer: 85	N.P. Healy: 4
Clontarf 2nds	Drawn	122	96/8			J. O'Donnell: 33	J. O'Donnell: 3
University College 2nds	Won	135/9	45			C. Little: 49	V.J. Cranley: 3

PROFILE: BILL RUMNEY

R-H dour batsman. Wicket-keeper. Bill played seventy-two games for Merrion 1sts between 1926–1933, scoring 786 runs @ 16.04, including 1*100 and 2*50s, and with a top score of 103*. He also took 28 catches and 8 stumpings as Merrion's first Senior wicket-keeper. He was captain of the 1sts in 1927 and president from 1947–49.

1923: INTERMEDIATE LEAGUE RUNNERS-UP

Junior: fixtures 16, reported 15, won 9, lost 5, drawn 1. Merrion 1sts lose the final of the Intermediate League to Sandymount in a closely fought game. A single 2nds fixture is mentioned, but not reported. J. O'Donnell, C. Little and F. Fryer represent Merrion on a Junior interprovincial Leinster team, which beats Ulster by 29 runs, Little scoring 40 out of a total of 92. Rollie Shortt starts off the season with Pembroke, but returns to Anglesea Road from Sydney Parade after the first Pembroke fixture. Did money change hands? A florin, perhaps? In a year of continuing bad weather, the civil war comes to an end and J. O'Donnell departs for America. *The Irish Field* of 25 August reports, 'J.A. O'Donnell played his last league match for Merrion on Sat, Aug 18th, as he leaves to take up an appointment in America. Blackrock College will also suffer by his absence, as he was a very useful centre three-quarter.' C. Little takes a hat-trick against Leinster 2nds. F. Fryer repeats the trick against Pembroke 2nds. Little scores over 500 runs, including 1 century and 3 fifties. Fryer takes 44 wickets:

Opponent	Result	Mer. 1st	Opp. 1st	Mer. 2nd	Opp. 2nd	Best Batting: Runs	Best Bowling: Wickets
Richmond	Lost	155	162/7			C. Little: 106	F. Fryer: 6
Pembroke 2nds	Won	63/9	41			C. Little: 39	Fryer/Little: 5 each
R & SPU	Won	102	53			Smith: 27*	F. Fryer: 8
Somerville	Won	69	49			F. Fryer: 39	F. Fryer: 7
Sandymount	Won	165	38			C. Little: 52	R. Shortt: 6
Leinster 2nds	Won	160	88			F. Fryer: 56	F. Fryer: 5
Pemb. Wand.	Lost	96	131			R. Shortt: 39	R. Shortt: 4
Clontarf 2nds	Drawn	189	102/8			F. Fryer: 60	P. Kenny: 4
Richmond	Lost	104	107			C. Little: 40	R. Shortt: 5
YMCA	Won	203	195			C. Little: 73	P. Kenny: 4
Leinster 2nds	Won	129	25			C. Little: 57	R. Shortt: 6
Clontarf 2nds	Won	147	23			P. Kenny: 48	C. Little: 6
Pembroke 2nds	Won	182/7	34			C. Moran: 70	F. Fryer: 7
Richmond	Lost	34	54			D. Moran: 12	C. Little: 6
Sandymount	Lost	137	146			C. Little: 46	F. Fryer: 6
Intermediate							
League final							

1924: INTERMEDIATE LEAGUE WINNERS

Junior: fixtures 19, reported 16, won 14, lost 2. E.T. Cochrane captains Merrion 1sts, with C. Little as vice-captain. After years of being beaten by teams such as Leinster 2nds, Civil Service 2nds and Pembroke 2nds, at last the wheel begins to turn, and Merrion start trouncing them, dismissing Leinster 2nds for 7 runs on one occasion. New knockout competitions are introduced for the Intermediate and Junior Cups, with the League winners earning only caps. Merrion are forced to yield a walkover to Sandymount in the semi-final of the Intermediate Cup, having failed to complete the rain-affected fixture in time. During yet another wet summer, Merrion 1sts win the Intermediate League for the first time, breaking Sandymount's three-year stranglehold. Merrion 2nds start in the Junior League, but fail to turn up for certain matches and are forced to pull out. Little and Fryer represent Leinster in a Junior interprovincial match against Ulster. Shortt, Little, Fryer, D. Moran and R.P. MacGarrigle also play friendly cricket for Mr Stanley's XI. Shortt gets 65 not out against Leinster 2nds and D. Moran scores 51 against Civil Service 2nds, while Fryer and Shortt get most of the wickets:

Opponent	Result	Mer. 1st	Opp. 1st	Mer. 2nd	Opp. 2nd	Best Batting: Runs	Best Bowling: Wickets
Clontarf 2nds	Won	70	37			D. Moran: 23	F. Fryer: 7
Leinster 2nds	Won	170/6	46			R. Shortt: 65*	Fryer/Shortt: 5 each
Balrath (F)	Won	57/3	53			C. Little: 27*	
St Columba's Coll. (F)*	Lost	48	204			E. Extras: 11	E.T. Collins: 7
Pemb. Wand.	Won	38	33				

St Pauls*	Lost	24	65/4			Hudson: 13	E.T. Collins: 3
YMCA	Won	61	43			C. Little: 21	R. Shortt: 6
King's Hospital (F)	Won	85	52			R.T. Jones: 24	
Sandymount 2nds*	Won	40	24	31	46	E.T. Collins: 13	J. Peat: 6
Civil Service 2nds	Won	174/9	40			D. Moran: 51	F. Fryer: 6
Pemb. Wand.	Won	87/5	51			R. Shortt: 47	R. Shortt: 6
YMCA	Won	149	121			E.W. Morris: 36	R. Shortt: 4
Leinster 2nds	Won	60	7			R. Shortt: 21	R. Shortt: 6
Sandymount (F)	Won	118	69			F. Fryer: 42	R. Shortt: 6
Pembroke 2nds	Won	122/7	63			N.P. Healy: 34	F. Fryer: 3
Sandymount	Won	165	67			C. Little: 37	Little/Fryer: 4 each

**Intermediate
League Final**

LEINSTER INTERMEDIATE LEAGUE FINAL 1924, SANDYMOUNT V. MERRION

Merrion			Sandymount		
D. Moran	b. Byrne	34	P.J. Byrne	b. Fryer	0
F. Fryer	b. Keating	0	R.J. Michals	st. Jones b. Fryer	11
C.J. Little	c. Byrne b. Knowles	37	N.W. Kavanagh	c. Jones b. Fryer	3
E.W. Morris	c. H. Williams b. Byrne	0	E. Branson	c. P. Kenny b. Little	5
N.P. Healy	b. Knowles	18	E. Holland	b. Fryer	2
B.G. Kenny	b. Knowles	5	H. Williams	c. Morris b. P. Kenny	11
P.B. Kenny	l.b.w. b. Knowles	27	M.H. Maher	b. Little	2
R.H. Shortt	b. Keating	12	E. Head	c. Cuthbert b. Little	7
P. MacGarrigle	c. & b. Knowles	0	J.E. Killen	b. Little	12
R.T. Jones	not out	12	M. Knowles	b. P. Kenny	0
H. Cuthbert	b. Keating	1	P. Keating	not out	1
	Extras	19		Extras	13
	Total	**165**		**Total**	**67**

1925: INTERMEDIATE LEAGUE WINNERS

Junior: fixtures 30, reported 26, won 18, lost 7, drawn 1. In their last season in Junior cricket, Merrion 1sts win the Intermediate League again, captained by one R.T. Jones, a pseudonym for the ever-present E.T. Cochrane. Presumably his disguise is necessary for professional reasons, and I.P. Freely is already taken. A strong 2nds re-emerges to finish fourth in Division B of the Junior League. The Minor League restarts, with just five teams. Merrion are not represented. Merrion 1sts beat a strong Phoenix side – including several Gentlemen of Ireland players – in a friendly match, dismissing that year's Senior League winners for 14 runs, a result that influences their efforts to join the ranks of Senior cricketers. J. O'Donnell returns from America to play the last few games, while Fred Fryer spends part of the year in the USA. Shortt takes 52 and Fryer 46 scalps. Little scores 474 runs, including 4 fifties and 1 century. At the end of another wet season, Merrion's application to join the Leinster Senior League is accepted, provided the club undertakes certain improvements to the wickets and outfield. The troublesome journey that began in 1892, with the enthusiasm of John Aloysius Swaine, has come to an end at last:

Opponent	Result	Mer. 1st	Opp. 1st	Mer. 2nd	Opp. 2nd	Best Batting: Runs	Best Bowling: Wickets
Clontarf 2nds (F)	Won	237	58			R. Shortt: 54	P.B. Kenny: 6
Sandymount	Lost	75	82			R. MacGarrigle: 26	P.B. Kenny: 5
St Columba's Coll. (F)	Won	63/3	41			N.P. Healy: 32	C. Little: 5
Malahide*	Won	74	50			J. Brown: 26	W. Walker: 7
Sandymount (C)	Lost	47	49			N.P. Healy: 9	R. Shortt: 6
CYM 2nds*	Lost	23	36			G. Dowling: 9	J. Peatt: 6
Richmond	Won	144/8	136			C. Little: 51	Little/Walker: 3 each
YMCA 2nds*	Won	113	54			F. Pierce: 31	F. Pierce: 5
R & SPU	Won	148	68			R. MacGarrigle: 48	P.B. Kenny: 5
St Johns*	Won	73	36			F. Pierce: 35	Walker/Pierce: 5 each
Civil Service 2nds	Won	129	86			C. Little: 58	Shortt/Fryer: 3 each
St James's*	Lost	27	144	60/8		C. Moran: 11	F. Pierce: 7
Dundrum Asylum (F)	Drawn	140	76/5			E.W. Morris: 35	F. Fryer: 3
CYM	Won	106/4	28			R. Shortt: 33*	F. Fryer: 6
Richmond	Won	196/6	118			C. Little: 74	F. Fryer: 7
Pemb. Wand. 2nds*	Lost	67	179			J. Alleyne: 25	M. Nicholson: 6
Monkstown*	Lost	81	89			R. MacGarrigle: 13	W. Walker: 6
St James's*	Won	107	47			W. Walker: 38*	M. Nicholson: 6
Phoenix (F)	Won	191	14		52/3	C. Little: 78	Fryer/Shortt: 4 each
Pemb. Wand. 2nds*	Lost	86	90				
CYM	Won	224/2	33			C. Little: 111*	Fryer/Shortt: 5 each
CYM 2nds*	Won	47	38			G. Darling: 13	M. Nicholson: 5
Sandymount	Won	217	81			D. Moran: 44	F. Fryer: 5
Wills*	Won	81	63				V.J. Cranley: 4
Leinster 2nds	Won	146	92			F. Fryer: 59	R. Shortt: 6
Intermediate							
League Final							
Pembroke (F)	Won	169	70			N.P. Healy: 40	Fryer/Shortt: 5 each

LEINSTER INTERMEDIATE LEAGUE FINAL 1925, LEINSTER 2NDS V. MERRION

Merrion			Leinster 2nds		
J.A. O'Donnell	b. Frazer	0	F.W. Fox	c. & b. Shortt	5
F. Fryer	st. Hession b. O'Kelly	59	A.E. Bex	c. Little b. Shortt	3
C.J. Little	b. Despard	0	J. O'Connor	b. Fryer	1
D.D. Moran	b. Nicholson	5	P. Hession	b. Shortt	11
R. MacGarrigle	c. Hession b. O'Kelly	27	A. Morton	c. Jones b. Shortt	15
E.W. Morris	b. Frazer	4	M. Nicholson	c. Pierce b. O'Donnell	22
R.H. Shortt	c. Frazer b. O'Kelly	9	R. Cunningham	c. Healy b. Fryer	9
N.P. Healy	b. O'Kelly	4	J. Graham	not out	7
P.B. Kenny	c. Despard b. Nicholson	29	B. O'Kelly	st. Jones b. Shortt	1
F. Pierce	b. Nicholson	2	A. Frazer	run out	1
R.T. Jones	not out	1	W. Despard	b. Shortt	2
	Extras	6	Extras		15
	Total	**146**	**Total**		**92**

NB Other teams playing between 1919 and 1925: School of Musketry, Lady of the Rose, The Beavers.

MERRION FIRST XI. C.C. AVERAGES, 1925.

Matches played 17, won 14, lost 2, drawn 1.
Runs for—2,445 for 140 wickets. Average per wicket, 17.46.
Runs against—1.132 for 162 wickets. Average per wicket, 6.99.

BATTING.

	Inns.	Runs.	Most in Inns.	Times not out.	Aver.
C. J. Little	17	474	111*	2	31.60
R. P. MacGarrigle	11	205	48	1	20.50
F. W. Fryer	10	198	59	0	19.80
R. T. Jones	13	119	26	6	17.00
N. P. Healy	15	242	41	0	16.13
R. H. Shortt	12	171	54	1	15.54
D. D. Moran	13	174	44	0	13.38
E. W. Morris	13	161	35	0	12.38
P. B. Kenny	12	143	39	0	11.91
C. Moran	6	58	23	0	9.44
L. J. Cranley	10	39	12*	3	5.57

* Not out.

BOWLING.

	O.	M.	R.	W.	Aver
F. W. Fryer	117.8	26	254	46	5.52
P. B. Kenny	79.5	28	153	27	5.66
R. H. Shortt	179.3	64	304	52	5.85
C. J. Little	76	17	183	20	9.14

Senior status is achieved.

3

THE MIDDLE YEARS

3.1. SENIOR STATUS: 1926-1939

This period represented the growth of Merrion as a Senior club, culminating in the Leinster Senior League/Cup double wins of 1940 – the first team to achieve this – and followed by twenty seasons during which the club was consistently challenging for, and winning, Leinster cricket competitions.

The early years in the Senior League were characterised by adequate performances, with the 1sts usually placed around the middle of any table. However, they finished runners-up to Leinster in 1931, in a year the Senior League had been suspended. They also narrowly missed winning the Senior League in 1934 by a fraction of a percentage point, losing to the winners, Leinster, in the last game of the season, when a draw would have seen them home. In 1936, they were the losing finalists in the newly formed Leinster Senior Challenge Cup, won by Leinster, who were obviously the team to beat.

Junior Merrion improved gradually during this period. Merrion 2nds were runners-up to Clontarf 2nds in the Intermediate Cup final of 1928, but beat YMCA to win it in 1929, before losing another final to Railway Union in 1939. From 1934 onwards, Merrion 3rds, after a difficult start, continued to participate fully in both the Junior League and Cup, winning nothing.

From 1926, only Senior games are detailed, together with a summary of the performance of the Junior teams.

1926: SENIOR LEAGUE DEBUTANTS

Senior: fixtures 17, reported 17, won 7, lost 5, drawn 5. Captain: J.A. O'Donnell. This is Merrion's first year in the Leinster Senior League. They replace University College Club, who have disbanded. Work continues on improvements to the playing area during yet another damp summer. The club imports a ton of marl to treat the wickets. This is so successful that they supply other clubs – Leinster, Grangecon and Clontarf – with the excess mudstone. It is 10 July before the first of only two Senior matches is played this year at Anglesea Road, resulting in a draw against Clontarf. The other home game is against R & SPU, also in July. Merrion 1sts adjust well to the higher standard, and the team finishes 5/8, with 14 points, having played 12, won 4, lost 6, drawn 2. O'Donnell, Little, Rumney and P.B. Kenny all score 50s, while Shortt – 45 wickets @ 9.24 – and Fryer – 30 wickets @ 10.80 – finish second and third respectively in the Leinster bowling analyses. Fryer takes 7 wickets on his Senior League debut against Civil Service. Little and Fryer play for Leinster against Ulster, Fryer taking 4 wickets. A tour to Kilkenny is arranged and a team from Carlow visits Anglesea Road:

Opponent	Result	Mer.	Opp.	Best Batting: Runs	Best Bowling: Wickets
YMCA (F)	Won	180	114	J. O'Donnell: 53	W. Rumney: 4
Civil Service	Won	93	46	D. Moran: 33	F. Fryer: 7
St Columba's Coll. (F)	Drawn	49/7	121/8	C. Little: 22	J. O'Donnell: 3
Gowran Castle (F)	Won	89	58	C. Little: 22	R. Shortt: 6
Phoenix	Lost	94	107	P.B. Kenny: 27	R. Shortt: 7
Leinster	Lost	186	199/5	C. Little: 61	Kenny/Short: 2 each
Leinster	Lost	91	154	Kenny: 21	R. Shortt: 4
Phoenix	Won	147	110	J.A. Stokes: 33*	F. Fryer: 4
Clontarf	Drawn	173	34/3	J. O'Donnell: 26	F. Fryer: 2
Carlow (F)	Won	203/5	147	W. Rumney: 59	C. Little: 5
R & SPU	Won	171/5	63	P.B. Kenny: 54	Shortt/Little: 5 each
Pembroke	Drawn	105/8	212/3	V.J. Cranley: 31	R. Shortt: 2
Civil Service	Lost	47	114	Kenny/Little: 11 each	F. Fryer: 5
Pembroke	Drawn	105/8	212/6	P.B. Kenny: 50	C. Little: 3
R & SPU	Won	200/8	54	J. O'Donnell: 79*	R. Shortt: 6
Dundrum (F)	Drawn	204/4	98/9	W. Rumney: 73*	C. Little: 3
Clontarf	Lost	71	80	J. O'Donnell: 34*	R. Shortt: 7

Junior: Merrion 2nds are in the Intermediate League and perform poorly, playing 9 games, winning 3, losing 6. They beat Dublin University 2nds twice and are knocked out of the Intermediate Cup by Pembroke 2nds in the first round. J.A. Stokes (a pseudonym for O. Healy, who also played for Civil Service) is their best batsman, scoring a brace of 50s. H. Cuthbert, a Superintendent in the Church Property Department at 21 Upper Merrion Street, is the most effective bowler. No Merrion team enters the Junior and Minor Leagues. First appearance of future stalwart and president, J. McAlinden.

1927: THORNTON IS MERRION'S FIRST INTERNATIONAL

Senior: fixtures 18, reported 18, won 3, lost 4, drawn 9, tied 2. Captain: W.V. Rumney. Yet another wet season, when several weekends are lost entirely to rain, and half the games are drawn. Merrion 1sts finish 6/8 in the Senior League, with 15 points, having played 13, won 2, lost 3, drawn 7, tied 1. As an indication of how times have changed since 1892, the 1sts tie with and beat Civil Service, the club the old Land Commission cricket team had aspired to conquer. The ground is not entirely acceptable yet, so Merrion must play Dublin University, Leinster and Pembroke away twice. Merrion tour the Kilkenny area again, playing Maryborough and Leix, and Bennett's Bridge.

The accounts for this year show a figure of £5 4s 0d allocated to a 'horse for rolling'; £4 4s 0d for 'bowling screens'; total subscription income as £42 0s 0d; income from 'Cullen grazing' as £3 3s 0d; and £44 2s 4d as a hefty profit from the 'Stop Watch Competition'. R.P. MacGarrigle and P. Thornton join Merrion from Trinity during the long vacation. Thornton and Little represent Leinster versus the visiting Cambridge Crusaders. Thornton gains his first of six international caps against the MCC at Lord's. Little scores a century against Monkstown and several other 50s in a summer total of over 600 runs, including friendlies. O'Donnell and Kenny also score 50s. Shortt, Little and Thornton dominate the bowling, with Little grabbing 36 wickets:

Opponent	Result	Mer.	Opp.	Best Batting: Runs	Best Bowling: Wickets
R & SPU	Won	106	41	J. O'Donnell: 23	R. Shortt: 7
Civil Service	Tied	49	49	J. O'Donnell: 11	R. Shortt: 8
DU	Lost	97	199/3	C. Little: 33	C. Little: 2
Bennett's Bridge (F)	Drawn	180	72/5	C. Little: 78	C. Little: 3
Clontarf	Drawn	126/5	175/8	C. Little: 57*	C. Little: 3
Leinster	Drawn	85/4	124	J. O'Donnell: 25	R. Shortt: 6
Phoenix	Drawn	68/4	167	J. O'Donnell: 32	C. Little: 5
Clontarf	Lost	76	166	C. Little: 18	P. Thornton: 4
Leinster	Drawn	107/8	197/3	W. Rumney: 37*	P. Thornton: 2
Maryboro & Leix (F)	Tied	73	73		
Bennett's Bridge (F)	Drawn	180	72/5	C. Little: 78	C. Little: 3
Civil Service	Won	93/7	53	W. Rumney: 32	C. Little: 4
DU	Drawn	78/4	176/6	J. O'Donnell: 46*	Little/Keegan: 3 each
Pembroke	Drawn	146	41/6	C. Little: 34	P. Thornton: 4
R & SPU	Drawn	216/3	115/8	P.B. Kenny: 77	C. Little: 6
Pembroke	Lost	68	202/2	P.B. Kenny: 32*	Shortt/Keating: 1 each
Maryboro & Leix (F)	Lost	177	179/4	J. O'Donnell: 75	Cuthbert/Muldoon: 2 each
Monkstown (F)	Won	228/2	61	C. Little: 104*	C. Little: 5

Junior: Merrion 2nds are in Division B of the Intermediate League. They play 13 games, winning 6, losing 4 and drawing 3. Carlisle knock them out of the Intermediate Cup. A. Keegan and A. Keating score 50s. P. Muldoon and H. Cuthbert take most wickets. A Merrion 3rds team makes a first appearance, but play only two friendlies and lose them both comprehensively.

PROFILE: PATRICK THORNTON

R-H forceful batsman. R-A medium-pace swing bowler. Brilliant fielder. Played ten games for Merrion between 1927-1930, scoring 199 runs @ 22.11 and taking 20 wickets @ 12.30. Won Marchant Cup in 1928 while playing for Dublin University, with 446 runs @ 64, including 2 centuries, 1 in 55 minutes against Pembroke. Also played for Cape Town University, Western Province, and six times for Ireland, scoring 120 runs @ 13.33, with a highest score of 37 against the West Indies, and taking 14 wickets @ 15.50, with best figures of 4/64. Son of George Thornton, a South African Test player. Patrick, who was a doctor by profession, died in 1961, aged fifty-six, at East London, Cape Province, South Africa.

1928: LITTLE SCORES LIGHTNING TON AGAINST CIVIL SERVICE; INTERMEDIATE CUP RUNNERS-UP

Senior: fixtures 19, reported 19, won 8, lost 7, drawn 4. Captain: J.A. O'Donnell. Merrion 1sts are strengthened by the return of Fred Fryer from England. An experiment is made with the Leinster Senior League, to prevent a player from assisting two clubs. *The Irish Field* reports, 'Each club will only play one league match each season, home and away, in alternate years, with every other Senior club.' All matches must be completed before the second Saturday in July and so Merrion undertake tours for the remainder of the season. The new structure doesn't help their performance much, as they finish joint 6/8, with 7 points, having played 7, won 2, lost 4, drawn 1. Nevertheless, Little is second in the Leinster batting averages, with 304 runs @ 60.8. He scores 102 not out against Civil Service in fifty-five minutes, the first Merrion Senior League century and one of the fastest ever recorded in that competition. Ninety-four of the runs come in boundaries, with 60 off 14 consecutive balls – 12*4s followed by 2*6s. J.A. Delaney scores 50 on debut against Leinster. Shortt and Fryer take 47 wickets between them in only seven games. Little plays for Leinster in two interprovincial games. Against Ulster he scores 46 not out in the 2nd innings. With 442 runs @ 63.14, Thornton wins the Marchant Cup for batting, based mainly on his performances for Dublin University. He plays four times for Ireland, taking a total of 12 wickets:

Opponent	Result	Mer.	Opp.	Best Batting: Runs	Best Bowling: Wickets
DU	Won	185/6	183/5	C. Little: 87*	R. Shortt: 3
Leinster	Lost	110	229/7	J.A. Delaney: 50	Shortt/Fryer: 2 each
Civil Service	Won	163/1	50	C. Little: 102*	F. Fryer: 7
Clontarf	Lost	66	111	C. Little: 23	R. Shortt: 8
King's Hospital (F)	Drawn	61/4	154/8	R.T. Jones: 18	F. Fryer: 3
Phoenix	Lost	71	78	C. Little: 20	R. Shortt: 5
Cork Co. (F)	Lost	92	97/9	C. Little: 26	R. Shortt: 5
R & SPU	Lost	92	94	J. O'Donnell: 29	F. Fryer: 6
Pembroke	Drawn	171	105/5	C. Little: 47	F. Fryer: 4
Co. Meath (F)	Won	116/3	84	R. MacGarrigle: 58*	R. Shortt: 4
Leinster (F)	Lost	41	219	R. MacGarrigle: 11	F. Fryer: 4
DU Long Vacation (F)	Drawn	88	44/4	J. O'Donnell: 22	F. Fryer: 3
Crotanstown (F)	Won	154	57	A. Elkins: 42	F. Fryer: 7
Co. Wexford (F)	Won	205/6	84	C. Little: 88	G.T. Kenay: 4
Clontarf (F)	Lost	91	210/7	G.T. Kenay: 52	R. Shortt: 3
Pembroke (F)	Drawn	179	156/7	P. Thornton: 74	F. Fryer: 5
Raheny (F)	Won	72	50	E. Barber: 26	R. McCartan: 5
Queen's Co. (F)	Won	199/9	87	E. Barber: 48	P.B. Kenny: 6
Grangecon (F)	Won	229/4	59	C. Little: 77	G.T. Kenay: 7

Junior: Merrion 2nds are in the Intermediate League, B Division, and lose to Clontarf 2nds in the Intermediate Cup final, 108 to 148. In a game against Sandymount, they walk off the field when the ball is lost – having already been beaten – rather than play with a new ball, prompting censure from the writer of the 'Irish Notes' section of *The Cricketer Annual*, and a subsequent letter from G.V.S. Ireland, the Merrion Hon. Secretary, pleading that it had been too cold to continue and both captains agreed to end the game anyway! Ah, Sandymount, Sandymount. A. Keegan, J. Walker and R. McCartan score 50s. P. Muldoon and H. Cuthbert share most of the wickets. A 3rds is entered in the Minor League, but the club struggles to put out a team, and only three games are recorded, all losses.

PROFILE: RALPH McCARTAN

R-H elegant batsman. R-A swing bowler. Educated at CUS. Chartered Accountant with Hodgson, Harris & Company. Also played rugby for Bective. A swimmer, until rheumatic fever forced him to give it up. Played cricket at Junior interprovincial level for Leinster. Played eighty-five times for Merrion 1sts, scoring 800 runs @ 11.26 and taking 53 wickets @ 15.26, including a hat-trick against Phoenix in 1934. Took 24 catches. Went down the ranks and played many times for the 2nds and 3rds. Hon. Treasurer for many years in the 1930s. During the Emergency, Ralph was responsible for managing the Theatre Royal and Gaiety, and arranging for actors such as Donald Wolfit, Jimmy Durante and Ben & Bebe Lyons to come to Dublin to entertain the bored neutrals. (See Collage 1 for photos of Ralph playing rugby against the great Jimmy O'Dea, Biddy Mulligan, the pride of the Coombe.)

1929: A NEW PAVILION; INTERMEDIATE CUP WINNERS

Senior: fixtures 14, reported 14, won 7, lost 2, drawn 5. Captain: J.A. O'Donnell.
The previous year's experiment with the Senior League seems to have been forgotten, as there are now two Divisions of four teams, with Merrion in Division B. All league matches are to be played in May and June, with a League final between the two section winners on 13 July. Merrion finish 3/4 with 8 points, having played 6, won 2, lost 2, drawn 2. The season is done and dusted by 4 July, so Merrion 1sts amuse themselves with friendlies for the remainder, touring the Kilkenny region again. J. O'Donnell wins the first of two international caps when he plays against the Catamarans in College Park. Loughery and Thornton join Merrion from Dublin University after the Senior League has finished, but only play a couple of friendly matches in late summer, each scoring centuries. Loughery plays twice for Ireland this year, against the Catamarans and Scotland, while Thornton gains his last cap against Scotland. W. Rumney also hits a century and Little, O'Donnell and Rumney score 50s. G.T. Kenay takes 20 wickets in the six Senior games, but T. O'Neill Kiely is the provincial leader with 16 wickets @ 5.68, and would have won the O'Grady Cup if it had existed then (it won't be introduced until 1937). C. Little takes most catches in the Leinster Senior League, with 6 from 6.

Another ton of marl is purchased, at a cost of £16, and again some of this is sold on to other clubs. A new galvanized-tin pavilion is purchased for £72 from Bective Rugby Club, complete with wooden floors and a tea room at the back. In 1935 this will be extended to include a separate tea room, some scary toilets and a machinery shed, at a cost of £70 14s 0d, and in 1936 it will be wired for electricity, at a cost of £11 14s 0d. This building will last until it is deliberately burned down in 1971. 'Who done it?' Read on:

Opponent	Result	Mer.	Opp.	Best Batting: Runs	Best Bowling: Wickets
R & SPU	Drawn	168	64/8	W. Rumney: 103*	T. Kiely: 3
Bennett's Bridge (F)	Drawn	41; 34/9	87; 29		C. Little: 6
Castlecomer (F)	Won	101/8	86	C. Little: 36*	C. Little: 8
R & SPU	Won	139/5	106	W. Rumney: 67	T. Kiely: 8
Phoenix	Lost	64	143/6	R. McCartan: 30	Little/Shortt: 2 each
Pembroke	Drawn	27/3	109	J. O'Donnell: 14	R. McCartan: 5
Phoenix	Lost	113	172/5	J. O'Donnell: 66	Kiely/McCartan: 2 each
Pembroke	Won	222	113	J. O'Donnell: 86	R. Shortt: 7
Clontarf (F)	Won	184/4	116	C. Little: 54*	T. Kiely: 4
Bennett's Bridge (F)	Won	192	90	P. Thornton: 112	G.T. Kenay: 4
Clontarf (F)	Won	148/9	137	W. Rumney: 32*	G.T. Kenay: 7

Merrion's home ground at Anglesea Road in 1929.

Curragh (F)	Drawn	133	61/8	J.A. Stokes: 34	T. Kiely: 6
Queen's Co. (F)	Won	221/8	48	P.A. Thornton: 71	Kiely/Kenay: 5 each
Leinster (F)	Drawn	226/7	113/5	W. Loughrey: 120	R. Shortt: 2

Junior: Merrion 2nds have an excellent run, bolstered by volunteers from the 1sts pleading for a game. They win the Intermediate Cup, thanks to a late attacking innings of 55 by P.B. Kenny in the final. They are in Division B of the Intermediate League, where they play 15, win 6, lose 7, draw 2. A. Keegan scores a century against Phoenix 2nds in the Intermediate Cup. T. Kiely and J.A. Delaney score 50s, while Kiely also shines with the ball, scalping over 50 victims. R. McCartan plays for Leinster versus Ulster in a Junior interprovincial. First appearance of Des O'Connor, future 1sts captain and stalwart. A 3rd eleven is entered into Division C of the Junior League, but fielding three teams proves to be a struggle again, and they fail to turn up on several occasions. Only four matches are recorded, including a 1st win against Sandymount 2nds.

1930: LOUGHERY AND O'DONNELL PLAY FOR IRELAND

Senior: fixtures 19, reported 19, won 8, lost 4, drawn 7. Captain: J.A. O'Donnell.
More rain, rain, rain. Many games are cancelled. This doesn't matter much to the 1sts, as there's no Senior League at all this season. Technically, all games are friendlies. The results are maintained, but don't count in provincial statistics. The published tables do not include Dublin University(#) games. In this supposedly non-competitive season, Merrion finish 3/7 with 54.54 per cent, having played 11, won 5, lost 2, drawn 4. Although he averages less than 10 runs this season for Merrion, J. O'Donnell plays for Ireland against the MCC at the Mardyke, Cork. W. Loughery plays three times for Ireland, and his sole Senior match for Merrion against Civil Service. There's another Whitsuntide tour of the Kilkenny area, where Merrion beat both Carlow and Bennett's Bridge. P. Thornton plays seven games for Merrion this season. Little, Thornton and Kenay play for Leinster against Ulster. O'Donnell, Little, Thornton and Shortt play for a Free State XI against the touring Civil Service Crusaders. Delaney, Barber and Kenny score 100s, with 50s from Little and Loughery. Shortt takes 36 league wickets:

Opponent	Result	Mer.	Opp.	Best Batting: Runs	Best Bowling: Wickets
Leinster	Drawn	171/9	65/8	C. Little: 40	R. Shortt: 5
Railway Union	Drawn	140/4	10/0	P. Thornton: 36	
Phoenix	Drawn				
Clontarf	Won	103	21	P. Thornton: 34	R. Shortt: 7
The Curragh (F)	Won	167/3	66	J.A. Delaney: 101	R. Shortt: 5
Pembroke	Drawn	222/7	188/9	J.A. Delaney: 50	R. McCartan: 4

Clongowes Coll. (F)	Lost	170	183/1		
DU#	Lost	132	190	C. Little: 57	P. Thornton: 6
Phoenix	Won	144/3	113	C. Little: 51*	T. Kiely: 5
DU#	Drawn	195/7	173/4	C. Little: 80	
Civil Service	Won	205/9	103	E. Barber: 101*	R. Shortt: 7
Clontarf	Lost	119	120/8	E. Barber: 37	G.T. Kenay: 6
Cork Co. (F)	Drawn	138/7	102/7	E. Barber: 38	G.T. Kenay: 4
Spike Island (F)	Drawn	111	102/9	G.T. Kenay: 26	Little/McCartan: 5 each
Cork Bohemians (F)	Won	222/8	79	J.A. Delaney: 67	G.T. Kenay: 7
Pembroke	Won	63	45	E. Barber: 30*	C. Little: 7
Leinster	Lost	65	127	J.A. Delaney: 25	J. Henry: 4
Civil Service	Won	188/8	43	W. Loughrey: 64*	R. Shortt: 6
Queen's Co. (F)	Won	207/8	104	P.B. Kenny: 103*	T. O'Carroll: 7

Junior: Merrion 2nds are in Division B of the Intermediate League. They finish 4/8 with 23 points, having played 14, won 7, lost 4, drawn 2, no result 1. Leinster 2nds knock them out of the Intermediate Cup, 306/3 to 100. H. Cuthbert scores a couple of 50s, while T. O'Carroll takes 25 wickets. Merrion 3rds are in Division C of the Junior League and complete a season's cricket for the first time. They finish 4/6 with 7 points, having played 10, won 2, lost 2, drawn 1, no result 5. Malahide dispose of them in the Junior Cup, 55 to 234/5.

PROFILE: BILL LOUGHERY

R-H opening batsman. Brilliant cover fielder. Played one game for Merrion, scoring 64 not out against Civil Service in 1930. Educated at Campbell College. Later a mathematics teacher and cricket master at Rugby School, the setting for *Tom Brown's Schooldays*. Also played the game of rugby, at fly-half and wing. Played for Dublin University, NICC, Ireland. Played six games for Ireland between 1929 and 1933, due mainly to his college performances, scoring 134 runs @ 12.18, with a top score of 29 against the MCC at College Park. A popular figure, Bill was born in Belfast and died in Hertfordshire in 1977, aged sixty-nine. He was widely mourned.

1931: THE RIVER DODDER OVERFLOWS ITS BANKS

Senior: fixtures 14, reported 14, won 9, lost 2, drawn 3. Captain: C.J. Little. For the second season in succession there is no formal Leinster Senior League and the games are categorised as 'club matches'. This is unfortunate, as Merrion finish runners-up, having played 10, won 6, lost 1, drawn 3. It's their best performance so far as a Senior team. They have five matches cancelled (four due to rain), while Leinster, the winners, only have three matches cancelled. Railway Union depart voluntarily from the Senior ranks, not to return until 1945. Little plays for Leinster versus Ulster, scoring 43 in the 2nd innings. Shortt and Little play for Leinster versus Munster. Barber, O'Donnell and Delaney score 50s. Shortt and Little take 50 wickets between them. This is in spite of the River Dodder overflowing its banks and flooding the ground in autumn, depositing rocks and silt, submerging the pavilion and sweeping away the boundary wall. The enthusiasm of the members saves the day, as it will do on two subsequent occasions. First appearances of K. Dempsey and W. Lindsay, future stalwarts and members of the double-winning side of 1940:

Opponent	Result	Mer.	Opp.	Best Batting: Runs	Best Bowling: Wickets
Pembroke	Won	87	79	C. Little: 30	C. Little: 5
Leinster	Drawn				
Civil Service	Lost	125	137/5	J.A. Delaney: 34	Shortt/Little: 2 each
Clontarf	Won	80/6	71	J. O'Donnell: 30	R. Shortt: 4
Cork Bohemians (F)	Won	87/5	67	C. Little: 27*	
Phoenix	Won	149/5	112	J.A. Delaney: 79	R. Shortt: 7
Leinster	Won	145/4	141	J. O'Donnell: 49	Delaney/Little: 3 each
Civil Service	Won	138	80	J. O'Donnell: 53	C. Little: 7
Pembroke	Won	73	60	R. Shortt: 20*	R. Shortt: 7
Phoenix	Drawn	70	41/3	A.D. Barber: 23	R. Shortt: 2
Cork Co. (F)	Won	112	104	C. Little: 22	C. Little: 5
Co. Meath (F)	Lost	68	135/8	J. O'Donnell: 14	
Clontarf	Drawn	183/6	75/2	A.D. Barber: 60	C. Little: 1
Pembroke (F)	Won	110/4	101	J. McDonagh: 34*	T. Byrne: 4

Junior: Merrion 2nds are in Division B of the Intermediate League, but fare poorly. Only four games are recorded, with one win and three losses. They lose to Royal Bank in the first round of the Intermediate Cup, 128 to 130/5. Merrion 3rds are in Division D of the Junior League, but also win one and lose three. St Paul's 2nds thrash them in the Junior Cup, 28 to 127. J. McDonagh scores a century against North Kildare 2nds.

PROFILE: P.B. KENNY

R-H batsman. R-A medium pace bowler. Worked in the Electricity Supply Board. *Paddy* played eighty games for Merrion 1sts between 1926–1934, scoring 826 runs @ 14.00, including 3*50s and with a top score of 77. He took 23 wickets @ 26.52, and 9 catches. He was 1sts captain in 1932.

1932: SENIOR LEAGUE RESTORED

Senior: fixtures 16, reported 16, won 4, lost 6, drawn 6. Captain: P.B. Kenny. The Leinster Senior League is officially restored and played on a percentage basis, with eight points for a win, four for a tie, three for a draw. Merrion finish 4/7, with 40.38 per cent, having played 13, won 3, lost 4, drawn 6. In a year when the batting lets them down badly, only 2*50s are scored, both by C. Little. R.H. Shortt, the dentist, extracts over 40 wickets from reluctant batsmen. Little plays for Leinster against Ulster and Munster. Shortt plays for Leinster against Munster, taking 6 wickets, including 3 in 4 balls. Cork County are well beaten on tour. Income from subscriptions has risen to £72 2s 0d. The season ends in an August washout:

Opponent	Result	Mer.	Opp.	Best Batting: Runs	Best Bowling: Wickets
Pembroke	Drawn	70	59/4	J.D. O'Connor: 27	R. Shortt: 2
Leinster	Drawn	51/7	164/8	J.D. O'Connor: 15	Shortt/Little: 3 each
Clontarf	Lost	73	108	W. Rumney: 12	R. Shortt: 4
DU	Lost	71	146/9	J.A. Delaney: 26	C. Little: 4

Phoenix	Lost	117	189/4	J. O'Donnell: 34	A. Keegan: 3
Civil Service	Won	114	67	T. Byrne: 30	R. Shortt: 5
DU	Drawn	167/5	201/6	C. Little: 84*	Shortt/Kenny: 2 each
Clontarf	Won	148	124	Kenny/Delaney: 40 each	Shortt/Little: 3 each
Leinster	Drawn	49/5	155/5	J. Nesbitt: 16*	C. Little: 2
Pembroke	Won	113	109	J.D. O'Connor: 21	R. Shortt: 6
Cork Co. (F)	Won	105/2	104	J. O'Donnell: 38	G.T. Kenay: 5
Cork Bohemians (F)	Lost	55	105		G.T. Kenay: 5
Phoenix	Drawn	141/5	172/7	W. Rumney: 48	C. Little: 3
Civil Service	Lost	93	136	J.D. O'Connor: 30	Kenny/Nesbitt: 3 each
Leinster (F)	Lost	59	99	R. Shortt: 18	R. Shortt: 6
Phoenix	Drawn	184/8	109/6	C. Little: 78	R. Shortt: 5

Junior: Merrion 2nds are in Division B of the Intermediate League. There are reports of 5 games, with 1 win, 3 losses, 1 draw. Raheny knock them out of the Intermediate Cup, 72 to 93. Merrion 3rds are in Division C of the Junior League. Only three of their games are reported, suggesting a possible withdrawal from the league. They win one and lose two and are beaten by Parkheath in the Junior Cup, 109 to 196. J. Widger and C. Boland score 50s. Keegan and Dempsey take most of the wickets.

PROFILE: JOHN DELANEY

R-H batsman. Wicket-keeper. He played sixty games for Merrion 1sts between 1931 and 1937, scoring 108 runs @ 3.48, with a top score of 11. He took 27 catches and 12 stumpings as wicket-keeper, and was the brother of Joe Delaney.

1933: JOE DELANEY SCORES WHIRLWIND 95 AGAINST PHOENIX

Senior: fixtures 17, reported 17, won 7, lost 5, drawn 5. Captain: R.H. Shortt. The Senior League regulations are the same as in 1932, except that 26 August is set as the closing date, to allow a Champions versus the Rest match to be played on 1/2 September. For the sixth successive season, Leinster win the league. Merrion finish 5/7, with 37.50 per cent, having played 12, won 3, lost 5, drawn 4. Little scores 48 for Leinster against Munster. The return of T. Kenny changes the fortunes in a season that finishes strongly, with three wins in the last four games, to lift the team off the bottom of the table. Delaney, O'Donnell and Little are the best batsmen. J.A. Delaney almost beats Phoenix on his own with an electric 95 not out. Shortt, Kenny, Little, Kiely take the wickets:

Opponent	Result	Mer.	Opp.	Best Batting: Runs	Best Bowling: Wickets
Pembroke (F)	Won	123/8	121/9	J.A. Delaney: 72	R. Shortt: 4
Phoenix	Lost	125	143	J.A. Delaney: 41	T. Kiely: 6
Leinster	Drawn	114	102/9	C. Little: 49	T. Kiely: 5
Clongowes Wood (F)	Won	133	23; 46/1	J. O'Donnell: 57	R. Shortt: 7
Clontarf	Lost	69	100	J.A. Delaney: 15	R. Shortt: 5
DU	Lost	62	148	J.A. Delaney: 30	R. Shortt: 5

Castlecomer (F)	Won	87	52	J.A. Delaney: 20	C. Little: 5
DU	Drawn	154	129/9	C. Little: 47	R. Shortt: 5
Civil Service	Lost	125	128/7	C. Little: 29	R. Shortt: 3
Pembroke	Lost	148	161/7	C. Little: 44	C. Little: 4
Clontarf	Drawn	93	72/7	R. McCartan: 23	T. Kenny: 5
Phoenix	Won	174	157	J.A. Delaney: 95*	T. Kenny: 5
Leinster	Drawn	207/9	175/7	J. O'Donnell: 57	C. Little: 5
Pembroke	Won	149	108	G.T. Kenay: 39	J.A. Delaney: 4
Civil Service	Won	174/7	110	J.A. Delaney: 49	C. Little: 4
Clontarf (F)	Won	193/5	49	J. Widger: 67	J.A. Delaney: 5
Leinster (F)	Drawn	58/3	117	C. Little: 30*	R. Shortt: 6

Junior: The Intermediate League comprises Merrion 2nds, YMCA, Carlisle, Raheny, Monkstown, St James's Gate, Civil Service 2nds. Merrion 2nds play 12, win 5, and lose 7 to finish mid-table. Leinster 2nds, the eventual winners, defeat them easily in the Intermediate Cup, 122 to 207. Dempsey, Cuthbert and Widger score most of the runs, while E.P. Mara takes over 40 wickets. There is no record of a 3rd eleven in the year a Junior Cup final is played at Anglesea Road for the first time.

PROFILE: JOE DELANEY

R-H batsman. R-A medium pace seam bowler. He played eighty-one games for Merrion 1sts between 1928 and 1936, scoring 1,636 runs @ 22.41, with 5*50s and a top score of 95*. He took 77 wickets @ 15.02, with 5 wickets in an innings on 4 occasions, and 16 catches. Firsts captain in 1935. He was the brother of John Delaney and, by all accounts, one of the finest cricketers ever to play for Merrion, whose all-round talents were exhorted to younger players like Derek Hayden many years later. He may be another Merrion player who was forced to abscond to England looking for work after 1936.

1934: SENIOR LEAGUE RUNNERS-UP

Senior: fixtures 18, reported 18, won 11, lost 6, drawn 1. President: R.J. Duggan. Captain: J.A. O'Donnell. The Senior League accepts YMCA into its ranks, provided they play all their league games away. R. Shortt takes 9 wickets in the opening friendly against Pembroke, with 7 batsmen clean-bowled. He finishes the Pembroke innings with a hat-trick. Merrion chase 156 in two hours in the Phoenix Park to beat Phoenix in a midweek match. On Saturday 14 July, Merrion are top of the Senior League, having played 9, won 6, lost 2, drawn 1, with 70.83 per cent. A succession of wins brings them to the last match of the season, against perennial winners Leinster, when a draw will be enough to win the Senior League. They are shot out for 42, and have to be content with second place. Their final record is: played 14, won 10, lost 3, drawn 1, with 74.10 per cent. So Leinster make it seven in a row. R. Shortt gains his sole international cap against the MCC at College Park. J.A. Delaney plays for Leinster v. Ulster. Little scores a century against Phoenix. Little, O'Connor and Dempsey score 50s. Ralph McCartan takes 20 wickets @ 11.40, including a hat-trick against Phoenix. Little takes 42 wickets, while Shortt notches up a paltry 35:

Opponent	Result	Mer.	Opp.	Best Batting: Runs	Best Bowling: Wickets
Pembroke (F)	Won	107	44	J.A. Delaney: 33	R. Shortt: 9
Leinster	Won	108/7	106/6	J.D. O'Connor: 63	T. Kiely: 2
Clontarf (F)	Lost	86	89	A.E. Bex: 14	R. Shortt: 5
YMCA	Won	182	54	J.A. Delaney: 42	C. Little: 6
Pembroke	Won				
Phoenix	Lost	80	215	J.D. O'Connor: 20	R. McCartan: 5
Bective (F)	Lost	223	224	C. Little: 83	R. McCartan: 3
Civil Service	Lost	169	224	A.E. Bex: 36	R. Shortt: 5
Phoenix	Won	160/8	156/7	C. Little: 105	C. Little: 3
DU	Won	154	103	C. Little: 59	R. Shortt: 5
Clontarf	Drawn	73/9	140	P.F. Craig-Martin: 16	J.A. Delaney: 5
DU	Won	198/8	108	K. Dempsey: 79*	R. Shortt: 8
YMCA	Won	180	166	E.P. Mara: 30	R. McCartan: 5
DU (F)	Lost	94	107	J.A. Delaney: 23	J.A. Delaney: 5
Civil Service	Won				
Clontarf	Won				C. Little: 8
Pembroke	Won				
Leinster	Lost	42	43/1		

Junior: Merrion 2nds continue to occupy the centre of the Intermediate League table. First appearance in Merrion colours of future legends, Chris Mara, Simon Curley and Paddy Waldron. P.B. Kenny and A. Keegan score 50s, while E.P. Mara takes most wickets. Merrion 3rds play a full season and win as many matches as they lose. They beat Cabra in the Junior Cup, but lose badly to Parkheath 2nds in the next round, 24 to 93. J. Dorgan and H. Cuthbert score 50s. H. Keegan and K. Dempsey take the wickets. In a game against Cremore they score 17 runs, batting first. Yet they win, skittling the opposition for 15.

Merrion 1sts, 1934 Senior League runners-up. Back row: J.A. Delaney, E.P. Mara, K.C. Dempsey, J.C. Delaney, R.F. McCartan, P.B. Kenny, A.E. Bex, K. Brown (S). Front row: J.G. Dorgan, C.J. Little, J.A. O'Donnell (C), R.H. Shortt, P.F. Craig-Martin.

1935: SIMON CURLEY AND CHRIS MARA DEBUT

Senior: fixtures 19, reported 19, won 9, lost 6, drawn 4. President: C.E. Gildea. Captain: J.A. Delaney. A decision is made to continue Senior League matches onto another day, if five hours' play is not possible on the scheduled date. The percentage system is dropped, in favour of a simple points system. Dublin University are to play each side once. A new knockout competition is introduced, the Leinster Senior Challenge Cup, to be played midweek by the eight Senior clubs. Merrion are drawn against Clontarf, but fail to progress beyond the second round. In the Senior League, Merrion finish 5/8, with 59 points, having played 13, won 7, lost 5, drawn 1. Little scores 108 against Phoenix, including 3*6s and 16*4s. He is picked to play for Leinster against Ulster. First appearance of a dour auctioneer called Louis McMullan, on a free transfer from Pembroke. He scores 186 runs @ 26.57. Joe Delaney scores 82 in a losing cause against Leinster. Simon Curley scores a single 50 in the season that he and Chris Mara move up from Junior to Senior cricket. The cost of the groundsman's wages this year is £51 8s 8d, out of a total expenditure of £141 12s 3d. The club makes £19 11s 6d from the sale of marl. Rollie Shortt finishes second in the Leinster bowling analyses, with 40 wickets @ 10.05:

Opponent	Result	Mer.	Opp.	Best Batting: Runs	Best Bowling: Wickets
DU (F)	Lost	107	112/8	C. Little: 43	E.P. Mara: 3
Phoenix	Lost	91	169	C. Little: 34	C. Little: 4
Leinster	Drawn	206	94/8	K. Dempsey: 39	C. Little: 3
YMCA	Lost	74	183/8	C. Little: 14	Delaney/Shortt: 3 each
DU	Lost	116	198/8	L. McMullan: 32	R. Shortt: 3
Civil Service	Won	222	73	L. McMullan: 44	R. Shortt: 8
Clontarf (C)	Won	134/8	88	J.D. O'Connor: 33	Shortt: 7
Clontarf	Drawn	135	89/6	L. McMullan: 43	McCartan/Shortt: 2 each
Pembroke	Won	120/7	78	L. McMullan: 27	J.A. Delaney: 5
Leinster	Lost	222	247/4	J.A. Delaney: 82	C. Mara: 2
YMCA	Won	130/5	99	J. O'Donnell: 46	Little/Shortt: 3 each
Pembroke	Lost	121	183	A.E. Bex: 23	R. Shortt: 5
Phoenix	Won	198/6	192	J.A. Delaney: 57	R. Shortt: 6
Phoenix (F)	Won	240	145	C. Little: 108	C. Mara: 6
Clontarf	Won	130/8	123	C. Little: 43	Little/Meenan: 3 each
Civil Service	Won	203/9	72	S. Curley: 55*	J.A. Delaney: 4
Cahir Park (F)	Won	315	274	C. Little: 82	R. Shortt: 4
Leinster (F)	Drawn	103/5	220/7	J.A. Delaney: 32*	S. Curley: 3
Phoenix (F)	Drawn	66/5	148/8	C. Mara: 18	R. Shortt: 3

Junior: Merrion 2nds are in Division A of the Intermediate League. J.C. Dorgan's team finishes 7/8, with 13 points, having played 14, won 4, lost 9, drawn 1. His team includes H. McCarthy, C.J. Russell, J.D. O'Connor, D.P. Keady, P. Waldron, P.R. Leahy, M.R. Leahy, A. Grimston, G. Nash. They lose to Parkheath in the second round of the Intermediate Cup, 150 to 182. Merrion 3rds are in Division C of the Junior League and finish 4/6, having played 8, won 3, lost 5, points 9. Des Wilson's side loses to Leinster 3rds in the first round of the Junior Cup, 110 to 147. Haigh scores a century and Russell, Nash and Byrne score 50s. P. Muldoon features strongly for both teams in an all-round capacity.

PROFILE: SIMON CURLEY

L-H cultured middle-order batsman. L-A slow bowler. Educated at CUS. A manufacturing agent and representative for Stuart Surridge gear in Ireland. Corinthians hockey fullback and CUS hurley player. *Si* met his wife Una in Cork, and married there, with Paddy Waldron as his best man. Played 360 Senior games for Merrion between 1934 and 1966, scoring a phenominal 9,510 runs @ 29.35, including 8*100s and 59*50s. Also took 356 wickets @ 18.60 and 138 catches. Captain in 1948, 1949, 1952, 1960, 1961, over 79 games, of which he won 43, drew 17, lost 19. During his five seasons of captaincy, Merrion won both the Senior League and Cup, and were runners-up in the League twice, and the Cup once. President 1969-1975, 1984-1987, and also effectively from 1960-1962, due to the absence of Tom Quinn. Won the Marchant Cup for batting in 1951, 1958. First Merrion player to 5,000, 6,000, 7,000, 8,000, 9,000 runs. Once got Sir Learie Constantine out LBW in a representative match in Cork. He played eight times for Ireland, scoring 208 runs @ 14.86, with a top score of 43 against Scotland.

Simon is first in the Merrion all-rounders' table. Although he was undoubtedly Merrion's giant of giants, he could also be a difficult taskmaster, with a litigious nature that benefitted Merrion hugely on most occasions. But he surely 'looked not on wine when it was red' and his opposition to proper bar facilites may have been partially responsible for the decline of the club after the 1950s. His running battle with schoolboys would certainly make him an anachronism nowadays, when such species are feted and coddled until they retire at twenty-one, discover women cricketers or move to a more successful club where there is inexplicably less white line fever.

1936: SENIOR CUP RUNNERS-UP; JUNIOR D LEAGUE RUNNERS-UP

Senior: fixtures 22, reported 22, won 8, lost 9, drawn 5. President: J.J. Boland. Captain: J.A. O'Donnell. Phoenix break Leinster's stranglehold on the Senior League, but the Rathmines team manage to beat Merrion in the final of the Senior Challenge Cup, 86 to 121. The final is played for league points also, and extends over several evenings. Merrion are unlucky in having to bat on a rain-affected wicket. Dublin University return to a full programme of matches in the Senior League. Merrion finish 6/8 in the league with 41 points, having played 13, won 4, lost 6, drawn 3. Little plays for Leinster versus Ulster. Little, Curley and Dempsey score 50s. Shortt takes 43 league wickets, including 8 in a single outing against Civil Service. Bective Rangers start using the ground at Anglesea Road to play rugby matches during the winter. The sale of marl continues, this year to the Postal Services, Pioneers, Thoms, Bellshire and Carlisle Cricket Clubs. CUS pay £10 0s 0d for the use of the ground:

Opponent	Result	Mer.	Opp.	Best Batting: Runs	Best Bowling: Wickets
Pembroke	Lost	85	133/9	J.A. Delaney: 27	J.A. Delaney: 3
Phoenix	Lost	97	197/7	J. O'Donnell: 26	C. Mara: 2
Leinster	Lost	179	214/7	C. Little: 72	Shortt/Delaney: 2 each
Civil Service	Won	129	53	C. Little: 55*	Shortt/Little: 5 each
DU	Lost	82	140	C. Little: 46	R. Shortt: 4
YMCA	Drawn	166	117/6	J.A. Delaney: 39	K. Dempsey: 2
DU (F)	Drawn	127/5	200/8	K. Dempsey: 55*	R. Shortt: 4
Civil Service (C)	Won	108	52	T. Hession: 30	R. Shortt: 6

YMCA	Lost	80	110	J.A. Delaney: 28	R. Shortt: 5
Clontarf	Won	108	59	K. Dempsey: 38	C. Little: 6
Phoenix (F)	Lost	115	228/6	K. Dempsey: 45	C. Mara: 4
Phoenix	Drawn	119/4	161	K. Dempsey: 50*	J.A. Delaney: 5
Civil Service	Won	124/3	45	K. Dempsey: 66	R. Shortt: 8
Pembroke (C)	Won	130/7	127	C. Little: 43	
Clontarf	Won	112/7	102	C. Little: 34	C. Mara: 3
Leinster	Lost	86	121	J.A. Delaney: 24	C. Mara: 6
Senior Cup final					
Mount Juliet (F)	Drawn	156	94/8	S. Curley: 64	S. Curley: 3
Cahir Park (F)	Lost	106	296	K. Dempsey: 81	P. Muldoon: 4
Pembroke	Drawn	174	166/7	C. Little: 83	Curley/Delaney: 2 each
DU	Lost	94	107	J.A. Delaney: 23	J.A. Delaney: 5
Civil Service (F)	Won	159	104	R. Shortt: 29*	Little/Shortt: 4 each
YMCA (F)	Won	196/5	55	C. Little: 68*	C. Little: 6

Junior: Merrion 2nds are in Division C of the Intermediate League and finish bottom of the table of six teams, with nine games played, and nine games lost. No points. Nevertheless, P. Waldron is picked to play for Leinster in a Junior interprovincial against Ulster. Merrion 3rds are in Division D of the Junior League and finish 2/6, with 18 points, having played 10, won 5, lost 3, drawn 2. Byrne and Cuthbert score 50s and the wickets are shared between Waldron, Muldoon, Hession and Boland.

Merrion 1sts, 1936 Senior Cup runners-up: P. Waldron, J.C. Delaney, T.F. McMahon, K.C. Dempsey, M.J. O'Higgins, J.A. O'Donnell (C), J.A. Delaney, J.D. O'Connor, A.E. Bex, S. Curley (hidden).

1937: THE ACCIDENTAL INTERNATIONAL

Senior: fixtures 20, reported 20, won 7, lost 7, drawn 6. President: J.B. Stephenson. Captain: C.J. Little. A new Constitution for the country is drawn up, but in Anglesea Road, things remain much the same. Subscriptions now amount to £83 13s 0d, out of a total income of £162 13s 11d. The club sells marl to YMCA, Monkstown, Imperials, Clontarf and the Royal Bank Cricket Clubs, and earns £2 10s 6d from the gates for Senior games. Merrion beat Clontarf in the first round of the Cup, but lose to Dublin University in the second round, 197 to 319/6. In the Senior League, they finish 5/8, with 57 points, having played 13, won 6, lost 4, drawn 3. At the end of the season, YMCA and Civil Service are relegated, and the following season they join Monkstown, Malahide, Carlisle and the Imperial Tobacco Company in a new Qualifying League. All six teams will play in the Senior Challenge Cup. A current Merrion player becomes our fifth international cricketer by accident, when A.E. Bex, then Secretary of the Irish Cricket Union, has to step into the breach at Nottingham against Sir Julian Cahn's XI, due to injuries in the Irish squad. The O'Grady Cup for bowling is introduced. Although the Samuels Cup is not presented until 1963, C. Little is the province's leading all-rounder, with a batting average of 30.75 and 32 wickets @ 13.37. He scores a chanceless 100 against Clontarf, with 15*4s and 1*6. Curley, Dempsey, Barber and MacMahon also score 50s. C. Mara takes 35 wickets. S. Curley takes 4/1 against Civil Service:

Opponent	Result	Mer.	Opp.	Best Batting: Runs	Best Bowling: Wickets
DU (F)	Drawn	129	97/9	J. O'Donnell: 38	C. Little: 5
Phoenix	Lost	39	191/8	J.D. O'Connor: 14*	S. Curley: 4
Civil Service	Won	97/4	37	K. Dempsey: 46	S. Curley: 4
DU	Lost	111	185/7	A.D. Barber: 26	C. Mara: 4
YMCA	Won	157/7	58	A.D. Barber: 51	C. Little: 6
Clontarf (C)	Won	144	101	A.D. Barber: 91*	C. Little: 5
Civil Service Crusaders (F)	Drawn	189/6	176/4	S. Curley: 77	C. Mara: 2
Leinster (F)	Lost	119	125/4	A.D. Barber: 41	R. Shortt: 2
Clontarf	Won	173	106	C. Little: 100	R. Shortt: 6
DU (C)	Lost	197	319/6	J.D. O'Connor: 45	R. Shortt: 2
Pembroke	Lost	163	196/4	K. Dempsey: 52	P. Waldron: 1
Phoenix	Drawn		123/7		C. Little: 4
Leinster	Lost	156	168/5	C. Little: 65	C. Little: 2
Leinster (F)	Lost	142	182	S. Curley: 37	C. Mara: 6
Clontarf	Won	194/7	190/6	T. MacMahon: 59	C. Mara: 3
Leinster	Drawn	125/6	206/4	S. Curley: 44	C. Mara: 2
Civil Service	Won	185/7	54	K. Dempsey: 41	C. Mara: 6
Pembroke	Drawn	117/4	173/7	S. Curley: 62*	Mara/Little: 3 each
Long Vacation (F)	Drawn	130/6	150/6	C. Little: 48*	C. Mara: 3
YMCA	Won	122/8	54	K. Dempsey: 30	R. Shortt: 4

Junior: Merrion 2nds are in Section B of the Intermediate League. They start well but fall away to finish in the bottom half of the table. They lose to Malahide in the second round of the Intermediate Cup, 133 to 135/1. T.P. Byrne and J. D'Arcy perform well with the bat. M. O'Higgins and P. Muldoon take the wickets. Merrion 3rds are in Division 2 of the Junior League, but lose most of their games. They lose to CYM 2nds in the second round of the Junior Cup, 81 to 130. Scaife and D'Arcy score 50s, while Boland and McAlinden take most wickets.

PROFILE: CHRIS MARA

R-H batsman and R-A fast bowler. Educated at O'Connell Schools. Civil Servant in the Department of Industry and Commerce. Played for Clontarf before joining Merrion in 1934. Bowled a good length with a high release and could get great lift from the wicket. Missed out on an international cap as his best years were during the Second World War. Between 1940 and 1945 he took 288 wickets @ 12.00, an average of 48 wickets per season. Leinster interprovincial. Also played hockey. Featured in 313 Senior matches for Merrion, scoring 2,104 runs @ 11.56 and taking 699 wickets @ 14.65, including 9/52 against Phoenix in 1940 and 4 wickets in consecutive balls against Civil Service in 1941. Captain in 1944/45, 1953/54. Chris is second in the Merrion all-rounders' table. He went down the ranks and played over six decades, his last match being for Merrion 3rds against Civil Service in 1981 at the age of seventy, when he took a wicket with the last ball he bowled. Chris never married. We hesitate to call him a misogynist, but he did once claim that the best team he ever played on in Merrion was made up of eleven bachelors. This was possibly in 1935. Just short of ninety, Chris shuffled off his mortal coil in 2001. We shall not look upon his like again.

1938: MERRION ON CORK TOUR

Senior: fixtures 19, reported 19, won 6, lost 6, drawn 7. President: P.J. McEvoy. Captain: J.A. O'Donnell. There are only six teams in the Leinster Senior League this year. In a poor season, characterised by some fighting draws, Merrion finish 4/6, with 26 points, having played 9, won 1, lost 2, drawn 6. They beat Monkstown and Civil Service to reach the semi-final of the Senior Challenge Cup, in which they are trounced by Dublin University, 188 to 194/1. C. Mara plays for Leinster against Munster. The club undertakes its customary Whitsuntide tour of Cork, where they beat both Cork County and Spike Island. P.J. McEvoy is President this year. He had been a third-class clerk in the Land Commission back in 1894. Dempsey, Little, O'Donnell and Curley score 50s. Mara and Curley emerge as wicket-takers to join Little and Shortt:

Opponent	Result	Mer.	Opp.	Best Batting: Runs	Best Bowling: Wickets
Pembroke (F)	Lost	136/3	137/6	S. Curley: 45	R. Shortt: 3
Clontarf	Won	99/7	97	C. Little: 28*	C. Little: 4
Phoenix	Drawn	97/9	189/6	S. Curley: 39	C. Little: 3
Pembroke	Drawn	130/8	206/5	J.D. O'Connor: 32	Mara/Shortt: 2 each
Leinster	Lost	147	157/9	K. Dempsey: 54	Little/Shortt: 3 each
Monkstown (C)	Won				
DU	Drawn	130/7	214/9	S. Curley: 47	Mara/Curley: 3 each
Civil Service (C)	Won	228	95	C. Little: 87	C. Little: 4
Cork Co. (F)	Won	81	53	J.D. O'Connor: 23	Shortt/McAlinden: 3 each
Spike Island (F)	Won	67	46	A.E. Bex: 22	S. Curley: 4/13
Clontarf	Drawn	127/5	143	T. MacMahon: 35	C. Little: 7
DU (C)	Lost	188	194/1	J.A. O'Donnell: 51	
Pembroke	Lost	139	142/7	P. Waldron: 31	C. Mara: 4
Pembroke (F)	Lost	135	191/5	C. Mara: 32	J. McAlinden: 3
Clontarf (F)	Drawn	98/6	113	S. Curley: 30	S. Curley: 4
Carlisle (F)	Won	197/9	108	C. Little: 70*	M. O'Higgins: 3

Leinster	Drawn				
Phoenix	Drawn	122/4	217/6	S. Curley: 64*	R. Shortt: 3
Civil Service (F)	Lost	94	100	T. MacMahon: 27	C. Mara: 6

Junior: Merrion 2nds are in Division 2 Section B of the Intermediate League, but can only finish mid-table again. They lose to Pembroke 2nds in the second round of the Intermediate Cup, 90 to 188/4. D. Lindsay scores 83 against Civil Service 2nds. J. McAlinden takes 7 wickets in the same match, and also takes 7 against Clontarf 2nds. Merrion 3rds are in Division 2 Section A of the Junior League. They are drawn against North Kildare 2nds in the Junior Cup, but do not progress. First appearance of future legends, Billy Lindsay and Paul Warren. Stan Greer takes 7 wickets against Cremore 2nds. The Leinster Women's Cricket Union is founded by Isolda Howard, but Merrion will not have a women's team until 1976.

1939: BOTTOM OF THE SENIOR LEAGUE; INTERMEDIATE CUP RUNNERS-UP

Senior: fixtures 20, reported 20, won 5, lost 8, drawn 7. President: P.J. McEvoy. Captain: J.D. O'Connor. There are still only six teams in the Leinster Senior League. The 1sts have an atrocious season, finishing 6/6, with 20 points, having played 10, won 1, lost 5, drawn 4. YMCA, a qualifying team, beat them in the first round of the Challenge Cup, 103 to 185. S. Curley plays for Leinster versus Ulster in a Senior interprovincial match. Curley, Little, Dempsey and O'Donnell score 50s and dominate the batting. Curley scores 82 against the Imperial Tobacco Company (Imperials), residents of Merrion's first cricket ground in Dolphin's Barn. Curley and Little take 25 league wickets apiece. On 3 September, the day that Britain, France, Australia and New Zealand declare war on Germany, Merrion play a friendly against Phoenix. The *Emergency*, known to everyone else on Planet Earth as the Second World War, begins:

Opponent	Result	Mer.	Opp.	Best Batting: Runs	Best Bowling: Wickets
Pembroke (F)	Drawn	167/9	62/1	S. Curley: 42	M. O'Higgins: 1
Phoenix (F)	Lost	99	108/5	S. Curley: 42	M. O'Higgins: 2
Cigany (F)	Drawn	156/8	50/2	O.V. Mooney: 31	
Phoenix	Lost	123	143	C. Little: 53	R. Shortt: 5
Leinster	Lost	126	160/9	C. Mara: 28	S. Curley: 3
YMCA (C)	Lost	103	185	T. MacMahon: 24	S. Curley: 7
Imperials (F)	Drawn	180/5	165/9	S. Curley: 82	C. Mara: 3
DU	Drawn	116/8	189/9	C. Mara: 22	S. Curley: 3
Leinster (F)	Won	155/5	119	C. Little: 63	Little/Shortt: 5 each
Clontarf	Drawn	193/8	133/8	K. Dempsey: 60	
DU	Drawn	188/3	204/8	K. Dempsey: 75	F. Boland: 4
Phoenix	Lost	50	179/7	K. Dempsey: 14	McAlinden/Little: 3 each
Malahide (F)	Won	230/3	131	C. Little: 74	R. Shortt: 5
Carlisle (F)	Won	140	99	W. Lindsay: 34	R. Shortt: 8
Pembroke	Lost	127	130/8	C. Little: 30	C. Little: 4
Cahir Park (F)	Lost	195	155	J. O'Donnell: 59*	S. Curley: 5
Clontarf	Drawn	149/9	230/8	C. Little: 57	S. Curley: 4
Pembroke	Won	160/4	159	S. Curley: 48	C. Little: 5
Leinster	Lost	97	215/3	R. Shortt: 27	
Phoenix (F)	Won	91	81	J. O'Donnell: 21	C. Mara: 6

Junior: Merrion 2nds are in Division 3 of the Intermediate League, along with Monkstown 2nds, Carlisle 2nds, Ierne, Richmond, Malahide 2nds, and Imperials 2nds. They finish mid-table. They lose to Railway Union in the final of the Intermediate Cup, 102 to 116/8, O.V. Mooney scoring 40 and M. O'Higgins taking 3/47. D. Lindsay, P. Waldron, A.E. Bex play for Leinster against Ulster in a Junior interprovincial match. T.P. Byrne and P. Waldron score 100s and 50s. Byrne gets a hat-trick against Malahide 2nds. Merrion 3rds are in Division 2 Section A of the Junior League, but only three games are reported. They lose to Jacobs in the first round of the Junior Cup, 46 to 124. McAlinden and Dove take most wickets.

NB Other teams playing between 1926 and 1939: Bellshire, Clonmore, Duleek, Melrose.

3.2. THE DOUBLE: 1940

The Emergency continued as the Nazis made their way towards Britain and Ireland, where one of their primary objectives was the dismantling of the Gaelic Athletic Association. YMCA joined the ranks of Senior cricket in the year an experiment with 8-ball overs was introduced. Merrion 1sts won both the Leinster Senior League and the Senior Challenge Cup; the first team to achieve this double since the Cup had been introduced five years earlier. It was reported that their bowling and fielding won the two competitions, and the fielding in the cup final was unsurpassed in Irish cricket until that time. But a question remains: apart from the usual sporting luck, how did a team that had failed to win more than one league match in 1938 and 1939, and which had not undergone any substantial change in its players, manage to go through the following season unbeaten?

1940: SENIOR CUP WINNERS; SENIOR LEAGUE WINNERS

Senior: fixtures 16, reported 16, won 11, lost 0, drawn 5. President: P.J. McEvoy. Captain: J.A. O'Donnell. Perhaps a combination of factors supplies the answer. Jack O'Donnell replaces Des O'Connor as captain, but then O'Donnell has been captain in 1938. O'Connor, relieved of the burden of captaincy, makes a strong personal contribution to the season's success with 345 runs @ 31.36. Only one new face appears in the team, that of Paul Warren, who takes 16 wickets @ 19.81, and his youthful presence (he has just turned seventeen) would certainly improve the fielding in a side that boasts at least three players around the forty mark. The younger players, like Waldron, D'Arcy, Curley and Dempsey, are starting to mature into more solid performers, who place a high price on their wicket. Simon Curley and Kevin Dempsey put together a match-winning stand in the cup final, scoring 84 runs for the 3rd wicket. Joe D'Arcy and Paddy Waldron also stand firm against YMCA in the league decider on 31 August, with a partnership of 71 runs when 6 wickets have been lost for 50 runs. Billy Lindsay is impressive behind the stumps with 16 catches and 8 stumpings, and is the leading wicket-keeper in Leinster, although the Hopkins Cup will not be introduced until 1974.

Cecil Little celebrates entry into his fifth decade by leading the provincial all-rounders' statistics, with 346 runs @ 31.45 and 29 wickets @ 16.86. Curley scores 442 runs @ 31.57, including an unbeaten century against YMCA. Dempsey blasts 409 runs @ 27.26 in his last season with Merrion. Chris Mara is a towering figure with the ball, taking 46 wickets @

12.13, including 9/52 against Phoenix – Merrion's best-ever figures – while also scoring some useful runs. Little and Mara play for Leinster against Munster in an interprovincial match, with Leinster being captained by Little. Despite the exhausting 8-ball overs, Rollie Shortt manages 40 wickets @ 10.40, including 7 for 14 against Dublin University at College Park. Of the eleven players on this team, five are internationals, not including Chris Mara, Billy Lindsay and Cecil Little, who should have been. The other three will become interprovincials. The *Evening Herald* of 10 July 1940 reports:

> *Merrion's present form is no flash in the pan; they have a really well-balanced team. It contains a certain number of sound, experienced cricketers, not yet at the end of their careers, and they have as well many young players of the highest promise, amongst whom S. Curley, P. Waldron and P. Warren stand out. They should be even stronger next season.*

THE WINNING OF THE CUP

First Round: Merrion draw Junior club Cremore at Anglesea Road. Batting first, they post 281, with Cecil Little (68), Kevin Dempsey (50), Des O'Connor (46), Simon Curley (22), Jack O'Donnell (20) getting the runs. There is one young newcomer in the side, Paul Warren (5*), a CUS schoolboy like J. D'Arcy and S. Curley before him. In reply, Cremore have no answer to the bowling of Shortt (4/16), Warren (3/20), Little (2/5) and Mara (1/21), and are dismissed for 92.

Second Round: Merrion come up against the old enemy (one of many) Phoenix at Anglesea Road. Merrion bat first again and total 158, thanks chiefly to Dempsey (61) and D'Arcy (34). A mighty 7 wickets for 61 from Chris Mara causes Phoenix to pull up 7 runs short.

Semi-final: Merrion play Dublin University again at Anglesea Road, and extending over the following Monday and Tuesday evenings. P. Waldron, another product of the CUS cricketer factory, replaces H. Bligh in the team. Batting first again, Merrion accumulate 257 runs (there is no limit in terms of overs), with the main contributors being Curley (55), O'Connor (44), D'Arcy (37), Little (30). The students fall 54 runs short, due to the bowling of Shortt (4/58), Little (3/60) and Curley (3/20).

Final: Merrion play another old enemy, Leinster, at Sydney Parade. Leinster bat first and find runs hard to come by on an awkward wicket, taking 2¾ hours to get 121. Warren, coming on late, takes 4/49, with backup from Mara (3/36), Little (2/7) and Shortt (1/27). It's a tight finish, with Merrion losing early wickets, but Curley remains obdurate at 61, Dempsey chips in with 24, and Little (17*) and Warren (8*) bring home the first of only two Leinster Senior Cups won by Merrion in the seventy-six-year history of the competition. A disgraceful statistic.

LEINSTER SENIOR CUP FINAL 1940, MERRION V. LEINSTER

Merrion			Leinster		
J.A. O'Donnell	c. Cuffe b. Boland	0	F.G. Connell	b. Shortt	35
W. Lindsay	c. Cuffe b. Murphy	3	F.W. Fox	c. O'Connor b. Warren	11
K.C. Dempsey	l.b.w. b. Graham	24	J.R. Gill	c. Curley b. Warren	0
S. Curley	c. Cuffe b. Graham	61	M.D. Burke	c. O'Donnell b. Warren	19
J.D. O'Connor	b. Graham	7	N.H. Lambert	c. Lindsay b. Mara	22

J.D'Arcy	l.b.w. b. Graham	3	P.C. Mannion	c. D'Arcy b. Mara	2
C.J. Little	not out	17	C.R. Cuffe	c. O'Donnell b. Warren	0
C. Mara	b. Graham	2	J.R. Graham	b. Mara	13
P. Warren	not out	3	P. Boland	st. Lindsay b. Little	11
P. Waldron	d.n.b.		P.B. Murphy	b. Little	2
R.H. Shortt	d.n.b.		W.C. Pemberton	not out	4
	Extras	3		Extras	2
	Total (for 7 wickets)	**123**		**Total**	**121**

PROFILE: BILLY LINDSAY

R-H dour batsman and wicket-keeper. Played field hockey for Scotland, appearing in the 1948 Olympic Games, where he won a silver medal with Great Britain. Played 203 games for Merrion 1sts, scoring 2,539 runs @ 15.38, including 6*50s. As a wicket-keeper, he took 120 catches and had 60 stumpings. Leading provincial wicket-keeper in 1940, with 16 catches and 8 stumpings. Firsts captain in 1943. When he gave up keeping and Maurice Gaynor became the 1sts keeper, Billy kept his place on the team as a batsman. Married to Avril, one of the most dedicated members of the Merrion ladies' tea committee in the 1950s. A fellow of most excellent fancy, Billy was a talented comic cartoonist, most of whose drawings of the 1940s teams disappeared in the 1970s fire that burnt down the old tin pavilion, except for those of Tom Quinn, Paddy Waldron and Cecil Little. So thanks a lot, SEWENVESVY.

THE WINNING OF THE LEAGUE

Merrion draw the first two league matches in 1940, in the second of which Pembroke need 2 runs to win with 4 wickets in hand when time is called. Phoenix win 5 and draw 1 of their first 6 matches and have a long lead by mid-June. Then Merrion beat Phoenix and begin a sequence of five consecutive wins. The fifth win in the sequence is also over Phoenix, on 17 August, the day the Germans establish an operational area around Britain. This carries Merrion into a three-point lead over Phoenix. Merrion then beat YMCA by 3 wickets on 31 August to clinch the championship. They finish the season with a draw against Leinster on the day the Battle of Britain begins. They play 12, win 7, lose 0, draw 5. They use only fifteen players throughout the season and three of these play in eight matches between them. But for all the glory of this successful season, and despite the *Evening Herald*'s views, it's a fact that for the three giants of Merrion's early period – Rollie Shortt, Geke O'Donnell and Cecil Little – their best years are already behind them:

Opponent	Result	Mer.	Opp.	Best Batting: Runs	Best Bowling: Wickets
Clontarf	Drawn	151/7	85/9	C. Mara: 39*	C. Little: 5/35
Pembroke	Drawn	137	136/6	J.D. O'Connor: 39	Little: 2/31; Shortt: 2/28
DU	Won	208/4	96	J.D. O'Connor: 74*	R. Shortt: 7/14
DU	Drawn	190/6	162/4	C. Little: 55*	Little: 2/53; Shortt: 2/29
Phoenix	Won	144	118	C. Little: 55	C. Mara: 5/32
Clontarf	Won	86/3	83	K. Dempsey: 32	Shortt: 4/13; Warren: 4/39
Leinster	Won	135/7	134	J.D. O'Connor: 47*	C. Mara: 4/31
YMCA	Won	191/6	123	S. Curley: 112*	C. Mara: 5/24

Phoenix	Won	127	115	J.D. O'Connor: 36	C. Mara: 9/52
Pembroke	Drawn	167/3	190/6	K. Dempsey: 72*	Shortt: 2/36; Little: 2/54
YMCA	Won	141/7	140	P. Waldron: 50*	C. Mara: 4/30
Leinster	Drawn	103/6	152/7	K. Dempsey: 34	R. Shortt: 3/39

LEINSTER SENIOR LEAGUE 1940, MERRION V. YMCA

Merrion			YMCA		
K.C. Dempsey	c. Peake b. Hirst	7	G.J. Balmer	c. Waldron b. Little	46
W. Lindsay	c. Balmer b. Hirst	0	A. Beatty	l.b.w. b. Little	0
S. Curley	b. Hirst	8	G.A. Boate	c. Curley b. Mara	0
J.A. O'Donnell	b. Hirst	12	B.W. Peake	c. D'Arcy b. Little	17
J.D. O'Connor	b. Dobson	12	F.L. Wolfe	b. Mara	22
C.J. Little	b. Dobson	1	V. Dobson	b. Shortt	10
P. Waldron	not out	50	F.W. Hirst	c. Lindsay b. Mara	30
J. D'Arcy	b. A. Beatty	18	W. Hanna	c. Dempsey b. Shortt	1
P. Warren	not out	11	W. Rowe	run out	4
C. Mara	d.n.b.		H. Beatty	b. Mara	0
R.H. Shortt	d.n.b.		J.H. Ross	not out	1
	Extras	22		Extras	9
	Total (for 7 wickets)	141		Total	140

Junior: Merrion 2nds are in Division 3 of the Intermediate League. They finish 5/8, with 16 points, having played 12, won 5, lost 6, drawn 1. Clontarf 2nds knock them out of the Intermediate Cup in the third round, 68 to 76/5. H. Bligh, T. MacMahon and H. Dove score 50s. P. Waldron, F. Montgomery and J. D'Arcy also score runs. R.H. Browett, P. Meenan and S. Greer take the wickets. First appearance of future captain T. Burke. Merrion 3rds are in Division 1 of the Junior League. They finish 5/8, with 13 points, having played 13, won 4, lost 8, drawn 1. Cremore 2nds defeat them in the first round of the Junior Cup, 48 to 97. T. Burke scores 75* against Clontarf 3rds. Davcy, Meenan and Montgomery also feature strongly with the bat. Browett and Greer take most of the wickets.

PROFILE: KEVIN DEMPSEY

R-H attacking batsman, with a lavatorial stance like Danny Parkinson. Occasional R-A bowler. A fiery, temperamental personality, who, like Rollie Shortt, enjoyed journeying through Sandymount. After winning the double with Merrion in 1940, presumably he felt, and rightly so, that nothing quite so great could ever happen again at Anglesea Road, and left to join Pembroke, with whom he won his sole international cap in 1947 against the Craven Gentlemen in Muirfield, Yorkshire, before finishing his career with Railway Union from 1951 to 1963. Kevin played eighty-eight times for Merrion 1sts between 1932 and 1940, scoring 1,692 runs @ 20.38, with a best score of 79* and including 11*50s. He took 7 wickets @ 20.85 and held 36 catches. In the double-winning year of 1940, his contribution with the bat was 409 runs @ 27.26 in all games.

NB Other teams playing in 1940: Harding, Hammond Lane, Sackville Press, 3rd OBU.

Left: Merrion 1sts, 1940 Senior League and Cup winners. Back row: Paul Warren, Joe D'Arcy, Paddy Waldron, Chris Mara, Simon Curley, Cecil Little. Front row: Billy Lindsay (W), Rollie Shortt, Jack O'Donnell (C), Des O'Connor, Kevin Dempsey.

Below: Merrion 1sts, 1940 Senior League winners. Back row: S. Greer (S), W. Lindsay, S. Curley, C. Mara, P. Warren, P. Waldron, K. Dempsey, P.J. McEvoy (P). Front row: J. D'Arcy, J.D. O'Connor, J. O'Donnell (C), R. Shortt, C. Little.

3.3. THE GOLDEN ERA: 1941-1960

After achieving the double in 1940, during this successful period the 1sts won three more Senior Leagues, in 1945, 1952, and 1958, and were runners-up in 1941, 1949, and 1960. They won the Senior Cup in 1960 and were runners-up in 1944, 1946, 1948, and 1951. Despite the fact that selection for a Junior team involved at least three players who owned cars, and this might be their only qualification, the 2nds won Division 3 of the Intermediate League in 1942 and the full Intermediate League in 1943, to gain promotion to Division 2 of the Senior 2 League in 1944. They won the Senior 2 League in 1945 and were promoted to Division 1. In 1954, they were runners-up in Section B of the Senior 2 League, and runners-up in the full Senior 2 League in 1955 and 1957. The 3rds were runners-up in Division 1 of the Junior League in 1942 and won the Junior League outright in 1943, to gain promotion to the Intermediate League in 1944, only to be demoted back to Junior status in 1945, in which year they were runners-up in the Junior Cup. In 1956, back in the Intermediate League, they were runners-up to Harding, and in 1960 they won the Intermediate League outright. Merrion 4ths made a first appearance in 1943, when they were runners-up in the Minor Cup. They won the Minor League in 1944. They won the Minor Cup in 1953, having been runners-up in 1952. They won the Junior League in 1958 and were runners-up in 1959. Merrion's Schoolboys won the Vacation League in 1942 and were runners-up in 1943.

Some important club developments took place during this period. In 1948, the use of the full ground for the parking of cars during the Spring and Horse Shows was introduced, although the parking was run by Irish Car Parks. In 1952, Merrion took the significant step of purchasing the ground – Area **A** – at Anglesea Road. A Ground Purchase Fund was set up with a mortgage on the ground and loans from individual members. In 1955, a club crest and foundation date was assigned, new blazers and caps were ordered and a club banner – with the erroneous foundation date of 1879 – was stitched up. Also in 1956, a ninety-year licence was signed with Bective Rangers Rugby Club, allowing them to play rugby on the ground during the winter. In 1956, the Hazeldene field was leased to provide extra playing area and practice wickets. Subsequently the wickets were changed to run from Dunluce to Hazeldene.

In 1960, the clubhouse was extended to include improved dressing rooms and a limited bar, despite the obvious temptations to lady members and the continued nuisance of schoolboys. The pace of this development meant additional problems for a club that already had its share of difficulties in getting competent groundsmen, mowers that actually worked (the problems with the Ransom and Allen mowers were too numerous to detail here; a separate book might be needed for that), subscriptions paid and help from members in the hard grind of rolling the wickets.

1941: SENIOR LEAGUE RUNNERS-UP

Senior: fixtures 18, reported 18, won 11, lost 3, drawn 4. President: J.B. Stephenson. Captain: J.A. O'Donnell. The Emergency continues during a rain-affected summer in Dublin. Civil Service return to the Leinster Senior league, Division 1, which now has eight teams, Carlisle having refused promotion. The Qualifying League has been replaced by Division 2 of the Senior League, a precursor of the Senior 2 League. Merrion play Phoenix in the first round of the Senior Cup, but are skittled for 64 by J. Boucher. After another hard-fought season, Merrion finish runners-up to Leinster in the league, with 81 points, having played 14, won 9, lost 2, drawn 3. Curley scores 507 runs @ 36.21, including a century and several 50s. He is the first Merrion Senior cricketer to score 500 runs in a season. O'Connor scores 320 runs @ 35.55, including a century against Civil Service. Mara takes 60 wickets @ 9.28, including 4 wickets in 4 consecutive balls against Civil Service. Shortt and Little take only 17 wickets apiece and their absence for part of this season may have been the difference between success and failure:

Opponent	Result	Mer.	Opp.	Best Batting: Runs	Best Bowling: Wickets
Leinster	Drawn	214/5	157/6	S. Curley: 79	Mara: 2/33; Little: 2/49
Clontarf	Won	131	94	P. Waldron: 40	C. Mara: 6/18
DU	Drawn				
YMCA	Won	178/1	72	S. Curley: 100*	
Phoenix (C)	Lost	64	65/3	J. O'Donnell: 23	
Civil Service	Won	145/5	75	P. Warren: 39*	Waldron: 3/12; Mara: 3/17

Civil Service	Won	228/3	62	J.D. O'Connor: 103*	Mara: 4/19; Shortt: 4/24
Pembroke (F)	Won	196/7	156	J. O'Donnell: 45	P. Warren: 5/36
Leinster	Lost	76	77/2	J. D'Arcy: 21	Warren: 1/17; Mara: 1/42
Clontarf	Drawn	162/9	142/9	T. Burke: 35*	R. Shortt: 5/46
Pembroke	Won	62/8	53	S. Curley: 27	C. Mara: 8/35
Phoenix	Lost	185/6	187/7	S. Curley: 88	C. Little: 5/70
YMCA	Won				
Pembroke	Won	174	150	J.D. O'Connor: 36*	C. Mara: 5/46
Phoenix	Won	110/6	105	S. Curley: 27	C. Little: 6/44
Imperials (F)	Won	93	64		S. Curley: 3/10
DU	Won	110/4	89		
Leinster (F)	Drawn	156/6	181/8	J. D'Arcy: 50	P. Warren: 3/46

Junior: Merrion 2nds are in Division 3 of the Intermediate League, along with Irish Times, Portrane, Carlisle 2nds, Monkstown 2nds, Civil Service 2nds, Leinster 3rds and Pembroke 3rds. They finish in the bottom half of the league table and lose to Richmond in the first round of the Intermediate Cup, 52 to 67. Tommy Burke makes most runs. Merrion 3rds are in Division 1 of the Junior League, with Thoms, Clontarf 3rds, St Mary's College 2nds, Parkheath 2nds, North Kildare and Stradbrook. They lose to Hammond Lane in the first round of the Junior Cup and finish towards the bottom of the league table. Jimmy McAlinden and Stan Greer remain the figureheads of this side.

PROFILE: TOMMY BURKE

R-H batsman and occasional R-A leg-break bowler. Educated at Blackrock College. Also played rugby for Blackrock. Manager of a container company, a subsidiary of Hammond Lane, who had their own cricket team. Played interprovincial cricket for Leinster. He started playing in the early '40s, but missed several seasons due to tuberculosis. Captain of Merrion 1sts in 1957-59, 64, 67. Won the Senior League in 1958 as captain and played on the 1960 cup-winning

Merrion 1sts, 1941 Senior League runners-up: S. Curley, P. Waldron, C. Little, J.D. O'Connor, T. Burke, J. O'Donnell (C), B. Cunningham, R. Shortt, C. Mara, W. Lindsay, J. D'Arcy.

team. Played 247 times for Merrion 1sts, scoring 2,514 runs @ 13.66, with a top score of 90. Also took 29 wickets and 72 catches. A quiet revolutionary, he was responsible for bringing Rodney Bernstein, the club's first Jewish player, to Merrion, against considerable opposition from the powers-that-be. Tommy died one evening in 1985, again far too early, from a heart attack, after helping out a neighbour with a flat battery and pushing their car to get it started. A good Samaritan, underrated Merrion cricketer and a key influence in the development of the club, he was a fine singer, whose party piece at the annual Merrion suppers was 'On The Street Where You Live' from *My Fair Lady*. '*I have often walked…*'

1942: INTERMEDIATE LEAGUE, DIVISION 3 WINNERS; JUNIOR LEAGUE, DIVISION 1 RUNNERS-UP; SCHOOLBOY VACATION LEAGUE WINNERS

Senior: fixtures 18, reported 18, won 9, lost 6, drawn 3. President: J.B. Stephenson. Captain: J.A. O'Donnell. Despite the Emergency, this is a great season for cricket. The weather is good and large crowds attend. There is a compelling race for the league and some splendid cup ties. But Merrion lose again to Phoenix in the first round of the Senior Cup, which no longer includes Division 2 teams. They now have their own competition, the Senior 2 Cup. The Anglesea Road side come 5/8 in the Senior League, with 57 points, having played 14, won 6, lost 5, drawn 3. In one game, Phoenix chase 210 in two hours. This year, which is the last full season on the 1sts for the captain, J.A. O'Donnell, begins the ascendancy of Paddy Waldron, one of Merrion's most elegant batsmen. Waldron hits 2*50s, including 65 against Queen's University. Little and Murphy score single 50s, while Curley continues to improve, with several match-winning innings. Tommy Burke moves from the Junior teams to the 1sts, averaging 30.57 over 8 innings. First appearance of Tommy's brother and future international, Joe Burke. Des O'Connor scores 339 runs @ 26.07. In a poor season for Rollie Shortt, he can only manage 36 wickets @ 15.16, but Chris Mara thunders on, taking 48 wickets @ 11.93, including 2*7 wicket hauls:

Opponent	Result	Mer.	Opp.	Best Batting: Runs	Best Bowling: Wickets
Leinster	Won	138	112	Brockway/Curley: 22 each	C. Mara: 5/50
Phoenix	Won	190/3	70	C. Murphy: 84*	R. Shortt: 4/21
DU	Lost	115	200	S. Curley: 49	C. Mara: 7/75
Pembroke	Won	60/4	59	W. Lindsay: 30	C. Mara: 7/29
Phoenix (C)	Lost	107	168	P. Waldron: 30	C. Mara: 5/53
Clontarf	Lost	74	182	P. Waldron: 23	C. Mara: 3/53
YMCA	Drawn	215/5	120/3	W. Lindsay: 91	R. Shortt: 1/22
Civil Service	Won	115/3	86	S. Curley: 57*	C. Mara: 4/24
Phoenix (F)	Won	137/4	130	S. Curley: 82*	P. Waldron: 5/36
Pembroke	Drawn	201/7	177/5	C. Little: 54	C. Mara: 2/55
Phoenix	Lost	210/7	218/5	T. Burke: 76*	P. Warren: 2/11
QU (F)	Won	245/4	66	P. Waldron: 65	R. Shortt: 5/4
Leinster	Lost	121	122/4	S. Curley: 28	C. Little: 2/22
YMCA (F)	Won	95/3	92	S. Curley: 42	P. Warren: 4/24
Clontarf	Won	214	70	P. Waldron: 67	C. Mara: 5/23
DU	Won	132/1	122	P. Waldron: 63*	R. Shortt: 5/24
YMCA	Drawn				
Civil Service	Lost	142	145	C. Little: 47	R. Shortt: 5/69

Junior: Merrion 2nds win Division 3 of the Intermediate League, with 88 points. Raheny win the play-off. They lose to Leinster 3rds in the first round of the Intermediate Cup, 129 to 178. Tommy Burke scores 282 runs @ 35.38. Joe Burke takes 44 wickets @ 6.02. Merrion 3rds are runners-up to Thoms in Division 1 of the Junior League, with 56 points. They lose to Cremore 2nds in the first round of the Junior Cup, 110 to 114/5. Ralph MacGinty scores 132 runs @ 26.4 and Hubert Warren hits 161 runs @ 16.1. Aiden O'Kelly gets 12 wickets @ 6.17 and Mick O'Connell snaffles 25 @ 10.08. Merrion's Schoolboys win the Vacation League, with 64 points. Their better players include S. Wright, M. Hillary, P. MacAuley, T. Burke, M. Gaynor, D. McCourt, and H. Warren.

PROFILE: PADDY WALDRON

R-H artistic opening batsman, who played the ball very late. R-A slow swing bowler. Educated at CUS (where he learnt his cricket and hurling), Trinity College (courtesy of a special dispensation from the Catholic Archbishop of Dublin) and King's Inns. Later a barrister in the Four Courts, where he also served as Admiralty Marshall. Played 216 times for Merrion 1sts, scoring 4,994 runs @ 27.74, including 4*100s and 32*50s. Won the Marchant Cup for batting in 1943. Took 86 wickets @ 18.98, and 55 catches. Firsts captain in 1947. Played also for Dublin University and was selected five times for Ireland, scoring 100 runs @ 11.11, with a top score of 32. He was replaced on the Irish side by Kevin Dempsey. Paddy retired from cricket early due to the pressure of work. He rarely appeared in Merrion after his retirement, as he spent his summers in his house in County Clare. Would deliberately throw his wicket away once he'd reached 50, much to Simon Curley's fury, so that he could go to the dogs (head down to the greyhound track). Related by marriage to Kathleen Talty, who baked the cake containing the key that allowed Éamon DeValera to escape from Lincoln Gaol. But we cannot blame him for that.

1943: INTERMEDIATE LEAGUE WINNERS; JUNIOR LEAGUE WINNERS; MINOR CUP RUNNERS UP; SCHOOLBOY VACATION LEAGUE RUNNERS-UP

Senior: fixtures 17, reported 17, won 5, lost 6, drawn 6. President: T.J. Collins. Captain: W.L. Lindsay. While the Emergency continues and the Allied Forces capture Italy, Merrion 1sts win nothing. They finish 5/8 in the Senior League, with 47 points, having played 14, won 4, lost 5, drawn 5. They lose to Clontarf in the semi-final of the Senior Cup. S. Curley features only once, as he is working in Munster, where he plays for Bohemians. He is selected to play for Munster against Leinster. Little is also absent for part of the season. Mara, Waldron and D'Arcy play for Leinster against Munster. Waldron scores 2 centuries and wins the Marchant Cup for batting, with an average of 40.50. D'Arcy has his best season with the bat, scoring 363 runs @ 33, including 3*50s, and finishes third in the provincial statistics. Des O'Connor belts 274 runs @ 19.57. Ralph McCartan strokes 163 runs @ 27.16. Mara procures 40 wickets @ 14.97, while Shortt extracts another 42 batsmen @ 13.14:

Opponent	Result	Mer.	Opp.	Best Batting: Runs	Best Bowling: Wickets
Clontarf	Lost	74	100	M. Gaynor: 18	C. Mara: 5/30
DU	Won	139	102	J.D. O'Connor: 59*	C. Mara: 5/41
YMCA (C)	Won	35/4	34	D'Arcy, T. Burke: 8	C. Mara: 6/24

Phoenix	Lost	111	184/6	J. D'Arcy: 38	C. Mara: 2/34; R. Shortt: 2/66
YMCA	Lost	95	107/1	P. Waldron: 24	R. Shortt: 1/38
Leinster	Drawn	127/6	186/7	P. Waldron: 38	R. McGinty: 3/34
Clontarf (C)	Lost	67	68/6	W. Lindsay: 28	C. Mara: 5/30; R. Shortt: 5/31
YMCA	Drawn	199/7	107/7	J. D'Arcy: 63	C. Mara: 3/27
Civil Service	Won	100/4	81	J. D'Arcy: 55*	R. Shortt: 5/24
Waringstown (F)	Drawn	151/6	97/6	C. Mara: 62*	K. Henry: 3/36
Pembroke	Drawn	206/8	86/3	P. Waldron: 101*	P. Waldron: 1/11
Clontarf	Won	123/2	112	J. D'Arcy: 54*	R. Shortt: 6/39
Leinster	Drawn	150/9	248/5	J. D'Arcy: 42	R. McGinty: 3/85
Phoenix	Lost	86	164	C. Little: 19	C. Mara: 5/44
Civil Service	Won	196/3	71	P. Waldron: 111	
Pembroke	Drawn	138/4	218/4	R. McCartan: 65	R. Shortt: 3/52
DU	Lost	146	154/9	P. Waldron: 47	R. Shortt: 5/24

Junior: Merrion 2nds beat Leinster 3rds to win the Intermediate League and gain promotion to the Senior 2 League. S. O'Sullivan leads the batting averages, with 249 @ 31.13. S. Wright heads the bowling averages, with 18 wickets @ 5.78. Merrion 3rds defeat Harding to win the Junior League and gain promotion to the Intermediate League. Pierce MacAuley has 133 runs @ 26.6, and Aiden O'Kelly scores 206 @ 22.89. M. O'Connell seizes 24 wickets @ 6.54. Merrion 4ths make their debut and finish 4/5 in Division 2 of the Minor League, with 32 points. Des Wilson scores 126 against Harding 2nds. They lose the Minor Cup final to Leinster 4ths by 1 run, 185 to 186, in which A. Burrowes scores 64 and R.H. Browett takes 7/71. The Schoolboys are runners-up to Pembroke in the Vacation League, with 40 points.

PROFILE: PAUL WARREN

R-H cultured batsman and slow R-A leg-break bowler. Occasional wicket-keeper. Educated at CUS. Career civil servant in the Departments of Finance and Posts and Telegraph, reaching department secretary status. Also played rugby for Lansdowne, winning the cup in the 1940s. Medals were presented to the players, but Paul was conspicious by his absence, as he was playing an important cup match for Merrion on the same day. Also played tennis. Would probably consider swimming his main pastime. The sole surviving member of the 1940s double-winning side, and of the 1945 league-winning side. Played interprovincial cricket for Leinster. Featured in 128 games for Merrion 1sts, taking 59 wickets @ 21.49 and scoring 1,400 runs @ 16.27. At the time of writing, Paul Warren is eighty-seven and unfortunately suffering from Alzheimer's Disease. Strangely enough, what he clearly remembers from his Merrion days is the following mantra, '*Bowl up, Geke. In the gulley, Ces. Rollie, long on. Pitch them up in the sun, Muldoon. D.G., wet the tea.*'

1944: SENIOR CUP RUNNERS-UP; MINOR LEAGUE WINNERS

Senior: fixtures 18, reported 18, won 7, lost 6, drawn 4, tied 1. President: E.T. Cochrane. Captain: C.J. Mara. Merrion experience their own 'Emergency', with a poor season in the Senior League, finishing 6/8, with 52 points, having played 14, won 5, lost 5, drawn 4. The title is shared between Leinster and Pembroke for the first time, as rain prevents play in the decider. Civil Service, in their last season in Senior cricket, lose their first thirteen league matches, as well as a cup match. However, Merrion have a good cup run during the Normandy invasion before losing out to Pembroke in the first final to start at 11a.m. Pembroke are captained on the day by ex-Merrion stalwart Kevin Dempsey. P. Waldron and R. Shortt play for Leinster against a Munster side that includes S. Curley. Waldron scores 530 runs @ 33.12. D. O'Connor scores 339 runs @ 28.25, including a century against YMCA. Paul Warren and Dermot McCourt get 50s. C. Mara continues his own personal war against all batsmen, with 50 wickets @ 13.74 in his first year as captain. R. Shortt proves that even authors can get it wrong, and that his best years are far from behind him, with 50 wickets @ 12.66:

Opponent	Result	Mer.	Opp.	Best Batting: Runs	Best Bowling: Wickets
DU	Drawn	136	96/8	P. Warren: 60	R. Shortt: 6/28
DU	Lost	195/9	200/6	P. Waldron: 76	R. Shortt: 5/61
QU (F)	Tied	118	118	C. Little: 24	S. Curley: 4/31
Clontarf	Lost	152	154/2	J. Burke: 48	C. Mara: 1/46
YMCA	Drawn	190/6	133/8	J.D. O'Connor: 115*	R. Shortt: 4/25
Leinster	Lost	105	206	P. Waldron: 32	P. Waldron: 5/37
DU (C)	Won	83/1	70	P. Waldron: 34	C. Mara: 7/34
Pembroke	Lost	105	121/6	S. Curley: 20	C. Mara: 5/41
Civil Service	Won	111/2	68	P. Warren: 33*	R. Shortt: 5/28
Phoenix (C)	Won	228/8	176	P. Waldron: 54	R. Shortt: 6/59
Civil Service	Won	136	45	P. Waldron: 50	C. Mara: 8/20
Pembroke	Lost	164	243	T. Burke: 37	C. Little: 5/49
Senior Cup final					
Phoenix	Won	140/0	138	P. Waldron: 80*	C. Mara: 3/31
Clontarf	Drawn	190/6	111/4	P. Waldron: 62	T. Burke: 1/10
Leinster	Won	138	109	C. Mara: 43	C. Little: 6/40
Phoenix	Drawn	227/7	115/6	J.D. O'Connor: 75	R. Shortt: 4/28
Pembroke	Lost	106	121/5	J.D. O'Connor: 26	C. Mara: 3/43
YMCA	Won	153/7	97	D. McCourt: 51	R. Shortt: 7/39

Junior: Merrion 2nds play in the Senior 2 League and finish 7/8 with 43 points. Having beaten the Imperials in the first round, they lose to Phoenix 2nds in the semi-final of the Senior 2 Cup, 178 to 181/9. Merrion 3rds finish 6/7 in Division 3 of the Intermediate League, with 24 points. Malahide beat them in the third round of the Intermediate Cup. Merrion 4ths defeat R & SPU 3rds to win the Minor League. St Mary's 2nds beat them in the second round of the Minor Cup.

PROFILE: JIMMY McALINDEN

R-H batsman, more ferret than rabbit. R-A wristy leg-break bowler. Educated at CUS and Clongowes. Trained as a draughtsman and worked as an estate agent with McArthurs, Battersby & Co., and J.D. Valentine & Co. Also played schools tennis and rugby as out-half for Monkstown and Seapoint. Later was a non-playing member of Bective Rangers Rugby Football Club. Born in Bangor, Northern Ireland in 1911 and moved south in 1915. Went to England during the Second World War, along with Hugh Coleman and Louis McMullan, looking for work. Used his experience as a draughtsman to become an inspector of tanks,

Merrion 1sts, 1944 Senior Cup runners-up. Back row: D. McCourt, S. Curley, J. Burke, D. McEvoy, P. Warren, P. Waldron. Front row: J.D. O'Connor, C.J. Little, C. Mara (C), W. Lindsay, R.H. Shortt.

prior to their deployment in the war. Jimmy played mainly for Merrion Junior teams and took 10/22 for the 3rds against Harding in 1957. He also officiated in many roles for Merrion down the years. When asked, in 1976, if he would like to score for the 1sts, he suggested politely that he would actually prefer to be President. And so he was, in 1977 and 1978. A gentle man, and a true gentleman.

1945: SENIOR LEAGUE WINNERS; SENIOR 2 LEAGUE WINNERS; JUNIOR CUP RUNNERS-UP

Senior: fixtures 16, reported 16, won 9, lost 3, drawn 4. President: J.J. Boland. Captain: C.J. Mara. Merrion play their first league match of the season against Clontarf on 5 May and two days later all German forces surrender unconditionally to the Allies. The Emergency is over, and Merrion have drawn their match, thanks to the umpire calling time with the last ball of an over still to be bowled. Those were the days. Yet Merrion surprisingly emulate their 1940 success by winning the Senior League for a second time, with a late surge that brings them four wins and two draws. They play 14, win 8, lose 2, draw 4, and finish with 76 points. This might be regarded as a greater achievement than the 1940 League win, as the team, according to the Hon. Secretary, Stan Greer, was 'not in the same class'. Railway Union replace Civil Service in the Senior ranks, having won the Senior 2 League in 1944. Qualifications for the Marchant and O'Grady Cups are changed, and it is now necessary to bat or bowl in seven league matches – not just play in seven.

In the Cup, Merrion are stymied in the semi-final by Pembroke, for whom Alan Murray scores 87. O'Connor, Curley, Warren, Waldron and Mara play for Leinster against Munster. P. Waldron scores 537 runs @ 35.80, including 100 against YMCA and a brace of 50s, while J. Burke and S. Curley supply the backup with 50s. The ever-reliable, gutsy Des O'Connor also plays some important innings, while compiling 236 runs @ 21.45. Billy Lindsay scores a century against Phoenix in a 'club game'. Paul Warren has a hat-trick in the same game. Mara takes 44 wickets @ 10.86. Shortt could only manage 41 @ 15.02. Little struggles to 35 @ 14.74. They average 7.5 wickets per game between them over sixteen games. It's worth noting that in 1945, Roland Henry Shortt is forty-six, Cecil John Little a mere stripling at forty-five and Christopher Mara a mewling baby at thirty-four. And they are bowling 8-ball overs! But that is all about to change:

Opponent	Result	Mer.	Opp.	Best Batting: Runs	Best Bowling: Wickets
Clontarf	Drawn	160/9	162	P. Waldron: 53	C. Little: 3/33
DU	Won	139	109	C. Little: 40	C. Mara: 6/28
YMCA	Lost	53	132	E. Extras: 13	R. Shortt: 6/39
Railway Union	Won	266	55	J. Burke: 57	C. Mara: 5/27
Leinster	Won	120	95	W. Lindsay: 44	C. Mara: 4/20
Railway Union (C)	Won	168/9	52	P. Waldron: 56	M. O'Higgins: 6/17
YMCA	Won	181/2	64	P. Waldron: 100*	C. Mara: 5/24
Pembroke	Drawn	96/8	187/9	P. Warren: 42	C. Mara: 4/59
Pembroke (C)	Lost	235	330	S. Curley: 55	C. Mara: 5/77
Leinster	Lost	63	97/3	D. McCourt: 15	R. Shortt: 3/36
Phoenix	Won	169/7	165	J.D. O'Connor: 43*	C. Little: 7/70
Railway Union	Won	112	83	J.D. O'Connor: 26	J. Burke: 7/28
Pembroke	Won	103/7	98	D. McCourt: 26*	C. Mara: 5/44
Phoenix	Drawn	267/4	174/9	S. Curley: 92*	C. Little: 4/70
Clontarf	Won	166/8	125	P. Waldron: 47	R. Shortt: 5/50
DU	Drawn	31/2	155	J. D'Arcy: 16	R. Shortt: 3/52
Phoenix (F)	Won	226/5	130	W. Lindsay: 113	P. Warren: 3/7

Merrion need just 3 points from the last match to secure the championship, and the Irish weather duly obliges:

LEINSTER SENIOR LEAGUE 1945, MERRION V. DUBLIN UNIVERSITY

Merrion			Dublin University		
J. D'Arcy	c. Steede b. Hool	16	R.H. Drennan	c. Lindsay b. Shortt	3
P. Waldron	c. Steede b. Kelly	14	D.A. Joughin	c. D'Arcy b. Mara	31
P. Warren	not out	0	N.B. Hool	c. Warren b. Mara	3
C. Mara	not out	0	W.E. Haughton	c. O'Connor b. Shortt	79
D. McCourt	d.n.b.		P.R. Oliver	l.b.w. b. Little	5
W. Lindsay	d.n.b.		V. Kelly	b. Little	27
J. Burke	d.n.b.		R.S. Crone	c. Burke b. Shortt	0
S. Curley	d.n.b.		R. Glynn	c. O'Connor b. Little	2
C.J. Little	d.n.b.		S. Steede	b. D'Arcy	2
J.D. O'Connor	d.n.b.		R.P. Willis	c. Curley b. D'Arcy	0
R.H. Shortt	d.n.b.		G.P. Jeffares	not out	0
	Extras	1		Extras	3
	Total (for 2 wickets)	31		Total	155

Junior: Merrion 2nds win Division 2 of the Senior 2 League, winning 6, losing 2, and drawing 1 games. They are awarded the Senior 2 League, as the winners of Division 1 refuse to play in the final over a matter that is, according to the Hon. Secretary, 'nothing to do with our club'. They are promoted to Division 1 in 1946. Malahide defeat them in the first round of the Senior 2 Cup. Merrion 3rds are demoted to Division A of the Junior League. They lose to Cremore 2nds in the final of the Junior Cup, 65 to 109. Merrion 4ths do not play in any league this year, despite winning the Minor League in 1944. The pressure of fielding four teams is just too much. They lose to YMCA 3rds in the first round of the Minor Cup.

CLUB NOTES

The AGM is held in the Red Bank Restaurant on 27 September. There is a feeling that more seating might be needed at the ground, as gate receipts are down on the previous year. Mr R. Shortt is elected 1sts Captain for 1946 'with acclamation'. Mr J. O'Donnell is elected 2nds Captain. Mr D. Wilson is voted in as 3rds Captain, to the joy of Mr S. Greer, who has been doing the job for the previous nine years, and can now look forward to being dropped.

PROFILE: J.D. O'CONNOR

R-H stoical batsman, with a strong straight drive, who called 'Yip' when he wanted a run. Veterinary surgeon. Des also played rugby for Bective Rangers and Edinburgh Wanderers at out-half, to near international standard. Firsts captain in 1939 and 1950. Played 219 Senior matches, scoring 3,182 runs @ 18.18, including 2*100s and 12*50s. Took 73 catches. Played interprovincial cricket for Leinster versus Munster at Cork in 1945. When the going got tough, Des O'Connor got going. In helmetless days, he would head the ball down to fine leg if it meant a run, regardless of the damage to his brain. He kept his wicket close to his heart and probably saved more matches for Merrion than any other single player, in that unmourned era of timed cricket, when a draw was a result that could help his team win a trophy. Merrion's unsung hero.

Merrion 1sts, 1945 Senior League winners: S. Curley, W. Lindsay, J.D. O'Connor, C. Mara, M. O'Higgins, P. Waldron, D. McCourt, P. Warren.

1946: SENIOR CUP RUNNERS-UP

Senior: fixtures 15, reported 15, won 7, lost 3, drawn 4, tied 1. President: J.J. Boland. Captain: R.H. Shortt. A dismal, wet summer in which Merrion come third in the Senior League, with 55.68 per cent, a return to percentage rating having been agreed in 1945. They play 11, win 4, lose 2, draw 4, tie 1, and are still in the hunt at the end of July. But their only two losses come within the last four games, and so another league title goes to Pembroke. Merrion are runners-up to the Sydney Parade side in the Senior Cup, having been 55/6 chasing 113 in the semi-final against Railway Union, before Paul Warren brings the team home. The final is a one-sided affair, with Pembroke batting first and winning by a margin of 137 runs. P. Waldron, C. Little, T. Burke and S. Curley play for Leinster against Munster. Waldron plays for Leinster against Ulster and for Ireland against Scotland. Waldron, Curley and J. Burke score 50s in a season of some poor team performances with the bat. Shortt celebrates a return to 6-ball overs with a modest 25 wickets @ 20.68. Mara has 38 @ 12.94, while Little, in his last full season on the 1sts, takes 26 wickets @ 18.19:

Opponent	Result	Mer.	Opp.	Best Batting: Runs	Best Bowling: Wickets
Clontarf	Drawn	148	139/8	P. Waldron: 81	R. Shortt: 3/27
Railway Union	Tied	151/9	151/7	S. Curley: 31	C. Little: 3/45
Clontarf (C)	Won	151	126	P. Waldron: 55	C. Mara: 4/40
YMCA	Drawn	103/7	190/1	S. Curley: 30	C. Mara: 1/31
Pembroke	Drawn	173	103/8	R. Woodhouse: 30	C. Little: 6/55
Leinster	Won	155/7	150	R. Woodhouse: 39	R. Shortt: 5/49
Railway Union (C)	Won	114/9	113	P. Warren: 25	C. Little: 4/43
Phoenix	Drawn	76/8	203/6	J.D. O'Connor: 19	R. Shortt: 3/83
YMCA	Won	105/0	85	J. Burke: 65*	C. Mara: 6/40
Pembroke	Lost	144	281	J. Burke: 29	C. Mara: 4/60
Senior Cup Final					
Clontarf	Lost	104	105/6	C. Little: 31*	C. Little: 5/47
DU	Won	121	106	D. McCourt: 38	C. Mara: 6/36
Cahir Park (F)	Won	149	124		
Railway Union	Lost	107	112/4	P.R. Oliver: 38	C. Mara: 3/23
Leinster	Won	149	62	S. Curley: 51	C. Mara: 6/17

Junior: Merrion 2nds finish mid-table in Division A of the Senior 2 League. They are drawn against Cremore in the second round of the Senior 2 Cup. Merrion 3rds finish mid-table in Division A of the Junior League. They beat Leinster 4ths in the first round of the Junior Cup, thanks to Mick O'Connell's 7 wickets for 5 runs, but lose in a subsequent round. Merrion 4ths beat Pembroke 4ths in the first round of the Minor Cup, but lose narrowly to St James's Gate in the second round.

CLUB NOTES

The Hon Secretary, Mr T.E. Murphy, comments on the effect this year's soft wickets have on Merrion's famous 'blitz attack'. This is Little, forty-six, Shortt, forty-seven, and Mara, thirty-five. The problems of petrol rationing continue to worry him, as he says 'but for the generosity of some of our car owner members, we would have been in a sorry plight'. At the AGM in the

Red Bank Restaurant on 26 September, Mr R.V. Stanford states that the 'lavatory is in a bad state and in his opinion needs close attention with a view to improved cleanliness'. (That's the Merrion lavatory, not the Red Bank one.) One speaker complains that on 'at least 2 occasions when the 1st XI have important matches at Anglesea Road, there is nobody on the gate, and quite a number of people come in and don't pay at all'.

PROFILE: JOE BURKE

R-H elegant opening batsman and R-A fast swing opening bowler with a high action. Educated at Blackrock College. Worked in the Bank of Ireland, St Stephen's Green. Once, after a campaign by Chris Mara, with whom he did not get on and who felt he was too slow in scoring his runs, Joe was dropped to the 2nds. His response was to score one of the fastest tons ever in Rathmines, thereby creating problems for Merrion with the starring list. Brother of Tommy, he played six times for Ireland, scoring 62 runs @ 8.86 and taking 5 wickets @ 39.60, including that of that great New Zealander John Reid. Captained Merrion 1sts in 1951 and 1955. Joe was an important member of the three league-winning sides of 1945, '52 and '58. He played 208 times for Merrion 1sts, scoring 3,626 runs @ 22.38, with a highest score of 89*, and taking 280 wickets @ 14.97 and 81 catches. Joe is seventh in the Merrion all-rounders' table. He played his last game in 1962, retiring completely, perhaps to avoid having to play with Chris on the 2nds, 3rds or 4ths. A man of considerable wit, if asked why he was out in a particular match, like Diogenes he would reply that he was 'practising disappointment'. If stopped by a policeman after breaking a traffic light, he would regally claim that, 'I was committed to the stroke, sir.'

Merrion 1sts, 1946 Senior Cup runners-up: S. Curley, R. Shortt (C), J. Burke, P. Waldron, R. Woodhouse, C. Mara, C. Little, P. Warren, D. McCourt, T. Burke, W. Lindsay (W).

1947: DEATH OF MERRION FOUNDER

Senior: fixtures 11, reported 11, won 3, lost 5, drawn 3. President: W. V. Rumney. Captain: P.H. Waldron. The appalling weather of 1946 continues well into August, leading to a truncated season of cricket. Only twenty-five of forty scheduled league matches are played, due to rain. There's yet another manic experimentation with the league structure – each team to play ten matches, one against four teams and two against three teams – to be decided by ballot! Merrion finish 6/8, playing 7, winning 2, losing 4, drawing 1, with 33.92 per cent. Dublin University play 6, winning 6 and the league with a 100 per cent record, without playing Merrion at all! The students play them in the first round of the Senior Cup, however, and chase down 243 to win. Nobody shines with bat or ball for Merrion in a season best forgotten. P. Waldron plays for Ireland against Scotland and South Africa. '*Billy the Poke*' Lindsay and '*Simon the Scold*' Curley are chosen to play for Leinster versus Derbyshire. Curley, Lindsay and Little play for Leinster against Munster. R. Shortt is Merrion's best bowler, with only 16 wickets @ 15.81. Jack (Geke) O'Donnell, architect of Merrion's early years in Senior cricket, plays his last Senior game against Pembroke. John Aloysius Swaine, ex-Land Commission cricketer and the father of Merrion Cricket Club, dies at the age of seventy-seven:

Opponent	Result	Mer.	Opp.	Best Batting: Runs	Best Bowling: Wickets
YMCA	Lost	122	123/5	J.D. O'Connor: 29	R. Shortt: 2/24
Leinster	Won	132	102	S. Curley: 51	C. Little: 6/35
Clontarf	Lost	132/8	146/6	P. Warren: 27	C. Little: 2/34
DU (C)	Lost	243	253/9	S. Curley: 70	R. Shortt: 6/96
Clontarf	Drawn	173/7	179/3	P. Waldron: 64	P. Warren: 1/28
Railway Union	Won	129/9	75	C. Little: 44	R. Shortt: 5/15
Watsonians (F)	Drawn	212/3	126/8	P. Waldron: 110*	R. Shortt: 5/38
Leinster (F)	Drawn	127	134/9	G.T. Kenay: 40	G.T. Kenay: 5/31
Cahir Park (F)	Won	79	69		
Pembroke	Lost	106	110/3	W. Lindsay: 24	T. Campbell: 2/21
Phoenix	Lost	84	149/4	W. Lindsay: 22	J. Burke: 1/4

Junior: Merrion 2nds win 7, lose 4 of their 11 games in the Senior 2 League. They are beaten by Pembroke 2nds in the second round of the Senior 2 Cup. J. O'Donnell wins the Louis Bookman Memorial Cup for Senior 2 batting, with an average of 42.87. T. Campbell, T. Burke, M. O'Connell and P. McCauley also do well at this level. J. Burke is picked for Leinster versus Ulster in a Junior interprovincial. Merrion 3rds finish mid-table in Division A of the Junior League. Malahide 2nds beat them in the second round of the Junior Cup. Merrion Schoolboys finish in third place in the Vacation League.

CLUB NOTES

The main subject for discussion this year is the need to provide a bar in order to earn extra income. Even Simon Curley is in favour of this. A motion is carried unanimously, 'That no ladies shall be admitted to the club bar nor shall any lady be supplied with intoxicating liquor for consumption on any part of the club premises.' R.H. Shortt suggests keeping the bar shut on Sundays due to the proximity of the church. Geke O'Donnell says he would vote against it if he were on the executive committee, but is in favour of it since he is not. The vote is carried by fourteen to four. Stan Greer has been persuaded to captain the 3rds again, the official captain, J. Doyle, having resigned. The club raffle this year shows a profit of £50, although the dances are a failure, being poorly attended by the club members. Some things never change. A note is made of the improvement in the wickets, due to the employment of a full-time groundsman. At the AGM, Mr C. Little suggests that, 'with a view to making money, the club should consider the idea of running a car park on the ground during the Spring and Horse Shows'.

PROFILE: JOE D'ARCY

R-H wristy batsman and R-A medium pace swing bowler. Brilliant short-leg fielder. Educated at CUS. Also played hockey for Pembroke Wanderers, rugby for Lansdowne, and tennis. A bookie, cricket coach, groundsman and general Merrion dogsbody. Once cut down the trees from the Dodder bank and sold the logs from a horse and cart. Times were hard then. From a humble background, he grew up with his two aunts above their shop at the entrance to Pembroke Cottages in Donnybrook. Played to interprovincial level with Leinster at cricket. Member of the 1940 double-winning side. Played 106 times for Merrion 1sts, scoring 1,406 runs @ 18.50, with a top score of 72*. Took 44 catches. Went down the ranks and played consistently for the 2nds and 3rds before retiring. If the Duckworth-Lewis method had existed then, Joe would have been able to work out any requirement like lightning, as his bookie's experience was used by the team to work out how to get the best of Dublin University under whatever rules prevailed for the students that year. Like Paddy Waldron, Joe had a taste for the dogs, and owned a couple of greyhounds. He later owned a bookie's shop in Palmerstown. He married a gorgeous blonde called Cregan, who was the subject of the juvenile lustful admiration of at least one of the authors of this book. Or maybe both.

1948: SENIOR CUP RUNNERS-UP

Senior: fixtures 14, reported 14, won 7, lost 5, drawn 2. President: W. V. Rumney. Captain: S. A. Curley. In one of those seasons where a little luck might have seen Merrion win both the league and cup, they finish 4/8 in the Senior League, with 52.27 per cent, having played 11, won 5, lost 4, drawn 2. Merrion disappoint with the bat in the Cup final against Phoenix, after comprehensive victories over YMCA and Dublin University. The students win their second successive league by 26 June, resulting in an anti-climactic end to the season. S. Curley plays for Ireland against Yorkshire, Scotland and the MCC. He captains Leinster versus Munster and Ulster, in a side that includes Ralph McGinty and Joe Burke. A team tours Cahir Park, Mount Juliet, Kilkenny and Coolattin. Curley gets 271 runs @ 30.11. Waldron hits 262 @ 29.11 and plays for Ireland against Scotland, Derbyshire, South Africa and Yorkshire. Warren scores 221 @ 24.55. Joe Burke emerges as a formidable all-round talent, with 209 runs @ 19.00 and 22 wickets @ 12.45. R. McGinty, who subsequently moves to England and plays for Cambridge University, takes 26 wickets @ 9.57. Billy Lindsay, a Scotsman, is away playing field hockey for Great Britain in the Olympic Games. Mara has a lean season, with 20 wickets @ 18.70. In his last full season on the 1sts, Shortt takes 21 wickets @ 14.95, including his 1,000th victim in competitive cricket in the last match of the season, against Railway Union:

Opponent	Result	Mer.	Opp.	Best Batting: Runs	Best Bowling: Wickets
Railway Union	Won	185/5	48	S. Curley: 53	R. Shortt: 4/14
Clontarf	Drawn	145/6	194/4	S. Curley: 47	C. Mara: 3/55
YMCA	Won	178/3	140	J. Burke: 89*	J. Burke: 4/22
Leinster	Lost	61	240/7	P. Waldron: 18	T. Campbell: 4/60
Phoenix	Lost	136	176	R. McGinty: 28	J. Burke: 3/42
Pembroke	Won	65	54	P. Warren: 19	C. Mara: 4/22
YMCA (C)	Won	300	77	P. Warren: 76	R. McGinty: 5/16
DU	Lost	120	127/9	P. Waldron: 27	S. Curley: 3/17
DU (C)	Won	55/0	54	P. Warren: 54*	R. McGinty: 3/11
Pembroke	Won	172/6	112		R. Shortt: 6/18
Phoenix	Lost	92	95/4	W. Lindsay: 29	J. Burke: 2/33
Senior Cup Final					
Clontarf	Lost	167	171/5	S. Curley: 57	R. McGinty: 3/48
YMCA	Drawn	135/4	132/8	J.D. O'Connor: 53*	R. McGinty: 5/47
Railway Union	Won	128/2	115	P. Waldron: 52*	C. Little: 3/7

Junior: Merrion 2nds are in Division A of the Senior 2 League, along with Carlisle, Cremore, CYM, Leinster 2nds and Malahide. They play 9 games, win 4, lose 4, draw 1. Cremore beat them in the first round of the Senior 2 Cup. R. Craig, T. Campbell and D. Barber are their chief contributors. Merrion 3rds are in Division A of the Junior League. They beat St James's Gate in the first round of the Junior Cup, 115 to 98, but lose to UCD in the second round, 63 to 66/4, the third of the Curley brothers, Frank, scoring 27.

CLUB NOTES

Mention is made of S. Curley's suggestion that the Cup final be postponed to enable some of the Phoenix team to recover from a car accident. They recover. The new Spring and Horse Show car parks are a great success. At the AGM, Mr Greer and Mr Curley are in agreement that too many balls are lost during the season. To Stan Greer's immense relief, Jimmy McAlinden accepts the captaincy of the 3rds for 1949. Messrs Curley and Rumney speak at length on the need for a winter club, consisting of table tennis, cards, etc. A subcommittee, consisting of M. Gaynor, S. Curley and S. Greer is formed to look into the matter, but this subject disappears from the minutes altogether, as it does on several subsequent occasions. Same as it ever was.

PROFILE: TOM QUINN

An enthusiastic member of Junior and touring sides. Educated at St Malachy's College, Belfast and the Institute of Engineering in Birmingham, where he qualified as a mechanical engineer. Started his successful engineering business in Dublin in the 1930s. Met his wife, Eileen, the sister of Ralph McCartan, at one of the Merrion *hops* of that time. He was an accomplished sculler with Dublin Rowing Club crews and also a keen swimmer and ruiner of good walks. A member of Bective Rugby Football Club, he became well known as a rugby referee after he finished playing. Later, he also bred Sealyham Terriers. A Peace Commissioner and a member of the Military History Society of Ireland, Tom gave active service to the ARP during the

Merrion 1sts, 1948 Senior Cup runners-up. Back row: R. McGinty, D. McEvoy, R. Shortt, J. Burke, C. Mara, D. McCourt. Front row: P. Warren, M. Gaynor (W), S. Curley (C), T. Campbell, P. Waldron.

Second World War. President of Merrion from 1955 to 1963, although illness prevented him from fulfilling his duties in the last three years, when Simon Curley stood in for him.

Tom's generosity in all aspects of his life was legendary, but in Merrion it was spectacular. He forewent his 1951 loan to the Ground Purchase Fund, which constituted 25 per cent of the cost of the area marked **A** on the diagram of the Anglesea Road plot. As well as paying for countless tours and expenses, for a gang mower and a tractor, he also offered a loan to build a proper *bar*, which the members of the committee had to refuse, presumably to avoid too much embarrassing obligation. He was instrumental in rebranding the club in 1955, with a new flag and new crested caps and blazers replacing the old egg and bacon striped ones, even though the foundation date was about twenty-five years too early. In the 1940s and '50s, the Littles and the Quinns would spend their summer holidays in Poulshone, County Wexford, where Tom would summon his family of seven children from the beach to their house, *MacArt's Fort*, by a different number of rings of a bell for each child – one for Dan, two for Malachy, three for Deirdre, four for Eileen-Siobhan, etc.

1949: SENIOR LEAGUE RUNNERS-UP

Senior: fixtures 17, reported 17, won 10, lost 3, drawn 4. President: W.V. Rumney. Captain: S.A. Curley. In a dry, hot summer, Ireland declares a Republic and it's another nearly season for Merrion, who finish runners-up to Phoenix in the Senior League, with

69.64 per cent, having played 14, won 9, lost 2, drawn 3. YMCA beat them in one match by 5 runs. They bat for more than two hours and thirty minutes (half the playing time of five hours) against Dublin University at College Park and get no points for the draw, but are granted 8 points as a walkover in the return match. Merrion leave it too late with a surge that sees them win seven of their last eight games. Phoenix win the league, despite being beaten twice by Merrion.

The story in the Senior Cup is much the same, with Railway Union beating Merrion in the first round by 12 runs. S. Curley and J. Burke play for Leinster versus Munster. Curley plays for Ireland against Scotland and Yorkshire. He scores 379 runs @ 42.11 and narrowly misses winning the Marchant Cup to S. Bergin of Pembroke. He tops the provincial catches table, with 14. Having played for many years with Civil Service and in England, Vinny Holloway starts his cricket career with Merrion by scoring 267 runs @ 38.14, including an undefeated century against Leinster. On tour, he scores 158 against County Kilkenny, having refused an LBW decision from the umpire at 10. J. Burke makes 265 runs @ 29.44 and takes 31 wickets @ 13.54, coming second in the provincial all-rounders. P. Waldron returns to bowling and takes 16 wickets @ 13.43, as well as scoring 322 runs @ 32.20. C. Mara is injured and plays only eight games this season, taking 16 wickets @ 15.18 and averaging 25.20 with the bat. In a second emotional reaction to being dropped from Merrion 1sts, and in complete ignorance of the notion of time, Rollie Shortt moves through Sandymount to join YMCA for a season. At fifty years of age, he could surely only claim to be a Christian male:

Opponent	Result	Mer.	Opp.	Best Batting: Runs	Best Bowling: Wickets
Phoenix	Won	157/2	152	P. Waldron: 76*	C. Mara: 3/17
Pembroke	Drawn	168/7	192/9	J. Burke: 62*	S. Curley: 4/28
DU	Drawn	125	114/8	M. Gaynor: 32*	C. Mara: 3/37
Clontarf	Lost	100	151/7	C. Mara: 32*	C. Mara: 4/41
Leinster	Drawn	223	93/3	S. Curley: 69	D. McLoughlin: 1/9
Phoenix	Won	175	134	S. Curley: 60	P. Warren: 3/7
Railway Union (C)	Lost	154	166	J. Burke: 39	J. Burke: 5/56
Leinster	Won	200/5	196/7	V. Holloway: 112*	J. Burke: 2/36
YMCA	Won	85/2	79	P. Waldron: 45	P. Waldron: 4/27
Railway Union	Won	89/1	86	V. Holloway: 38*	J. Burke: 4/26
Watsonians (F)	Drawn	124/5	79/5	B. Cunningham: 49	R. Craig: 2/12
YMCA	Lost	111	116	D. McEvoy: 29	C. Little: 3/18
Clontarf	Won	128/2	113	V. Holloway: 51*	P. Waldron: 4/27
Cahir Park (F)	Won	97	72		
Pembroke	Won	156/5	153/9	S. Curley: 83	J. Burke: 4/44
Railway Union	Won	111/1	109	S. Curley: 54*	J. Burke: 5/33
DU	Won			Walkover	

Junior: Merrion 2nds have a bad season, winning only one of their thirteen games in Section A of the Senior 2 League. Brian Cunningham averages 26.78 over 9 innings. Mick O'Connell takes 25 wickets @ 13.40. They lose to Pembroke 2nds in the first round of the Senior 2 Cup, 110 to 259/7. Merrion 3rds are back in Section A of the Intermediate League, but finish the season in the wrong half of the table. In addition to being the most consistent batsman, Gerry Doyle achieves the ultimate for a bowler when he takes all 10 wickets for 25 against Clontarf 3rds. The team loses to Railway Union 3rds in the first round of the Intermediate Cup, 165 to 182.

CLUB NOTES

Joe Burke, the Hon. Secretary, reports on the resignation of R.H. Shortt, 'despite the fact that a few members did not always see eye-to-eye with Rollie, all regretted his action and I am sure we all wish him good luck with his new club'. Burke complains about the scarcity of volunteer labour in the maintenance of the wickets and ground. At the AGM in September, none of the three proposed members, J. Burke, P. Warren, S. Curley, are willing to allow his name to go forward for captain of the 1sts, so a decision is postponed until the following April. A recommendation is made to the incoming committee that a telephone be installed in the pavilion. Nobody mentions the words 'bar' or 'intoxicating liquor'. The ladies are safe for another year.

PROFILE: BRENDAN CURLEY

R–H attacking batsman, prone to scoring runs on the leg side, and one of the few batsmen in Leinster cricket to regularly dismantle the bowling of Alec O'Riordan, the best Irish cricketer of his time. R–A occasional slow-medium seam bowler. Educated at CUS. Industrial Officer in Dublin Gas. Younger brother of Simon, he also played hockey for Pembroke Wanderers and soccer for Oaklands in the Dublin Amateur League. Once scored fifty goals in a season. Interprovincial cricketer for Leinster. Played 362 games for Merrion 1sts between 1952 and 1979, scoring 5,665 runs @ 18.51, including 21*50s and with a top score of 87*. Took 112 catches. Continued playing far too long on the 1sts, because *'there was no-one else'*. Also went down the ranks to 2nds and 3rds level. Life Member. Brendan never forgot some good advice that Paddy Waldron gave him as a newcomer to the 1sts, *'it's not enough to watch the ball. You have to smell it.'*

Merrion 1sts, 1949 Senior League runners-up. Back row: C. Mara, R. Craig, V. Holloway, D. McEvoy, B. Cunningham. Front row: A. O'Kelly, P. Warren (W), D. McCourt, S. Curley (C), P. Waldron, J. Burke, W. Rumney (P).

1950: WORRIES ABOUT ANGLESEA ROAD LEASE

Senior: fixtures 14, reported 14, won 4, lost 7, drawn 3. President: T.E. Murphy. Captain: J.D. O'Connor. In a poor season, Merrion finish 7/8 in the Senior League, with 37 per cent, having played 13, won 4, lost 6, drawn 3. They bat over time against Clontarf and get no points for the draw. Making a valiant effort to chase 309 against Clontarf in the first round of the Senior Cup, Merrion struggle to 276 over several evenings in bad light, falling short by 33 runs. O'Connor is injured for half the season, so vice-captain Little takes over. S. Curley is subbed onto the Irish team to play MCC at College Park, and almost guides his country to a thrilling victory, falling short by 3 runs. He scores 516 runs @ 43, but is 20 runs short of Stanley Bergin's average of 63.62, which wins the Marchant Cup. Yet again, he leads the provincial catches table, with 13. J. Burke scores 263 runs @ 29.22. P. Waldron glides 428 runs @ 32.92. Rollie Shortt bows to the inevitable and makes a triumphant return to Merrion 2nds, cured forever of his Sandymount wanderlust. His absence may be a factor in the season's poor performance. A fifty-year-old Cecil Little tweaks 6/47 against Railway Union. C. Mara snaffles 36 wickets @ 14.19. Tommy Campbell, who achieves fame later in the *Guinness Book Of Records* for the longest drive by an amateur golfer (392 yards, in his first full round of eighteen holes, at Dún Laoghaire Golf Club), wheedles 5/40 against Leinster:

Opponent	Result	Mer.	Opp.	Best Batting: Runs	Best Bowling: Wickets
Phoenix	Won	139	135	J. Burke: 37	J. Burke: 3/23
Railway Union	Drawn	113/8	147/9	D. McCourt: 24	C. Little: 6/47
Clontarf	Lost	158/6	162/4	P. Waldron: 55	C. Mara: 3/52
YMCA	Drawn	163	142/9	S. Curley: 83	S. Curley: 5/22
Leinster	Won	150/2	149	J. Burke: 63*	T. Campbell: 5/40
DU	Lost	83	86/4	C. Mara: 27*	C. Mara: 2/20
Leinster	Lost	169/7	178/6	J. Burke, P. Waldron: 63	P. Warren: 2/26
Clontarf (C)	Lost	276	306	P. Waldron: 70	C. Mara: 6/68
Pembroke	Lost	145	148	W. Lindsay: 64	C. Mara: 3/41
Phoenix	Lost	175	210/8	S. Curley: 92	C. Mara: 4/39
Clontarf	Drawn	169/1	75/4	P. Waldron: 80*	A. O'Kelly: 1/4
Railway Union	Won	177/2	173	P. Waldron: 63	C. Mara: 4/55
YMCA	Won	162/6	96	J.D. O'Connor: 56	C. Mara: 4/20
Pembroke	Lost	151/9	152/8	V. Holloway: 77	S. Curley: 3/39

Junior: Merrion 2nds are in an expanded Section B of the Senior 2 League, along with Clontarf 2nds, Phoenix 2nds, 3rd OBU, YMCA 2nds, Railway Union 2nds, Civil Service, St James's Gate, and UCD. They play 11, win 5, lose 6, and finish mid-table, with 40 points out of a possible 88. Maurice Gaynor scores a century. Jimmy McAlinden takes 6/18 against Phoenix. Des McLoughlin takes 29 wickets @ 9.20. Having beaten St James's Gate in the first round of the Senior 2 Cup, 91 to 51, they lose to Leinster in the second round. Merrion 3rds finish 8/8 in Section A of the Intermediate League, with 12 games played, 1 won, 10 lost, 1 drawn, 11 per cent. Niall McEvoy takes 7 wickets for 31 runs in one game. They lose to Belvedere in the first round of the Intermediate Cup.

CLUB NOTES

The April meeting elects Des O'Connor as captain of the 1sts. A question is asked about renewing the lease on the ground. Ominously, the Chairman replies that there is a legal hold-up. The club is £50 in debt. Vinny Holloway suggests that the groundsman is an unnecessary expense, and that he is overpaid for the amount of work done. His idea is that the members should do the work. The Chairman bemoans the continued defacing of the dressing-room walls with paint and the breaking open of club lockers, and pleads for 'a better club spirit among the younger members'. At the AGM in September, the Hon Secretary, C. Mara wishes that Mr Louis McMullan were available on Saturdays, as his presence would improve the 1sts considerably (Louis worked in his furniture auction rooms in Rathmines on a Saturday). Mr Mara also suggests that more spin should be used on the 1sts, as there is far too much reliance on 'dismantled fast bowlers'. At the end of the season J. Burke is elected captain for 1951, with V. Holloway as vice-captain.

PROFILE: VINNY HOLLOWAY

R-H attacking batsman. R-A occasional slow bowler. Known as '*Hurricane Holloway*'. Bookkeeper with GKN and ambulance driver with the Civil Defence in England during the Second World War. Hockey player for Railway Union. He was also somewhat of a star player as a teenager for Civil Service, from 1935 to 1943, for West Bromwich Dartmouth (with Alf Gover) and Smethwick in the Birmingham League from 1944 to 1948, and Merrion from 1949 to 1966, where he played ninety-six times for the 1sts, scoring 1,603 runs @ 21.09, with a top score of 112* and including 8*50s, and taking 30 catches. Interprovincial for Leinster and Munster. President in 1968, after which he returned to live in England for about thirty years, returning to Ireland in the late 1990s. A notorious practical joker, he was once suspected of filling Jimmy Boucher's car with a flock of Stan Greer's hens from the Hazeldene farm, but the real culprit was actually a Phoenix player, Donald Pratt. At ninety-one years of age, *The Doc* is still on the lookout for the Clantons as he continues his gunfight at the OK Corral. He is undoubtedly Merrion's eldest statesman.

1951: GROUND PURCHASED; SENIOR CUP RUNNERS-UP

Senior: fixtures 12, reported 12, won 3, lost 5, drawn 4. President: T.E. Murphy. Captain: J.P. Burke. Merrion have another poor season, finishing 7/8 in the Senior League, with 27.77 per cent, having played only 9 games due to bad weather, winning 1, losing 4, drawing 4. Yet the team are runners-up again in the Senior Cup, losing in the final to Phoenix and the guile of Jimmy Boucher. This is the first final to be played at Park Avenue, whose residents are beaten in the semi-final by Merrion, successfully defending 80 runs. S. Curley wins the Marchant Cup with 536 runs @ 59.55, including a chanceless 107 against Dublin University and a second big century against Leinster. He plays for Ireland against South Africa and Scotland. P. Waldron has 381 runs @ 38.10. Curley takes most wickets also, with 19 @ 17.21. C. Mara is close behind, with 18 @ 16.88. First Senior appearance of future stalwart Gerry Doyle, who takes 5 Pembroke wickets in the league:

Opponent	Result	Mer.	Opp.	Best Batting: Runs	Best Bowling: Wickets
DU	Drawn	193/6	155/8	S. Curley: 107	S. Curley: 4/33
Pembroke	Drawn	196/6	203/8	V.J. Holloway: 74*	G. Doyle: 2/5
Railway Union	Lost	151	197/9	V.J. Holloway: 45	S. Curley: 3/33
Leinster	Lost	169	175/6	C. Mara: 60	T. Campbell: 2/30
YMCA	Drawn	254/2	155/6	P. Waldron: 108*	C. Mara: 3/28
Leinster (C)	Won	307	239	S. Curley: 175	S. Curley: 3/40
Phoenix	Won	223/7	221/7	P. Waldron: 77	S. Curley: 3/63
Railway Union (C)	Won	80	76	J. Burke: 38	C. Mara: 4/25
Phoenix	Lost	137	138/5	J. Burke: 32	J. Burke: 3/42
Senior Cup final					
Pembroke	Lost	181/6	185/9	N. Flood: 49*	G. Doyle: 5/62
YMCA	Drawn	159/8	136/5		
Clontarf	Lost	96	103/4		

Junior: Merrion 2nds finish mid-table in Section B of the Senior 2 League. R. Craig takes 23 wickets @ 9.60. They lose to Civil Service in the first round of the Senior 2 Cup. Merrion 3rds finish third in Section B of the Intermediate League. M. O'Connell, H. Warren, J. McAlinden and J. McDermott are the main wicket-takers. Although they beat Railway Union 3rds in the first round of the Intermediate Cup, 50/5 to 47, and Civil Service 2nds in the second round, they lose to Rush in the semi-final.

CLUB NOTES

A Special General Meeting is held on 18 May to discuss the purchase of the ground – Area **A**. As the club has no fixity of tenure and the owners want to sell, an offer of £1,000 is made on the spot by the Chairman and Mr O'Donnell. It is accepted and the purpose of the meeting is to find ways of raising the money, despite Chris Mara's warning that the club should be neither a lender nor a borrower. Mr O'Donnell states that a loan of £500 has been offered by the Property Loan Company, and £300 has been contributed by members, of which £250 comes from Tom Quinn. A discussion ensues on ways of finding the balance, repaying the loan and running the club at the same time. The word '*bar*' is mentioned again, but any further discussion is postponed. The meeting decides to approach the members more actively, with a view to getting everyone to contribute more. At the AGM in September, Mr Mara identifies the absence of organised practice as the root cause for the decline of the 1sts this year. Mr O'Donnell reports that £617 18s od has been subscribed towards the Ground Purchase Fund, but the deeds are still with the solicitors. Only thirty-nine of the members have contributed so far and the meeting agrees to make a stronger appeal to the defaulters. Mr Greer, the Sheriff of Dublin, suggests that a '*bar*' will be a great source of revenue and that Merrion are the only Senior club without one.

PROFILE: CATHAL McALINDEN

R-H opening batsman. Occasional R-A seam bowler and wicket-keeper. Educated at CUS. Worked as an estate agent with Battersby & Co., Lambert Smith Hampton and occasionally with Louis McMullan in his furniture auction rooms in Rathmines. Also played rugby for

Merrion 1sts, 1951 Senior Cup runners-up. Back row: D. McEvoy, J.P. Clifford, C. Mara, S. Curley, D. McCourt, W. Lindsay (W). Front row: W.T. Campbell, V. Holloway, J. Burke (C), C. McAlinden, P. Waldron.

Lansdowne as flanker, tennis, and in his later years went to ruining good walks. Although he played twenty-seven times for Merrion 1sts, like his elder brother Jimmy, Cathal played mainly for the Junior sides, captaining the 2nds over many years and scoring several centuries for them. Holding a plethora of offices within the club, including trustee, Cathal's gruff exterior hid a warm heart and he did as much as anyone in Merrion to encourage and develop younger players in the days when a coach was something you travelled in to get to an away match, and anybody under the age of eighteen wasn't allowed near the pavilion.

1952: SENIOR LEAGUE WINNERS; MINOR CUP RUNNERS-UP

Senior: fixtures 14, reported 14, won 9, lost 4, drawn 1. President: P.J. Brennan. Captain: S.A. Curley. In a dry, sun-filled summer, and after finishing seventh in the previous two seasons, Merrion win their third Senior League title, with 78.12 per cent, having played 12, won 9, lost 2, drawn 1. Simon Curley's captaincy is obviously an important factor in this success, considering their second placement in 1949, his previous year as captain. A newspaper strike in July and August prevents the full reporting of this season. In a close match, Pembroke knock Merrion out of the Senior Cup in the first round, despite a last-wicket stand by R. Craig and G. Doyle, which ends in a disastrous misunderstanding and Craig being run out. First appearance of future legend and younger brother of Simon, Brendan Curley. S. Curley scores 343 runs @ 42.87, including 123 not out against Phoenix, and is third in the provincial batting averages. He takes 24 wickets @ 16.20 and is the leading provincial all-rounder. J. Burke is not far behind him, with 392 runs @ 39.20 and 23 wickets @ 16.95. P. Waldron scores 428 runs @ 35.66. John Clifford takes 24 wickets @ 13.25 and the ever-reliable Chris Mara chips in with 31 wickets @ 13.67, to finish third in the provincial bowling averages:

Opponent	Result	Mer.	Opp.	Best Batting: Runs	Best Bowling: Wickets
YMCA	Won	141	126	J.P. Clifford: 41	J.P. Clifford: 4/44
Pembroke	Won	145/8	128	J. Burke: 60*	S. Curley: 4/36
DU	Won	158/6	72	J. Burke: 52	J.P. Clifford: 6/35
Leinster	Lost	116	120/5	S. Curley: 47	S. Curley: 2/26
Pembroke (C)	Lost	203	215	P. Waldron: 55	C. Mara: 4/43
Railway Union	Won	134/5	132	W. Lindsay: 46*	S. Curley: 3/25

Cahir Park (F)	Lost	79	92/6		
Leinster	Won	129/1	125	P. Waldron: 69*	C. Mara: 4/23
YMCA	Won				
Phoenix	Lost				
Phoenix	Won				
Railway Union	Won				
Pembroke	Won				
Clontarf	Drawn	204/4	131/8	J. Burke: 83	S. Curley: 4/34

Merrion have already won the league title when they play Clontarf, with this victory over Leinster on 5 July:

LEINSTER SENIOR LEAGUE 1952, MERRION V. LEINSTER

Merrion			Leinster		
P.H. Waldron	not out	69	J.R. Gill	c. Mara b. Curley	14
W. Lindsay	b. Metchette	43	A.B. Curtis	l.b.w. b. Mara	4
J. Burke	not out	3	J. Caprani	l.b.w. b. Burke	5
S. Curley	d.n.b.		F.G. Connell	c. McEvoy b. Burke	13
G. Doyle	d.n.b.		B.A. Kelly	c. Waldron b. Clifford	4
N. Flood	d.n.b.		J. Spencer	run out	55
D.B. McEvoy	d.n.b.		G.A. Duffy	l.b.w. b. Burke	0
C. Mara	d.n.b.		P.C. Mannion	b. Mara	2
P.A. McGilligan	d.n.b.		F. Metchette	b. Mara	11
R. Craig	d.n.b.		J. Notley	b. Mara	7
J.P. Clifford	d.n.b.		C. Fagan	not out	0
	Extras	14		Extras	10
	Total (for 1 wicket)	**129**		**Total**	**125**

Junior: Merrion 2nds finish 5/8 in Section B of the Senior 2 League with 44 per cent, having played 10, won 4, lost 5, drawn 1. They beat Railway Union 2nds in the first round of the Senior 2 Cup, but lose to Malahide in the second round. Merrion 3rds finish 7/8 in Section B of the Intermediate League with 24 per cent, having played 8, won 2, lost 5, drawn 1. They lose to Harding in the first round of the Intermediate Cup, 137 to 138/6. Danny Parkinson debuts for Merrion, having watched the '*posh folk*' from the far side of the Dodder, and decided that playing for St James's Gate is simply no longer good enough. What he thinks when he meets Rollie Shortt cannot be remembered. Vincent Finnegan, yet another auctioneer, scores 66* against Old Belvedere. Merrion 4ths make a reappearance in the Minor Cup, beating Civil Service 3rds and Leinster 5ths, before succumbing to Balrothery 2nds in the final.

CLUB NOTES

A Special General Meeting is held on 9 May. Mr O'Donnell outlines the position as regards the purchase of the ground. It now belongs to Merrion, and £1,100 has been raised. This money must somehow be paid back, with interest, over a twenty-year period. A discussion ensues as to how this should be done – an extra 6d on teas, raffles, increased subscriptions, twenty-week draws – the usual suspects. Mr Mara suggests dances. After much debate it is agreed that a letter be written to all defaulting members, asking for a donation, and a subcommittee is formed to investigate the matter. At the AGM in September, Mr O'Donnell reiterates his appeal to those members who have not yet contributed to the Ground Purchase Fund. Mr Curley asks that all cricket balls be returned to the club. At an Executive Committee Meeting (ECM), Schoolboy P. Butler is suspended for leaving the field before the end of a match. At the same meeting, Mr Curley deplores an anonymous letter he has received, in connection with a midweek league match. The meeting agrees that the sender should be traced. Miss Marple has a complicated pullover to knit, so it is Hercule Poirot that must be notified.

PROFILE: GERRY DOYLE

R–H batsman. L–A slow leg-break bowler. Educated at CUS. Insurance official, who worked with Gerry Duffy. Played 101 games for Merrion 1sts between 1950 and 1964, scoring 525 runs @ 9.72, and taking 24 wickets @ 25.45, with 17 catches. But it was at a Junior level that Gerry made his biggest mark, captaining the 2nds and 3rds for many years, and capturing all 10 wickets for 25 runs for Merrion 3rds against Clontarf 3rds in 1949. He tells us that he and Brendan Curley were very fast runners between the wickets. Their favourite trick was to tap the ball to a close-in fielder, call 'Two' loudly, watch the fielder fumble the ball in alarm, and take a second run. Gerry's father, Stephen, was involved in the administrative and social side of the club for many years during the '40s, '50s and '60s and probably umpired every single game played during that period. Gerry's daughter also played for Merrion women's teams over several years. Nowadays, he has become a Life Member and a 'hurler on the ditch', who shares happy memories of pushing pens with Gerry Duffy as they chant abuse at the antics of the 1sts from the trenches.

1953: MINOR CUP WINNERS

Senior: fixtures 14, reported 14, won 6, lost 4, drawn 4. President: P.J. Brennan. Captain: C.G. Mara. In the year that Malahide enter the Senior League and Cup for the first time, Merrion finish 4/9 in the league, with 57.69 per cent, having played 13, won 6, lost 3, drawn 4. Phoenix beat them in the first round of the cup, having chased 279 to win. Simon Curley scores 5 half-centuries in getting 482 runs @ 37.07. He also has a fine season with the ball, with 27 wickets @ 17.77, being beaten to the O'Grady Cup by Merrion's nemesis, Gerry Duffy of Leinster. Joe Burke scores 336 runs @ 42.00 and is picked to play for Ireland against Scotland. Paddy Waldron, in his last season in Senior cricket, grooves 179 runs @ 17.90. S. O'Sullivan, in his only season for Merrion, scores 207 runs @ 23.00. C. Mara and newcomers R. Craig and M. O'Connell ('The Bomber') take most of the remaining wickets:

Opponent	Result	Mer.	Opp.	Best Batting: Runs	Best Bowling: Wickets
DU	Drawn	152/7	220/5	J. Burke: 62	C. Little: 2/16
Phoenix	Drawn	175/5	188/6	S. Curley: 65	G. Doyle: 3/66
Pembroke	Lost	135	141/7	P. Waldron: 33	S. Curley: 5/29
Railway Union	Won	161/4	160	S. Curley: 73	S. Curley: 6/63
Leinster	Lost	159/8	160/1	J. Burke: 41	C. Mara: 1/55
Clontarf	Won	167/6	166/7	S. Curley: 77	J. Burke: 2/21

Leinster	Lost	136	137/5	S. O'Sullivan: 44	C. Mara: 2/43
Phoenix (C)	Lost	278	279/8	S. Curley: 98	D. Hayden: 2/27
Pembroke	Won	170/6	166/7	S. O'Sullivan: 44*	R. Craig : 3/29
Malahide	Drawn	115/9	205/9	W. Lindsay: 55	S. Curley: 5/51
YMCA	Won	179/8	178/3	S. Curley: 39	C. Mara: 2/29
YMCA	Won	157/5	154/7	S. Curley: 51	M. O'Connell: 4/46
Clontarf	Won	106/3	104	P. Waldron: 54*	M. O'Connell: 5/19
Railway Union	Drawn	179/7	155/7	J. Burke: 78*	P. Waldron: 2/28

Junior: Merrion 2nds finish 3/8 in Section B of the Senior 2 League, with 75 per cent, having played 4, won 3, lost 1. Rollie Shortt's team loses narrowly to Railway Union 2nds in the first round of the Senior 2 Cup, 83 to 84/9. Merrion 3rds finish mid-table in Section B of the Intermediate League. Vinny Finnegan's team are beaten by Phoenix 3rds in the first round of the Intermediate Cup. Merrion 4ths are captained by Geke O'Donnell, and win the Minor Cup, beating Leinster 5ths, Civil Service 3rds, Belvedere 3rds and then Hammond Lane in the final. They make no league appearances.

CLUB NOTES

At an ECM in February, an offer of a £500 loan from Tom Quinn to instal a bar is rejected, due to the large addional debt. At a subsequent meeting, Mr T. Soraghan suggests the erection of garages inside the entrance gate, as a source of revenue. No decision is made on this matter. In April, Mr Curley volunteers to talk to Mr Greer, tenant of Hazeldene, about the messy problem of his cattle straying onto the club ground. Meetings are held with the RDS in order to get a flat rate for car-park usage, but nothing comes of this. Bective propose a payment of £200 for a ninety-year licence to play one rugby match per week during the football season, in addition to the existing rent of £60, but this is rejected. An archery club asks to use the ground for practice on Sunday mornings during the winter, but subsequently withdraws their application. At the AGM in September, a lively discussion is held into ways of getting more members to pay their subscriptions on time, especially the Schoolboys. Mr O'Donnell reports that no real progress has been made with the Ground Purchase Fund. The situation is the same as at the last meeting. The members agree that all outstanding monies from CUS should be collected, in order to satisfy the year's £60 loan repayment.

1954: TOM QUINN ELECTED PRESIDENT; SENIOR 2 B LEAGUE RUNNERS-UP

Senior: fixtures 12, reported 12, won 2, lost 7, drawn 3. President: P.J. Brennan. Captain: C.G. Mara. Proof that not every year is successful during this period is provided by this wet summer's results. Merrion experience their worst season for some years, finishing 8/9, with 28.40 per cent, having played 11, won 2, lost 6, drawn 3. They use twenty-five play-ers. Phoenix defeat them in the second round of the Senior Cup. The premature retirement of Paddy Waldron due to work pressures is felt keenly, as Simon Curley manages only 225 runs @ 18.75 and 20 wickets @ 17.20, including 7/59 against Malahide. Joe Burke scores 180 runs @ 22.50 and plays for Ireland against Lancashire and Scotland. Vinny Holloway tops the Merrion batting averages with 222 runs @ 27.75 and revels in his new position as opener. All-rounder Mike Ward provides a useful stopgap before returning to England. In his fourth and final year of captaincy, Chris Mara takes a modest 14 wickets @ 19.42:

Opponent	Result	Mer.	Opp.	Best Batting: Runs	Best Bowling: Wickets
DU	Lost	82	85/1	E. Extras: 16	G. Dagg: 1/17
Railway Union	Won	108	84	J. Burke: 29	S. Curley: 4/26
Pembroke	Lost	109	112/2	B. Curley: 25	J. Burke: 1/33
Malahide	Won	171/9	106	V.J. Holloway: 61	M. Ward: 3/18
Leinster	Drawn	178/8	159/8	V.J. Holloway: 54	M. Ward: 3/37
Phoenix (C)	Lost	172	173/3	M. Ward: 31	S. Curley: 1/37
YMCA	Lost	93	95/4	J. Burke, S. Curley: 22	R. Craig: 1/6
Malahide	Lost	62	147/8	N. Flood: 15	S. Curley: 7/59
YMCA	Lost	43	45/1	S. Curley: 20	C. Mara: 1/23
Clontarf	Drawn	182/6	158/7	S. Curley: 57	D. Hayden: 2/27
Phoenix	Drawn	167/5	110/3	B. Curley: 66	C. Mara: 2/16
Pembroke	Lost	138	139/1	B. Curley: 37	M. Ward: 1/47

Junior: Merrion 2nds are runners-up in Section B of the Senior 2 League. Richmond beat Cathal McAlinden's team in the first round of the Senior 2 Cup, 21 to 22/0. They also use twenty-five players. Bobby Booth tops the 2nds averages with 99.00 @ 33.00. Mike Ward takes 10 wickets @ 2.00. Merrion 3rds finish mid-table in Section A of the Intermediate League. They are defeated by Pembroke 3rds in the first round of the Intermediate Cup. The schoolboys in this team show great promise, especially Sean Pender, Brendan Byrne and Michael Leahy. Merrion 4ths make no league appearances and are defeated by Hammond Lane in the second round of the Minor Cup, 70 to 71/9, having disposed of Balrothery 2nds along the way.

CLUB NOTES

At the AGM in September, Gordon Aston, the Hon. Secretary, reports on the poor state of the ground and wickets this season, due to 'trouble with the mower' and the difficulty in getting a suitable groundsman. He hopes the new groundsman will perform his duties more effectively next year. Tommy Soraghan, the Hon. Treasurer states that total subscriptions – £3 3s 0d for a Senior, and £1 10s 0d for a Junior member – are up £50 on the previous year, and very few are outstanding. It is decided to write a letter to Mr D. Hand, a schoolboy defaulter for two years running, stating that he is no longer entitled to the privileges of a member of the club. A draw for a £100 note has realised £54 during the season. Tom Quinn is elected as President for a term that will turn into nine consecutive years. After some discussion about Schoolboy members leaving to join other clubs, it is decided to enter a 4ths in the Minor League in 1955.

PROFILE: MAURICE GAYNOR

R-H elegant batsman. Wicket-keeper. Educated at Blackrock College. Also played rugby for Blackrock. He played fifty games for Merrion 1sts between 1943 and 1955, scoring 230 runs @ 9.20, with a top score of 32*. He took 15 catches and 11 stumpings as wicket-keeper when Billy Lindsay was away and after he had finished, and was Hon. Secretary for several years in the late 1940s.

1955: CLUB CREST AND FOUNDATION DATE CONCOCTED; SENIOR 2 LEAGUE RUNNERS-UP

Senior: fixtures 14, reported 14, won 3, lost 7, drawn 4. President: T.A. Quinn. Captain: J.P. Burke. Another poor season in a glorious summer sees Merrion finish 8/9 again in the Senior League, with only an uncharacteristic Phoenix below them. With 29.14 per cent, they play 12, win 2, lose 6, draw 4. Leinster beat them easily in the semi-final of the Senior Cup. Simon Curley is back to his all-round best, with 302 runs @ 23.23, and 25 wickets @ 21.64. Joe Burke also turns in a decent all-round performance, with 220 runs @ 27.50 and 19 wickets @ 16.89. In September he plays for Ireland against the MCC at Lord's, taking 1/43. Vinny Holloway scores 232 runs @ 29. Derek Hayden takes 15 wickets @ 21.00:

Opponent	Result	Mer.	Opp.	Best Batting: Runs	Best Bowling: Wickets
Leinster	Lost	106	234/4	S. Curley: 67	S. Curley: 3/48
Railway Union	Lost	155/5	156/8	S. Curley: 64*	R. Craig: 3/30
DU	Lost	119	123/5	V.J. Holloway: 27	D. Hayden: 3/42
Phoenix	Lost	123	203/9	J. Burke: 33	J. Burke: 3/28
Clontarf	Drawn	94/9	177/7	B. Curley: 28	J. Burke: 4
YMCA (C)	Won	86	49	B. Curley: 40	D. Hayden: 6/25
Malahide	Lost	55	175/4	T. Burke: 22	S. Curley: 2/48
YMCA	Won	204/5	203/5	N. Flood: 45	S. Curley: 2/86
Railway Union	Lost	137	162	S. Curley: 39	C. Mara: 7/48
Leinster (C)	Lost	88	92/2	J. Burke: 20	D. Hayden: 1/24
Malahide	Drawn	174/9	223/2	V.J. Holloway: 87	T. Burke: 2/57
Clontarf	Drawn	211/2	190/8	J. Burke: 80*	J. Burke: 4/36
Phoenix	Drawn	140/7	178/9		
Pembroke	Won	117	94	N. Flood: 26	G. Doyle: 3/15

Junior: Merrion 2nds win their first seven league matches, but lose to 3rd OBU in the Senior 2 League final. Cathal McAlinden's team loses to CYM in the first round of the Senior 2 Cup, 134 to 155. C. Little takes all 10 wickets for 30 runs in a league match against YMCA 2nds, and 8 for 34 against Railway Union 2nds a few weeks later. Vinny Holloway hits 76 runs in 45 minutes against Malahide. Shortt, O'Connor and Lindsay continue their Merrion cricketing life on the Junior sides, while Paul Warren returns after a lengthy absence. Merrion 3rds are in Section A of the Intermediate League. Having beaten YMCA 3rds in the first round of the Intermediate Cup, they succumb to Cremore in the next round, 70 to 71/6. Vinny Finnegan makes 50 against Pembroke 3rds. Sean Pender, Des Barber and Barry MacMahon also get runs for this team. Merrion 4ths are back in Section C of the Junior League. They play North Kildare in the first round of the Junior Cup. John Leonard, Jack O'Donnell, Tony Sulzmann and Aidan O'Kelly feature strongly in this league.

CLUB NOTES

At a Special General Meeting held in May, the subject of the foundation date is discussed. Mr Mara suggests that Merrion should have a foundation date on their fixture cards. Mr O'Donnell points out that 'the name of the club was changed to Merrion, prior to which it was known as the Land Commission Cricket Club'. (This statement is not exactly accurate, as shown at the end of chapter 2.1.) The Chairman states that it should just be a question of finding out when the Land Commission came into existence, and using that date. (Somebody confused the Land War date – 1879 – with the true date of the Land Commission formation 1881 and didn't check to see whether there had been a cricket team between 1879 and 1891.)

During the year, extra seating to hold the crowds is ordered from CIE, in the form of old railway sleepers costing £3. These are placed mainly up against the Hazeldene bank. New toilets are built, using £100 from the Ground Purchase Fund, now in a healthy state, and another loan of £172 10s 0d from Mr T. Quinn. The next stage is to organise a water supply from the Dodder. At one of the meetings, Mr Soraghan reports that Mrs Barnes, the tea lady, has asked for an increase of 2s 6d. The matter is left in abeyance. At another meeting, it is agreed to plant a hedge at the entrance to the ladies' toilet, and Mr O'Donnell undertakes to supply cuttings.

In connection with creating a club crest, correspondence with the Arms Office reveals that they can find no entry in their records of a Land Commission or Merrion Cricket Club. As a result of an inspection of the wickets by the LCU, who claim that they resemble an unweeded garden that grows to seed, a supply of weedkiller is ordered. This is further evidence that cricket in these days is a bowling competition. The committee agrees to a ninety-year licence with Bective Rangers Club for them to play rugby at Anglesea Road on Saturdays from 1 October to 1 March only, for an annual rent of £60 (subject to a *pro rata* revision in the event of a fluctuation in the value of the pound sterling in relation to the value of the United States dollar) and a once-off *fine* of £1,000. (This licence contains a termination option for the licencors at the end of either thirty or sixty years, provided the licensees have been given twelve months' previous notice in writing.)

PROFILE: RODNEY BERNSTEIN

R-H middle-order batsman. R-A opening, very fast bowler. Educated at Stratford College. Worked as a diamond-setter. Also a soccer player, and played cricket for Leinster and Carlisle. Between 1958 and 1966, he featured 102 times for Merrion 1sts, scoring 1,089 runs @ 13.12, and taking 271 wickets @ 11.83, the best bowling analysis in the history of the club. Rodney played hugely important roles in 1958, when Merrion won the Senior League and in 1960, the last time they won the Senior Cup. He took 5 wickets in an innings on 19 occasions, and his 8/22 against Dublin University in 1962 included a hat-trick. He had 50-wicket hauls in 1960 and in 1963, when another cup win was just missed, with Chris Anderson of Dublin University gaining a ludicrous reprieve from the umpire '*when he was absolutely plumb*' and with 1 wicket to go in the final.

He played eight times for Ireland, scoring 96 runs @ 7.38 and taking 21 wickets @ 25.62. This included 4/23 against the MCC in his first match, when he caused problems for, among others, Len Hutton. It's arguable that he also gained Joe Hopkins his single cap as wicket-keeper. Small in stature, Rodney's low trajectory, combined with a speed of up to 80 miles per hour, made life extremely difficult for batsmen, especially the tail, which was usually swept up rapidly when he was playing. '*The wickets were dead slow in those days. The ball would just lob through to Joe.*' Right. As slip fielders to this bowler, we can both testify to his misuse of the word 'lob' here. The word is 'zip'.

1956: HAZELDENE FIELD LEASED; INTERMEDIATE LEAGUE RUNNERS-UP

Senior: fixtures 14, reported 14, won 1, lost 7, drawn 6. President: T.A. Quinn. Captain: B.C. Curley. Merrion Cricket Club (MCC) now has a telephone, but this doesn't stop the 1sts' disastrous slide through the 1950s as they prop up the Senior League in ninth place, with 25 per cent from 13 games played, winning 1 (by the margin of 3 runs), losing 6, drawing 6. The foul summer has certainly reduced the number of matches lost, as new regulations stipulate that once a game has started, it is a draw if abandoned. Of the 110 Senior league games started this year, 46 are drawn. Leinster beat them in a close thriller in the second round of the Senior Cup, in which game Merrion's arch-nemesis, Gerry Duffy takes 5 Merrion wickets for 41. First appearance of Joe Hopkins, future Irish wicket-keeper, on a long-term loan from Pembroke. Although it is the batting that lets the side down, Simon Curley has another fine season, scoring 312 runs @ 24, and taking 34 wickets @ 14.08, just missing out on qualification for the O'Grady Cup for bowling (35 wickets), which is not awarded this season. Brendan Curley hockeys 233 runs @ 17.92. Despite being picked for Leinster against Munster, Joe Burke has a poor season with the bat, but he takes 26 wickets @ 16.76. Vinny Holloway slams 194 runs @ 24.25. Rollie Shortt makes his final, grumbling appearance for Merrion 1sts. Chris Mara manages 23 wickets @ 16.73:

Opponent	Result	Mer.	Opp.	Best Batting: Runs	Best Bowling: Wickets
Pembroke	Drawn	104/9	187/8	N. Flood: 33	J. Burke: 5/57
DU	Lost	108; 84/6	167/9	B. Curley: 38	S. Curley: 4/31
Railway Union	Lost	105	153	J. Burke: 33	J. Burke: 5/56
Phoenix	Lost	117	233/9	S. Curley: 40	S. Curley: 3/75
Railway Union	Lost	123	125/8	S. Curley: 62	C. Mara: 5/33
Leinster (C)	Lost	181	185/9	S. Curley: 56	C. Mara: 5/38
Leinster	Drawn	93/5		V.J. Holloway: 28	
Clontarf	Lost	121	144	C. Mara: 25	P. Meade: 3/54
YMCA	Drawn		115/6		S. Curley: 3/32
Pembroke	Won	167/9	164	B. Curley: 66	S. Curley: 7/81
Malahide	Drawn	146	69/4	J. Hopkins: 56	J. Burke: 3/32
Clontarf	Lost	96	191/8	V.J. Holloway: 36	S. Curley: 4/60
Phoenix	Drawn	215/9	25/0	B. Curley: 52	
Leinster	Drawn		39/5		J. Burke: 4/15

Junior: Merrion 2nds finish near the bottom of Section A of the Senior 2 League. Carlisle beat them by 8 wickets in the first round of the Senior 2 Cup, a competition they go on to win. Joe D'Arcy returns after several years out of the game. Cecil Little takes 8 for 35 in a losing cause against Leinster 2nds, in which match Paddy Dowling scores 52 out of 100. Merrion 3rds win Section A of the Intermediate League, but lose to Harding in the play-off. Des Mara, brother of Chris, home on holidays, takes 5/44 against Leinster 3rds.

CUS SCHOOLBOYS – 1

1: Note Ralph McCartan (centre).

2: Note Ralph McCartan (front row, end left).

3: Note Des O'Connor (back row, end left) and Jimmy McAlinden (middle row, end left).

4: Note Paddy Waldron (sitting).

5: Note Paddy Waldron (second from left, sitting) and Simon Curley (end right, sitting).

6: Note Simon Curley (middle row, end left) and Paddy Waldron (middle row, second from right).

CUS SCHOOLBOYS – 2

1: Note Paddy Waldron (sitting, second from left) and Simon Curley (sitting, end right).

2: Note Joe D'Arcy, Simon Curley.

3: Note Paul Warren.

4: Note Joe D'Arcy, Paul Warren.

5: Note Cathal McAlinden, Paul Warren.

6: Note Brendan Curley, Joe Hopkins.

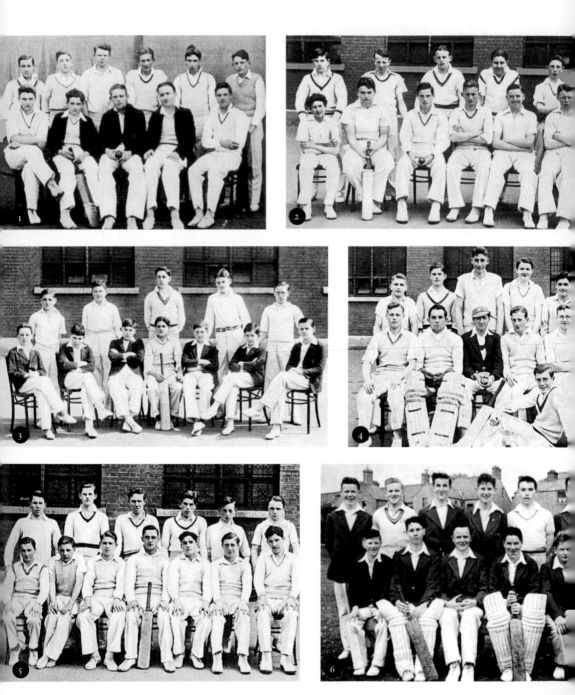

CUS SCHOOLBOYS – 3

1: Note Barry MacMahon (standing, third from right), John Leonard (sitting, end left), Brendan Byrne (sitting, second from left), Joe Hopkins (sitting, centre), Freddy Gaynor (sitting, second from right).

2: Note R. Fair (standing, end left), G. Doyle (sitting, end left), Louis McMullan (sitting, centre), Cathal McAlinden (sitting, second from right), Jimmy McAlinden (sitting, end right).

3: Note Ray Hogan (sitting, end right), John Bastable (standing, end left), Gary Hynes (standing, centre).

4: Note Mick Bolger (standing, second from left), Jim Furlong (standing, third from left), Jack Ormonde (standing, third from right), Arthur Short (sitting, third from left), Dave Bolton (sitting, third from right).

5: Note Gene Parkinson, John Bastable, Gary Hynes, Brian Hynes, Stan Parkinson, Ray Hogan.

6: A CUS Practice in 1950 at Anglesea Road.

TEAMS – 1

1: 1sts, 1929.

2: 1sts, 1943.

3: 1sts, 1944.

4: 1sts, 1950.

5: 1sts, 1953.

6: 1sts, 1955.

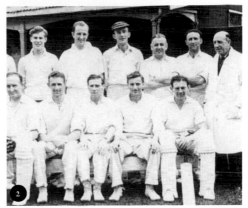

TEAMS – 2

1: 1sts, 1956.

2: 1sts, 1957.

3: 1sts, 1964.

4: Singles Team, 1953.

5: Marrieds Team, 1953.

6: Taverners, 1963 – the end of an era.

TOURS

1: Kilkenny tour, 1926.

2: Cork Tour, 1938.

3: 1939.

4, 5: Halverstown, 1947.

6: Cork.

RALPH McCARTAN

1: Welcoming Winifred Shotter, Donald Wolfit.

2: Welcoming Margaretta Scott.

3: Tossing with Jimmy O'Dea for charity rugby match.

4: Jimmy O'Dea goes for the ball.

5: Celebrating with Jimmy O'Dea.

6: Biddy Mulligan, the pride of the Coombe.

PADDY WALDRON

1: Leinster v. Ulster, 1946. Copyright *The Irish Times.*

2: Merrion v. Queen's University, 1944. Copyright *The Irish Times.*

3: Merrion v. Phoenix, 1943. Copyright *The Irish Times.*

4: Merrion v. Trinity, 1944. Copyright *The Irish Times.*

5: Trinity v. Free Foresters, 1946. Copyright *The Irish Times.*

6: Merrion v. Trinity, 1943. Copyright *The Irish Times.*

GOING OUT TO BAT

1: Merrion v. Trinity. Paddy Waldron, Joe D'Arcy, 1943.

2: Merrion v. Trinity. Joe Burke, Paddy Waldron, 1944.

3: Simon Curley, Paddy Waldron.

4: Merrion v. Queen's University. Jack O'Donnell, Paddy Waldron, 1944.

5: Billy Lindsay, Simon Curley.

6: Brendan Curley, Tommy Burke.

LADIES COMMITTEE

1: Captain's dinner menu discussed. F. Byrne, B. Parkinson, C. Little, U. Curley, A Lindsay, 1952.

2: Captain's dinner to celebrate purchase of ground, 1952.

3: Captain's dinner, 1952.

4: Merrion Ladies Committee. C. O'Donnell, U. Curley, E. Balfe, B. Parkinson, B. McAlinden, C. Little, 1959.

5: Connie Little, Una Curley, Avril Lindsay, Betty McAlinden.

6: Connie Little, Una Curley.

HURLERS ON THE DITCH

1: Parkinsons and Littles.

2: Birdie Parkinson, Kay Soraghan, Tommy McAlinden.

3: Birdie Parkinson, Elaine Heffernan, Frank Morrison.

4: Tommy Soraghan.

5: Patsy Curley, Connie Little, Una Curley, Avril Lindsay.

6: Madeleine Parkinson.

'CECIL'
THE MAN WITH THE CALM DISPOSITION!

FEELING A BIT NERVOUS TODAY CECIL?

Bill

'TOM'
– and the Champ.!

Bill

LINDSAY

Paddy Waldron

THE GREATS

1: Billy Lindsay's drawing of Cecil Little.

2: Billy Lindsay's drawing of Tom Quinn.

3: Billy Lindsay's drawing of Paddy Waldron.

4: Vinny Holloway.

5: Merrion V Queen's University, by the Hazeldene wall.
J. D'Arcy, J. McDermott, J. O'Donnell, J.D. O'Connor,
P. Warren, B. Mathews, D. McCourt, S. Curley, J.B. Stephenson,
D. McEvoy, P. Waldron, 1944.

6: Rollie Shortt, Cecil Little, 1960s.

THE LITTLES

1: Alan and Barry Little, pushed by Des Wilson.

2: Barry Little.

3: Alan Little with Hazeldene in background.

4: Clifford Campbell and Barry Little, at the entrance.

5: Cecil Little.

6: Cecil Little, with Rollie Shortt's car in the background.

GAMES

1: Cathal McAlinden is not out. Proof that umpiring has improved.

2: An early example of sledging. John Leonard, Barry MacMahon and Henry Lafferty attack Alan Little.

3: Danny Parkinson's cover drive.

4: Danny Parkinson's forward defensive stroke.

5: Merrion v. Pembroke, 1970s.

6: Merrion v. Pembroke, 1970s.

MERRION CRICKET CLUB

Ground: **Anglesea Road, Ballsbridge**

You have been selected to play for:—

Merrion..1st...XI (League)	Merrion....1st...XI (LEAGUE)
v.Railway..Union	v. PEMBROKE...
at Park Avenue	at ANGLESEA Rd W60 & THURS
on..Sat..15th May	on..19 & 20th Ma
start....2.30.p.m.	start....6P.M.

practice.......................................

If unable to play please notify me immediately.

C. McALINDEN (Team Sec.)
37 North Avenue. Mt. Merrion,
Blackrock, Co. Dublin.

Phone 889109 (Evening 6 p.m. to 7 p.m.)

Merrion Cricket Club.

Ground Purchase Fund.

Certificate of Loans Received.

This is to certify that *Thos Seaghan (*

of 47, *Anglesea Road* has contributed the sum

of *Twenty five Pounds* (£25).

as a Loan to this fund.

Signed on behalf of Merrion Cricket Club

on this 11 day of *June* 1951.

[signatures] ⎱ Trustees

These Loans will be repaid at the earliest possible moment

MERRION CRICKET CLUB
CAR PARK

The Operators do not accept responsibility for any injury, damage or loss incurred.

2/6

MERRION CRICKET CLUB

The Committee request the pleasure of the company

of..

at a *Marquee Dance*, at *Anglesea Lawn Tennis Club*, Anglesea Road, on

SUNDAY, SEPTEMBER 19th, 1943

Music by	Dancing
Joe Bonnie and his Band	9 p.m—1 a.m.

Member's Signature..................................

Subscription - (including Tax) - 2/6

WOT! No GIRLS?

THEY'RE ALL GONE TO THE MERRION C.C. MARQUEE DANCE

AT ANGLESEA L.T.C. AUGUST 18TH ADMISSION (INCLUDING TAX) 2/6
DANCING FROM 9 — 1

Oh, my Merrion and my Anglesea Road, long ago!

82 Mounttown Av.,
Dn Leary
4 April 1995

Dear Vincent,
The enclosed will bring back memories.
"The field is full of shades as I near the shadowy coast,
And a ghostly batsman plays to the bowling of a ghost"
Regards Blair.

CLUB LIFE

MISCELLANY

1: 1950s game in Merrion.

2: Pushing the heavy roller.

3: The tractor and gang mower.

4: The heavy and light rollers.

5: Pushing the heavy roller again.

6: The tree.

They beat Civil Service 2nds in the first round of the Intermediate Cup, 240 to 70, in which John Leonard wheedles 8/25. However, Deanhill dispose of them in the semi-final, 58 to 176. Sean Pender takes 7/17 against Cremore. Merrion 4ths are in Section B of the Junior League. They lose to Old Belvedere 3rds in the first round of the Junior Cup. CUS schoolboy Cormac Byrne and Henry Lafferty score the runs and Jimmy McAlinden takes the wickets for this team. Barry Little makes his debut for Merrion against Bellew, edging 7 runs and snaffling a catch.

CLUB NOTES

An Executive Meeting in April reports that an agreement has been reached with the tenants of Hazeldene, to rent the adjoining field – Area **E** – in order to lay two concrete bases for practice wickets and to extend the cricket playing area. Pipes are to be laid simultaneously, which will supply water to the pavilion from the Dodder. A pump is to be installed. The party wall is to be removed, with the qualification, granted by Tom Quinn in a private letter to her, that it be rebuilt to a height of five feet, should the owner, Mrs Honor Prendergast of 75 Anglesea Road, ever wish it. The Chairman submits designs for a club flag and crest, but a decision about this is deferred. S. Curley recommends that a notice be put up to the effect that 'Schoolboy members are not permitted in the vicinity of the pavilion during a match'.

On 14 July, the ninety-year licence with Bective Rangers that is to later become so troublesome is signed. The rugby club can play one match per weekend, either on Saturday or Sunday, between 1 October and 1 March each year. The lump sum received from the rugby club is invested, with the view that the interest gained, together with the rent received from both Bective and CUS, be paid each year into the Ground Purchase Fund. A subsequent meeting suggests that worm treatment on the wickets be carried out before March, and a few days before the next rugby match. (Note: rugby is played *across* the wickets.)

The Chairman states that he has arranged with Saville & Co. to have the tree stumps removed from the area adjoining Hazeldene, and that Crampton & Co. will undertake the task of removing the intervening wall – Area **C**. He also confirms that the 'club flag is finished, except for the sewing of the two sides together, and that Mrs Morris has very kindly undertaken to do this work'. At a winter get-together in the Red Bank Restaurant, Chris Mara vows abstinence from the demon drink for the rest of his life, which means another forty-five years without alcohol. Did he know this?

PROFILE: DEREK HAYDEN

R-H batsman who was never allowed to bat as high as he wanted. R-A fast swing bowler who made a dangerous opening partnership with Rodney Bernstein. Educated at Mountjoy College, he became a chartered accountant with KPMG. Derek played ninety-six games for Merrion 1sts, from 1953 to 1963, scoring 118 runs @ 4.53, with a highest of 22. He took 144 wickets @ 17.85, with 5 wickets in an innings on 6 occasions, and 12 catches. He played on the 1958 league-winning and 1960 cup-winning sides, and was captain in 1963. In 1964 he emigrated to the West Indies where he worked for eight years, giving up cricket altogether as the standard was too high there. When he returned, he went to spoiling good walks and outdoor bowling. Derek has now retired to live in Poulshone in County Wexford, where he remembers his difficult early time on Merrion 1sts with amusement. This was in the early 1950s, when Merrion was a cold place for a Schoolboy player, and a dropped catch or mis-field on the 1sts might generate screams of abuse from Simon Curley and Chris Mara. Nowadays he'd get a kiss on the cheek from the skipper and be offered group therapy in a psychiatric counselling course.

1957: EXTENSION TO PAVILION PLANNED; SENIOR 2 LEAGUE RUNNERS-UP

Senior: fixtures 17, reported 17, won 4, lost 6, drawn 7. President: T.A. Quinn. Captain: T.J. Burke. Another wet season, with thirty-two of seventy-eight league matches drawn. The Senior League and Cup are extended to ten teams by the inclusion of Old Belvedere, who celebrate by beating Merrion to record their first Senior win. All league matches, except for Malahide at home, now start on a Friday evening. Merrion finish 6/10, with 41.66 per cent, playing 15, winning 4, losing 5, drawing 6. They are knocked out of the Senior Cup in the first round by Railway Union. Vinny Holloway plays for Munster against Leinster. Sean Pender plays a game for Merrion this year under the pseudonym M. Collins. Should he have been at work? Or was he just a revolutionary at heart? Simon Curley tops the Merrion batting averages with 301 runs @ 33.44. Brendan Curley hockeys 352 runs @ 32. Joe Hopkins scores 216 runs @ 24. Joe Burke blossoms as a bowler under his brother Tommy's captaincy, taking 37 wickets @ 13.00 and coming sixth in the provincial bowling averages. Paddy Meade takes 22 wickets @ 14.50. Chris Mara is back to his blistering best, with 41 wickets @ 12.24, and is fifth in the provincial averages:

Opponent	Result	Mer.	Opp.	Best Batting: Runs	Best Bowling: Wickets
Leinster	Won	202	178	S. Curley: 57	C. Mara: 5/36
YMCA	Lost	106	208	J. Hopkins: 35	S. Curley: 4/31
Railway Union	Drawn		150/8		J. Burke: 4/45
Old Belvedere	Lost	128	183	T. Burke: 41	J. Burke: 4/49
Railway Union (C)	Lost	155	197	S. Curley: 54	C. Mara: 5/56
Pembroke	Drawn	128	99/5	T. Burke: 39	C. Mara: 3/60
Phoenix	Drawn	288/6	106/8	D. McEvoy: 70	C. Mara: 7/31
DU	Won	112	89	S. Curley: 26	P. Meade: 6/23
Clontarf	Drawn	216	134	B. Curley: 77	J. Burke: 4/24
Malahide (F)	Drawn	196/5	209/8		
Clontarf	Won	93/1	92	S. Curley: 58*	J. Burke: 6/21
Malahide	Drawn	143	107/9	T. Burke: 34	C. Mara: 4/20
Pembroke	Lost	65	221/8	S. Curley: 18	J. Burke: 5/50
Railway Union	Won	147	86	J. Burke: 57	P. Meade: 4/15
Old Belvedere	Lost	123	187	J. D'Arcy: 44	J. Burke: 4/41
Phoenix	Drawn	14/0	228/6	J. Burke: 9*	J. Burke: 3/67
YMCA	Lost	67	167	V. Finnegan: 17	T. Burke: 3/34

Junior: Merrion 2nds finish runners-up in the Senior 2 League, losing a play-off to 3rd OBU, in which Jimmy McAlinden takes 5/72. Cathal McAlinden scores 101* against Railway

Union 2nds. Tom MacMahon wins the Bookman Cup for batting, with an average of 42.87. They beat Old Belvedere 2nds in the first round of the Senior 2 Cup, but lose to 3rd OBU in a match that is replayed after a tied encounter. Merrion 3rds are in Section A of the Intermediate League. Jimmy McAlinden takes all 10 wickets for 22 runs against Harding. Joe D'Arcy's team beats Railway Union 3rds in the first round of the Intermediate Cup, 134/1 to 133, but is defeated in the next round. Des Hughes, Jack McDermott and Peter McNally are among their better batsmen. Merrion 4ths finish well in Section B of the Junior League. They lose to CYM 3rds in the first round of the Junior Cup, 73 to 125. First appearance of Jim Furlong, yet another product of the conveyor belt of talent that is known as the Catholic University School.

CLUB NOTES

A plan is made to have Saville & Company erect a new pavilion down by Dunluce House in return for parking rights every year and a place to display their machinery each Spring Show, but fortunately this is shelved when Saville pull out. The question of the members running the car park themselves, instead of Irish Car Parks – who organise the annual parks for Merrion each year – is discussed and a decision deferred until the rates for public liability insurance have been established. Another new groundsman needs to be employed and it is decided that Mr Little will supervise the preparation of wickets and cutting of the outfield from then on. Mr S. Curley raises the issue of the CUS net needing repair, and Mr J. Burke suggests talking to a fisherman he knows. As the new field is being levelled and made ready for use, a subsequent meeting agrees to construct a path through to the piggery in Hazeldene. An issue that remains topical is discussed when the Chairman, Mr T. Quinn, states 'all the right of ways, excepting the one at the corner house, have been granted by the club as an act of grace to particular persons living in houses abutting the ground, but the privilege has been abused because the front gates are seldom shut at night'. The corner house was then occupied by the Balfe family, and their right of way was given verbally in return for a small portion of the ground at the bottom of their garden. This is subsequently returned to the owners. New plans are made for the extension of the current pavilion, to include a 'bar' and a new kitchen.

PROFILE: TOMMY McALINDEN

Due to an ankle injury in his youth, Tommy, the youngest of the McAlinden brothers, played no sport whatsoever. He was educated at CUS and worked as a bookie for the family book-making firm, before moving to *The Irish Press* in the 1950s, where he became Head of Competitions. A keen photographer, Tommy was the 1sts scorer for almost thirty years, starting as a teenager. His beautiful, multicoloured scorebook resembled the paintings of Willem De Kooning, and fortunately were a lot easier to read. Tommy the artist never moved or had his tea until he had finished the statistics for an innings completely. He scored for all the Junior sides as well, and served as Hon. Secretary from 1951 to 1958. He died, far too young, in that year of terrible change for Merrion, 1966. But thanks to him, Merrion has a full album of photos from the mid-1930s to the mid-1960s.

1958: SENIOR LEAGUE WINNERS; JUNIOR LEAGUE WINNERS

Senior: fixtures 16, reported 16, won 8, lost 2, drawn 6. President: T.A. Quinn. Captain: T.J. Burke. In this very wet season, Merrion win the Senior League for the fourth time. It's so wet that twenty matches out of a possible eighty-one are never started. Merrion lose only once, to Old Belvedere at Anglesea Road, in the first match of the season, when Simon Curley is absent. They finish with 60.41 per cent, having played 12, won 5, lost 1, drawn 6. They lose to Phoenix in the semi-final of the Senior Cup, after victories against the 3rd Old Boy's and Railway Unions. First appearance of future Irish international Rodney Bernstein, the fastest bowler of his day. Final, final appearance of Cecil Little, who has obviously made the fatal mistake of packing his gear in the boot. Simon Curley nurdles and drives 652 runs (250 more than the next, younger brother Brendan) @ 59.27 to win the Marchant Cup for the second time. He is the first Merrion player to score over 600 runs in a season. Brendan Curley keeps it in the family by totalling 402 runs @ 36.54, and is third in the provincial averages. Joe Burke is the leading all-rounder in Leinster, scoring 278 runs @ 23.16 and taking 34 wickets @ 9.14. His bowling average is lower than the O'Grady Bowling Cup winner, A.B. Robertson, at 9.44, but he is 1 wicket shy of qualifying for the trophy. He is recalled to the Irish team to play against New Zealand and the MCC. Tommy Burke scores 244 runs @ 22.18. Rodney Bernstein takes 29 wickets @ 10.37:

Opponent	Result	Mer.	Opp.	Best Batting: Runs	Best Bowling: Wickets
Old Belvedere	Lost	113	220/7	M. Boyle: 43	J. Burke: 3/47
Railway Union	Won	230/2	71	S. Curley: 155*	D. Hayden: 5/23
Leinster	Won	128/2	125	S. Curley: 92*	J. Burke: 5/33
Clontarf	Drawn	173/9; 81/2	107; 89/5	J. Burke: 78	J. Burke: 5/33
3rd OBU (C)	Won	189	124	T. Burke: 90	R. Bernstein: 5/31
Railway Union (C)	Won	139	103	B. Curley: 51	P. Meade: 5/26
YMCA	Drawn	125/7		B. Curley: 42	
DU	Drawn	125/5		J. Burke: 40	
Phoenix (C)	Lost	92	93/6	T. Burke: 39	J. Burke: 3/36
Pembroke	Won	223	131	S. Curley: 75	R. Bernstein: 3/15
Leinster	Won	114/2	111	S. Curley: 64	R. Bernstein: 5/25
Railway Union	Won	107/5	105	J. Hopkins: 25*	J. Burke: 6/30
Pembroke	Drawn	108/2		S. Curley: 70*	
Phoenix	Drawn	141/7	178/6	B. Curley: 45	C. Mara: 3/26
Malahide	Drawn	178	109/6	B. Curley: 37	J. Burke: 4/14
Adastrians (F)	Won	131/6	70	B. Curley: 71	R. Bernstein: 5/19

Merrion have only to draw against Malahide on 22/23 August to win the league for the fourth time:

LEINSTER SENIOR LEAGUE 1958, MERRION V. MALAHIDE

Merrion			Malahide		
S.A. Curley	c. Gilmore b. Goodwin	26	P.A. Neville	c. Hopkins b. Burke (J)	30
J.P. Burke	c. Neville (P) b. Robertson	21	H. Darlington	b. Burke (J)	2
B.C. Curley	c. Dawson b. Goodwin	37	W. Behan	b. Dorgan	8
J.K. Hopkins	b. Dawson	9	J.D. Caprani	c. Burke (T) b. Burke (J)	5
T.J. Burke	c. Neville (J) b. Goodwin	28	T. Dawson	lbw b. Burke (J)	0

R.E. Bernstein	c. Neville (P) b. Dawson	1	R.J. Gilmore	not out	37
G.T. Doyle	c. Behan b. Dawson	3	J.J. Neville	c. & b. Dorgan	3
M.J. Boyle	c. Dawson b. Goodwin	7	C. Burgess	not out	5
D. Dorgan	b. Goodwin	21			
C.G. Mara	c. Burgess b. Dawson	5			
E.D. Hayden	not out	4			
	Extras	16		Extras	19
	Total	178		Total (for 6 wickets)	109

Junior: Merrion 2nds are in Section A of the Senior 2 League, which now has a total of seventeen teams split over two sections. The two McAlinden brothers provide the main batting and bowling, along with Rollie Shortt (still trundling away at fifty-nine) and Paddy Meade. Des Hughes scores 50 against Clontarf 2nds. They lose to Cremore in the first round of the Senior 2 Cup, 47 to 48/3. Merrion 3rds are in Section A of the Intermediate League. They beat YMCA 3rds in the first round of the Intermediate Cup, 151 to 58, in which match Jack O'Donnell makes 53 and Cecil Little takes 5 for 9. Schoolboy Eddie Rafter debuts for the 3rds this season. Merrion 4ths win the Junior League, with the help of Jack Ormonde, Ken Gunn, Jim Furlong, Dave Bolton, Mick O'Connell, Eddie Rafter, Peter McNally, Michael Murdoch, Louis McMullan and Terry McNally. Danny Parkinson's team loses to CYM 3rds in the first round of the Junior Cup, 66 to 67/9.

CLUB NOTES

Early in the year, a letter is sent to members, asking for a £1 contribution to the extension of the pavilion to include 'an additional room where light refreshments, such as sandwiches, beer, minerals may be obtained'. The committee agree that this new 'bar' must close by 10p.m. In May, a meeting agrees that the groundsman should cut the square as well as the outfield with the motor-mower, allowing Mr D'Arcy to finish the wickets with a hand-mower. A letter is read from Mr Greer, insisting that a boundary fence be erected between matches, once the Hazeldene field becomes part of the playing area. At a subsequent meeting, an application from the Dodder Anglers' Club, to be allowed to fish the river from Merrion's ground, is rejected. An end-of-season match is arranged between the 1940 double-winning side and that year's league-winning team – result unknown, but guessable. Plans are made for a new cricket square, facing between Hazeldene and Dunluce. Mr S. Curley recommends that covers be included in the costing. Club income is now £500 per annum. A decision is made to redeem the mortgage on the ground with the Property Loan Company, and to pay off the loans made by members into the Ground Purchase Fund. Plans are drawn up for new dressing rooms, and an application for another loan of £1,500 is made, this time from the Munster & Leinster Bank.

PROFILE: TOMMY SORAGHAN

Tommy was born in Dundalk in 1916 and educated there. He came to Dublin in 1933 and lived for a number of years on Stradbrook Road in Blackrock before buying 47 Anglesea Road. He owned and ran one of the most successful wholesale toy and stationery businesses

Merrion 1sts, 1958 Senior League winners. Back row: T. McAlinden (S), G. Doyle, M. Boyle, R. Bernstein, D. Hayden, P. Meade, J. Hopkins (W), S. Doyle (U). Front row: J. Burke, B. Curley, T. Burke (C), S. Curley, C. Mara.

Merrion 4ths, 1958 Junior League winners. Back row: T. McAlinden (S), M. O'Connell, M. Murdoch, J. Furlong, K. Gunn, J. Ormonde, P. McNally, S. Doyle (U). Front row: T. McNally, L. McMullan, D. Parkinson (C), E. Rafter, D. Bolton.

in Ireland for most of his life. He participated in sports from cricket at Merrion to athletics with Donore Harriers. Despite not having played at Senior level, he often went on tour with Merrion and played on the Junior sides and in Married versus Singles matches. He became involved at various committee levels and eventually ended up as a trustee of the club. He personally assisted the club in times of financial constraint, as did others, such as Tom Quinn and Simon Curley. He and Simon effectively organised the running of the lucrative car parking at Merrion during the Spring and Horse Shows at the RDS up to the 1970s. He assisted in organising Merrion's annual Dinner Dance in the 1950s and 1960s, and in fundraisers to continually improve both the ground and the clubhouse facilities.

One of his main hobbies was producing many variations of apples, which proved to be a big hit, especially with many of Merrion's younger members, whether invited to taste them or not. He also organised groups of people each summer from cricketing families to pick blackberries in the Dublin Mountains. The fruits of their work were enjoyed with Tommy's very own blackberry jam. He was a keen photographer and actually recorded a movie clip of Merrion 1sts playing in Anglesea Road as far back as 1959. He organised an annual Halloween bonfire at the big tree stump on the bank near the boundary with Hazeldene. This was followed by games afterwards in Soraghan's kitchen with many of Merrion's younger members. Tommy's sons Dermot (a Merrion trustee himself), Pat and Paul played for Merrion teams, as well as his youngest daughter Joan, who featured for Merrion women's 1sts, along with his daughter-in-law Maureen. Tommy's life on Anglesea Road was dedicated to protecting the interests of Merrion members at its present location, not just for the benefit of the current generation of players but for those who followed in the future. The club lost one of its longest serving members when Merrion's gatekeeper passed away in 1999.

1959: JUNIOR LEAGUE RUNNERS-UP

Senior: fixtures 18, reported 18, won 7, lost 6, drawn 5. President: T.A. Quinn. Captain: T.J. Burke. This hot, dry season starts well, with four wins and two draws in the first six games, but falls apart after a close loss to Dublin University. A brace of wins at the end pulls Merrion back to a creditable third place in the Senior League, with 16 games played and 49.21 per cent, winning 6, losing 5, drawing 5. They are routed again by Gerry Duffy of Leinster in the semi-final of the Senior Cup. First appearance of future stalwart Paddy Willis, who plays for Leinster against Munster, along with Brendan Curley and Rodney Bernstein. Future captain and noisy hurler-on-the-ditch Danny Parkinson scores his first runs in Senior cricket, with a match-winning 64 against the young christian men. '*Simon told me just to stay there, and I did.*' The Curley brothers dominate the batting, with Simon scoring 399 runs @ 30.69, and Brendan, 262 runs @ 20.23. Joe Burke, Vinny Holloway and Rodney Bernstein also make important contributions with the bat. George Murdoch takes 28 wickets @ 13.92. Bernstein takes 38 wickets @ 9.07. Derek Hayden takes 32 wickets @ 16.93:

Opponent	Result	Mer.	Opp.	Best Batting: Runs	Best Bowling: Wickets
Leinster	Won	151	63	G. Doyle: 26	J. Burke: 3/9
Railway Union	Won	73/3	71	B. Curley: 36*	R. Bernstein: 7/22
Pembroke	Lost	73	82/5	G. Doyle: 15*	R. Bernstein: 3/27
Malahide	Won	119/5	118	J. Burke: 46*	D. Hayden: 4/30
Old Belvedere	Drawn	134/7	70/8	B. Curley: 57	G. Murdoch: 3/16

Phoenix	Won	96/4	95	R. Bernstein: 32*	R. Bernstein: 7/23
DU	Lost	142	148	V.J. Holloway: 38	G. Murdoch: 6/55
Clontarf	Lost	154	157/4	D. Craig: 34	P. Willis: 1/7
Railway Union (C)	Won	49/2	47	S. Curley: 30*	J. Burke: 4/4
YMCA	Drawn	109/6		D. Craig: 30	
Leinster (C)	Lost	85	257	T. Burke: 35	R. Bernstein: 4/64
Old Belvedere	Drawn	50/5	136/9	S. Curley: 15	R. Bernstein: 3/23
Phoenix	Lost	86	88/3	V.J. Holloway: 27	G. Murdoch: 2/17
Clontarf	Drawn	128/9	169	S. Curley: 58*	K. Gunn: 7/48
YMCA	Won	155/9	117	D. Parkinson: 64	D. Hayden: 4/28
Railway Union	Drawn	136/7	180/9	S. Curley: 55*	R. Bernstein: 3/40
Leinster	Lost	147	148/5	J. Burke: 39*	D. Hayden: 4/57
Pembroke	Won	217	215/7	J. Hopkins: 59	E. Rafter: 2/17

Junior: Merrion 2nds are in Section A of the Senior 2 League. Boyle, MacMahon, McAlinden and Parkinson continue to contribute at this level. They are drawn against Malahide 2nds in the first round of the Senior 2 Cup. Merrion 3rds are in Section A of the Intermediate League, along with Balrothery, Leinster 3rds, CYM 2nds, 3rd OBU 2nds, Clontarf 3rds, Harding, Railway Union 3rds, Deanhill, and Pembroke 3rds. They beat Clontarf 3rds in an exciting first round of the Intermediate Cup, 144/9 to 143, but lose the next round. John Leonard and Joe D'Arcy provide the backbone to this side. Merrion 4ths lose a play-off for the Junior League to Harding 2nds, 78 to 80/5, at Sydney Parade. John Stephens, Pierce Butler, Barry Little, Dave Bolton and Mick O'Connell are the mainstays of this team. They are also drawn against Harding 2nds in the first round of the Junior Cup.

CLUB NOTES

An early meeting votes on the proposals for new dressing rooms, which are carried, but not unanimously. There are problems with the difference between the quote for the extension of the wickets by McDermotts and the final invoice. Notices for occasional bar licences are lodged for the first time in Merrion history. The Hazeldene field is not yet ready for play-ing, as it needs to be cut, have soil put on it, be seeded and levelled. A decision is made to buy a scythe for the groundsman, and to use the tea bell during matches, if it can be found. New toilets and a urinal are built. It is noticeable that during this season, both the President and Captain are frequently absent from meetings. Although the committee is not happy with the work done on the new wickets, the last match of the season against Pembroke is the first game to be played on them, as laid north to south, but without the Hazeldene extension. No more jammy wickets for slow bowlers tossing the ball into the sun as it sets over Herbert Park. All of the loans for the Ground Purchase Fund have now been repaid, except for Tom Quinn's, which he has forgone. At the last meeting of the year, D. Parkinson reports that due to illness, Mr Quinn, the President, 'will not be taking an active part in the running of the club during the coming year'. The overdraft with the Munster and Leinster Bank is now £1,500.

PROFILE: JOE HOPKINS

R-H batsman. Wicket-keeper. Came to Merrion from Pembroke as Harry Hill was the established Sydney Parade keeper. Another product of the CUS cricketer factory. Auctioneer with Morrissey's. Also an international tenpin bowler. Played centre-half at soccer with Oaklands in the Dublin Amateur League. Played 104 games for Merrion as keeper between 1956 and 1964. Scored 1,527 runs @ 16.78, with a top score of 70 and including 7*50s. Took 61 catches and 19 stumpings. Captain in 1962. He featured in the 1958 Senior League and 1960 Cup-winning sides, where Rodney Bernstein's pace helped Joe win his single international cap in 1961 against the visiting Australians at College Park, in which he scored 13 runs and took 2 catches and 1 stumping, that of Alan Davidson. Joe returned to Pembroke in 1965 as a fielder (Harry Hill was still behind the stumps there) and continued his playing career with the club his father had played for before him. In 1974, the provincial wicket-keeping cup was named after Joe's father, and Joe became its presenter.

1960: SENIOR CUP WINNERS; SENIOR LEAGUE RUNNERS-UP; INTERMEDIATE LEAGUE WINNERS

Senior: fixtures 19, reported 19, won 11, lost 3, drawn 5. President: T.A. Quinn. Captain: S.A. Curley. Friday-night play in league matches is abandoned. Normal hours are now from 2.15p.m. to 8.30p.m. on a Saturday. Merrion have a good season in the league, finishing runners-up to Railway Union. They play 15, win 7, lose 3, draw 5 and gain 59.14 per cent of their possible points. Although they have a chance of catching the leaders with five games to play, a rain-affected draw against Phoenix sets them back, and they fall off the pace, winning only one of their last six matches. So near and yet so far from another glorious double to end this period. Railway Union gain 85 per cent, losing 1 game, to Merrion. The Anglesea Road side extract some vengeance in the Senior Cup, winning a close final against Clontarf, having narrowly defeated the Park Avenue side in the semi-final. Chasing a modest total of 104 in the final, Merrion are 25 for 4 thanks to an onslaught by Ernie Bodell, when Simon Curley is joined by Rodney Bernstein to fight for the remaining 80 runs. Both Curleys have remarkable seasons with the bat. Elder brother Simon comes third in the provincial statistics, with 560 runs @ 43.07. Brendan is fifth, with 396 runs @ 33.00. Bernstein gets his share of runs – 192 @ 13.71 – as well as 51 wickets @ 9.31, and debuts for Ireland against the MCC. He is second to Alec O'Riordan in the provincial bowling statistics, who repeats his 1959 triumph by winning the O'Grady Cup again. Last Senior appearance of fast-bowling legend, Chris Mara, who takes 9 wickets @ 5.11 in just 2 games. Paddy Willis looks set to pick up the giant's baton, with 28 wickets @ 12.21. George Murdoch takes 27 wickets @ 11.77:

Opponent	Result	Mer.	Opp.	Best Batting: Runs	Best Bowling: Wickets
DU	Lost	60	82	G. Murdoch: 15	G. Murdoch: 6/22
YMCA	Won	123	69	R. Bernstein: 40	R. Bernstein: 5/17
Old Belvedere	Won	177/6	73	B. Curley: 79	R. Bernstein: 3/18
Railway Union	Won	121	105	S. Curley: 74	P. Willis: 6/19
Pembroke (C)	Won	112/7	110	B. Curley: 82*	P. Willis: 4/31
Pembroke	Lost	120	121/3	B. Curley: 31	R. Bernstein: 2/41
Leinster	Drawn	138/6		S. Curley: 43	
Malahide	Won	104/9	101	D. Parkinson: 62	C. Mara: 6/21

Railway Union (C)	Won	196/8	193	S. Curley: 50	P. Willis: 4/70
Clontarf	Won	100/1	99	D. Dorgan: 49*	P. Willis: 5/22
YMCA (C)	Won	78/2	77	D. Dorgan: 37*	R. Bernstein: 5/34
Clontarf	Won	105/6	104	S. Curley: 48*	R. Bernstein: 7/41
Senior Cup Final					
Old Belvedere	Won	113/7	112	D. Bolton: 30	R. Bernstein: 5/41
Malahide	Drawn	81/4	177/6	B. Curley: 31*	R. Bernstein: 2/40
Phoenix	Drawn	175/3		S. Curley: 82*	
Railway Union	Lost	102	105/7	B. Curley: 29	R. Bernstein: 4/31
Clontarf	Drawn	128/9	129	T. Burke: 31	R. Bernstein: 5/37
Leinster	Drawn	192/7	88/9	S. Curley: 121*	K. Gunn: 3/23
Pembroke	Won	79/6	77	D. Bolton: 18	D. Hayden: 6/27

LEINSTER SENIOR CUP FINAL 1960, MERRION V. CLONTARF

Merrion			Clontarf		
D. Dorgan	b. Bodell	8	L. Jacobson	c. Dorgan b. Bernstein	34
D. Parkinson	b. Bodell	5	G. Carroll	l.b.w. b. Bernstein	6
J. Hopkins	b. Bodell	0	D. Sweeney	c. Dorgan b. Bernstein	10
B. Curley	b. Hughes	5	S. Mullen	b. Bernstein	0
S. Curley	not out	48	D. O'Sullivan	b. Bernstein	20
R. Bernstein	c. Bell b. Bodell	17	A. Spence	c. Hopkins b. Bernstein	0
T. Burke	b. Bodell	6	E. Bodell	b. Murdoch	14
G. Murdoch	not out	4	V. Savino	l.b.w. b. Murdoch	4
D. Williams	d.n.b.		J. Bell	c. Hayden b. Murdoch	7
P. Willis	d.n.b.		P. Hughes	c. Hopkins b. Bernstein	0
D. Hayden	d.n.b.		R. Buckley	not out	0
	Extras	12		Extras	9
	Total (for 6 wickets)	105		Total	104

Junior: Merrion 2nds are in Section A of the Senior 2 League. Chris Mara becomes the 2nds best bowler. Jim Furlong and Ken Gunn also contribute with the ball. David Craig, Dan Rogers and Gerry Doyle score the runs. They are drawn against Malahide 2nds in the first round of the Senior 2 Cup. Merrion 3rds beat College of Surgeons to win the Intermediate League under the captaincy of Frank Curley, with Noble, Furlong and Fuller taking wickets. They are drawn against Leinster 3rds in the first round of the Intermediate Cup. Merrion 4ths are in Section A of the Junior League. They lose to Clontarf 4ths in the semi-final of the Junior Cup, 75 to 85.

CLUB NOTES

With the continued absence of Tom Quinn, Simon Curley effectively acts as President this year. At an ECM in January, the Team Secretary is instructed to arrange the first couple of league matches away, after which, presumably, the Hazeldene extension will be ready. New sightscreens are planned for the coming season. At a later meeting, Simon Curley agrees to put up a 'Trespassers Will Be Prosecuted' sign, to deal with the problem of children on

Merrion 3rds, 1960 Intermediate League winners. Back row: D. Noble, N. Fuller, B. Byrne, J. Leonard, J. Stephens, J. D'Arcy, J. McAlinden (U). Front row: J. Furlong, L. McMullan, F. Curley (C), D. Bolton (W), E. Rafter.

Merrion 1sts, 1960 Senior Cup winners. Back row: P. Willis, D. Dorgan, D. Hayden, J. Hopkins, G. Murdoch, D. Williams. Front row: R. Bernstein, D. Parkinson, S. Curley, T. Burke, B. Curley.

the ground. '*Schoolboy members should not remain on the ground after 8.30p.m.*' It is agreed that all members must wear whites during net practice. On 16 May, Danny Parkinson reports that the first night of the '*bar*' is very successful, with a profit on the bottled beer of £13. Obviously no ladies have been tempted into this den of iniquity. Yet.

There are complaints from opposing teams about the state of the new wickets. Simon Curley says it is impossible to get help from members in the preparation and rolling of wickets. Joe D'Arcy is called upon once again to prepare the wickets. The cinder practice wickets also need work. There is contention with Stan Greer concerning the use of the Hazeldene part of the new ground for the parking of cars. Pierce Butler makes a motion to a meeting that 'a committee be appointed to inquire into the possibility of building an indoor recreation hall in Merrion for the playing of cricket, tennis and badminton in the winter, and the running of dances in the summer'. An application is granted for the use of the club premises for the sport of fencing during the winter. Mills Circus apply for the use of the ground the following July. The committee are broadly in favour of additional highwire artists at Anglesea Road, but a decision is deferred. Stan Greer refuses to allow Bective Rangers to play rugby on the Hazeldene extension.

PROFILE: PADDY WILLIS

R-H batsman. R-A bowler of fast off-cutters. Started playing cricket for Bagnelstown at the age of ten. Educated at St Columba's College, where he was coached by Cecil Little, who encouraged him to join Merrion. Paddy also played rugby for Carlow. Worked as a book retailer in Ireland and England. Played cricket for Trinity College, with whom he won the Senior Cup in 1961, having won the 1960 Senior Cup with Merrion. Played 102 games for Merrion 1sts from 1959 to 1976, with breaks every two to three years, when he was unable to play on Saturdays due to work commitments. He scored 386 runs @ 5.76 and took 148 wickets @ 22.41, with a best of 7/35 against Phoenix in 1974. Took 5 wickets in an innings 6 times and 19 catches. Played interprovincial cricket for Leinster. President in 2002 and 2003, during the period that saw the hosting of the Middlesex match. Paddy obviously had second thoughts about small families, as his son Richard played twenty games for Merrion 1sts between 1979 and 1982 and twenty years later, another son, Robin played fifty-eight games from 1998 to 2006, taking 60 wickets @ 24.00, before taking that well-trodden London trail.

NB Other teams playing between 1941 and 1960: Virginians, Bellew, Deanhill, Barony of Forth.

4

THE LATER YEARS

4.1. THE SIXTIES: 1961-1970

For Merrion 1sts, the '60s did anything but swing. They curdled. They curdled Merrion into a bleak and barren period of thirty-five years without a single trophy. Thirty-five years. Not one piece of silver. Nada. Aucune. Niente. Not only that, but the 1sts won exactly 140 out of 659 games during this period, excluding 20-overs and Irish Senior Cup cricket. And fourteen of them were won in 1995! More disgraceful statistics. And it means that between 1926 and 1995, a period of seventy years, Merrion 1sts won 6 of the 176 or so Senior trophies available, and all of these were won between 1940 and 1960. Of the ten years covered in this section, Merrion propped up the Senior League on six occasions – 1964, '65, '66, '67, '69 and '70.

It was no coincidence that these dark ages began as Simon Curley eased himself into retirement from Senior cricket after thirty-three years of an unquantifiable contribution to Merrion Cricket Club, playing his last three games in 1966. Another major factor in this downturn was the simultaneous departure of Rodney Bernstein to Carlisle and Leinster, where he continued to play until 1982.

Junior Merrion suffered a similar fate, despite the continued involvement of past heroes such as Chris Mara, Des O'Connor, Joe D'Arcy, the McAlinden brothers, Gerry Doyle and Mick O'Connell. In 1961, the 4ths won the Junior League; in 1962, the 3rds were runners-up in the Intermediate Cup; in 1968, the Schoolboys won the Vacation League. A new influx of CUS products came off the assembly line – John Bastable, Ray Hogan, Dave Bolton, Stan, Danny Jnr and Eugene Parkinson, Ken Gunn, Mick Bolger, Gerry and Jack Ormonde, Jim Furlong, the Hynes brothers. Other schools provided Eddie Rafter, David Fair, Alan Little, Eddie Bohane and Noel Hayden. The second half of the decade introduced John O'Hagan, Eddie Lewis, Joe Morrissey Snr, Alex Burns and Dermot Soraghan. Some of these players had long careers as Senior cricketers, but it's a fact that most of this genera-tion disappeared fairly rapidly, providing one of the main reasons for the prolonged trophy diaspora. The topical reason for this might be found in the short-sightedness of a manage-ment committee that failed to provide adequate social facilities for its younger players, but it's also true that only Stan Parkinson, who left Merrion to play for Leinster from 1970 to 1984, before returning home; Noel Hayden, who retired early for business reasons in 1971; Dennis Noble, who played 249 times between 1961 and 1977, taking 417 wickets; and Eddie Lewis, who played 351 times for Merrion 1sts from 1967 to 1994, scoring 7,183 runs and taking 186 wickets, had the potential to match Simon Curley, Paddy Waldron, Chris Mara and Rollie Shortt in terms of class.

During this period, Merrion lost their best bowler in Rollie Shortt, their most influential and generous President in Tom Quinn and their most artistic scorer in Tommy McAlinden.

Senior: fixtures 19, reported 19, won 8, lost 5, drawn 6. President: T.A. Quinn. Captain: S.A. Curley. Merrion 1sts start well but finish badly in the Senior League, in fifth place, with 51.56 per cent, having played 16, won 6, lost 4, drawn 6. The last 8 games result in 4 losses, 3 draws and 1 win. However, the season is not without its compensations, as Merrion deprive Pembroke of the league title in the last match. One more run and the title would have gone to Sydney Parade, rather than Castle Avenue, where Clontarf win two matches more than Merrion, who lose two matches by margins of 5 and 14 runs, and draw another with the scores even. (At that time, a *tie* occurs only when the team batting second has lost *all* their wickets.) Twenty runs. Four cricket shots. A taverner's total. So near and yet so far again.

In the Senior Cup, Merrion dispatch Pembroke (when night-watchman Danny Parkinson stands his ground for a dour, thrillingly edge-filled 54) and Malahide, before falling to Railway Union in a record-breaking, high-scoring semi-final, wherein 863 runs are scored for the loss of 17 wickets over a period of six days. Rodney Bernstein plays five times for Ireland this year, and is joined by Joe Hopkins, in his only international, against Australia at College Park. Simon Curley scores a ton against YMCA, and several 50s. Victor Dorman-Smith, Les Bloomer and Joe Burke also score 50s. Curley totals 512 runs @ 32.00 and takes 19 wickets @ 20.15. Joe Burke, in his last full season on the 1sts, takes 27 wickets @ 14.00, and is sixth in the provincial all-rounders averages. Dorman-Smith scores 425 runs @ 32.69. Rodney Bernstein dominates the bowling, with 47 wickets @ 12.31, while Derek Hayden helps out with 22 wickets @ 11.22. Jim Furlong takes 13 wickets @ 19.84. First appearance of stalwart Dennis Noble, who snaffles 6 wickets for 6 runs in 7.5 overs against Pembroke in the league, and who will go on to take over 400 wickets for Merrion:

Opponent	Result	Mer.	Opp.	Best Batting: Runs	Best Bowling: Wickets
Leinster	Won	77/8	76	J. Hopkins: 23	J. Burke: 4/18
YMCA	Won	151	138	S. Curley: 112	R. Bernstein: 5/35
Clontarf	Drawn	164/5	140/7	S. Curley: 70	R. Bernstein: 3/44
Old Belvedere	Lost	50	55	D. Noble: 13	J. Burke: 4/13
Phoenix	Drawn	152/7	162/6	J. Burke: 63	J. Furlong: 2/37
Pembroke (C)	Won	234	112	D. Parkinson: 54	R. Bernstein: 7/40
Malahide	Drawn	115/8	174/8	V. Dorman-Smith: 32	R. Bernstein: 4/54
Leinster	Won	203/4	81	S. Curley: 62	R. Bernstein: 4/20
Malahide (C)	Won	124/2	123	V. Dorman-Smith: 72*	J. Burke: 3/32
Pembroke	Won	177/8	65	T. Burke: 34*	D. Noble: 6/6
Railway Union (C)	Lost	378	485/7	L. Bloomer: 85*	D. Hayden: 3/85
Railway Union	Won	207/5	206/3	V. Dorman-Smith: 67	J. Burke: 1/43
Clontarf	Drawn	40/3	91	S. Curley: 25*	R. Bernstein: 4/34
DU	Drawn	147/9	174/8	V. Dorman-Smith: 54	D. Hayden: 6/39
Old Belvedere	Lost	92	106	B. Curley: 23	D. Hayden: 4/37
YMCA	Lost	116	117/5	D. Dorgan: 45	G. Murdoch: 2/17
Phoenix	Lost	162	164/2	S. Curley: 31	R. Hogan: 2/35
Malahide	Won	154	127	B. Curley: 49*	J. Burke: 6/30
Pembroke	Drawn	152	152/7	T. Burke: 34	R. Bernstein: 6/56

Junior: In a poor season, Merrion 2nds finish 7/10 in Section A of the Senior 2 League, with 41.34 per cent, having played 13, won 5, lost 7, drawn 1. Chris Mara, Norman Fuller, Dave Bolton,

Des McEvoy and Joe D'Arcy (who bats ninety-five minutes for 5 runs to force a draw against Pembroke) provide whatever runs they manage to get, while George Murdoch, Jim Furlong and David Craig take the wickets. They lose to Railway Union 2nds in the first round of the Senior 2 Cup, 66 to 141. Merrion 3rds finish in the bottom half of Section A of the Intermediate League, despite the best efforts of Peter McNally, David Fair and Gerry Doyle with the bat, and Ken Gunn and Frank Curley with the ball. They lose to College of Surgeons in the first round of the Intermediate Cup, 87 to 91/6. Mick O'Connell's 4ths win Section A of the Junior League and then beat Bray Parish in the league decider, 142 to 130, David Fair scoring 40 and Frank Curley 30. Ray Hogan takes 3/49. Frank Curley takes 6/45 in a losing cause against Phoenix. They also beat Bray Parish in the first round of the Junior Cup, 234 to 71, but fail to progress any further.

CLUB NOTES

Although the President, Tom Quinn, is absent again for most of this year, he makes an appearance in October. Concern is expressed at the assurance he has given regarding the rebuilding of the dividing wall between Merrion and Hazeldene. Members present feel that such an undertaking should not have been granted without the committee's knowledge. A motion that the phone be cut off, as it has cost the club £20 the previous season, is defeated. A suggestion is made that a house be built at the entrance to the club, as there is so much waste space there. Cathal McAlinden agrees to investigate the value of the site. A decision is made to apply for a full licence for the bar, as temporary licences cannot be used on Sundays or after 10p.m. on weekdays. At one of the meetings, Chris Mara reports that the toilets are in a deplorable state. It is decided to purchase some disinfectant and a brush, as a matter of urgency. Finally Stan Greer agrees to the Bective rugby pitch being at right angles to previous years. As some of the ladies are not prepared to help with the annual supper, it is decided to use, for the first time, outside caterers in the shape of Ormond Hotels Ltd, who will provide everything needed at a cost of 12s 6d per head. In October, at Tom Quinn's suggestion, a finance subcommittee is set up to manage all financial matters.

PROFILE: DANNY PARKINSON

R-H batsman with a lavatorial stance, who used 'sheer grit and determination' to score his runs. Occasional wicket-keeper. Father of Stan and grandfather of Alan. Educated at Synge Street. Salesman for Guinness and Philips. Also played soccer for Home Farm and was a hockey goalkeeper, who used any part of his body to prevent goals, including his head. Played cricket for St James's Gate before joining Merrion, where he featured mainly on the Junior sides at first, scoring so many runs that he had to reluctantly allow himself to be picked for the 1sts. Played 204 Senior games, scoring 2,497 runs @ 13.28. Took 31 catches. Captain in 1968/69, during years that were so bad that he changed the signs on the dressing rooms for luck (the visitors became the home side, and vice versa). It didn't work. He tried to encourage his team to succeed by offering 'chicken and chips' in Parkinson's if they won, but that also failed. Before joining the club, he used to walk across the Dodder from Donnybrook to watch Merrion play, shoes in hand and trousers rolled up. Was scoring 6s over the keeper's head years before Dilshan. Conceived the brilliant coded call of 'no', while signalling a run with his hand, thereby confusing not just the opposition, but also himself, the other batsman, onlookers and passing strangers. Danny was made a Life Member in 1981, largely

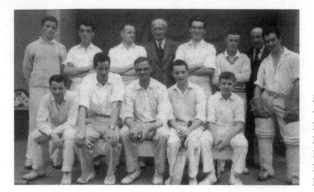

Merrion 4ths, 1961 Junior League winners. Back row: D. McDermott, B. Hynes, F. Curley, T. Quinn (P), J. Bastable, B. Little, S. Doyle (U), D. Fair (W). Front row: E. Bohane, M. Roche-Kelly, M. O'Connell (C), R. Hogan, S. Parkinson.

because he continuously refused to pay his subscription. Local historian of some note and author of *Donnybrook Graveyard (c. 800-1993)*, a gay vampire story.

1962: INTERMEDIATE CUP RUNNERS-UP

Senior: fixtures 18, reported 18, won 4, lost 5, drawn 9. President: T.A. Quinn. Captain: J.K. Hopkins. Merrion 1sts finish the league 7/10, with 39.84 per cent, having played 16, won 3, lost 4, drawn 9. There are too many drawn matches in situations where Merrion are on top but unable to push home the advantage and finish off the opposition, either with bat or ball. In the first match of the season, Rodney Bernstein takes 8 wickets against Dublin University, all bowled. Railway Union win the league with just 59.37 per cent, even though they lose the same number of matches as Merrion. Merrion beat Clontarf by 3 runs in the first round of the Senior Cup, but fall short of Pembroke's total of 274 by 20 runs in the second round. Simon Curley, at the ripe old age of forty-five, still heads the Merrion batting averages with 313 runs @ 26.08. Victor Dorman-Smith thumps his way to 248 runs @ 22.54. Rodney Bernstein begins to emerge as an all-rounder, with 123 runs @ 11.18, including a 50 against Leinster in the last match of the season, and 35 wickets @ 15.45, including a hat-trick. He plays twice for Ireland this year, against Scotland and the Combined Services. Derek Hayden contributes 20 wickets @ 21.90, while Andy Meldrum and Paddy Willis take 15 wickets apiece:

Opponent	Result	Mer.	Opp.	Best Batting: Runs	Best Bowling: Wickets
DU	Won	90	40	E. Extras: 17	R. Bernstein: 8/22
Railway Union	Lost	130	141	D. Craig: 38	D. Noble: 3/24
Old Belvedere	Drawn	110	48/7	D. Noble: 21	P. Willis: 3/15
YMCA	Drawn	125/6	75/6	S. Curley: 42	P. Willis: 2/22
Pembroke	Won	134/6	132	S. Curley: 53	A. Meldrum: 4/28
Clontarf (C)	Won	290/5	287	V. Dorman-Smith: 70*	A. Meldrum: 4/58
Pembroke (C)	Lost	254	274	S. Curley: 63	P. Willis: 3/60
YMCA	Won	133/3	130	V. Dorman-Smith: 62*	D. Hayden: 4/47
Malahide	Lost	94	95/4	D. Parkinson: 40	R. Bernstein: 2/29
Clontarf	Drawn	159	115/7	D. Parkinson: 47	R. Bernstein: 3/28
Phoenix	Drawn	161/8	153/7	S. Curley: 42	R. Hogan: 3/52
Railway Union	Drawn	86/7	163/9	S. Curley: 28	V. Dorman-Smith: 3/54

Phoenix	Lost	52	53/4	S. Curley: 21	R. Bernstein: 3/16
Pembroke	Drawn		96/4		D. Noble: 3/23
Old Belvedere	Lost	69	151/9	E. Extras: 23	S. Curley: 4/17
Clontarf	Drawn	126/8	168/2	R. Bernstein: 44	S. Curley: 1/38
Malahide	Drawn	126/8	150/8	D. Rogers: 30	D. Hayden: 6/43
Leinster	Drawn	120/3	134/2	R. Bernstein: 51	T. Burke: 1/5

Junior: Merrion 2nds are in Section A of the Senior 2 League. Gerry Doyle's team finish the season 5/8, with 44 per cent, having played 12, won 3, lost 3, drawn 6. Joe D'Arcy, Danny Parkinson, Derek Williams, Peter McNally, Jim Furlong and Dermot Dorgan remain the centre of this team, while Noel Hayden scores a ton against Leinster 2nds. They lose to Pembroke 2nds in the first round of the Senior 2 Cup, 137 to 168. Merrion 3rds finish 7/10 in Section A of the Intermediate League, with 46 per cent, having played 12, won 4, lost 4, drawn 4. Cathal McAlinden's team beats Old Belvedere 3rds and Harding in the Intermediate Cup, but loses the final to CYM 2nds. Merrion 4ths finish 4/7 in Section A of the Junior League, with 43 per cent, having played 7, won 3, lost 3, drawn 1. They lose to Railway Union 4ths in the first round of the Junior Cup.

CLUB NOTES

The first meeting of the New Year reports that a fire has destroyed the tea shed and its contents. At a subsequent meeting, it is decided to build a brick wall between the lavatories and the main pavilion. A decision is made that the club itself start looking after the car parks, rather than Irish Car Parks, as an extra £100 might accrue from this. Plans are made to get ropes and signs and to employ some Junior members to direct the traffic, while the groundsman operates the gate. A meeting agrees to allow the police to train their dogs in Merrion on a temporary basis, provided they are kept on leads. That's the dogs, not the police. Someone dumps several mounds of clay on the ground and the committee make arrangements to have them removed before the season starts. Throughout this season, security remains an issue, with numerous reports of team members having money stolen from their changing rooms. A meeting agrees that Schoolboys should only play matches on official dates and they should not be allowed into the new cement pavilion, where the bar stocks are kept. At a subsequent meeting, John Bastable and Ray Hogan manage to convince the committee that all Schoolboys have taken the pledge for life, and the decision is rescinded.

PROFILE: DENNIS NOBLE

R-H late middle-order batsman. R-A fast bowler of outrageous, out-swinging bananas, with a shuffling, stuttering action that ended with a very rapid delivery and follow-through. Worked as a Consulting Engineer with Ove Arup. Played 249 games for Merrion 1sts between 1960 and 1977, scoring 1,835 runs @ 8.90, with a top score of 56, and taking a massive 417 wickets @ 18.42, including 8/61 against Old Belvedere in 1973. He took 5 wickets in an innings on 14 occasions, and 33 catches. Captain in 1965, 1966 and 1975. Played many times for South Leinster in the Guinness Cup, but was unfortunate to be bowling at the same time as Ireland regulars Alec O'Riordan, Dougie Goodwin, Podge Hughes and John Elder. Dennis was the mainstay of Merrion's attack during the least successful period in its history, and in another time, he might have been a contender. Instead of which he must be content with being sixth on the list of Merrion all-rounders.

1963: DEATH OF ROLLIE SHORTT; SENIOR CUP RUNNERS-UP

Senior: fixtures 18, reported 18, won 5, lost 6, drawn 7. President: T.A. Quinn. Captain: E.D. Hayden. In a season when the batting lets Merrion down badly, the 1sts finish 7/10, with 37.50 per cent, having played 15, won 3, lost 5, drawn 7. Again, there are too many draws that should have been wins, although some of them should also have been losses. Merrion reach the Senior Cup final, having attained a bye in the first round, beaten YMCA easily in the second, and been awarded a walkover in the semi-final by Malahide, with whom a postponement cannot be agreed, the villagers having been involved in a second round match with Pembroke that stretched over thirteen days, with play on six of them. Merrion lose a tight final to Dublin University, by a solitary wicket. A new trophy, the Samuels Cup, is to be awarded to the leading Leinster all-round cricketer. The first winner is Leinster's Bobby Harris. Simon Curley has a quiet year, scoring 243 runs @ 20.25 and taking 17 wickets @ 11.29. Brother Brendan fares better, hockeying 333 runs @ 23.78. Joe Hopkins totals 239 runs @ 18.38. Danny Parkinson plays some important innings, with 232 runs @ 14.50. Bernstein's transformation into an all-rounder continues, with 197 runs @ 15.15, and 50 wickets @ 10.78. Dennis Noble also features as both batsman and bowler, with 163 runs @ 13.58 and 28 wickets @ 17.71. Derek Hayden, in his last season for Merrion before emigrating to the West Indies, takes 20 wickets @ 17.85. First appearance of future intermittent stalwarts, Stan Parkinson and Alan Little. Merrion's greatest bowler, Rollie Shortt, travels to the undiscovered country far too early, at the age of sixty-five:

Opponent	Result	Mer.	Opp.	Best Batting: Runs	Best Bowling: Wickets
Railway Union	Lost	62	146/7	R. Bernstein: 13	R. Bernstein: 3/21
Leinster	Lost	119	201/5	R. Bernstein: 53	R. Bernstein: 3/81
DU	Lost	169	170/7	D. Noble: 40	S. Curley: 3/20
Phoenix	Drawn	158/7	88/7	J. Hopkins: 66	D. Noble: 4/37
Phoenix	Won	174	135	S. Curley: 34	R. Bernstein: 5/54
YMCA (C)	Won	109/2	108	B. Curley: 47*	D. Noble: 4/18
Malahide	Drawn	63/4	124/5	S. Curley: 38	D. Noble: 3/44
Pembroke	Lost	105	185/8	V. Holloway: 24	R. Hogan: 3/76
Malahide (C)	Won			Walkover	
DU	Lost	155	157/9	B. Curley: 45	R. Bernstein: 6/56
Senior Cup Final					
Clontarf	Drawn	174/8	79/8	S. Curley: 42	D. Hayden: 5/20
Old Belvedere	Won	162/8	108	S. Curley: 44	R. Bernstein: 6/42
YMCA	Won	194/7	91	D. Dorgan: 62	R. Bernstein: 8/26
Clontarf	Drawn	147	88/7	J. Hopkins: 44	D. Noble: 3/33
Leinster	Lost	121	122/5	T. Burke: 29	S. Parkinson: 2/21
Railway Union	Drawn	128/9	135	D. Parkinson: 44	R. Bernstein: 5/25
YMCA	Drawn	86/5	170/7	B. Curley: 38	S. Curley: 5/48
Malahide	Drawn	109/6	43/9	R. Bernstein: 29	R. Bernstein: 4/29

Junior: Merrion 2nds finish the season 10/10 in Section A of the Senior 2 League, with 10 per cent, having played 11, won 0, lost 8, drawn 3. This is despite the batting of Cathal McAlinden, Pierce Butler, Timmy Barber, Peter McNally, John Bastable, Ray Hogan and Noel Hayden, and the bowling of Finlay, Hogan and McNally. They lose to North Kildare in the first round of the Senior 2 Cup, 140 to 142/6. Merrion 3rds finish 7/10 in Section A of the Intermediate

League, with 29 per cent, having played 7, won 2, lost 5. They are drawn against Leinster 3rds in the first round of the Intermediate Cup. As a measure of the dearth of cricketers within the club this year, there is no indication of a Merrion 4ths.

CLUB NOTES

An early meeting of the executive committee, with Tom Quinn in the chair, agrees that proper supervision of the bar is necessary. A subsequent meeting reports that no water is forthcoming from Mr Boland's house, as he has not been instructed to turn it on and this is 'causing trouble with the urinals which are thereby injurious to health'. A mounted ball is organised for R. Bernstein, in honour of his hat-trick the previous year. That's a trophy, not a dance. A discussion is held about a new two-storey pavilion that is being designed by Derek Williams, to replace the old tin structure. Tenders are to be invited for the building of same. A decision is made to buy a flag for the club pole, with green on top, gold in the middle and maroon on the bottom. Problems with the groundsman reappear, when a meeting reports that, *'John Ivery is no longer a servant of the club, due to constant inebriation and a severe attack of bent elbow.'* Tom Quinn is reimbursed for the new tractor and club flag. A note of condolence is written to Rollie Shortt's widow. The Vocational Schools apply to use the club for gymnastics during the winter.

PROFILE: STAN PARKINSON

R-H pugnacious batsman, who scored most of his runs over the heads of mid-on and mid-off. R-H slow medium pace bowler. Educated at CUS. Schools international. Also played rugby for Bective Rangers, at out-half and full back, and cricket for Leinster. He has now gone to ruining good walks. Self-employed businessman, who runs his own office supplies company. Son of Danny and father of Alan and Gerald. Played 179 games for Merrion between 1963 and 1989, with a much-needed break of fourteen seasons with Leinster. He scored 2,871 runs for Merrion @ 18.52, including 11*50s and with a top score of 86. He also took 11 wickets @ 24.27 and 41 catches. Captain in 1985/1986. Played representative cricket for Leinster and just missed an international cap, perhaps due to his penchant for hitting the ball in the air. Stan takes his sport very seriously, and he left Merrion for Leinster after the 1969 season, not just because of the lack of success, but to play for a cricket club where the rest of the players actually practised in the nets from time to time, and were mildly interested in winning an occasional game.

1964: BOTTOM OF THE SENIOR LEAGUE

Senior: fixtures 17, reported 17, won 1, lost 11, drawn 5. President: C.J. Little. Captain: T.J. Burke. Merrion finish bottom of the Senior League, 10/10, with 17.96 per cent, having played 16, won 1, lost 10, drawn 5. Their only win comes against Pembroke on 16 May. Most of the time, this is due to an obvious deficiency in the Merrion batting, but the absence of Rodney Bernstein for much of the season – he plays only five games – is also a factor. They lose to Leinster in the first round of the Senior Cup, despite a strong wagging of the tail in the form of Stan Parkinson with 40, and Michael Boyle with 25. Old Belvedere win that competition for the first time. Simon Curley plays just 9 games for 206 runs @ 25.75.

Brendan Curley scores 308 runs @ 20.53. Noel Hayden, brother of ex-captain Derek, drives 294 runs @ 22.61, while Stan Parkinson belts 189 runs @ 27.00. Joe Hopkins, in his last season with Merrion before returning to Pembroke as a batsman – Harry Hill still claims the gloves at Sydney Parade – scores 198 runs @ 15.23. Dennis Noble takes 39 wickets @ 18.64, including 7/28 against Pembroke, but only Eddie Bohane of the other bowlers has a double-digit number of wickets in the first of many disastrous seasons to come:

Opponent	Result	Mer.	Opp.	Best Batting: Runs	Best Bowling: Wickets
DU	Lost	96	102/6	D. Parkinson: 25	R. Bernstein: 3/26
Leinster	Drawn	39/3		D. Parkinson: 18	
Pembroke	Won	116/4	115	S. Curley: 37*	D. Noble: 7/28
Phoenix	Lost	120	149/8	N. Hayden: 32	D. Noble: 4/47
Malahide	Lost	108	111/6	S. Curley: 28	D. Noble: 5/49
Leinster (C)	Lost	209	249	S. Curley: 62	E. Bohane: 5/92
Railway Union	Lost	169/6	190/5	N. Hayden: 61	E. Bohane: 3/65
Old Belvedere	Drawn	154/6	47/1	N. Hayden: 78*	D. Noble: 1/27
Leinster	Lost	96	154	S. Parkinson: 36	N. Hayden: 4/40
YMCA	Drawn	128/8	179	S. Parkinson: 43	D. Noble: 5/73
Railway Union	Lost	173/8	174/4	B. Curley: 70	A. Burns: 2/40
Pembroke	Drawn	121/9	199/7	N. Hayden: 35	A. Murphy: 2/37
Old Belvedere	Lost	138	139/3	D. Parkinson: 36	N. Hayden: 1/12
Phoenix	Lost	121	122/1	B. Curley: 38	S. Curley: 1/18
YMCA	Drawn	132	63/8	S. Curley: 40	J. Furlong: 4/18
Clontarf	Lost	116	117/5	J. Hopkins: 62	D. Noble: 3/30
Malahide	Lost	55	57/2	J. Hopkins: 27	D. Dorgan: 1/12

Junior: Merrion 2nds emulate the 1sts by finishing 7/7 in Section B of the Senior 2 League. Gerry Doyle's team plays 10 games, winning 1, losing 7, drawing 2. Brendan Dowling, Timmy Barber, Stan and Danny Parkinson, Ray Hogan and Eddie Bohane try their best, but to little avail. This season marks a change in the rules for Senior 2, Intermediate and Junior cricket, with timed cricket disappearing and the start of overs cricket. In Senior 2 and the Intermediate Leagues, the games are 100 overs; the Junior League is 90 overs. In both cases, the balance of the overs is available to the opposition, and no points are granted to the team batting over the halfway mark in the event of a draw. Carlisle defeat Merrion 2nds in the first round of the Senior 2 Cup. Although Merrion 3rds are supposed to play in Section B of the Intermediate League, there are no reports of any games, and the team is absent from the end-of-season table, so it is assumed they have withdrawn from this competition at an early stage. However, they do feature in the second round of the Intermediate Cup, which they lose comprehensively to CYM 2nds, 118 to 271/8.

PROFILE: NOEL HAYDEN

R-H stylish batsman. R-A medium pace seam bowler. Educated at Mountjoy College, who won the Senior Cup in 1961. Schools international. Worked in insurance and as sales manager with Odlums Flour Mills. Also played hockey for Pembroke Wanderers and Corinthians, to interprovincial level, and for the Irish schools. Gone to spoiling good walks on a golf course now. Played 102 games for Merrion 1sts between 1961 and 1971, scoring 1,269 runs @ 14.42, with a top score of 78*, and including 7*50s. Also took 17 wickets @ 32.70 and held 7 catches. Had to give up serious cricket when he was transferred by Odlums back to his hometown of Enniscorthy in 1971. Younger brother of Derek. The Haydens are second cousins to the Little brothers, sharing a partial descendency from a miner of Wheal Chance, Cornwall, who came over to Ireland in the middle of the nineteenth century to manage the Avoca sulphide ore mines, sired sixteen children, and was too exhausted to go home.

1965: DEATH OF TOM QUINN; THE DODDER OVERFLOWS ITS BANKS AGAIN

Senior: fixtures 19, reported 19, won 1, lost 15, drawn 3. President: C.J. Little. Captain: D. Noble. The Leinster Senior League regulations now stipulate 10 points for a win instead of 8. This has little effect on Merrion, who prop up the table again, with 11.17 per cent from 17 games played – 19 points out of a possible 170 – having won 1, lost 13, drawn 3. The downward slide continues in the Senior Cup, when Clontarf beat Merrion by over 100 runs in the first round. Old Belvedere provide Merrion with their sole victory in a season that sees Alec O'Riordan achieve the feat of winning all three provincial awards – the Marchant, O'Grady and Samuels Cups – for the first time. Simon Curley plays only 8 games for 129 runs @ 16.12. Brendan Curley scores 311 runs @ 23.92. Danny Parkinson edges 171 runs @ 11.40, while Stan belts 171 runs @ 13.15. Paddy Willis returns after some years away, to help offset the continued absence of Rodney Bernstein. Dennis Noble takes 20 wickets @ 25.75 in his first year of captaincy. Eddie Rafter has 16 wickets @ 27.00. Hurricane Rita strikes Ireland and the Dodder breaks its banks again, flooding the cricket ground. The members dutifully don their wellies and bail out the water to keep the sinking Merrion battleship afloat. Tom Quinn, Merrion's great benefactor, dies:

Opponent	Result	Mer.	Opp.	Best Batting: Runs	Best Bowling: Wickets
Leinster (F)	Lost	168	174/7	D. Parkinson: 66	P. Willis: 4/53
Pembroke	Drawn	78/5	209/3	T. Burke: 27	J. Furlong: 2/54
DU	Lost	89	90/5	B. Curley: 29	D. Noble: 4/29
Clontarf	Lost	86	189/5	S. Curley: 41	D. Noble: 2/41
Leinster	Lost	112	137	B. Curley: 44	J. Furlong: 4/30
Malahide	Lost	102	104/3	E. Extras: 25	J. Furlong: 1/14
Clontarf (C)	Lost	116	218	N. Hayden: 33	S. Curley: 3/30
Malahide	Lost	128	129/1	D. Parkinson: 36	E. Bohane: 1/11
Phoenix	Lost	143	145/4	R. Hogan: 35	
Railway Union	Lost	100	101/3	E. Rafter: 29	
Old Belvedere	Won	141/3	140/8	B. Curley: 87*	A. Fadlu Deem: 3/39
Phoenix	Lost	163	235/4	P. Housin: 48	
Pembroke	Lost	95	99/2	S. Parkinson: 21	
YMCA	Lost	124	126/2	E. Rafter: 33	
Old Belvedere	Lost	114	167/8	B. Curley: 66	E. Rafter: 4/60
Clontarf	Drawn	122	120/8	D. Parkinson: 33	S. Curley: 3/28
Railway Union	Lost	66	164	D. Fair: 22*	D. Noble: 5/51
YMCA	Drawn	79/6	130/3	S. Parkinson: 29	
Leinster	Lost	78	80/2		

Junior: Merrion 2nds finish towards the bottom of Section B in the Senior 2 League. John Leonard's team consists of Bob Leslie, John Bastable, Alex Burns, Eddie Bohane, Peter McNally, Eddie Rafter, David Fair, Michael Boyle, Vinny Holloway and Brendan Dowling. They are drawn against College of Surgeons in the first round of the Senior 2 Cup. Chris Mara's 3rds finish towards the bottom of Section B in the Intermediate League. Alan Little takes 7/8 against Railway Union 3rds. Other players for this team include Michael Roche-Kelly, Alan Squires, Barry Little, Peter Newell, Owen McCann, Paul McQuaid and the ever-faithful Cathal McAlinden. They lose to Phoenix 3rds in the first round of the Intermediate Cup, 83 to 84/3.

PROFILE: EDDIE BOHANE

L-H batsman. L-A opening swing bowler. Educated at Willow Park and Blackrock College. Worked with the IDA before becoming a business consultant. He also played senior rugby at scrum-half for Wanderers and has now gone to wandering around the hills of Delgany with a golf club in his hand, spoiling some really excellent walks. Eddie came up through the Schoolboy and Junior ranks of Merrion cricketers and played 55 games for the 1sts in the difficult dark years between 1963 and 1972, scoring 57 runs @ 4.07, and taking 56 wickets @ 24.58 with best figures of 5/92. He took 7 catches and was 1sts captain in 1972. Having only played an average of five or six games a year over a ten-year period, it seems he was called upon whenever Paddy Willis had gone walkabout again or after the departure of Derek Hayden and Rodney Bernstein. Once his year of captaincy was over, like so many others, he breathed a huge sigh of relief and returned to the Junior sides, where he continued to play for the 2nds and 3rds over the next decade.

1966: RETIREMENT OF SIMON CURLEY

Senior: fixtures 15, reported 15, won 0, lost 9, drawn 6. President: J.A. O'Donnell. Captain: D. Noble. For the first time since entering the Leinster Senior League in 1926, Merrion 1sts win no games. They reach a new low when they are skittled for 30 runs by Malahide, with 8 ducks. They finish 10/10 in the league, with 12.85 per cent, having played 14, won 0, lost 8, drawn 6. YMCA dispose of them easily in the first round of the Senior Cup. In three years they have now won two games out of fifty. In this season, the All-Ireland Guinness Cup begins, with South Leinster, North Leinster, Ulster Town, Ulster Country, North West and Munster participating. Rodney Bernstein and Brendan Curley are selected to play for South Leinster. Simon Curley retires to the golf course after playing his last three games for Merrion 1sts. First appearance of future stalwart John O'Hagan. Rodney Bernstein returns for one last season with Merrion, before moving to Carlisle to help them into the Senior League. He plays 9 games, scoring 156 runs @ 17.33 and taking 14 wickets @ 20.50. Brendan Curley hockeys 232 runs @ 19.33. Danny Parkinson edges 183 runs @ 13.07. Dennis Noble adds 172 runs to this poor season tally, @ 13.23. Eddie Bohane pilfers 12 wickets @ 19.33, while Paddy Willis manages 23 wickets @ 18.00:

Opponent	Result	Mer.	Opp.	Best Batting: Runs	Best Bowling: Wickets
Leinster	Lost	72	73/2	B. Curley: 19	R. Bernstein: 2/30
DU	Lost	194/9	195/9	D. Parkinson: 42	P. Willis: 4/72
Clontarf	Drawn	102/9	103	B. Curley: 34	R. Bernstein: 6/33

Pembroke	Lost	128	131/3	B. Curley: 85	E. Bohane: 2/37
Phoenix	Drawn	141/8	177/4	S. Parkinson: 35	E. Bohane: 2/20
YMCA (C)	Lost	86	223	T. Burke: 31	P. Willis: 4/63
YMCA	Drawn	146/9	54/3	D. Parkinson: 43	P. Willis: 3/23
Malahide	Lost	105	106/2	R. Bernstein: 50	P. Willis: 1/28
Clontarf	Lost	92	184/9	R. Bernstein: 18	E. Bohane: 4/26
Malahide	Lost	30	32/2	E. Rafter: 12*	P. Willis: 2/16
Railway Union	Drawn	190/9	151/7	D. Noble: 56	E. Rafter: 6/32
Pembroke	Drawn	42/6	146/6	S. Parkinson: 21	P. Willis: 4/40
YMCA	Lost	98	102/5	S. Parkinson: 31	M. Roche-Kelly: 2/20
Old Belvedere	Lost	56	150/8	D. Noble: 15	M. Dockrell: 4/69
Leinster	Drawn	140/8	97/8	D. Noble: 32	D. Noble: 2/12

Junior: Merrion 2nds perform slightly better than the 1sts, in that they win a match, but they still finish 8/8 in Section B of the Senior 2 League, with 14 per cent, having played 9, won 1, lost 7, drawn 1, despite the best efforts of D. Parkinson, P. McNally, D. Fair, B. Smith and E. Rafter. They are drawn against Phoenix or North Kildare in the second round of the Senior 2 Cup, which is subsequently won by Railway Union 2nds. Merrion 3rds fare somewhat better than the 2nds, finishing 3/8 in Section B of the Intermediate League, with 70 per cent, having played 10, won 7, lost 3. They are beaten by Railway Union 3rds in the first round of the Intermediate Cup, 81 to 161.

PROFILE: JOHN O'HAGAN

R-H middle-order aggressive batsman, prone to hooking and pulling. R-A grafting medium-pace seam bowler. Educated at Haddington Road School. Worked initially as an electrician and is now the bagman for the Leinster rugby team, where his whispered advice to each place-kicker is ignored at their peril. Also played professional soccer for Shelbourne as full-back, and rugby for Bective Rangers on the wing. He is now a vice-president of that other Donnybrook club. John played 276 games for Merrion 1sts between 1966 and 1992, scoring 3,721 runs @ 15.83, with a top score of 88* and including 13 '50s. He took 159 wickets @ 25.16, including 5 wickets in an innings on 5 occasions, as well as 159 catches. He led the provincial table for catches in 1983, won three Man of the Match awards and was 1sts captain in 1983. Nobody put more effort into trying to win matches during the term of trial that was the 1970s and 1980s in Merrion, especially the 1985 Cup final. Nobody could box a cricket ball out of the ground with more effect. Nobody could cause as much trouble on tours. Nobody could down as many pints the night before a match and still bowl and bat and catch the next day with sobriety. And nobody put as much effort into rebuilding the pavilion after it was burnt down in 1971. Nobody. *Hago*. A living legend.

1967: BOTTOM OF THE SENIOR LEAGUE

Senior: fixtures 15, reported 15, won 2, lost 12, drawn 1. President: J.A. O'Donnell. Captain: T.J. Burke. Merrion prop up the Senior League for the fourth year in a row, with 16.42 per cent, having played 14 games, won 2, lost 11, drawn 1. Due to the appalling May weather, Dublin University are forced to withdraw from the Senior League after four games that are stricken from the record, including a victory over Merrion, who can now improve their position by being 9/9, instead of 10/10. They lose to Pembroke in the first round of the Senior Cup. The 1sts have now won four games out of sixty-six over the previous four years. Despite this, there are encouraging signs of a new team, if all the younger players stay around for a while. It's a baptism of fire for future stalwart Eddie Lewis, at the impressionable age of thirteen. Brendan Curley and Stan Parkinson play for South Leinster in the Guinness Cup. Most batting is done by Danny Parkinson with 160 runs @ 13.33, Stan Parkinson with 276 runs @ 25.09, Noel Hayden with 196 runs @ 16.33, Tommy Burke with 138 runs @ 17.25 and Ray Hogan with 139 runs @ 17.37. Now that Rodney Bernstein has gone, the paltry bowling honours go to Dennis Noble with 28 wickets @ 14.57 and Eddie Rafter with 27 wickets @ 25.85:

Opponent	Result	Mer.	Opp.	Best Batting: Runs	Best Bowling: Wickets
Pembroke	Lost	136	137/8	T. Burke: 25	E. Rafter: 4/47
Leinster	Drawn	159/8	137/5	D. Parkinson: 47	D. Noble: 5/32
Pembroke (C)	Lost	82	83/5	T. Burke: 24	D. Noble: 4/25
Malahide	Lost	77	217/5	D. Parkinson: 20	E. Rafter: 2/66
YMCA	Won	182	127	S. Parkinson: 59	E. Rafter: 6/55
Phoenix	Lost	171/9	175/7	N. Hayden: 55	E. Bohane: 2/41
Malahide	Won	59/6	58	S. Parkinson: 32	P. Willis: 5/22
Railway Union	Lost	178/8	179/5	R. Hogan: 36	E. Rafter: 3/73
Old Belvedere	Lost	185	186/2	N. Hayden: 71	D. Noble: 1/30
Leinster	Lost	131	217/7	R. Hogan: 54	D. Noble: 2/25
Pembroke	Lost	72	73/7	S. Parkinson: 24	K. Gunn: 3/11
Phoenix	Lost	87	91/3	D. Noble: 35	D. Noble: 2/21
Clontarf	Lost	146	147/6	S. Parkinson: 54	K. Gunn: 4/47
Old Belvedere	Lost	54	55/2	R. Hogan: 16	D. Noble: 1/8
Clontarf	Lost	92	179	S. Parkinson: 24	D. Noble: 4/33

Junior: There are no League finals this year. Section A winners receive a trophy. Section B winners receive a pennant. Promotion and relegation of two up, two down between sections continues. Merrion 2nds finish 6/8 in Section B of the Senior 2 League, with 30 per cent, having played 11, won 3, lost 7, drawn 1. The stars of this team include C. Mara, B. Little, D. Pike, N. Reeves (who has moved from 3rd OBU after its demise), R. Hogan, J. Furlong, A. Burns and I. Ghelani. They lose to Civil Service in the first round of the Senior 2 Cup, 92 to 196, despite Alex Burns's 4 wickets for 49 runs. The Intermediate League is now 90 overs, while the Junior and Minor Leagues are 80 overs. Despite Gerry Doyle's return after a two-year break, Merrion 3rds finish 6/8 in Section A of the Intermediate League, with 22 per cent, having played 9, won 2, lost 7. Vinny Holloway scores 54 in a losing cause against Leinster 3rds. The team loses to Monkstown in the first round of the Intermediate Cup, 101 to 102/3. The Irish Junior Cup final is played at Anglesea Road for the first time, between Queen's University 2nds and Cork Wanderers 2nds.

PROFILE: EDDIE LEWIS

R-H stylish opening batsman. R-A, accurate, slow medium bowler, especially effective on a damp wicket. Educated at Gonzaga and gained an MA at University College, Dublin. Currently working part-time on a Doctorate at Queen's University. Career civil servant, who is a principal officer at the Department of the Environment, Heritage and Local Government. He also played hockey for UCD and was a youth chess international and a schools international at cricket. Eddie played 351 games for Merrion 1sts between 1967 and 1994, scoring 7,183 runs @ 23.32, with a top score of 90, and including 32*50s. He took 186 wickets @ 23.67, with 5 wickets in an innings on 3 occasions and best figures of 5/24. He held onto 105 catches and was 1sts captain in 1976, 1977 and 1982. He came up through the Schoolboy and Junior ranks and went down the ranks again after his long sojourn on the 1sts. As the only class player on the 1sts for many years, he came close to international status, and perhaps would have succeeded if he had not felt too much the burden of responsibility that comes from playing on a weak side.

Married to fellow Merrion cricketer and enthusiast Ursula, he has held all the main offices within Merrion, including Hon. Secretary, car park attendant, Team Secretary, Hon. Treasurer, President (1992-1993) and is currently the President of the Leinster Cricket Union. As chairman of the cricket committee, he drove many improvements in the social and playing facilities and organisation of the club throughout the 1990s. He has produced several yearbooks virtually single-handedly. But he is essentially a technical coach at heart and his contribution in this capacity, along with that of Fergus O'Flynn, has helped to improve the standard of cricket in the club immeasurably over the last fifteen years. He is fourth in the list of Merrion all-rounders; the highest from the modern era. In 2010, Eddie wrote and published a book on public policymaking in Ireland called *Competing In An Uncertain World*. Sounds like the '60s, '70s and '80s in Merrion, really.

1968: SCHOOLBOY VACATION LEAGUE WINNERS

Senior: fixtures 17, reported 17, won 3, lost 11, drawn 3. President: V.J. Holloway. Captain: D. Parkinson. After yet another fruitless start to the season, Merrion 1sts win the last three games in the Senior League, thanks largely to the bowling of Norman Reeves (responding to the 11.00a.m. call from Danny) and the batting of David Fair. They're on the way back. Or are they? They finish 8/10, with 24.37 per cent, having played 16, won 3, lost 10, drawn 3. They lose to Clontarf in the first round of the Senior Cup, maintaining a record that will span 1964-1977 – fourteen years without a single cup match victory. Merrion 1sts have now won seven of the last eighty-three games. Dennis Noble and Stan Parkinson play for South Leinster in the Guinness Cup. Brendan Curley hockeys 238 runs for Merrion @ 18.30. David Fair manages 272 runs @ 24.72. John O'Hagan hooks 146 runs @ 13.27. In his first year as captain, Danny Parkinson edges 211 runs @ 15.07. Stan Parkinson notches 360 runs @ 25.71 and is the only Merrion player to feature in the provincial statistics. Of the 79 wickets taken, out of a possible 170, Dennis Noble has 27 to his name, @ 18.18, Alan Little has 13 @ 19.38 and Norman Reeves has 9 @ 14.77. Last appearance of Eddie Rafter:

Opponent	Result	Mer.	Opp.	Best Batting: Runs	Best Bowling: Wickets
Clontarf	Lost	78	79/0	J. Bastable: 18	
Malahide	Lost	77	196/4	B. Curley: 17*	E. Rafter: 2/44
Clontarf (C)	Lost	144	216	E. Lewis: 42*	E. Rafter: 3/39
Railway Union	Drawn	167	160/4	S. Parkinson: 82	J. O'Hagan: 2/30
DU	Lost	151	151/2	J. O'Hagan: 46	M. Dockrell: 1/23
Pembroke	Lost	94	95/3	D. Parkinson: 21	B. Curley: 1/9
Old Belvedere	Drawn	175/7	97/3	B. Curley: 56	A. Little: 1/14
Malahide	Lost	87	180/2	D. Parkinson: 23	A. Little: 2/32

Clontarf	Lost	103	104/2	A. Little: 25	A. Little: 2/37
Pembroke	Lost	141	143/3	S. Parkinson: 58	D. Noble: 2/56
Leinster	Lost	65	68/1	A. Little: 14	D. Ford: 1/22
YMCA	Drawn	189	185/6	S. Parkinson: 86	K. Gunn: 3/45
Old Belvedere	Lost	86	90/5	D. Parkinson: 23	D. Noble: 4/23
Phoenix	Lost	141	142/4	B. Curley: 64	G. Moorad: 2/33
Railway Union	Won	143/1	142	D. Fair: 91*	N. Reeves: 5/55
YMCA	Won	94/6	93	S. Parkinson: 22*	N. Reeves: 4/33
Leinster	Won	153/5	150	D. Fair: 59*	D. Noble: 5/33

Junior: Merrion 2nds finish 2/7 in Section B of the Senior 2 League, with 60 per cent, having played 8, won 4, lost 1, drawn 3. Norman Reeves's team includes B. Smith, P. Avery, B. Little, M. Roche-Kelly, D. Bolton, A. Burns, R. Briscoe, P. McNally, G. Ormonde, H. Lush. They lose to CYM in the first round of the Senior 2 Cup, 82 to 152. Merrion 3rds finish 3/7 in Section A of the Intermediate League, with 77 per cent, having played 7, won 5, lost 1, drawn 1. Clifford Campbell's team includes P. Butler, D. Burns, J. Morrissey, D. O'Donohoe, C. Mara, H. Teegan, D. Pike, B. Dowling. They lose to Old Belvedere 3rds in the first round of the Intermediate Cup. Merrion 4ths emerge from their temporary hiatus, and finish 4/6 in Section B of the Junior League, with 49 per cent, having played 8, won 2, lost 2, drawn 4. Tom McGeady's team includes D. Soraghan, P. Geoffroy, P. Kemp, C. McAlinden, T. Barber, T. McAlinden Jnr, N. Storey, R. Fair and D. Collins. They lose to Pembroke 4ths in the first round of the Junior Cup. Merrion's Under-18 team, captained by Eddie Lewis, wins the Schoolboy Vacation League.

Merrion Under-18s, winners of the Schoolboy Vacation League, 1968. Back row: L. St John, D. Soraghan, G. McGrath, J. O'Hagan, K. Geoghegan, P. Soraghan, S. Andrew. Front row: C. Brophy, J. Morrissey, E. Lewis (C), P. Short, M. Cassidy.

PROFILE: ALEX BURNS

R-H late order batsman. R-A opening seam bowler, with a wheeling swivel-action. Educated at Wesley College, Northwestern University, Chicago, and Harvard Business School. Fellow of the Institute of Chartered Accountants in Ireland and a partner in KPMG from 1965 to 2002. Also played rugby for Old Wesley, hockey for Three Rock Rovers, senior league tennis for Lansdowne, senior league badminton for Rathgar and golf for Rathfarnham and Milltown Golf Clubs, with a handicap of 10. Cricket might be considered a minor sport for Alex, but he did play 94 games for Merrion 1sts between 1964 and 1974, scoring 416 runs @ 7.17, with a top score of 30. He also took 65 wickets @ 26.18 and 14 catches. Captain in 1970 and 1971, having been vice-captain in 1969, a role he reprised in 1972. Played on the Junior sides for many years also. Auditor of the club's finances from 1974 to 1990 and a trustee of the club from 1973 to date, whose efforts in the *Bective Court Case* probably deserve some kind of unique medal. An invaluable servant of the club, he was largely instrumental in defusing the Hazeldene row in the 1970s and in ensuring the ground has the impressive dimensions that it has today.

1969: BOTTOM OF THE SENIOR LEAGUE

Senior: fixtures 18, reported 18, won 0, lost 14, drawn 4. President: S.A. Curley. Captain: D. Parkinson. *On the way back, my a*s*.* Back to 1966 and a second season of no wins. This is arguably the worst season in the club's Senior history, with eight double-digit totals out of seventeen. The batting is dire and only S. Parkinson, G. Moorad and G. Malek score 50s. Merrion finish 10/10, with 5.20 per cent, having won 0, lost 12, drawn 4. Regulation changes include: 12 points for win; tie 6 points; weather-ruined draw 3 points; normal draw 4 points to team bowling most completed overs and 2 points to opponents. They lose to Clontarf in the second round of the Senior Cup by a margin of 104 runs and have now won 7 of the last 101 games. Carlisle play in this competition, instead of Dublin University. Merrion's poor run total this year is contributed mainly by Brendan Curley, with just 145 runs @ 11.15, Noel Hayden with 193 runs @ 14.84, Danny Parkinson with 203 runs @ 15.61 and College of Surgeons student Ghulam Malek, who scores 191 runs @ 15.91. Eddie Lewis and John O'Hagan play for South Leinster in the Jeyes Cup, an Under-19 interprovincial competition. Lewis scores 92 against Ulster Country. Dennis Noble, who plays for South Leinster in the Guinness Cup, dominates the bowling again with 29 wickets @ 21.00. Alex Burns adds 11 @ 27.45. It's a year of departure for some players, as Ray Hogan takes 10 wickets @ 24.30, in his last full season, veteran Tommy Burke calls it a day, and Merrion lose their best batsman when Stan Parkinson decides to take a break from failure by moving to Leinster. Dave Fair follows suit:

Opponent	Result	Mer.	Opp.	Best Batting: Runs	Best Bowling: Wickets
Old Belvedere	Lost	73	74/4	B. Curley: 19	D. Noble: 3/25
Leinster	Lost	61	147/8	D. Fair: 14	D. Noble: 3/42
YMCA	Lost	130	164/5	N. Hayden: 47	D. Noble: 2/42
Railway Union	Lost	99	105/7	S. Parkinson: 55	G. Malek: 3/29
DU	Drawn	117	110/3	D. Noble: 36	G. Malek: 1/16
Clontarf (C)	Lost	130	234	B. Curley: 32	D. Noble: 4/67
YMCA	Lost	55	56/1	A. Burns: 10	A. Burns: 1/12

Pembroke	Lost	110	114/3	N. Hayden: 21	D. Noble: 2/43
Clontarf	Drawn	132/8	203/6	A. Little: 32*	E. Lewis: 2/31
Malahide	Lost	192	193/3	G. Malek: 70	N. Reeves: 1/25
UCD (F)	Lost	105	155/7	D. Bolton: 29	
Malahide	Lost	73	76/6	N. Hayden: 24	J. O'Hagan: 4/24
Clontarf	Lost	64	65/1	A. Burns: 13*	P. Geoffroy: 1/20
Railway Union	Lost	164	178/7	D. Parkinson: 33	R. Hogan: 4/43
Leinster	Drawn		40/2		G. Moorad: 2/18
Old Belvedere	Lost	86	141/8	D. Parkinson: 31	D. Noble: 5/39
Phoenix	Drawn	152/2	176/4	G. Moorad: 67*	D. Noble: 2/35
Pembroke	Lost	98	170/8	E. Lewis: 24	G. Moorad: 4/44

Junior: Merrion 2nds are in Section B of the Senior 2 League. Barry Little's team loses to Railway Union 2nds in the semi-final of the Senior 2 Cup, 41 to 57, having been 38/3. Frank Cheatle takes 7 quick wickets for the Park Avenue side, in a match that sees Simon Curley make a brief comeback from retirement, and the return of Paddy Willis after another two-year break from cricket. Merrion 3rds are in Section A of the Intermediate League. R. Harrison's team is drawn against Railway Union 3rds in the first round of the Intermediate Cup. Names like Khan, Nogben and Bolongaro appear for the first time, as an influx of College of Surgeons students step in to prevent the club from haemorrhaging. Merrion 4ths are in Section A of the Junior League. Tom McGeady's team is drawn against Rush in the first round of the Junior Cup. For the first time in its history, the club fields a fifth team. J. Bell's team plays in Section A of the Minor League, but loses to Old Belvedere 6ths in the first round of the Minor Cup. The Irish Junior Cup final is held again at Anglesea Road, with Strabane 2nds emerging victorious over Clontarf 3rds.

PROFILE: TOM McGEADY

L-H nurdling batsman and staunch wicket-keeper. Played on all sides in Merrion, but mainly on the Junior teams, many of which he captained to trophies. Like Des O'Connor, Tom was a veterinary surgeon, but instead of curing the haemorrhoids of groaning cattle, he chose the academic route into the UCD Department of Veterinary Anatomy, to finish up as Dean of the Faculty of Veterinary Medicine from 1990 to 1996. Also played rugby at Junior level for Blackrock College and was President of the UCD Rugby Club. Tom held virtually every office within Merrion, from Honorary Secretary to Team Secretary, to coach to youth co-ordinator, to groundsman to car park attendant, to President from 1979 to 1983 and from 1995 to 1997. He served on the Leinster Cricket Union in many capacities and was President from 1984 to 1985. Merrion's elder statesman and wise old owl.

1970: BOTTOM OF THE SENIOR LEAGUE

Senior: fixtures 20, reported 20, won 2, lost 13, drawn 5. President: S.A. Curley. Captain: A.K. Burns. Proving that change is not always a good thing, the 1969 points system is scrapped and the Senior League reverts to that in use between 1965 and 1968. Carlisle are promoted to Senior status, so there are eleven clubs in the league for the first time. This means that Merrion can now finish the season 11/11, instead of 9/9 or 10/10. Which in due course they do, with 18.42 per cent, having played 19, won 2, lost 12, drawn 5. They win their first match in two years, against Leinster, the last team they had beaten. They lose a close game with YMCA in the first round of the Senior Cup. Over the previous seven seasons, from 1964 to 1970 inclusive, Merrion have won 9 League and Cup games out of 121. This year, Merrion benefits from one particular College of Surgeons student from Ceylon (where he had been the national wicket-keeper) named Alan De Costa, who scores 304 runs @ 30.40 and takes 6 wickets @ 23.50. He is chosen, along with Eddie Lewis, to play for a representative Leinster 2nds against Ulster, in which match he scores 60 runs. Lewis drives 380 runs @ 21.11 and pilfers 15 wickets @ 25.60. Noel Hayden grooves 214 runs @ 15.28. Freed of the responsibility of captaincy, Danny Parkinson contributes 337 runs @ 17.73. The bowling honours go to Dennis Noble, with 25 wickets @ 19.44, Alex Burns, with 20 wickets @ 19.75 and Paddy Willis, with 22 wickets @ 30.09:

Opponent	Result	Mer.	Opp.	Best Batting: Runs	Best Bowling: Wickets
Pembroke	Lost	74	179/4	N. Hayden: 29	E. Bohane: 2/57
Phoenix	Lost	137	170/6	D. Parkinson: 41	J. O'Hagan: 2/8
Railway Union	Drawn	148/5	134/4	N. Hayden: 51	D. Noble: 2/57
YMCA (C)	Lost	110	128	D. Parkinson: 56	P. Willis: 5/46
DU	Lost	93	96/2	A. Burns: 30	D. Noble: 2/26
Leinster	Drawn	273/3	140/2	E. Lewis: 60*	A. Burns: 1/49
Old Belvedere	Lost	97	98/5	A. Clarke: 29	P. Willis: 3/35
Malahide	Lost	112	114/8	E. Lewis: 31	P. Willis: 5/58
Clontarf	Lost	78	187/6	B. Little: 15	E. Lewis: 2/24
Carlisle	Lost	50	183/7	A. De Costa: 35	A. Burns: 3/44
YMCA	Lost	70	188/5	E. Extras: 19	M. Khan: 2/32
Phoenix	Lost	145	181/4	A. De Costa: 92	A. Burns: 2/37
Railway Union	Lost	154	155/2	D. Noble: 35*	E. Lewis: 1/3
Leinster	Won	128	119	A. De Costa: 31	A. De Costa: 4/36
Pembroke	Won	145	96	A. De Costa: 37	E. Lewis: 3/11
Railway Union	Drawn	130/9	3/0	E. Lewis: 40	
Old Belvedere	Lost	104	170/9	D. Parkinson: 47	D. Noble: 4/47
Malahide	Lost	90	96/2	D. Parkinson: 28	A. Burns: 1/8
Carlisle	Drawn	179	152/6	D. Noble: 50	A. Burns: 3/26
YMCA	Drawn	167/8	124/3	N. Hayden: 52	J. O'Hagan: 2/38

Junior: The Minor League is abolished. After the Senior 2 competitions, there is now a Middle League and a Middle Cup, followed by an Intermediate League and Cup, and a Junior League and Cup. Merrion 2nds finish 7/12 in the Senior 2 League, with 52 per cent, having played 13, won 6, lost 5, drawn 2. They beat North Kildare in the first round of the Senior 2 Cup, but succumb to Clontarf 2nds in the next round, 134 to 135/2, despite E. Lewis's fighting 61. Merrion 3rds finish 6/8 in Section A of the Intermediate League, with 48 per cent, having played 7, won 3, lost 2, drawn 2. They lose to CYM 2nds in the first round of the Intermediate Cup. Merrion 4ths finish 8/8 in Section B of the Intermediate League, with 3 per cent, having played 7, lost 6, drawn 1. They are drawn against Balrothery in the first round of the Intermediate Cup. Merrion 5ths are scheduled to play in the Junior League, but as there is no sign of this team in the end-of-season tables, it must be assumed that they withdraw from the competition. They are drawn against Pembroke 5ths in the first round of the Junior Cup.

PROFILE: ALAN LITTLE

R-H aggressive finisher. R-A slow bowler with three speeds: slow; super-slow; and never quite arriving. There is some suggestion that he bowled slowly so that if he didn't like the ball, he could run after it and get it back, and umpires couldn't give an LBW decision as they weren't entirely sure that the ball would ever reach the stumps. Educated at St Andrews's and Trinity College. Worked as a systems analyst and is now a fully retired ex-computer manager. Also played squash (for Trinity and Universities of Ireland to 1969, and subsequently Mountpleasant and Guinness) and soccer (for Trinity 2nds and 3rds as goalkeeper). The third son of Merrion great C.J. Little. Like Rollie Shortt, he left Merrion twice. He walked off the field in 1965 in the middle of a 2nds game against Old Belvedere in Cabra, because the captain, one John Leonard, refused to bowl him. The following year, he played for Dublin University mainly as a bowler and took 27 wickets, including 8/32 against Leinster, and scored 180 runs in 10 games, batting at No.8 for the team that won the Leinster Senior League for the first time since 1948. During the 1966 season, Merrion won zero games. The second time was in 2002, when he tossed a coin between Bird Avenue and Laois and the splendid doubloon came down Laois. Captain of Merrion 1sts in 1978-79. Played 221 games, scoring 2,621 runs @ 14.72, with a top score of 77 and including 3*50s. Took 35 wickets @ 28.37. Went down the ranks and captained the 2nds and 3rds. Suffered from the 'rush of blood to the head' as a batsman, and could never quite keep his left elbow up high enough, unless it was to suffer from a 'severe case of the bent elbow'. Personally responsible for the downturn in the club's fortunes after the 1950s when he placed a promising young schoolboy's spanking new cricket ball under the heavy roller in a fit of jealousy. Michael Halliday left Merrion as a result, and joined Phoenix.

NB Other teams playing between 1961 and 1970: Eastern Command, Chapelizod, St Ita's.

4.2. THE SEVENTIES: 1971-1980

After a poor start, this decade saw a gradual improvement in the standard of performance of the 1sts, despite a lack of self-belief in some of the Senior players and an intermittent lapse in the will to win. To win or not to win, that was the question. Although no competitions *were* won during these ten years, from 1975-1980 there was the nucleus of a genuine Senior team, capable of taking arms against a sea of troubles called Phoenix, the outstanding side of this period. The addition of professionals at the end of the ten years helped to achieve this, but not as much it should have, and the experiment was swiftly abandoned. In 1980, the Schoolboys won the Under-18 Amoroso Cup, so the future looked bright enough. In 1978, the fourteen-year Senior Cup bogey was laid to rest with victories over Carlisle and Pembroke, followed by a cup final against that same Phoenix side. Having crushed them in a league match the previous week, Merrion 1sts failed to chase a modest total of 234 in 60 overs. The defeat raised the old chestnut of whether it was wise to put the opposition in on an adequate wicket, or whether, as Bradman advised, the captain should have thought very carefully about putting them in, and then batted, regardless of the state of the wicket, or the state of the professional. When interviewed for this book, the captain was asked if he would do the same again. He placed his hand on his heart and said no, but with a suspicious, defiant glint in his eye, which may well have been a reflection in the author's computer screen.

In 1979, the club undertook what was possibly its first overseas tour, of the London area. In between boating competitions and other childish forms of alcohol abuse, some tough games were played against teams like Fords of Dagenham, Sidcup, Orpington and Finchley, and a new trend was set. There would be six more tours over the following twelve years. Junior Merrion fared well during this period, with trophies in 1974 (Intermediate Cup), 1978 (Intermediate C League) and 1979 (Middle League), in addition to some narrow defeats in finals. The middle of this period also saw the welcome beginnings of women's cricket in Merrion.

It was a difficult decade for the club off the field, with much litigation. It began with a fire that destroyed the old corrugated tin pavilion. Suspicions of arson were raised when the gatekeeper Tommy Soraghan spotted members of the 1sts dancing around the ashes at dawn the following morning. After an intense investigation, conducted again by Hercule Poirot, using his little grey cells for about ten seconds, a suitable culprit was found. For legal reasons, he or she cannot be named. But a clue to the arsonist's identity is hidden within the following simple code: SEWENVESVY. This code is known henceforth as the Merrion code, and has nothing whatever to do with the sacred feminine. Damned masculine, more likely. A hint to its solution is provided in the word *Viginere*.

A new pavilion was built, with a proper bar, using the insurance claim and prize bonds, and the club bade farewell to the old tea room, the scary outdoor toilets, the olfactory urinals, the beer and sweets shop, the bearded wooden floors and all that curvy, curvy green tin, without looking back once. An ongoing issue raised its head when the new owners of 43 Anglesea Road, the former residence of the Balfe family, claimed a legal right of way through the ground, when no such right of way had ever been formally instituted. Problems with the abuse of their licence by Bective Rangers Rugby Football Club led to a court case that lingered over the decade like an ugly storm cloud, only to be resolved in 1980 with a judgement that allowed Bective to continue playing, provided they complied with the original agreement. Rather than appeal, legal advice recommended continuing the ninety-year licence until the first thirty-year break in 1986, which Merrion agreed to do.

The most serious issue of this decade involved the Hazeldene extension, when, in 1972, Merrion were given a legal Notice to Quit the one-acre field, by this time an integral part of the playing area. The Hazeldene property was being sold by Stan Greer (a trustee of the club at the time) and he wanted to include this portion of the ground in the sale. Thanks to some fast thinking and moving on the part of the other trustees, notably Tommy Soraghan, Simon Curley and Alex Burns, this outcome was avoided, and the affair resulted in the negotiation of a new boundary wall and a ninety-nine-year sporting lease being signed with the new owners later on in the decade. In 1979, the supposed centenary arrived without much kerfuffle, as no one could be sure when the club had actually started.

In addition to all these trials and tribulations, there were the usual ongoing problems with tractors, trailers and mowers, bar management, security, late subscriptions, the price of fertilizer, water supply, lost cricket balls, practice facilities, collecting tea money, deworming the wickets, irritating schoolboys, what to do about the women and not enough support from the members in the running of the club. Goes without saying, really.

1971: OLD PAVILION GOES UP IN SMOKE; INTERMEDIATE CUP RUNNERS-UP

Senior: fixtures 17, reported 17, won 2, lost 8, drawn 7. President: S.A. Curley. Captain: A.K. Burns. Regulation changes: qualification for the Marchant Cup is increased to 400 runs and for the O'Grady Cup to 40 wickets; in the league, a minimum of 20 overs must be bowled from a point starting one hour before close of play: the Senior Cup is now sponsored by Messrs John Player. Merrion finish 10/11 in the league, courtesy of an injury to Dublin University's main bowler, John Frankland. They play 16, win 2, lose 7, draw 7 and have 25.62 per cent. In one of their two wins, they chase a Railway Union total of 203 for 1. In a draw with Malahide, they are put into bat and leave their opponents 17 overs to bat, forcing Ray Daly to resort to under-arm bowling. Tough. That's what you got in those days, when you put the opposition in to bat. Actually, it can be argued that Merrion are instrumental, along with Clontarf a few weeks later, when Enda McDermott chooses to sacrifice a game rather than bat for some miserly period of time, in forcing the introduction of overs cricket in Leinster, which happens three years later with the introduction of the Wiggins Teape League. They lose to Old Belvedere by 180 runs in the first round of the Senior Cup. There are some fighting draws, but nevertheless, they have now won 11 games out of the last 138.

Alan De Costa is picked to play for South Leinster in the Guinness Cup. First appearance of Kevin O'Herlihy in Merrion colours. Last appearance of Noel Hayden before his return to Enniscorthy. Newcomer Sidney Chetty pummels 315 runs @ 24.23 and snaffles 15 wickets @ 17.46, in his sole season with Merrion. Eddie Lewis chips 436 runs @ 36.33 and comes third in the provincial batting statistics. Alan De Costa compiles 317 runs @ 28.81. In a season when the opposition is bowled out on just two occasions, Dennis Noble purloins 30 wickets @ 17.90 and A. Burns filches 12 wickets @ 26.16:

Opponent	Result	Mer.	Opp.	Best Batting: Runs	Best Bowling: Wickets
Phoenix	Lost	92	95/1	E. Extras: 16	D. Noble: 1/24
Carlisle	Lost	178/9	179/7	E. Lewis: 71*	G. Malek: 2/32
Railway Union	Won	206/7	203/1	A. De Costa: 58	D. Noble: 1/61
DU	Drawn	96/3		A. De Costa: 29	
Old Belvedere (C)	Lost	83	263	A. De Costa: 39	P. Willis: 4/88
YMCA	Won	144	75	E. Lewis: 62	S. Chetty: 4/16
Railway Union	Drawn	172/9	75/6	S. Chetty: 45	K.D. O'Herlihy: 2/9
Clontarf	Lost	129	131/5	N. Hayden: 36	D. Noble: 4/40
Malahide	Drawn	172/4	20/1	S. Chetty: 61*	K.D. O'Herlihy: 1/1
Pembroke	Drawn	122/9	201/8	A. De Costa: 41	E. Lewis: 3/23
Pembroke	Drawn	170/9	126/8	A. De Costa: 48	K.D. O'Herlihy: 3/30
Old Belvedere	Drawn	147	94/9	J. O'Hagan: 32	S. Chetty: 5/30
Leinster	Drawn	78/7	146/6	S. Chetty: 31	A. Burns: 4/40
Malahide	Lost	87	88/4	E. Lewis: 37	S. Chetty: 2/18
Phoenix	Lost	148	152/5	G. Malek: 34*	J. Sterry: 2/30
Old Belvedere	Lost	100	101/6	S. Chetty: 50	J. Sterry: 4/56
Clontarf	Lost	151	169/8	E. Lewis: 46	A. Burns: 2/41

Junior: Merrion 2nds finish 11/13 in the Senior 2 League, with 26.66 per cent, having played 12, won 2, lost 7, drawn 3. This is despite the efforts of a squad that consists of N. Reeves, B. Little, C. Brophy, P. Willis, J. O'Hagan, M. Khan, J. Keogh, E. Bohane, K. Geoghegan, B. Luther, J. Morrissey, M. Cassidy and G. Linehan. They lose to Clontarf 2nds in the first round of the Senior 2 Cup. Merrion 3rds finish 4/8 in Section A of the Intermediate League, with 60 per cent, having played 10, won 6, lost 4. Malahide 3rds chase 177 to beat Merrion in the final of the Intermediate Cup. Merrion 4ths finish 4/9 in Section B of the Intermediate League, with

50 per cent, having played 8, won 4, lost 4. They lose to Old Belvedere 4ths in the first round of the Intermediate Cup. There is no sign of a Merrion 5ths this year.

CLUB NOTES

The pavilion goes up in smoke, probably around November. In the absence of club minutes for this year, it is impossible to expand on this subject. But it did lead to a new pavilion, and many of the younger players were pleased to see the back of the old one. So many thanks, SEWENVESV Y.

PROFILE: DEREK KILPATRICK

R-H solid opening batsman. Very occasional R-A, slow medium bowler. Educated at Friends School, Lisburn and gained a degree in Chemistry at Glasgow University. He worked in the pet-foods industry for ten years, followed by another ten as Managing Director of Crest Foods and eight years as Commercial Director of Avondale Foods. He then moved to the UK to become Managing Director of Hibernia Foods. He retired in 2003 and now divides his time between his home near Edinburgh and winter holidays in Florida. Also played rugby and badminton at school, and squash, tennis and golf in later life. Derek played seventy-eight games for Merrion 1sts between 1970 and 1981, scoring 1,299 runs @ 18.04, with a top score of 74*, and including 3*50s. He also took 9 wickets @ 21.55, 19 catches and was 1sts captain of a weak side in 1973-1974, when the team was imbued with a certain fighting spirit. He remembers many funny moments from his time in Merrion, but one incident stands out:

> ... as if it was yesterday. We were playing Old Belvedere in a limited overs match and I was opening the batting with Danny. As Alec O'Riordan came in to bowl, Danny charged down the wicket. Alec stopped and walked back to his mark. This happened at least four times until a totally exasperated O'Riordan stood at the wicket, glared at Danny and bawled, 'Danny, this is not f-----g cricket.' I don't remember the result but it was immaterial.

1972: HAZELDENE PORTION OF GROUND UNDER THREAT

Senior: fixtures 18, reported 18, won 2, lost 10, drawn 6. President: S.A. Curley. Captain: E. Bohane. Merrion 1sts continue to circle the drain, as Dublin University again deprive them of last place in the Senior League, and they have to be satisfied with 10/11, with 22.35 per cent, having played 17 games, won 2, lost 9, drawn 6. In a game against Leinster, Gerry Duffy scores 51 and takes 5/43. The Senior Cup is now confined to 60 overs per side with 12 overs maximum per bowler, but this is irrelevent to Merrion, as they lose to YMCA in the second round (a bye in the first), after collapsing from 92/4 off 37 overs, chasing 197, to 136 all out. They have now won 13 games out of 156. This year sees the debut of Kevin Allwright and Raj Ramsaroop. Derek Kilpatrick scratches 249 runs @ 20.75. Alan De Costa notches 213 runs @ 21.30. W. Lee Kin steals 145 runs @ 18.12. Brendan Curley hockeys 115 runs @ 16.42. Eddie Lewis pulls 197 runs @ 13.13 and procures 19 wickets @ 17.84. In a season when the opposition is bowled out on three occasions, Dennis Noble pouches 34 wickets @ 16.67 and Joe Keogh wheedles 10 batsmen into throwing away their wicket @ 22.40. Eddie Bohane seizes 11 wickets @ 22.81 in his last season with Merrion 1sts (it's that captaincy thing):

Opponent	Result	Mer.	Opp.	Best Batting: Runs	Best Bowling: Wickets
Carlisle	Drawn	46/2		E. Lewis: 20*	
Railway Union	Lost	59	63/4	G. Malek: 36*	K.D. O'Herlihy: 2/8
Dublin University	Lost	70	148/6	D. Kilpatrick: 14	E. Lewis : 2/12
Leinster	Lost	154	155/8	A. De Costa: 62	D. Noble : 5/35
Phoenix	Drawn	33/3	136	D. Kilpatrick: 12	E. Lewis: 3/17
Railway Union	Drawn	161/6	65/7	D. Kilpatrick: 67*	E. Bohane: 3/12
YMCA (C)	Lost	136	196/8	D. Kilpatrick: 44	D. Noble: 3/28
Clontarf	Lost	69	70/3	E. Lewis: 17	E. Bohane: 1/18
Leinster	Lost	77	78/4	D. Kilpatrick: 20	D. Noble: 2/16
Carlisle	Drawn	173	162/6	D. Kilpatrick: 55	E. Bohane: 3/47
Pembroke	Lost	46	49/2	K. Geoghegan: 12	D. Noble: 2/8
Malahide	Lost	146	147/2	W. Lee Kin: 62*	J. Keogh: 2/50
YMCA	Won	173/8	111	W. Lee Kin: 59	D. Noble: 4/26
YMCA	Drawn	114/9	124	B. Curley: 37	D. Noble: 5/35
Clontarf	Drawn	170/7	192/5	J. O'Hagan: 59	D. Noble: 2/57
Malahide	Lost	70	74/3	D. Parkinson: 30	D. Noble: 2/36
Pembroke	Lost	79	217/2	K. Allwright: 29	A. Burns: 1/48
Old Belvedere	Won	151/7	152/9	D. Noble: 33*	E. Lewis: 4/41

Junior: Merrion 2nds finish 12/13 in the Senior 2 League, with 8 per cent, having played 15, won 1, lost 13, drawn 1. J. Keogh, M. Keogh, K. Gunn, K. Allwright and R. Malek play for this team. They are drawn against CYM in the first round of the Senior 2 Cup. Merrion 3rds finish 5/9 in Section A of the Intermediate League, with 42 per cent, having played 14, won 5, lost 6, drawn 3. They beat Guinness in the first round of the Intermediate Cup, but lose to Clontarf 4ths in the next round, 70 to 72/8, despite Rashid Malek's 40*. Merrion 4ths finish 6/8 in Section B of the Intermediate League, with 37 per cent, having played 12, won 4, lost 7, drawn 1. They are drawn against Rush 2nds in the first round of the Intermediate Cup.

CLUB NOTES

Drama comes to Anglesea Road shortly after 7.00a.m. on Thursday 1 June. The ever-vigilant Tommy Soraghan spies, from the window of his house, some workmen placing a fence along the boundary of the Hazeldene extension. *Que passe?* On 28 April, Merrion had received a Notice to Quit the extra one acre from Seymour (Stan) and Eileen Greer, owners of the Hazeldene property, who have sold the land. And who are also avid members of Merrion Cricket Club, by the way, Stan having been an Hon. Secretary and captain of the 3rds for many years, as well as godfather to at least one of the authors of this book (the atheist). He is also a current trustee, so he's basically sending a Notice to Quit to himself, as well as to Jack O'Donnell, Tommy Soraghan, Simon Curley, Cathal McAlinden and Thomas McAlinden.

The club has already been advised that they have three months from the date of the Notice in which to apply for a sporting lease on the property (area marked **E**). When Simon Curley and Alex Burns arrive at the ground, it transpires that a Mr Brian Leonard and some of his workers are erecting a fence to wire off the Hazeldene extension. Mr Leonard, a builder, claims his right to the property and threatens to plough up the ground during the afternoon. Simon *Schwarzenegger* Curley drives his car between the tripods set to erect the fencing posts, but to no avail. The press and Gardaí are called and Alex Burns informs Mr Leonard that the legal rights of the parties will be determined during the day. Leaving the Gardaí to prevent any rotivation, Simon Curley and Alex Burns spend most of that Thursday in the Four Courts, and by 5.00p.m. an injunction is granted to them to restrain any unauthorised person from entering the club grounds. They are also given the authority to remove the fence. This happens the following day and the ground is available for the weekend games. Phew!

Subsequently, maps are exchanged so that boundaries can be carefully marked out. Although the club doesn't quite own 75 per cent of the total ground, a deal is done with the eventual builders of the apartment block – Sheelin Homes – whereby Merrion get the ninety-nine-year lease in return for not opposing the development and allowing them to include the leased area in their plot ratio (this enables Sheelin Homes to build more apartments). The lease applies from 1 January 1974, and is negotiated under the Landlord and Tenant (Amendment) Act, 1971.

PROFILE: RAJ RAMSAROOP

L-H stroke-player with a wide array of shots. R-A slow leg-break bowler. Originally from South Africa, Raj played 103 games for Merrion 1sts between 1972 and 1983, scoring 1,999 runs @ 20.82, including 1 century and 8*50s, and with a top score of 125. He took 156 wickets @ 18.78, including 5 wickets in an innings on 7 occasions. His low tally of 19 catches in 103 matches illustrates his fielding ability, which might be regarded as the weakest part of his game. Played representative cricket for South Leinster in the Guinness Cup. Raj is the only player of the modern era to feature as both a Centurion and a Gladiator in the statistics, and is only the third in the club's history, after Simon Curley and Cecil Little. Many years after his return to South Africa, Raj was working in the security business, when tragedy struck. He was shot and badly wounded. His recovery led to his confinement to a wheelchair, for which we wish this talented Merrion all-round cricketer nothing but good thoughts.

1973: A NEW FIGHTING SPIRIT EMERGES

Senior: fixtures 17, reported 17, won 3, lost 6, drawn 8. President: S.A. Curley. Captain: D. Kilpatrick. Merrion achieve their best Senior League position since 1963 when they finish 7/11, with 33.75 per cent, having played 16, won 3, lost 5, drawn 8. Phoenix beat them in the first round of the Senior Cup. There is much evidence in this season of a more fighting attitude, with many draws and some stonewall batting. Nevertheless, they have now won 16 games out of 173. Dennis Noble plays for South Leinster in the Guinness Cup. Raj Ramsaroop plays for South Leinster in an Under-19 interprovincial match. Eddie Lewis grooves 235 runs @ 26.11 and snaffles 10 wickets @ 28.90. Derek Kilpatrick squirts 334 runs @ 23.85. Brendan Curley hockeys 237 runs @ 26.33. Ghulam Malek paddles 192 runs @ 32.00. Raj Ramsaroop cuts 146 runs @ 12.16 and pilfers 25 wickets @ 19.20. In a season when the opposition is bowled out once (largely due to Derek Kilpatrick's bowling), Dennis Noble is second in the provincial bowling statistics, with 41 wickets @ 17.60:

Opponent	Result	Mer.	Opp.	Best Batting: Runs	Best Bowling: Wickets
Pembroke	Lost	90	91/5	J. Keogh: 17*	J. Keogh: 3/45
Old Belvedere	Drawn	92/8	164/9	E. Lewis: 29	D. Noble: 8/61
Malahide	Drawn	90/7	152/4	D. Kilpatrick: 29	D. Noble: 3/61
Phoenix (C)	Lost	96	97/5	B. Curley: 25	R. Ramsaroop: 2/11
Carlisle	Lost	138	142/3	R. Ramsaroop: 39	R. Ramsaroop: 2/38
Clontarf	Drawn	157/8	184/4	E. Lewis: 77	R. Ramsaroop: 3/67
Leinster	Drawn	197/8	126/6	J. O'Hagan: 41*	J. O'Hagan: 2/17
Phoenix	Won	170/5	166/4	J. Keogh: 31	R. Ramsaroop: 3/34
YMCA	Drawn	54/4	138/6	D. Kilpatrick: 24*	J. O'Hagan: 2/22
Railway Union	Won	169/9	172/4	J. Morrissey: 55*	R. Ramsaroop: 6/53
YMCA	Drawn	59/5	135/9	D. Kilpatrick: 17*	D. Noble: 3/46
Carlisle	Drawn	196/9	164/7	G. Malek: 56	E. Lewis: 3/37
Clontarf	Lost	100	173/8	E. Lewis: 51	D. Noble: 4/46
DU	Lost	168/8	169/8	G. Malek: 37*	D. Noble: 4/51
Leinster	Drawn	133/8	179/4	D. Noble: 45	E. Lewis: 1/22
Old Belvedere	Lost	102	153/9	R. Malek: 30	R. Ramsaroop: 4/34
Railway Union	Won	122/7	120	G. Malek: 47	D. Kilpatrick: 4/20

Junior: Merrion 2nds finish 11/13 in the Senior 2 League, with 29 per cent, having played 16, won 3, lost 8, drawn 5. They lose to YMCA 2nds in the first round of the Senior 2 Cup, 30 to 96. Norman Reeves's team includes Donagh McDonald, Colm Brophy, Ken McDonald, Dermot Soraghan (who scores 58* against CYM) and Danny Parkinson. Merrion 3rds finish 8/9 in Section A of the Intermediate League, with 29 per cent, having played 13, won 3, lost 7, drawn 3. They beat Clontarf 4ths in the second round of the Intermediate Cup, 106 to 79, but lose to The Hills in the next round, 47 to 229/7. Peter Geoffroy's team includes Kieran and Derek O'Herlihy, Paul Short, Mick Keogh and C. O'Kelly. Merrion 4ths finish 10/10 in Section B of the Intermediate League, with 20 per cent, having played 16, won 2, lost 11, drawn 3. They lose to Rush 2nds in the first round of the Intermediate Cup, 84 to 174. Tom McGeady's team includes Patsy Keogh, Des Murray, Cathal McAlinden, Vinny Finnegan and Chris Mara, who, still shuntering away at sixty-two, claims a hat-trick against Man-O-War 2nds.

CLUB NOTES

A sign of the trouble that is to come with Bective Rangers is revealed in some acrimonious correspondence relating to the late payment of rent.

PROFILE: JOE KEOGH

R-H middle-order batsman. R-A steady, accurate, medium pace seam bowler. Educated at St Mary's College, although he didn't play cricket until the age of nineteen. Worked as a service engineer in the central heating business, initially for Heatovent and subsequently for himself. He also played table tennis for Glenalbyn in Division 1 of the Leinster League, and now plays tennis and recreational golf. Joe came up through the Junior teams in Merrion and featured in ninety-eight games for the 1sts between 1972 and 1978, scoring 585 runs @ 7.04, with a top score of 37. He took 119 wickets @ 24.25, with 5 wickets in an innings on 5 occasions, and best figures of 8/59, in addition to 44 catches. He was a part of the first South Leinster side to win the Guinness Cup and came close to international selection. In the middle of the 1978 season, he resigned from the club to join Railway Union, where he continued to take wickets regularly. He is a member of an extended family of ex-Merrion cricketers, which includes his brothers Mick and Patsy, his sister Anne and ex-brother-in-law Kevin O'Herlihy, and his brothers and children, all of whom contributed much to the history of Merrion over the years.

1974: A NEW PAVILION; INTERMEDIATE CUP WINNERS; UNDER-13 MINI-CRICKET CUP WINNERS

Senior: fixtures 19, reported 19, won 3, lost 10, drawn 5, no result 1. President: S.A. Curley. Captain: D. Kilpatrick. The season is split between the old Senior League, with everyone playing each other once, and a new 50-over competition, sponsored by Wiggins Teape for £1,000. This is bad news for Merrion, as draws are no longer an option. Dublin University don't play in the new competition. The Senior League rules are further changed: cancelled matches will be refixed; unfinished matches will be refixed if three or more hours are lost from the official starting time, due to weather; points will be awarded, rather than percentages (4 for a win, 2 for a tie, 1 for a draw), and there's a new trophy in memory of A. O'Donnell presented by Clontarf CC. Merrion tie with Railway Union at 9/11, with 9 points, having played 9, won 1, lost 3, drawn 5. Railway Union beat them narrowly in the second round (bye in the first) of the Senior Cup. In the Wiggins Teape League, they finish 9/10, with 22 points, and no money won, having played 9, won 2, lost 6, no result 1. Merrion have now won 19 games out of the last 192. Gerry Murphy of Phoenix is the winner of the first provincial cup for wicket-keepers, named after J. Hopkins of Pembroke, and presented by his son, ex-Merrion member J.K. Hopkins. Eddie Lewis plays for South Leinster. He grooves 462 runs @ 27.23 and fiddles 13 wickets @ 22.23. Derek Kilpatrick scrapes 246 runs @ 16.40. Dermot Soraghan nicks 146 runs @ 11.23. Kevin Allwright hoicks 156 runs @ 12.00. John O'Hagan hooks 241 runs @ 26.77 and delivers 10 wickets @ 31.30. Raj Ramsaroop swipes 242 runs @ 22.00 and snatches 12 wickets @ 31.50. Joe Keogh edges 168 runs @ 12.92 and snaffles 14 wickets @ 25.21, including 8/59 against Railway Union, his absolute favourite club. Paddy Willis returns from yet another two-year break, to grab 25 wickets @ 18.00. But it's Dennis Noble, by name and nature, who is the mainstay of Merrion's bowling yet again, with 37 wickets @ 14.91:

Opponent	Result	Mer.	Opp.	Best Batting: Runs	Best Bowling: Wickets
Malahide	Drawn	104/6	166/4	R. Ramsaroop: 27	
DU	Lost	57	133	D. Kilpatrick: 9	R. Ramsaroop: 6/40
Old Belvedere	Lost	89	161/6	J. Keogh: 35	D. Kilpatrick: 2/13
Phoenix	Won	125	92	K. Allwright: 48	P. Willis: 7/35
YMCA	Drawn	164/6	87/6	E. Lewis: 78	D. Noble: 4/25
Carlisle	Drawn	211/5	111/5	R. Ramsaroop: 78	P. Willis: 2/18
Railway Union (C)	Lost	183	189	D. Kilpatrick: 48	J. O'Hagan: 2/34
Clontarf	Lost	136	201/5	R. Ramsaroop: 49	P. Willis: 2/50
Leinster	Drawn	156/9	67/3	D. Soraghan: 49	E. Lewis: 3/9
Railway Union	Drawn	141	91/2	E. Lewis: 29	B. Curley: 1/1

Wiggins Teape

Carlisle	Lost	152/8	197/7	E. Lewis: 29	P. Willis: 4/76
Old Belvedere	Lost	110	133/8	J. O'Hagan: 32	D. Noble: 3/38
Clontarf	Lost	78	102	D. Soraghan: 31	D. Noble: 7/45
YMCA	Lost	143	144/6	E. Lewis: 36	D. Noble: 4/52
Pembroke	Lost	135	186/6	J. O'Hagan: 44	D. Noble: 6/53
Malahide	Won	180/9	167	E. Lewis: 56	J. O'Hagan: 5/43
Leinster	Won	189	173	J. O'Hagan: 64	D. Noble: 2/21
Railway Union	Lost	116/9	155	J. O'Hagan: 27	J. Keogh: 8/59
Phoenix	No Res.		91/0		

Junior: In their best season for years, Merrion 2nds finish 5/13 in the Senior 2 League, with 48 per cent, having played 12, won 5, lost 4, drawn 3. Danny Parkinson's side loses to YMCA 2nds, 161 to 162/5, in the first round of the Senior 2 Cup, despite Joe Keogh's 31 and John O'Hagan's 29. Alex Burns, Norman Reeves, Eddie Bohane, Donagh McDonald, Denis McKenna and Paul Short complete the make-up of this team. Merrion 3rds finish 6/9 in Section A of the Intermediate League, with 43 per cent, having played 7, won 2, lost 2, drawn 3. Philip Herron's team beats Clontarf 4ths, 129 to 84, in the first round of the Intermediate Cup, with the captain purloining 6/17. They continue to win games against Railway Union 3rds and Man-O-War 2nds to reach the final against YMCA 3rds. A close finish provides Merrion's first trophy win since 1961, as they chase 122, to win by 2 wickets. Simon Curley briefly relives his gilded youth with 36 runs, while Kieran O'Herlihy provides support with 21. Mick Keogh manages 3/22. Merrion 4ths finish 5/9 in Section B of the Intermediate League, with 46 per cent, having played 14, won 6, lost 8. Des Murray's team includes P. Keogh, C. O'Kelly, R. Clarke, J. Walsh, P. Soraghan, B. McArdle, D. Bartley, K. McDonald and L. St John. They lose to Leinster 4ths in the first round of the Intermediate Cup, 31 to 280/7. Under Paddy Willis's guidance, the Under-13s win the inaugural Mini-Cricket competition.

CLUB NOTES

This year the new pavilion is finished and it includes a real *bar*. Not just a beer and sweeties shop that has to be closed by 10.00p.m., but a proper den of iniquity. It is not recorded as to whether ladies are being served *intoxicating liquor* at this time. We can only hope that this is the case. Subscriptions for Senior playing members this season are £7. The signing of the new lease for the Hazeldene portion of the ground is delayed, as there are plans to have squash courts built by Squash Ireland at the side of the pavilion. Needless to say, these plans do not materialise. At a Management Committee Meeting (MCM) in November, it is reported that a planning application has been made to build a three-storey apartment block on the site of Hazeldene. Meanwhile the ongoing problems with Bective Rugby Club continue, with a forced entry to the toolshed and damage to the cricket square from the boundary markings of the rugby pitch.

PROFILE: PETER GEOFFROY

R–H batsman, a ferret at Senior level, but rather more than a rabbit on Junior teams. Slow L–A bowler who still makes an excellent job of pretending to spin the ball. Educated at Wilson's Hospital and Mountjoy College. Gained a PhD in Biochemistry. Worked in industry for many

Merrion 3rds, 1974
Intermediate Cup winners.
Back row: W. Brogan, C.
Campbell, K. McDonald,
F. O'Flynn, M. Keogh,
G. Doyle. Front row: K.J.
O'Herlihy, S. Curley, P.
Herron (C), T. McGeady,
R. Clarke.

years, before becoming a dealer in old collectibles, mainly coins and stamps. Also played squash and rugby. Peter joined Merrion in 1967 and since then has held the office of Hon. Secretary for seven years, first in the seventies and then in the noughties. He also held the position of Team Secretary over countless years. He captained the 2nds, 3rds and 6ths, and has played for all teams, including thirty-eight games for Merrion 1sts, when he was picked on a weak side mainly as a fielder. At gully, Peter saved many a certain 4 and pulled off many a spectacular catch. Married to ex-Merrion women's star Sandie, Peter spends his summer weekends patiently by the phone, dressed in his cricket gear and practising his shot, waiting for that last-minute call to action. From any captain. He is actually still available for the 1sts, believe it or not.

1975: BOTTOM OF BOTH LEAGUES

Senior: fixtures 19, reported 19, won 1, lost 14, drawn 4. President: S.A. Curley. Captain: D. Noble. In a season in which Phoenix win all three competitions, Merrion do the opposite. They finish last in the Senior League, with 7 points, having played 9, lost 5, drawn 4. They lose badly to Old Belvedere in the first round of the Senior Cup, the final of which is played at Anglesea Road for the first time. They finish joint bottom of the Wiggins Teape, with Carlisle, who also have 10 points and no money, having played 9, won 1, lost 8. Merrion 1sts have now won 20 games out of the last 211, and the counting has to stop, due to author fatigue. There are nine double-digit scores out of nineteen this year, indicating a problem with the batting, but the addition of Mike Bryce and Peter McWilliam does add depth, and it's true that Merrion fail to translate some close results into victories. Eddie Lewis plays for South Leinster in the Guinness Cup, scoring 94* against Ulster Country. For Merrion, he drives 243 runs @ 20.25. Derek Kilpatrick chips 161 runs @ 16.10. Brendan Curley hockeys 306 runs @ 20.40. Raj Ramsaroop has 346 runs @ 18.21 and 12 wickets @ 31.50. Dermot Soraghan hoicks 170 runs @ 17.00. Dennis Noble soldiers on for 31 wickets @ 15.61 in his last year of captaincy. Joe Keogh grabs 22 wickets @ 25.45:

Opponent	Result	Mer.	Opp.	Best Batting: Runs	Best Bowling: Wickets
DU	Drawn	143/9	97/6	E. Lewis: 75	D. Noble: 3/16
YMCA	Drawn	157/9	165	B. Curley: 49	J. Keogh: 5/34
Pembroke	Drawn	137/9	139/7	E. Lewis: 45	D. Noble: 3/21
Phoenix	Lost	94	174/7	D. Kilpatrick: 20	P. Willis: 3/48
Old Belvedere (C)	Lost	55	201/4	B. Curley: 25	D. Noble: 2/40
Clontarf	Lost	85	86/1	J. Morrissey: 23	A. Little: 1/41
Old Belvedere	Lost	138/9	142/6	D. Kilpatrick: 74	D. Noble: 3/39
Carlisle	Drawn	184/9	188/4	B. Curley: 56*	A. Little: 2/54
Malahide	Lost	162	163/2	R. Ramsaroop: 41	K.J. O'Herlihy: 1/6
Railway Union	Lost	160	161/4	D. Soraghan: 49	K.J. O'Herlihy: 2/28
Wiggins Teape					
Railway Union	Lost	68	69/2	R. Ramsaroop: 31	D. Noble: 1/17
Phoenix	Lost	95	208/2	B. Curley: 34	K.D. O'Herlihy: 1/36
Carlisle	Won	136/6	132	E. Lewis: 37	J. Stephens: 5/7
Clontarf	Lost	157	183/6	R. Ramsaroop: 68	D. Noble: 4/44
Pembroke	Lost	96	172/8	P. McWilliam: 27	J. O'Hagan: 4/57
Old Belvedere	Lost	133/9	136/4	M. Bryce: 46	D. Noble: 2/25
Malahide	Lost	83	172/9	R. Ramsaroop: 26	D. Noble: 3/36
YMCA	Lost	52	72	R. Ramsaroop: 16	J. Keogh: 7/26
Leinster	Lost	69	136	D. Parkinson: 27	R. Ramsaroop: 3/33

Junior: Merrion 2nds finish 8/13 in the Senior 2 League, with 35 per cent, having played 17, won 4, lost 8, drawn 5. Peter Geoffroy's team includes Barry Little, Mike Bryce, Kevin O'Herlihy, Joe Keogh, Alex Burns and Dermot Soraghan, who scores 107 against Leinster 2nds. Joe Keogh takes 8/22 against Man-O-War. They lose to Malahide 2nds in the first round of the Senior 2 Cup. Merrion 3rds finish 5/9 in Section A of the Intermediate League, with 53 per cent, having played 13, won 5, lost 4, drawn 4. Tom McGeady is their best batsman, with 320 runs, while Dick Clarke takes 25 wickets. Fergus O'Flynn's team loses to Leinster 4ths in the preliminary round of the Intermediate Cup. Merrion 4ths finish 7/9 in Section B of the Intermediate League, with 43 per cent, having played 13, won 5, lost 6, drawn 2. Des Murray's team includes Jim Scully, Frank Curley, Derek O'Herlihy, Denis McKenna, Frank Nugent, Jim Walsh and Geoff Smith. They beat Guinness in the first round of the Intermediate Cup, but lose in the next round.

CLUB NOTES

A suggestion that the collection and reselling of waste paper might be a means of increasing revenue, gets off the ground at an early MCM, when Simon Curley suggests that the waste paper could be stored in the old hen house at the back of Hazeldene. This matter is subsequently left up in the air. Merrion's ground is now being used occasionally to provide car parking for exhibitions in the RDS as well as the Spring and Horse Shows. A decision is made to build a wall from the end of the pavilion, across the entrance, to ensure privacy. A Taverners team is set up by Jim Scully. A meeting agrees that schoolboys should not frequent the clubhouse. A decision is made to form a women's committee. Dennis Noble resigns from the position of captain of the 1sts over the mishandling of a match with Leinster at Anglesea Road, when Merrion fail to turn up. The club receives plans for the new flats at Hazeldene and agrees to negotiate a more favourable boundary line.

At a meeting towards the end of this year, after several years of repeated breaches of the agreement, with late payments of rent, use of the ground on non-prescribed days and failure to maintain the playing fields, a decision is taken to revoke the licence dated 14 July 1956 with Bective, whereby they are permitted to play rugby on certain fixed, limited occasions. Bective arrive at the ground shortly afterwards to erect goal posts and are refused permission. Subsequently, Bective sue Merrion and solicitors are engaged on both sides, with the Supreme and High Courts getting involved. This problem spans the remainder of the decade. Simon Curley reports that schoolboys have been letting off fireworks in the changing rooms. The Hon. Secretary is empowered to write to the parents concerned. At the Annual General Meeting (AGM), both Simon Curley and Jim Byrne, the groundsman, are commended for their work on the wickets, especially the Cup final preparations. Danny Parkinson suggests that a professional be employed to strengthen the 1sts and to organise coaching. At a subsequent MCM, it is agreed that Robin Waters be approached with a view to coaching Merrion.

PROFILE: KEVIN O'HERLIHY

R-H late middle-order batsman, R-A, slow off-break bowler. Educated at Belvedere and Blackrock Colleges. Worked as a Meteorological Officer for Met Éireann until he was forced to retire in 1994, suffering from Multiple Sclerosis. Also played soccer, rugby and tennis, and now spoils good walks with a handicap of 4. Was in the Munster badminton and fishing squads. Kevin played 155 games for Merrion 1sts between 1971 and 1981, scoring 691 runs @ 9.21, with a top score of 40*. He took an impressive 208 wickets @ 20.05, with best figures of 7/71, including 5 wickets in an innings on 8 occasions and a hat-trick in 1980. He also managed to hang onto 56 catches. Captain in 1981, after which his job led him to Shannon Airport, where he played for Limerick and captained Munster in the Guinness Cup from 1983 to 1988, missing out on an international cap due to the ever-present Michael Halliday.

He and his cricketing spouse Anne captained Munster men and women at cricket on the same day – surely a unique achievement. Their four children, Patrick, Michael, Kevin Jnr and Ian all came up through the Schoolboy and Junior ranks of Merrion, before moving elsewhere. Also a unique achievement. Kevin went to Thailand in 2001 to see if the use of Thai traditional medicine could improve his condition. As a result, he is no longer confined to a wheelchair and can enjoy life in a hot climate with his new wife Marisa and their daughter Emma. Kevin's favourite trick after a few pints was to travel to the ground of an away match late the night before, and 'do a Poder' freely on the end of the wicket he would be bowling to the next day. Especially Phoenix. So now we know where all those wickets came from.

1976: MINI-CRICKET COMPETITION WINNERS; UNDER-13A LEAGUE WINNERS; UNDER-13B LEAGUE RUNNERS-UP; UNDER-15 LEAGUE RUNNERS-UP

Senior: fixtures 20, reported 20, won 8, lost 10, drawn 2. President: T. Soraghan. Captain: E. Lewis. The Senior League regulations are changed to cater for a situation where both sides bowl the same number of overs in a normal drawn match, in which case each gets 2½ points. This glorious summer is recorded elsewhere as the beginning of a false dawn, but for the players who struggle to win a competition over the following ten years, it seems like a real sunrise. For the first time in many bleak seasons, Merrion have the makings of a genuine 1sts, capable of competing with the likes of Phoenix, a team that wins 13/30 competitions between 1974 and 1983. Merrion finish 6/11 in the Senior League, with 53 points, having played 10, won 4, lost 4, drawn 2. They lose to Leinster in the second round (bye in the first) of the Senior Cup. In the Wiggins Teape, they finish 5/10, with 40 points, having played 9, won 4, lost 5. They win £65, along with Leinster, Pembroke and Railway Union, with whom they share fifth place. Yet they are just three close losses – by margins of 5 runs, 2 wickets, 3 wickets – away from winning this league, and the £300 jackpot.

A tour of Cork is undertaken. Joe Keogh, Raj Ramsaroop and Eddie Lewis play for South Leinster in the Guinness Cup. Raj Ramsaroop is tenth in the provincial batting rankings and second in the list of provincial all-rounders (qualification: 200 runs and 20 wickets). He notches 447 runs @ 31.92, including a ton against Carlisle, and grabs 40 wickets @ 15.55. Eddie Lewis is fourteenth in the provincial batting averages and fifth in the all-rounders' statistics, with 589 runs @ 31.00 and 22 wickets @ 18.36. Brendan Curley beavers on for 258 runs @ 18.42. John O'Hagan hooks 246 runs @ 27.33. Peter McWilliam nurdles a gritty 239 runs @ 17.07. Joe Keogh bores another 34 batsmen to death @ 17.35. Kevin O'Herlihy pilfers 30 wickets @ 15.73. Dennis Noble adds another 13 wickets to his growing tally, @ 17.00. He has now taken over 400 wickets for Merrion, and is the fourth and last player to do so:

Opponent	Result	Mer.	Opp.	Best Batting: Runs	Best Bowling: Wickets
Leinster	Drawn	148/8	191/4	E. Lewis: 63	J. Keogh: 2/48
Old Belvedere	Drawn	139	63/7	B. Curley: 51	J. Keogh: 3/20
Clontarf	Lost	182	188	R. Ramsaroop: 87	R. Ramsaroop: 5/60
Phoenix	Lost	112	113/3	A. Little: 42	R. Ramsaroop: 2/25
Malahide	Lost	73	183/6	D. Noble: 13	D. Noble: 3/51
Carlisle	Won	133	103	J. Bastable: 29	J. Keogh: 6/38
Railway Union	Lost	72	73/6	B. Curley: 19	D. Noble: 3/11
DU	Won	84/8	82	R. Ramsaroop: 36	J. Keogh: 4/23
YMCA	Won	162/3	160/6	P. McWilliam: 67*	J. Keogh: 4/55
Leinster (C)	Lost	107	108/3	E. Lewis: 30	E. Lewis: 2/16
Pembroke	Won	192/8	173	E. Lewis: 77	E. Lewis: 3/24
Wiggins Teape					
Railway Union	Lost	101	135/9	R. Ramsaroop: 29	R. Ramsaroop: 5/58
Carlisle	Won	265/2	148/8	R. Ramsaroop: 125	E. Lewis: 4/21
Old Belvedere	Lost	163/8	168/9	E. Lewis: 40	K.D. O'Herlihy: 7/71
Malahide	Lost	152	154/7	J. O'Hagan: 62	J. Walsh: 3/9
Pembroke	Lost	111	112/8	E. Lewis: 44	K.D. O'Herlihy: 5/47
Phoenix	Won	156/6	78	P. McWilliam: 37	J. Keogh: 4/41
YMCA	Won	185	136	E. Lewis: 45	R. Ramsaroop: 7/61
Leinster	Won	125	122	J. O'Hagan: 40	K.D. O'Herlihy: 7/42
Clontarf	Lost	135	181	R. Ramsaroop: 60	

Junior: Merrion 2nds finish 10/13 in the Senior 2 League, with 44 per cent, having played 15, won 6, lost 7, drawn 2. Danny Parkinson's team includes J. Bastable, B. Dowling, P. Coghlan, J. Morrissey, K.J. O'Herlihy, F. Curley, K. McDonald and K. Allwright, home from England on holiday, who wins the Bookman Cup for batting with an average of 76.00 from 5 games – 56,

121*, 107, 10, 10. The rules for this competition are changed as a result, to ensure that at least 8 innings are completed. They lose to Clontarf 2nds in the first round of the Senior 2 Cup, 169 to 170/8. The final of this competition is to be held at Anglesea Road the week after the Horse Show. Merrion 3rds finish 9/9 in Section A of the Intermediate League, with 11 per cent, having played 13, won 0, lost 9, drawn 4. Mick Keogh's team includes C. Campbell, E. Bohane, S. Adamson, B. Carter, J. Scully, K. Gunn, D. Heffernan, P. Willis, F. O'Flynn and P. Herron. They beat YMCA 3rds in the first round of the Intermediate Cup, 77 to 43, but lose to Clontarf 4ths in the next round, 77 to 78/3. Merrion 4ths finish 10/10 in Section B of the Intermediate League, with 14 per cent, having played 17, won 2, lost 13, drawn 2. Frank Nugent's team includes D. Murray, R. Clarke, J. McGeady, C. Mara, A. McKenna, A. Lydiat and E. Kearon. They are drawn against Man-O-War 2nds/Old Belvedere 4ths in the second round of the Intermediate Cup. Merrion Schoolboys are runners-up in the Under-15 League, with tons from Paul Coghlan and John McGeady. Coghlan, McGeady, Jim Walsh and Ken McDonald play for a successful South Leinster Under-19s. The Schoolboys win the Under-13A League and are runners-up in the Under-13B League; they also win the Mini-Cricket Cup. League medals are presented to the Under-13 side by Colin Cowdrey.

CLUB NOTES

An early meeting reports that Robin Waters is not available to coach Merrion this coming season. Later on, the tractor goes on fire, having been repaired by Massey Ferguson. The Bective issue rumbles along in the background all season, with the rugby club taking legal action against Merrion. The exact placement of the boundary wall is discussed with the builders of the new Hazeldene flats. The annual supper is organised, at £2 a head. At the AGM, Danny Parkinson suggests hiring out the ground in the winter to a hockey club. A centenary committee is set up, chaired by Danny Parkinson, to organise events for the coming 100-year anniversary in 1979. Jimmy McAlinden and Cecil Little are elected Life Members. A motion to allow associate status to women players is defeated, opposed by many members who feel that it would be wrong for female members to have voting rights. After all, as a majority at an AGM, they might imbibe some *intoxicating liquor* at the bar and vote to flog the joint!

PROFILE: KEN McDONALD

R-H opening batsman. Wicket-keeper. Educated at Blackrock College and UCD, where he qualified from medical school in 1981. He trained in Vincent's and worked at the University of Minnesota from 1988 onwards. He is now a Consultant Cardiologist in St Vincent's Hospital and lectures in heart failure at UCD. Ken came up through the Schoolboy and Junior ranks within Merrion and became 1sts captain in 1980. He played 178 games between 1974 and 1987, scoring 1,783 runs @ 13.01, with a top score of 132*, and including 2*50s. As wicket-keeper, he took 127 catches and 36 stumpings and is ranked third in the all-time list. Professor McDonald is a heart surgeon and chairman of the Irish Heart Foundation Council on heart failure, so if you wake up some day with him bending over you, scalpel in hand, and you hear the immortal phrase, '*ah, lads*', you will know that it is time to greet the great umpire in the sky.

1977: INTERMEDIATE LEAGUE RUNNERS-UP; INTERMEDIATE CUP RUNNERS-UP; NINETY-NINE-YEAR SPORTING LEASE FOR HAZELDENE EXTENSION AGREED

Senior: fixtures 20, reported 20, won 5, lost 11, drawn 4. President: J. McAlinden. Captain: E. Lewis. The false dawn is slightly dimmer this year, as Merrion finish 7/11 in the Senior League, with 37 points, having played 10, won 2, lost 4, drawn 4. Phoenix hammer them in the second round (bye in the first) of the Senior Cup. In the Wiggins Teape, they finish 8/10, with 30 points, having played 9, won 3, lost 6. They win £25 in prize money. Joe Keogh and Eddie Lewis play for South Leinster in the Guinness Cup. Eddie Lewis is third in the provincial all-rounders' statistics, with 425 runs @ 21.25 and 26 wickets @ 13.03. Raj Ramsaroop is ninth in the same table, with 381 runs @ 19.05 and 29 wickets @ 15.96. Brendan Curley hockeys 214 runs @ 11.88. Peter McWilliam nurdles 186 runs @ 13.28. John O'Hagan pulls 241 runs @ 15.06. In the season that the venerable Dennis Noble plays his last game for Merrion 1sts, Joe Keogh steals 24 wickets @ 26.37, Kevin O'Herlihy somehow fiddles 27 wickets @ 17.88 and Mick Mills delivers 13 wickets @ 26.38:

Opponent	Result	Mer.	Opp.	Best Batting: Runs	Best Bowling: Wickets
Clontarf	Drawn	94/9	138/6	E. Lewis: 48	K.D. O'Herlihy: 4/51
Pembroke	Lost	110	130/7	R. Ramsaroop: 33	K.D. O'Herlihy: 3/27
Phoenix	Lost	66	127	K.J. O'Herlihy: 20	E. Lewis: 5/24
DU	Lost	84	85/4	A. Little: 19	J. Keogh: 4/42
Malahide	Lost	74	151	D. Harkin: 16*	R. Ramsaroop: 5/27
Carlisle	Drawn	173	157/7	E. Lewis: 69	J. Keogh: 4/46
Railway Union	Drawn	148/8	162/9	J. O'Hagan: 66	K.D. O'Herlihy: 6/64
Phoenix (C)	Lost	60	62/2	D. Kilpatrick: 21	M. Mills: 2/22
YMCA	Won	174/8	171/7	E. Lewis: 60	K.D. O'Herlihy: 4/57
Leinster	Drawn	131	97/9	B. Curley: 41	R. Ramsaroop: 4/24
Old Belvedere	Won	134	64	E. Lewis: 54	M. Mills: 4/26
Wiggins Teape					
Pembroke	Lost	106	107/4	E. Lewis: 19	M. Mills: 2/39
Phoenix	Lost	76/6	170/2	P. Coghlan: 19	M. Mills: 1/61
Old Belvedere	Lost	67	68/4	J. Morrissey: 16	E. Lewis: 2/14
Carlisle	Won	189/8	116	E. Lewis: 60	E. Lewis: 5/25
YMCA	Lost	209/8	210/5	R. Ramsaroop: 88	R. Ramsaroop: 3/43
Malahide	Won	169/7	159	R. Ramsaroop: 56	J. Keogh: 5/41
Clontarf	Lost	121/7	122/3	P. McWilliam: 37	R. Ramsaroop: 3/32
Railway Union	Won	123/7	122	R. Ramsaroop: 50	R. Ramsaroop: 6/45
Leinster	Lost	85	88/3	J. O'Hagan: 22	J. Keogh: 2/47

Junior: Merrion 2nds finish 6/13 in the Senior 2 League, with 44 per cent, having played 16, won 6, lost 8, drawn 2. Danny Parkinson's team includes D. Noble, B. Little, A. Little, P. McWilliam, M. Mills, B. Carter and K.J. O'Herlihy. They lose to Pembroke 2nds in the second round of the Senior 2 Cup, 81 to 176, despite Denis McKenna's obdurate 24 and Paddy Willis's 5/42. Danny resigns during the season and Alan Little takes over. Merrion 3rds finish 2/10 in Section A of the Intermediate League, with 67 per cent, having played 14, won 8, lost 1, drawn 5. Mick Keogh's team includes P. Herron, D. Soraghan, D. O'Herlihy, J. Bryant, J. McGeady and B. Dowling. They beat Kilbride, Carlisle 3rds, Guinness (162 to 40) and Merrion 4ths, before reaching the final of the Intermediate Cup, which they lose to Mullingar, 112 to 135. Merrion 4ths finish 6/10 in Section B of the Intermediate League, with 35 per cent, having played 17, won 4, lost 7, drawn 6. Des Murray's team includes C. Mara, D. McKenna, M. Abrahams, A. McKenna, G. Curtis, J. O'Brien and the memorable Stafford Gordon. They lose the semi-final of the Intermediate Cup to Merrion 3rds. Merrion Schoolboys are 3/10 in the Under-18 League, with 10 points, having played 8, won 5, lost 3. Derek O'Herlihy, John McGeady and Paul Coghlan are selected to play for the South Leinster Under-19s. Merrion A come 5/12 in the Under-15 League, with 20 points, having played 7, won 5, lost 2. Merrion B come 10/12 in the same league, with 7 points, having played 8, won 1, lost 4, drawn 3. Robbie Stanton and Richard Willis play for the South Leinster Under-15s. Merrion finish 6/8 in the Under-13 League (Southern Section), with 6 points, having played 7, won 3, lost 4.

CLUB NOTES

A January meeting decides to ascertain the exact age of the club, in preparation for the 1979 celebrations. Priorities for the coming year include levelling the outfield, improving the pavilion and providing a bar storeroom. A letter is written to Mr John Stanton concerning his continuous misuse of the club's premises. An August meeting agrees that the bar needs better control, as people are observed leaving it in a drunken state, especially after Taverners matches and including the pair who are supposed to be managing it. A decision is made to sink a well that can be used to water the wickets in times of drought. Another meeting decides to give six cricket balls to the women's team in recognition of their tea making.

Danny Parkinson resigns from Merrion, as a reaction to his being disciplined for obstreperousness during a match, but is persuaded to withdraw his resignation by the Hon. Secretary. Simon Curley reports that some youths have damaged the aerial of his car. At the AGM, the Hon. Secretary reports that a decision on the Bective court case depends on whether the club's agreement is held to be a licence or a lease. A licence does not grant exclusive possession, whereas a lease does. The judicial decision remains outstanding. At the same time, the meeting approves a new ninety-nine-year sporting lease for the Hazeldene extension with Easky Investments, who have purchased the land. This lease is backdated to 1 January 1974. It's worth noting that the landlord warrants that there is no right of way for Hazeldene residents over the leased portion of the ground. The lease is signed in December. A motion to consider changing the rules to separate the jobs of Captain of the 1sts and Club Captain, is carried. The 1977 car-park takings are double those of the previous year.

PROFILE: BRENDAN DOWLING

L-H stroke-playing batsman. R-A slow, medium pace bowler. Educated at CUS and UCD. Economist and stockbroker. Also ruins good walks and has played softball in the past. Came up through the ranks of Merrion Schoolboys but played most of his adult cricket on the Junior sides. Acted as Hon. Secretary and Hon. Treasurer in the late seventies and was President from 1988 to 1991. During his period in office, he changed the role of President from that of geriatric chat-show host to hands-on chairman of a more efficient, businesslike committee. Over the four years of his tenure, the pavilion was redeveloped, the management of the club was reorganised on a functional basis, a drive for new members was instigated, new practice facilities were introduced and the social life of the club was expanded exponentially, with race nights, discos, karaokes, six–a–sides, etc. Since then he has become a trustee, whose valuable advice is sought on most major issues affecting the future of the club.

1978: SENIOR CUP RUNNERS-UP; INTERMEDIATE C LEAGUE WINNERS; MINI-CRICKET COMPETITION WINNERS; UNDER-13 JEYES CUP (SOUTHERN) WINNERS; UNDER-15 ROBERTSON CUP WINNERS; UNDER-15 YATES HALE CUP RUNNERS-UP

Senior: fixtures 22, reported 22, won 9, lost 10, drawn 3. President: J. McAlinden. Captain: A. Little. The Senior League has a new sponsor in Tyler's Shoes. £500 goes to the winner, £150 to the runner up and £100 to third place. New bowling bonus points are introduced, with 1 point for every two wickets taken. For the first time since the days of Fenner Brockway, Merrion employ a professional cricketer to bolster their team. Contrary to his curriculum vitae, which mysteriously removes ten years from his actual age, he is a mid-forties ex-Yorkshire league cricketer from Pakistan called Salim Uddin. Although his first year with Merrion is a success in terms of runs (667 @ 33.35) and wickets (13 @ 22.61), it is impossible to quantify the negative effect on younger players of a professional who constantly breaks wind in the changing room, before demanding '*ball, please*'. And a new trend is set, whereby cricket bats are flung across the dressing room, preferably smashing a window along the way, in response to the umpire's raised digit.

Despite this, Merrion finish 5/11 with 88 points, having played 10, won 4, lost 3, drawn 3. In the Senior Cup, Merrion win their first match since 1963, when they beat Carlisle in the first round. They go on to defeat Pembroke in the semi-final, when John McGeady's fine bowling wins him Merrion's first Man of the Match award. However, they lose to David Ensor's Phoenix in the final at the Park. This loss, according to Sean Pender, was due to Merrion's, 'immaturity, when, after winning the toss, they declined first use of a perfect wicket'. Thanks to David Pigot's century, Phoenix manage just 233 runs in 60 overs on this perfect wicket, with Kevin O'Herlihy bowling 12 overs for 17 runs. Despite a chase of less than 4 runs per over, Merrion's batting collapses and they are all out for 122. Unfortunately, too many of the Merrion players are just happy enough to be in a final for the first time in their lives. All the captain's father, ex-Merrion giant Cecil Little, can do is scratch his head and mutter to himself for the rest of his life (he dies the following year, possibly from disappointment) the mantra, '*He put them in, he put them in, he put them in.*' This is Phoenix's fifth Senior Cup win in six years.

In the Wiggins Teape, Merrion finish 8/10 with 30 points, having played 9, won 3, lost 6. Joe Keogh and Eddie Lewis help South Leinster to win the Guinness Cup. Eddie Lewis clips 363 runs @ 20.16. Alan Little hoicks 373 runs @ 17.76. The irreplacable Raj Ramsaroop, in his last full season with Merrion, comes seventh in the provincial all-rounders' table, with 398 runs @ 23.41 and 36 wickets @ 17.91. Kevin O'Herlihy procures 31 wickets @ 19.96. Mick Mills seizes 12 wickets @ 24.00. John McGeady steals 16 wickets @ 19.12:

Opponent	Result	Mer.	Opp.	Best Batting: Runs	Best Bowling: Wickets
Railway Union	Lost	123	124/2	D. Kilpatrick: 32	K.D. O'Herlihy: 1/22
DU	Won	69/5	66/9	R. Ramsaroop: 29*	K.D. O'Herlihy: 4/13
Leinster	Drawn	155/9	182/5	K. McDonald: 51	J. Keogh: 3/52
Malahide	Won	137	76	S. Uddin: 84	M. Mills: 6/35
Carlisle	Drawn	131/7	168/6	S. Uddin: 55	R. Ramsaroop: 4/65

Old Belvedere	Lost	112	178/9	R. Ramsaroop: 49	S. Uddin: 3/34
Phoenix	Lost	117	120/1	S. Uddin: 51	R. Ramsaroop: 1/35
YMCA	Won	159	144	D. McKenna: 33	J. O'Hagan: 3/25
Carlisle (C)	Won	218/3	215/9	S. Uddin: 87	E. Lewis: 3/40
Pembroke	Won	117	85	R. Ramsaroop: 37	K.D. O'Herlihy: 5/27
Pembroke (C)	Won	118/2	117	S. Uddin: 58	J. McGeady: 6/21
Clontarf	Drawn	125/4	203/5	S. Uddin: 37	M. Mills: 2/26

Wiggins Teape

Old Belvedere	Lost	106/9	146	E. Lewis: 41*	K.D. O'Herlihy: 2/37
Phoenix	Won	131/5	129	A. Little: 77	J. McGeady: 6/56
Phoenix	Lost	122	233/5	E. Lewis: 22	R. Ramsaroop: 1/37

Senior Cup final

Malahide	Lost	79	80/5	S. Uddin: 38	R. Ramsaroop: 4/24
Clontarf (run rate)	Lost	142/9	125/5	R. Ramsaroop: 39	R. Ramsaroop: 2/48
Leinster	Lost	117	118/3	E. Lewis: 25	K.D. O'Herlihy: 2/31
YMCA	Won	134/7	133/8	S. Uddin: 65	R. Ramsaroop: 3/20
Carlisle	Lost	137/9	138/4	S. Uddin: 69	S. Uddin: 2/43
Pembroke	Won	200/5	96/9	E. Lewis: 73*	R. Ramsaroop: 3/2
Railway Union	Lost	83	200/8	E. Lewis: 21	R. Ramsaroop: 4/90

Junior: Cricket at this level is restructured this year, with a smaller Senior 2 League, a Senior 3 League, Intermediate A, B and C Leagues and Junior A and B Leagues. Merrion 2nds finish 8/9 in the Senior 2 League, with 28 per cent, having played 10, won 2, lost 6, drawn 2, and so are demoted to Senior 3. Ken McDonald takes over the captaincy from Dennis Noble mid-season, but can't prevent relegation. His team is drawn against Leinster 3rds in the second round of the Senior 2 Cup. Merrion 3rds finish 8/9 in the Intermediate A League, with 32 per cent, having played 15, won 4, lost 8, drawn 3. Peter Geoffroy's side is drawn against Old Belvedere 5ths in the first round of the Intermediate Cup. Merrion 4ths finish 1/9 in the Intermediate League C, with 68 per cent, having played 11, won 7, lost 1, drawn 3. Newcomers John Hancock and Dick Whittington feature strongly for Des Murray's team, which is drawn against CYM 2nds in the first round of the Intermediate Cup.

Merrion Schoolboys are 9/12 in the Under-18 League, with 36 per cent, having played 7, won 2, lost 4, drawn 1. Paul Coghlan, Will Gibbs, John McGeady and Derek O'Herlihy play for South Leinster in the Under-19 interprovincial competition, sponsored by Esso. Merrion A win the Under-15 League, with 38 points, having played 12, won 9, lost 1, drawn 2, and the A.B. Robertson Cup. They are runners-up to YMCA in the Under-15 Yates Hale Cup. Merrion B come 8/14 in the Under-15 League, with 19 points, having played 10, won 4, lost 3, drawn 3. Merrion win the Under-13 Jeyes Cup (Southern Section) with 20 points, having played 12, won 10, lost 2. Merrion win the Mini-Cricket competition.

CLUB NOTES

An early meeting this year decides to advertise for a playing professional, who will also coach. A subsequent meeting selects Mr Salim Uddin, an experienced thirty-five-year-old Yorkshire League player. It is agreed that the price of teas be increased to 50p for Senior players. In March, Joe Keogh resigns from the position of vice-captain of the 1sts and the management committee, due to pressure of business. Midway through the season, he resigns from the club altogether and moves to Cold-Blow Lane. A Supplemental Lease with Easky Investments is signed in May. This provides for a small extra portion of land at the Dodder end, which has been used for practice wickets and to store equipment since then. A successful mixed six-a-side is held, along with a single-wicket competition, which is won by Brendan Curley. At the end of the season, it is decided to employ a younger and fitter professional for the 1979 season, with fewer stomach problems, and a Schoolboy organiser who can be co-opted onto the committee. A discussion is held about the behaviour of schoolboys, specifically their presence on the pavilion roof along with a bicycle. Mr McConnell explains the presence of the Hon. Treasurer there by indicating his desire to avoid being showered by water bombs. At the AGM in November, a suggestion is made that the women become pavilion members of Merrion. Alan Little agrees to organise a tour for the following season. Friday night jazz sessions are introduced successfully for the winter.

Above: Merrion 1sts, 1978 Senior Cup runners-up. Back row: J. O'Hagan, K.D. O'Herlihy, E. Lewis, M. Mills, R. Ramsaroop, J. McGeady, S. Uddin (Pro). Front row: J. Heavey (S), D. O'Herlihy, K. McDonald, A. Little (C), B. Curley, P. Coghlan.

Left: Merrion 4ths, 1978 Intermediate C League winners. Back row: S. Lewis, G. Quinn, A. McKenna, F. O'Flynn. Middle row: J. O'Brien, D. Murray (C), J. Bryant, G. Percival. Front row: S. Adamson, R. Willis, Siva.

PROFILE: PAUL COGHLAN

R-H elegant, stroke-playing batsman. R-A fast bowler, capable of extracting extreme bounce from the most docile of wickets. Educated at Willow Park and Blackrock College. He played senior rugby for UCD and Blackrock, where he captained the 1st XV to Leinster Cup honours. After university, Paul went into insurance and set up his own successful business. He was a cricket Schoolboy interprovincial for Leinster and Irish Youth international. He played 136 games for Merrion 1sts from 1976 to 1988, scoring 1,151 runs @ 11.17, with a best of 54, and including 2*50s. He took 100 wickets @ 26.28, including 5 wickets in an innings on 4 occasions, 47 catches and 2 stumpings. He retired early to focus on his business interests and ruining good walks.

1979: DEATH OF CECIL LITTLE; MIDDLE LEAGUE WINNERS; TOUR OF LONDON

Senior: fixtures 20, reported 20, won 7, lost 10, drawn 3. President: T. McGeady. Captain: A. Little. After the last-minute withdrawal of a West Indian cricketer called Guy Yearwood, Salim Uddin (now another year older than his curriculum vitae) is chosen again as professional, to be paid on a game-by-game basis. Merrion finish 6/11 in the Tyler League, with 83½ points, having played 10, won 3, lost 4, drawn 3. They lose to Malahide in the first round of the Senior Cup, in a game where John O'Hagan gets most runs and wickets, having crawled out of bed in the pavilion lounge at 10a.m., wanting to know who he is, where he lives and what are all these albinos doing in his room? Nowadays it'd be a matter for the disciplinary committee, but in those days, we could hold our drink and still perform. Merrion finish 7/10 in the Wiggins Teape, with 40 points and £83 prize money, having played 9, won 4, lost 5.

An overseas tour of London is undertaken. Not much is remembered of this, apart from one player getting particularly hosed. The club benefits hugely from the temporary presence of an Australian, David Gee, the Little Red Rooster, who takes 26 wickets @ 18.50. This year marks the first appearance of future veteran Robbie Stanton. Salim Uddin thumps 503 runs @ 25.15, as well as stealing 19 wickets @ 21.52 and 16 catches in the field. Eddie Lewis, who plays for South Leinster in the Guinness Cup, spanks 497 runs @ 27.61. Paul Coghlan manages 194 runs @ 16.16. Alan Little hoicks and edges 285 runs @ 17.81. John O'Hagan hooks 205 runs @ 20.50. Kevin O'Herlihy (playing sometimes as K. Doherty when mitching from getting the weather forecast wrong) scratches 194 runs @ 24.25 and filches 42 wickets @ 16.66, coming tenth in the Leinster provincial bowling statistics. In tune with the year, Merrion all-time great Cecil Little, the 'Don', at the age of seventy-nine throws his wicket away to a googly disguised as a massive heart attack:

Opponent	Result	Mer.	Opp.	Best Batting: Runs	Best Bowling: Wickets
DU	Drawn	148/3	113/7	S. Uddin: 72	J. McGeady: 3/16
Phoenix	Lost	49	122/7	S. Uddin: 22	E. Lewis: 4/34
Railway Union	Lost	146/8	152/5	S. Uddin: 56	K.D. O'Herlihy: 2/29
Leinster	Won	139	133	P. Coghlan: 39	M. Mills: 4/21
Malahide (C)	Lost	167/8	169/5	J. O'Hagan: 36*	J. O'Hagan: 2/36
Pembroke	Won	102/4	101	E. Lewis: 60	D. Gee: 6/33
Carlisle	Lost	159	166/9	E. Lewis: 56	M. Mills: 4/58

YMCA	Drawn	109/9	130	K.D. O'Herlihy: 24*	D. Gee: 6/43
Malahide	Won	82/6	78	E. Lewis: 21	K.D. O'Herlihy: 6/26
Clontarf	Lost	162/7	163/6	S. Uddin: 44	D. Gee: 3/62
Old Belvedere	Drawn	194/7	204/5	E. Lewis: 68	R. Stanton: 1/11
Wiggins Teape					
YMCA	Won	133/7	131	S. Uddin: 50	S. Uddin: 2/19
Pembroke	Won	193	156	S. Uddin: 81	K.D. O'Herlihy: 3/28
Clontarf	Lost	147	158/6	E. Lewis: 39	K.D. O'Herlihy: 3/57
Old Belvedere	Lost	120	126	K. McDonald: 28	S. Uddin: 3/27
Railway Union	Lost	133/7	137/6	K.D. O'Herlihy: 40*	S. Uddin: 2/18
Carlisle	Won	156/6	155/9	E. Lewis: 45	K.D. O'Herlihy: 5/57
Malahide	Lost	123	124/6	E. Lewis: 38	D. Gee: 3/53
Phoenix	Lost	111	130	J. O'Hagan: 39	K.D. O'Herlihy: 4/19
Leinster	Won	131/4	127	A. Little: 49*	D. Gee: 4/56

Junior: Merrion 2nds finish 3/10 in the Senior 3 League, with 56 per cent, having played 16, won 7, lost 5, drawn 4. John Hancock gets 93* in a reduced 20-over match against Carlisle 2nds. They lose to Leinster 2nds in the second round of the Senior 2/3 Cup, 145 to 147/6. Merrion 3rds win the Middle League, with 73 per cent, having played 17, won 11, lost 1, drawn 5. They lose to Pembroke 3rds in the second round of the Middle Cup, 107 to 157. Merrion 4ths finish 6/9 in Section A of the Intermediate League, with 39 per cent, having played 11, won 4, lost 5, drawn 2. They lose to Carlisle 3rds in the second round of the Intermediate Cup, 201/9 to 202/9. Paul Coghlan and Robbie Stanton play for South Leinster in the All-Ireland Under-19 Esso Cup. Coghlan also acquits himself well on the Irish Youths team.

CLUB NOTES

A January meeting proposes the employment of a West Indian all-round cricketer called Guy Yearwood as professional for the 1979 season. The motion is carried by a 7-1 majority, with Simon Curley objecting on the grounds that the money would be better spent on repayment of outstanding legal fees or of members' debt. It is planned to purchase a pump to provide water from the new well for the preparation of wickets. Crusaders Athletics Club start to use the club without formal permission. In the middle of April, at 4a.m., Guy Yearwood pulls out and an urgent meeting agrees to offer the position again to Salim Uddin, with payment on a match-by-match basis and extra fees for any coaching undertaken. John Byrne, the groundsman, who now has a permanent job, agrees to prepare wickets on Monday, Wednesday and Friday evenings. New sightscreens are planned. The women indicate they will organise teas in return for some coaching. At Simon Curley's request, a notice is put up stating that no golf is to be allowed on the club grounds. The Chief Superintendent of Donnybrook GS inquires if the grounds are available for the Pope's visit. A decision on this is deferred. Another single-wicket competition is held. At the AGM, the subscription for Senior playing members is increased to £20 per annum. Chris Mara queries the status of lady members and is told they are non-playing pavilion members, with their own club, within a club. A meeting in December agrees to offer the position of player-coach for the 1980 season to Andrew Lynch, a young Australian. By the way, this is not the centenary year.

PROFILE: JOHN McGEADY

R-H positive, attacking batsman. R-A medium pace seam bowler until a back injury forced him to give it up at an early stage. Educated at Willow Park and Blackrock College, where he played rugby for Blackrock College Junior and Senior Cup teams, losing four finals in a row. Played senior rugby for Lansdowne, won a Leinster Cup medal and gained an international cap at B level. Went straight from school into the world of business, and emigrated to Canada and the USA. For Merrion 1sts, John played eighty-nine games from 1978 to 1992, scoring 1,129 runs @ 15.25, with a best of 83 and 6*50s. He took 27 wickets @ 19.33, including 5 wickets in an innings on 5 occasions (illustrating the extent of his loss to Merrion as a bowler) and 18 catches. He was a Schoolboy interprovincial and played many games on Merrion's Junior sides. John was elected 1sts captain for the 1993 season, but was forced to return to America before the summer.

1980: SCHOOLBOY UNDER-18 RALEIGH CUP WINNERS

Senior: fixtures 20, reported 20, won 8, lost 9, drawn 3. President: T. McGeady. Captain: K. McDonald. Under a new young captain, Ken McDonald, Merrion employ a different professional in David Robinson, an Australian who is at least fifteen years younger than Salim Uddin's curriculum vitae, and twenty-five years younger than Salim Uddin himself. Nevertheless, they finish 8/11 in the Tyler League, with 64 points, having played 10, won 2, lost 5, drawn 3. Leinster beat them in the second round (bye in the first) of the Senior Cup. But they are serious challengers for the Wiggins Teape, until they lose the last two matches. They tie with Malahide, but gain full points on the basis of a faster run rate. Poor batting against Leinster is followed by the last match of the season, where rain curtails a plausible chase of 196, and YMCA take full points, also on a faster run rate. They finish 3/10, their best position in any league since 1960. Eddie Lewis, Ken McDonald, Kevin O'Herlihy and Will Gibbs play for South Leinster in the Guinness Cup. Dave Robinson finishes fourth in the provincial batting table, with 776 runs @ 38.80, fifth in the bowling statistics with 41 wickets @ 14.95, and third in the provincial all-rounders' table. He is the first Merrion player to score over 700 runs in a season. Eddie Lewis spanks 462 runs @ 30.80. Ken McDonald slaps 455 runs @ 23.94, including a chanceless ton against Carlisle in the pitch-black pouring rain. Alan Little hoicks 211 runs @ 15.07. Kevin O'Herlihy snaffles 30 wickets @ 21.16, including a hat-trick in the final match against Pembroke. Robbie Stanton pilfers 20 wickets @ 22.80. Will Gibbs wins 25 wickets @ 15.76 with his pacy off-cutters:

Opponent	Result	Mer.	Opp.	Best Batting: Runs	Best Bowling: Wickets
Carlisle	Lost	80	124	D. Robinson: 26	D. Robinson: 5/15
Leinster	Drawn	150/5	203/6	D. Robinson: 52	K.D. O'Herlihy: 3/59
DU	Won	235/3	102	D. Robinson: 133	W. Gibbs: 7/54
Old Belvedere	Drawn	192/8	195	E. Lewis: 90	W. Gibbs: 8/41
Phoenix	Lost	137	139/5	E. Lewis: 30	K.D. O'Herlihy: 2/31
Clontarf	Drawn	154/6	183/9	D. Robinson: 56	J. O'Hagan: 4/31
Leinster (C)	Lost	132	135/5	K. McDonald: 28	R. Stanton: 3/30
Pembroke	Lost	114	116/1	K. McDonald: 24	K.D. O'Herlihy: 1/31
Railway Union	Lost	177/7	178/4	E. Lewis: 52	P. Coghlan: 2/27
Malahide	Lost	77	79/6	D. Robinson: 27	K.D. O'Herlihy: 3/17

Wiggins Teape

YMCA	Won	185/4	183	D. Robinson: 54	K.D. O'Herlihy: 5/56
Old Belvedere	Won	134/9	127/9	K. McDonald: 27	J. O'Hagan: 5/69
Clontarf	Lost	143	155/7	K. McDonald: 32	D. Robinson: 4/43
Carlisle	Won	242/4	240/7	K. McDonald: 132*	W. Gibbs: 2/57
Phoenix	Won	97	78	D. Robinson: 35	D. Robinson: 7/24
Railway Union	Won	154/9	83	E. Lewis: 35*	R. Stanton: 5/25
Malahide	Won	162/5	162/8	D. Robinson: 74	K.D. O'Herlihy: 4/54
Leinster	Lost	104	109/1	D. Robinson: 35	D. Robinson: 1/29
YMCA	Lost	110/5	195/8	D. Robinson: 53	D. Robinson: 3/61
Pembroke	Won	163	112	D. O'Herlihy: 35	K.D. O'Herlihy: 4/11

Junior: Merrion 2nds finish 4/9 in the Senior 3 League, with 49 per cent, having played 16, won 5, lost 5, drawn 6, including a defence of 68 against Balrothery, who are shot out for 53. John Heavey takes 8/11 against Old Belvedere 3rds. Barry Little's team is drawn against Clontarf 2nds/Carlisle 2nds in the second round of the Senior 2/3 Cup. Merrion 3rds finish 7/10 in the Middle League, with 41 per cent, having played 17, won 6, lost 7, drawn 4. John Hancock's team is drawn against Man-O-War 2nds/The Hills 2nds in the second round of the Middle Cup. Merrion 4ths finish 9/9 in Section A of the Intermediate League, with 19 per cent, having played 14, won 1, lost 8, drawn 5. Tommy McGeady's team is drawn against Civil Service 2nds in the second round of the Intermediate Cup. Merrion Schoolboys beat Clontarf to win the Irish Raleigh Under-18 League (Amoroso Cup), John Heavey taking 5/19 and Robbie Stanton 3/3. Paul Coghlan, John Heavey, Richard Willis and Robbie Stanton play for South Leinster in the Under-19 interprovincial competition. Paul Meehan, Angus Hancock, David Heavey and Paul Neilsen play for South Leinster in the Smurfit All-Ireland Under-15 Cup.

CLUB NOTES

The pavilion is rented for two weeks to well-known English rock band Smokie, during which time they are almost living next door to Alice. A Leinster six-a-side competition in memory of the late Cecil Little is planned, but never gets off the ground. In February, Andrew Lynch declines the position of player-coach. Hurried exchanges with our liaison, Frank Tyson, produce another candidate in David Robinson, again a young Australian, who accepts the position. New sightscreens are planned. A letter is written to John Stanton, asking him to stop using the ground as a personal car park. At the beginning of the season, the committee considers the judgement handed down in the court case with Bective, which allows them to continue playing at Anglesea Road, provided they pay all outstanding rents, together with a sum of money to cover part of Merrion's costs, and agree to comply with the terms of the original agreement. Rather than risk the danger of an unsuccessful appeal due to a possible legal hiccup, they decide to continue with the licence until the thirty-year period is up. Nevertheless, the whole issue raises the question as to whether the problems couldn't have been solved out of court between two sporting clubs that have had such a close association. It is agreed that only the secretary of the women's committee be allowed to attend the MCMs. The LCU Umpires Association is to be approached to ask them to show more discretion in their actions. Hah! Chance would be a fine thing. A proposal for a new All-Ireland competition is accepted, amid reservations concerning a possible glut of fixtures. Another tour is planned for the 1981 season. At the AGM, the Treasurer notes that no subscriptions have been received from lady members in 1980. Chris Mara and Simon Curley are made Life Members.

PROFILE: KEVIN ALLWRIGHT

R-H, swashbuckling, middle-order batsman, prone to scoring most of his runs in the corner of the cows. Occasional wicket-keeper. Bowled when nobody was looking. Born in Hong Kong in 1955, where his father was head of the Dental Service of the Fragrant Harbour. Educated at Willow Park, Blackrock College and Rathmines College of Commerce. Currently Headmaster at Aravon Primary School, where he resides with his college sweetheart and wife, Irene and their three boys, Philip, Rory and Christopher, each of whom also plays cricket for Merrion. He played senior rugby for London Irish and Monkstown (captain for two years) and cricket for Northwood and Twickenham. *Ollie* came up through the Schoolboy and Junior Merrion ranks before disappearing to England in the mid-1970s to attend teacher training college and doss around Europe, exploring the university of life by driving lorries and working on oil rigs for about a decade, returning to Dublin in 1981. Overall he played 199 games for the 1sts between 1972 and 1998, scoring 2,913 runs @ 20.22, with a top score of 108*, and including 14*50s. As wicket-keeper, he took 23 catches and 1 stumping, a relatively modest return. But he did manage 69 catches in the outfield. As captain from 1994 to 1996, he was instrumental in turning the performances of the 1sts around, leading them to their first trophy since 1960, the 1996 Alan Murray 20 Overs Cup. Since then, he has gone willingly down to the Junior sides and anticipates his long sojourn in Bird Avenue with barely bated breath. A gifted impressionist and an avid student of Stephen Potter's book on *One-Upmanship*, he has been known to run members of the opposition out by pretending to call for a run when keeping wicket, fooling the batsman at the other end into leaping out of his crease in anticipation, only to end up trapped halfway down the wicket, and thence run out. *Yes, yes, yes!*

NB Other teams playing between 1971 and 1980: St John Bosco Boys' Club, Ardamine, Carlow.

Merrion Under-18s, Raleigh Cup winners, 1980. Back row: F. Geoghegan, R. Willis, M. Rutledge, J. Hourihane, S. King, P. McGeady, J. Heavey (C). Front row: P. Broughan (S), G. Percival, R. Stanton, D. Heavey, P. Hourihane, J. Kingston, D. Lang.

4.3. THE EIGHTIES: 1981-1990

In Merrion lore, this was known as the fun decade, when activities off the field tended to cloud the poor performances on the field. There were five tours, several six-a-side and single-wicket competitions, race nights, discos, and problems with the running of a very active bar. Rumours abounded of a secret drinking club, *The Syndicate*, whose initiation ceremony included downing a pint containing a live goldfish, eating raw squid and wearing kippers around one's neck. Needless to say, none of these fishy activities helped to improve the standard of cricket on the 1sts, whose teams were known to include at least three members, and possibly more. At one stage it seemed that participation in this private club was a condition for selection, unless, of course, you were a rugger-bugger or Eddie Lewis.

The false dawn came to a premature end after the 1981 season, and the remainder of the period saw the standard of play return at times to that of the '60s and early '70s, with 33 games won out of 169 between 1982 and 1990. In retrospect, the decision by the club's management, and subsequently the LCU, to turn their backs on professional cricketers, might be considered a mistake of titanic proportions. Although Merrion 1sts frequently propped up both leagues, the 1985 Senior Cup final provided a single highlight, with a tense thriller against Leinster at Anglesea Road, which the club lost narrowly. Merrion's batting was strong throughout this period. From 1985 onwards, the failures were due mainly to the absence of a strong bowling lineup to support Robbie Stanton and the aging, but match-winning, John O'Hagan. As the decade came to a close, there were promising signs for the '90s, in the shape of a prolific cricketing dynasty named Joyce.

Junior Merrion experienced a more successful '80s, with trophies in 1981 (Senior 3 League), 1982 (Middle Cup), 1985 (Middle B League), 1986 (Junior and Whelan Cups), 1987 (Intermediate A and Junior B Leagues), and 1990 (Intermediate A League), in addition to many near misses. The club added a 5ths and 6ths during this period, but found it difficult to field enough players and finished with five teams. The Schoolboys won the Under-13 Jeyes Cup in 1984. Women's cricket continued to grow during the first half of this period, but fell away towards the end, with some Senior players leaving to join other clubs. There were two new Taverners social teams, with the Theatrical Cavaliers coming forward to add a much-needed touch of artistry to the shorter format in 1987.

As use of the bar grew, the issue of security became more important. Several break-ins occurred and alcohol was stolen, despite improved alarm systems and procedures. This problem was eventually solved by placing a locked gate at the entrance to the club, which in turn led to the hoary old chestnut of rights of way for Anglesea Road residents to enter their rear gardens through the club premises. Expensive law suits came to nothing, and the club lost the slight area at the back of No.43, which had been in use since 1952. Ducks may have the right of way in all traffic, but not the residents whose houses back onto Merrion. At last the Bective issue was solved, when the ninety-year licence came to a natural end at the first thirty-year break point in 1985. In 1986, Hurricane Charlie caused the Dodder to fill the ground with mud and silt and almost destroy the pavilion. Members worked hard through the winter to have the club ready for the following season. The decade saw new sightscreens, covers, practice wickets and a redevelopment of the pavilion. Attempts were made to improve the functional organisation of the club.

Sadly, this period also saw the deaths of Merrion stalwarts Jack O'Donnell, Tommy Burke and Simon Curley.

1981: SENIOR 3 LEAGUE WINNERS; SENIOR 2/3 CUP RUNNERS-UP; TOUR OF NOTTINGHAM

Senior: fixtures 22, reported 22, won 8, lost 9, drawn 3, tied 1, no result 1. President: T. McGeady. Captain: K.D. O'Herlihy. Changes in regulations for the Tyler League include: for a normal draw the team bowling least overs now gets 2 points, not 1; the team batting first may bat for 55 overs maximum, or for 60 overs, if put in to bat. Merrion do well this season, coming 4/11 in the Tyler League, with 103 points, having played 10, won 5, lost 2, drawn 3. They beat Pembroke easily in the first round of the Senior Cup, with Dave Robinson securing a Man of the Match award, but lose to Old Belvedere narrowly in the next round, with John McGeady getting his second Man of the Match award. CYM join the Wiggins Teape League, wherein Merrion's season falls away badly, as they finish 11/11, with 27 points, having played 10, won 2, lost 6, tied 1, no result 1. Another tour is undertaken. This time it's Nottingham's turn to be razed.

Dave Robinson, Merrion's Australian professional for the second year running, is picked for South Leinster, but the game is cancelled due to the troubles in Northern Ireland. He finishes fifth in the provincial batting table, with 746 runs @ 39.26, including a brace of tons, and is eight in the O'Grady Cup for bowling, with 45 wickets @ 14.73. He wins the Samuels Cup for all-rounders. Paul Coghlan gets 176 runs @ 13.53 and blasts out 24 batsmen @ 16.29. Eddie Lewis contributes 298 runs @ 18.62. Alan Little hoicks 252 runs @ 18.00. Denis McKenna nudges 233 runs @ 15.53. John McGeady biffs 321 runs @ 26.75. Last appearance for Merrion 1sts of K. Doherty, aka Kevin O'Herlihy, before heading for Munster. He whiffles 25 wickets @ 19.04. Ross Porter grabs 19 wickets @ 17.68. Robbie Stanton filches 18 wickets @ 22.72:

Opponent	Result	Mer.	Opp.	Best Batting: Runs	Best Bowling: Wickets
YMCA	Won	128/4	124	E. Lewis: 55	K.D. O'Herlihy: 3/7
DU	Won	100/2	96	D. Robinson: 38*	D. Robinson: 6/27
Railway Union	Drawn	120	97/4	E. Lewis: 54	D. Robinson: 2/14
Pembroke (C)	Won	115/2	114/9	D. Robinson: 66	R. Stanton: 3/17
Phoenix	Drawn	143/9	178/8	P. Coghlan: 54	D. Robinson: 4/52
Leinster	Won	190/4	186/7	D. Robinson: 109	K.D. O'Herlihy: 3/37
Clontarf	Drawn	201/6	183/5	D. Robinson: 117*	D. Robinson: 3/39
Old Belvedere (C)	Lost	186	192/9	J. McGeady: 52	R. Stanton: 3/35
Old Belvedere	Lost	115	197/6	K. McDonald: 22	R. Stanton: 2/42
Carlisle	Lost	148	151/3	J. McGeady: 79	D. Robinson: 2/37
Malahide	Won	114/7	110	D. Robinson: 36	R. Porter: 6/25
Pembroke	Won	114/5	112	D. Robinson: 47	P. Coghlan: 5/37
Wiggins Teape					
Carlisle	Lost	133	136/4	D. McKenna: 35	D. Robinson: 2/42
Phoenix	No Res.				
YMCA	Lost	141	144	D. McKenna: 51	D. Robinson: 5/56
Railway Union	Won	193/9	143	J. McGeady: 55	P. Coghlan: 5/24
Malahide	Tied	193/5	193/9	J. McGeady: 60*	R. Porter: 4/57
Old Belvedere	Won	176/8	175	J. Heavey: 31	D. Robinson: 5/42
CYM	Lost	102	104/1	P. Coghlan: 33	K.D. O'Herlihy: 1/33

Pembroke	Lost	85	136/9	D. Robinson: 35	J. McGeady: 5/47
Clontarf	Lost	170	185/5	D. Robinson: 55	P. Coghlan: 3/56
Leinster	Lost	110	211	J. McGeady: 31	R. Porter: 4/36

Junior: Merrion 2nds win the Senior 3 League, with 79.4 per cent, having played 15, won 11, lost 2, drawn 2. Jim Walsh's team, which includes Dick Clarke, Richard Willis, John McGeady, Brendan Curley, Paul Coghlan and John Heavey Jnr, is promoted to Senior 2. Denis McKenna nudges 111* against Clontarf, while Jim hoicks 74* against the same team. They beat YMCA 2nds, Man-O-War and Railway Union 2nds, to reach the Senior 2/3 final, which they lose to CYM, despite a fighting 59 from Barry Little. As CYM have only been accepted this year into the Wiggins Teape for the first time, they are allowed to play their West Indian club professional Marlon Tucker in the Cup, and this is probably the difference between the teams. Merrion 3rds finish 7/10 in the Middle League, with 37.8 per cent, having played 13, won 4, lost 5, drawn 4. Joe Morrissey Snr scores 76* against Malahide, while Andy Atkinson, Paul Meehan, Derek Kilpatrick, Stephen King and Tommy McGeady also contribute 50s. Chris Curley takes 8/63 in a match and Jimmy O'Cleirigh surprises everyone with 4/3 in another. Peter Geoffroy's team is drawn against Old Belvedere 4ths/Pembroke 3rds in the second round of the Middle Cup. Merrion 4ths finish 3/9 in Section B of the Intermediate League, with 54.6 per cent, having played 11, won 6, lost 5. Jimmy O'Cleirigh's team includes Des Murray, Andrew Dixon, Paul Hourihane, David Heavey and Leo Clear. They lose to Leinster 6ths, 149 to 150/9, in the second round of the Intermediate Cup. The Under-19 Schoolboys tour Strabane. The Under-15s withdraw from the league before the end of the season. Robbie Stanton is named in the fourteen-man squad for the Irish team in the International Youths Tournament in Denmark.

CLUB NOTES

The question of insurance against damage to windows and cars in the Hazeldene flats is raised. The club's overdraft is extended to pay for future tarmacing of the drive and parking area, and for a new shed, tractor, sightscreens and practice wickets. Kevin O'Herlihy gets the job of disposing of a car that has been dumped at the entrance to the ground. A drive to attract new members is undertaken. The question of women's membership is raised again. It's decided to run the bar on a rota system. John Stanton is invited to captain a Taverners team, for players who can't get on the 4ths. It is also planned to encourage more caravans to park on the ground during Horse Show week, with advertisements in *The Field*. A concrete practice wicket is placed in the corner of the ground. Andy Atkinson is employed to assist with the preparation of wickets. At last the new sightscreens arrive, having been rolled up from Sandymount. Their painting is organised. It is agreed to field a 5ths, provided St Columba's College can be used for their home games. Problems with the running of the bar are reported. At a meeting after the Horse Show, a letter from a caravan-owner is read, politely suggesting some improvements that might be made to the toilet facilities. It is agreed that Bective should be allowed back for the duration of the licence, under certain conditions, including the settlement of all outstanding financial matters. A new Memorandum of Agreement is agreed between the two clubs, and a joint committee is set up. The long-running *Bective Court Case* is coming to an end at last. There are some changes to the original document, including roping off the cricket square during the rugby season,

Merrions 2nds, Senior 3 League winners/Senior 2-3 Cup runners-up, 1981. Back row: B. Little, S. King, J. Heavey, J. O'Hagan, R. Clarke, P. Broughan (S), J. McGeady. Front row: J. Hourihane, P. Geoffroy, R. Willis, J. Walsh (C), B. Curley, D. Heavey.

the annual rent going up to £85 per annum and Bective not using the ground for matches of Division 1 or 2 standard. At the AGM, Danny Parkinson is elected a Life Member with acclamation, thereby proving that bad behaviour carries its own rewards. The cost of insuring against break-ins, loss of bar stock and installing alarm systems is discussed.

PROFILE: DENIS McKENNA

L-H nurdling batsman, heavily influenced by Tom McGeady, with an elegant cover drive. R-A awkward bowler of accurate non-leg breaks. Excellent fielder, with many nicknames, the cleanest of which was 'buckets'. Educated at CBS, Westland Row and the Dublin Institute of Technology, where he gained a Bachelor of Science degree in Management and Law. A civil servant, he is currently employed in the Law Library. He played competitive soccer and hurling as a youngster, and didn't get 'into' the foreign sport of cricket until the 1970s, when his father persuaded him to join Merrion, a club that Al McKenna Snr had apparently been supporting since the 1950s. Denis came up through the ranks in Merrion, playing 184 games for the 1sts from 1977 to 1992 and scoring 2,088 runs @ 13.21, with a top score of 60* and including 6*50s. He took 77 wickets @ 28.16, including a stumping job on Jack Short in Den's 2nd over in Senior cricket, thereby depriving the international of the Marchant Cup for batting. Buckets held onto 61 catches, captained the 1sts in 1984, and won the Oulton Cup for Senior 2 bowling in 1988, the only Merrion player to achieve this feat. He is one of a Merrion family of McKennas that includes ex-Merrion women's player Grace and that cavalier priest from Fair City, Al McKenna Jnr, who also played a little cricket for the Junior sides in his time. Denis was another fully paid-up member of The Syndicate, but as he couldn't handle his drink, was finally debarred from it.

1982: MIDDLE CUP WINNERS

Senior: fixtures 21, reported 21, won 5, lost 14, drawn 2. President: T. McGeady. Captain: E. Lewis. After four years of professionals and no trophies, Merrion decide to go it alone again. A new All-Ireland knockout competition is introduced, sponsored by Schweppes. Merrion lose to Eglington in the first round, 69/8 to 73/2. Regulation changes to the Tyler League: CYM are admitted to full Senior status; Tylers withdraw prize fund, but contribute

£250 to the LCU; individual batting and bowling awards are discontinued; weather abandoned matches are no longer to be replayed; four and a half hours' play is necessary for a match to count; the final table is to be worked out on averages, taking into account the number of games played. Merrion finish 11/12 in the Tyler League, with 59 points, and an average of 5.90, having played 10 (the game against CYM is a washout), won 2, lost 6, drawn 2. Parliament Printing/Sportsgear take over sponsorship from John Player for the Senior Cup. The prize fund is now £1,000. Merrion lose narrowly to Clontarf in the first round of this competition, despite a resilient 52 from Denis McKenna, for which he wins the Man of the Match award.

They fare badly again in the limited-overs competition, finishing 11/11, with 30 points, having played 10, won 3, lost 7. Ross Porter takes 6/71 for South Leinster, in a losing cause against Munster. Robbie Stanton and Ken McDonald also play for South Leinster. The captain, Eddie Lewis is injured for part of the season and the vice-captain, Paul Coghlan, takes over. Nevertheless, Eddie Lewis manages 259 runs @ 19.92. Alan Little hoicks 326 runs @ 19.17. John Heavey flicks 400 runs @ 19.04, including 3*50s, and tweaks 13 wickets @ 30.76. Paul Coghlan nabs 240 runs @ 12.63 and purloins 17 wickets @ 29.41. John O'Hagan hooks 200 runs @ 25.00 and poaches 10 wickets @ 24.20. Denis McKenna nudges 334 runs @ 23.85, including 3*50s. Richard Willis, one of Paddy's many sons, grabs 157 runs @ 26.16. Ross Porter squirts 151 runs @ 13.72 and snaffles 26 wickets @ 19.42, after which he disappears to join the baton-wielding Royal Ulster Constabulary, thereby proving that fast bowling is not all about intelligence. Robbie Stanton persuades 36 batsmen to part with their wicket for an average of 18.47 runs:

Opponent	Result	Mer.	Opp.	Best Batting: Runs	Best Bowling: Wickets
DU	Drawn	200/6	237/6	J. Heavey: 55	M. Mills: 2/20
Pembroke	Lost	145	146/8	K.J. O'Herlihy: 42	R. Porter: 3/34
Leinster	Lost	137	138/4	E. Lewis: 55	P. Coghlan: 2/32
Old Belvedere	Lost	112	113/3	E. Extras: 18	R. Porter: 2/26
Clontarf (C)	Lost	184	210/8	D. McKenna: 52	R. Stanton: 2/23
Malahide	Lost	121	125/6	R. Porter: 30	R. Stanton: 3/24
YMCA	Won	136/2	133	D. McKenna: 54*	R. Stanton: 4/30
Railway Union	Lost	192/9	194/5	J. Heavey: 31	R. Porter: 2/27
Clontarf	Lost	111	192/5	R. Willis: 19	J. Heavey: 2/32
Phoenix	Drawn	199/7	118/8	J. Heavey: 60	P. Coghlan: 4/19
Carlisle	Won	138/6	135	A. Little: 37*	R. Stanton: 4/37
Wiggins Teape					
Leinster	Lost	83	84/0	J. Heavey: 20	
Railway Union	Lost	129/6	135/5	A. Little: 59	R. Porter: 3/65
YMCA	Lost	138	139/6	J. McGeady: 39	P. Coghlan: 3/36
Old Belvedere	Lost	171	218/7	K. McDonald: 47*	R. Porter: 3/33
Carlisle	Won	141/9	122	R. Willis: 31*	J. Heavey: 4/28
CYM (run rate)	Lost	187/6	164/4	E. Lewis: 76*	R. Stanton: 2/48
Malahide	Lost	126/8	127/2	R. Willis: 51*	J. Heavey: 2/35
Pembroke	Won	186/6	183/5	J. Heavey: 90	P. Coghlan: 2/55
Phoenix	Won	146	121	J. O'Hagan: 69	R. Porter: 4/10
Clontarf	Lost	130	131/5	P. Coghlan: 30	R. Stanton: 5/62

Junior: Merrion 2nds finish 3/10 in the Senior 2 League, with 50 per cent, having played 14, won 5, lost 3, drawn 6. John McGeady biffs 100 against Leinster 2nds and whiffles 8 wickets against Pembroke. Stephen King wallops 61* against Malahide 2nds. Kieran O'Herlihy hits 51 against Pembroke 2nds. Will Gibbs takes 6/8 against Rush. Derek O'Herlihy's team lose to Phoenix 2nds in the first round of the Senior 2 Cup, 223 to 228/2, despite Richard Willis's 108 runs. Merrion 3rds finish 6/11 in the Middle League, with 43.8 per cent, having played 18, won 6, lost 6, drawn 5, tied 1. Angus Hancock scores 72 against Civil Service 2nds. Eamonn Ryan steals an energetic 6/40 in the same game. Jimmy O'Cleirigh's team beats Railway Union 3rds, Rush 2nds and North Kildare (with Paul Neilsen grabbing 6/18 on a dodgy wicket) on their way to a low-scoring final against Mullingar in the Middle Cup, which they win, 81/6 to 79. Eddie Bohane takes 6/18 to help win this match. Merrion 4ths finish 4/8 in Section B of the Intermediate League, with 46.5 per cent, having played 11, won 3, lost 3, drawn 5. Johnny Kingston scores 68 in a losing cause against Railway Union 4ths. Dermot Soraghan, Johnny Hourihane and Angus Hancock also score 50s. Frank Nugent's team is drawn against Leinster 5ths in the second round of the Intermediate Cup. For the first time, a Merrion 5ths competes in the Junior C League, and finishes 4/7, with 50 per cent, having played 12, won 6, lost 6. John Hancock, Martin Curley and Kevin Kenny are the backbone of Jack McConnell's team. They lose to Phoenix 4ths in the first round of the Junior Cup, when some blow-in called Hank Stephens, bowling off the wrong foot, riddles them for about 50.

CLUB NOTES

At the early meetings, there is much discussion about the cost of extending the practice nets. The women ask politely for improved kitchen facilities. John Smyth is given the task of getting rid of more wrecked cars at the ground entrance. Players are banned from practising on the tarmac in the car park after yet another window in the flats is demolished. At a meeting in March, it's agreed that all unused draught beer be returned and credited to Merrion's account. Simon Curley volunteers enthusiastically to get the necessary plastic buckets and funnel.

The corner of the ground is ploughed up, in preparation for the new artificial practice wickets. There are continuing problems with the alarm system. A pump is purchased for the 135-foot well. Merrion is billed £113 by a Strabane hotel for damage done during their stay at the Irish Senior Cup. Room 104 is apparently responsible for quite a lot of this. At a meeting Simon Curley raises questions about the condition of the wickets, the outfield, the practice wickets, the toilets, the kitchen, car-park signs, women practising near the flats, an eleven-year-old driving the roller and the kitchen cooker being left on. He maintains there is a slackness in the running of the club. In addition, the pavilion roof needs repairing. A truck hits the entrance wall to the ground and does a bunk, despite the presence of a policeman across the road. It is agreed that playing cards for money in the pavilion will not be allowed. Late-night drinking has also resumed and needs to be controlled.

Subscriptions for Senior playing members will be £30 for the 1983 season. A Special General Meeting is held in September to amend the club rules to ensure that properly audited accounts are available at the end of each season. An activities subcommittee is formed, chaired by Frank Dolan. One of their first jobs is to organise a Christmas party. Another tour is planned for 1983. At the beginning of the winter, Bective return to Anglesea Road, even though the legal consent document remains unsigned by one of Merrion's trustees for a further two years.

PROFILE: JOHN HEAVEY JNR

R-H cultured opening batsman. R-A slow, off-break bowler, capable of giving the ball an outrageous tweak. Occasional wicket-keeper. Educated at Blackrock College and UCD, where he gained a BSc. Honours in Computer Science and Mathematics. Works as an information technology consultant. He played 204 games for Merrion 1sts between 1980 and 1994, scoring 3,146 runs @ 16.64, with a top score of 90, and including 13*50s. He took 43 wickets @ 31.30, and 53 catches in the outfield. As wicket-keeper, he took 6 catches and 7 stumpings. He came up through the Schoolboy and Junior ranks of Merrion, scoring for the 1sts in 1978 – a team he was to captain himself in 1991. *Speed* followed in his father's footsteps to become a hard-working Hon. Secretary from 2001 to 2007 and is currently a trustee of the club. Rumoured to have been the President and founding father of *The Syndicate*, John's turbulent, hell-raising youth within Merrion certainly affected his development as a cricketer, and perhaps deprived him of the representative honours that his ability deserved. But if making whoopee was an international sport, John would certainly have opened the batting for Ireland. And despite his seven years as club secretary and current status as trustee, his transformation from uber-partying *bête noir* to establishment figure is far too sudden for many, who have elected to wait for at least another forty years before they will begin to believe it. He's quite good at nicknames, too.

1983: TOUR OF SOMERSET; JUNIOR C LEAGUE RUNNERS-UP

Senior: fixtures 19, reported 19, won 4, lost 10, drawn 4, tied 1. President: T. McGeady. Captain: J. O'Hagan. Merrion beat Lurgan in the first round of the Schweppes Cup, 179/8 to 156, thanks to Kevin Allwright's 33* and Dave Gee's 4/23. However, they lose to The Hills in the second round. Belvedere Bond take over sponsorship from Tyler in the Senior League; £500 goes to the league winners and £250 to the runners up; The Hills are promoted to Senior status; thirteen teams are divided into two sections by ballot; Dublin University to be in the seven team section; the winners of the two sections are to meet in a final on 2 July; in the event of a tie, the winner is the team with most wins; if still level, the team with the higher runs per wicket average, wins; if rain prevents less than five hours cricket, the match must be refixed; if more than ten minutes' play is lost in the second innings of a drawn match, it will be considered a weather-ruined draw. Merrion finish 6/7 in Section A, with 33 points, having played 6, lost 2, drawn 4. Man-O-War are accepted into the Sportsgear/Parliament Cup, in which Merrion beat YMCA by 5 runs in the first round, with Denis McKenna getting his second Man of the Match award. But they fall to Phoenix in the next round in a high-scoring match at Anglesea Road. In the Wiggins Teape League, Merrion finish 9/12, with 35 points, having played 11, won 3, lost 7, tied 1.

A successful tour of Somerset takes place, despite the scary presence at Bath University of '*The Phantom*', who quotes the Old Testament frequently and causes beds to mysteriously disappear. For the first time since 1950, when Simon Curley won this award, John O'Hagan tops the provincial catches table, with 15. Eddie Lewis is fourth in the provincial all-rounders' statistics, with 350 runs @ 25.00, and 20 wickets @ 17.65. John O'Hagan is thirteenth on the same table, with 249 runs @ 22.63, and 29 wickets @ 21.24. Paul Coghlan manages 167 runs @ 10.43 and grabs 22 wickets @ 27.95. Last full season for Alan Little, who hoicks 318 runs @ 22.71. Kevin Allwright makes a welcome return from England, to plunder 276 runs @ 17.25. John McGeady has his best season with the bat, biffing 365 runs @ 24.33. Denis McKenna manages to nurdle

252 runs @ 13.26. Derek O'Herlihy swipes 266 runs @ 22.16. John O'Hagan, in his only season as captain, hooks 249 runs @ 22.63, and pilfers 29 wickets @ 21.24. Dave Gee returns briefly, to take 10 wickets @ 27.00. Robbie Stanton buys 20 wickets @ 18.70:

Opponent	Result	Mer.	Opp.	Best Batting: Runs	Best Bowling: Wickets
DU	Drawn	173/8	157/6	J. McGeady: 83	J. O'Hagan: 3/43
YMCA	Drawn	163	76/8	E. Lewis: 54	P. Coghlan: 2/11
YMCA (C)	Won	179/9	174/8	D. McKenna: 59	J. O'Hagan: 2/18
Pembroke	Lost	67	125	K. Allwright: 21	E. Lewis: 3/10
Clontarf	Lost	129	171/8	E. Lewis: 39	E. Lewis: 2/20
Malahide	Drawn	162/8	114/8	J. O'Hagan: 85*	R. Stanton: 3/7
Phoenix (C)	Lost	214	280/3	D. Gee: 47	J. O'Hagan: 2/79
The Hills	Drawn	183/6	97/6	A. Little: 64*	J. O'Hagan: 3/25
Wiggins Teape					
Leinster	Lost	170	183/8	D. O'Herlihy: 51	J. O'Hagan: 4/78
Railway Union	Tied	175/9	175/7	J. McGeady: 62*	J. Walsh: 3/30
YMCA	Lost	155	156/5	J. McGeady: 40	P. Nielsen: 4/60
The Hills	Won				
Malahide	Won	146/5	143	J. O'Hagan: 5/36	J. Heavey: 37
Phoenix	Lost	215/9	225	J. Heavey: 86	P. Nielsen: 3/45
CYM	Lost	221/8	293/4	K. Allwright: 46	J. O'Hagan: 2/59
Clontarf	Lost	129	150/8	K. Allwright: 41	R. Stanton: 3/38
Pembroke	Lost	120/8	122/6	D. O'Herlihy: 27	P. Coghlan: 5/43
Old Belvedere	Lost	106	108/4	K. McDonald: 34	C. Curley: 2/33
Carlisle	Won	213/7	205/9	D. O'Herlihy: 58	E. Lewis: 4/30

Junior: Merrion 2nds finish 5/10 in the Senior 2 League, with 58.2 per cent, having played 17, won 8, lost 7, drawn 2. Jim Walsh's team lose to Clontarf 2nds in the first round of the Senior 2 Cup, 101 to 247. Merrion 3rds finish 3/9 in the Middle League, with 63.8 per cent, having played 13, won 6, lost 3, drawn 4. Jimmy O'Cleirigh's team is drawn against Leinster 3rds in the first round of the Middle Cup. Merrion 4ths finish 6/10 in Section B of the Intermediate League, with 53 per cent, having played 15, won 4, lost 7, drawn 4. Frank Nugent's team is drawn against Carlow in the first round of the Intermediate Cup. Merrion 5ths finish 2/8 in Section C of the Junior League, with 75 per cent, having played 12, won 9, lost 3, and are promoted to Junior B. Mark Rutledge's team is drawn against Civil Service 4ths in the second round of the Junior Cup.

CLUB NOTES

A cash register is purchased for the bar. Improvements to the dressing rooms and showers are planned, along with the redecoration of the bar and dining areas. New club ties are ordered. A letter is received from the residents of the Hazeldene flats, complaining about the level of noise at discos. Forrest Hills Fruit Farms stump up for the damage to the entrance wall. Bective Rugby Club offer a payment to comply with the conditions of the court settlement, but do not repair the ground properly at the end of the 1982/83 season. A small liaison committee is formed from both clubs to ensure the satisfactory maintenance of the ground by

Bective in the future. Another break-in is reported. The alarm system is dismantled, a window broken, the till damaged and about £300 of bar stock stolen. A sympathy letter is written to his next of kin after the death of Eddie Daly, a vice-president. An award for Player of the Month is introduced. Crates of empties are stolen from the back of the pavilion. The occupants of 63 Anglesea Road erect a door between their garden and the club premises, without permission, and are asked to restore the wall. There are more problems with the operation of the bar, with drinks not being paid for and it not closing on time. The management committee's views on the restructuring of the Senior leagues is conveyed to the LCU: A) there are too many Senior 1 teams; B) promotion and relegation to and from Senior 1 is acceptable, provided professionals are not allowed. The status of lady cricketers is discussed once again, without conclusion. Tommy McGeady is congratulated on his appointment as President of the LCU in the following year. It's planned to play some Junior and Women's fixtures at Gonzaga College in 1984. Other ideas include a gate for the main entrance, a new scorebox, covers and an extra cage net for practising.

PROFILE: ANDREW NIXON

R-H middle-order batsman with a powerful, straight drive. R-A occasional bowler of slow tempting leg breaks that don't break. Educated at Downside School in Somerset. Moved to Ireland in 1984. Didn't bring his gear, as he wasn't expecting any cricket to be played here. He found himself in Sandymount, with four clubs within walking distance. Worked for many years as a stockbroker, before retiring to Thomastown and Portugal, just before the bubble burst. Also played rugby and tennis and now spoils good walks. He played 148 games for Merrion 1sts from 1982 to 2001, scoring 2,004 runs @ 16.56, with a top score of 109* (in 1994 against Dublin University) and including 3*50s. He took 49 catches and 1 stumping. Andrew spent his first year in Ireland playing cricket for YMCA, noticed the absence of a bar, and moved up Simmonscourt Road to Merrion, not knowing that Rebecca Rutledge was lying in wait for him. But he's not the only Merrion cricketer to marry another Merrion cricketer, nor is he the only player to begin his honeymoon by featuring for the 1sts the day after his wedding. This precedent had already been set by Cecil Little in 1936. Andrew's wonderful idea of fun was to use the Merrion scoreboard to 'mark' the ladies for pulchritude as they parked their cars on the Thursday of each Horse Show, and to follow anyone with a score of eight or more down to the RDS. Sad. Yet strangely compelling.

1984: DEATH OF JACK O'DONNELL; UNDER-13 JEYES CUP WINNERS

Senior: fixtures 18, reported 18, won 2, lost 11, drawn 4, tied 1. President: S. Curley. Captain: D. McKenna. Merrion thrash Cork Church of Ireland in the first round of the Schweppes Cup, 284/6 to 127, thanks largely to an aggressive 133* from John Heavey, including 2*6s and 16*4s. But they lose easily to Ballymena in the next round, 130 to 133/1. Belvedere Bond regulation changes: reverts to a single league; no final; if the side winning the toss bats, the innings may not exceed 55 overs; if it inserts the opposition, the innings may not exceed 60 overs; 14 points to be awarded for a win, 7 for a tie, 3 for a draw; 1 bonus point will be awarded for each 20 runs scored over 80 to a maximum of 5, and one bonus point for each wicket taken after the fifth; matches of less than five hours play will be refixed. Denis

McKenna is elected captain on the anti-O'Herlihy ticket and Stanley Parkinson returns to the fold after fourteen quite successful seasons with Leinster. In the Belvedere Bond League, Merrion finish 11/13, with 90 points and no money, having played 12, won 1, lost 6, drawn 4, tied 1. They lose comfortably to Malahide in the first round of the Sportsgear Senior Cup.

The Wiggins Teape is now split into two sections with an end-of-season final. Merrion finish joint 4/6 in Section A, with Railway Union and The Hills, on 10 points each, having played 5, won 1, lost 4, including a match against Malahide which Merrion refused to play in the absence of official umpires, the game being awarded to Malahide. Another poor season, and it's time to start counting again. Not including the Schweppes Cup or any 20-over competitions, Merrion 1sts have now won eleven games out of their last fifty-eight. Plenty of runs are scored in a season whose results may be due mainly to the absence of quality bowlers to back up Robbie Stanton. The runs come from skipper McKenna, with 265 @ 16.56, John O'Hagan, with 357 @ 23.80, Stan Parkinson, with 339 @ 24.21 and Paul Nielsen, with 201 @ 16.75. Eddie Lewis grooves his customary 234 runs @ 16.71 and seizes 16 wickets @ 29.00. John Heavey flicks 242 runs @ 14.23 and filches 15 wickets @ 24.53. In a season when the opposition is bowled out on three occasions, Robbie Stanton manages 37 wickets @ 21.97, including 7/49 against Pembroke. Dick Clarke poaches 11 wickets @ 31.90:

Opponent	Result	Mer.	Opp.	Best Batting: Runs	Best Bowling: Wickets
Leinster	Drawn	164/9	226/4	J. O'Hagan: 53	J. O'Hagan: 1/2
Pembroke	Lost	182/8	183/8	J. O'Hagan: 57*	R. Stanton: 7/49
Old Belvedere	Lost	153	187/8	E. Lewis: 39	J. Heavey: 4/90
CYM	Drawn	223/5	240/3	S. Parkinson: 62*	R. Stanton: 2/77
Clontarf	Lost	75	200/7	P. Neilsen: 22	R. Stanton: 3/80
DU	Won	125/4	124	D. McKenna: 41	R. Clarke: 4/7
Railway Union	Drawn	208/8	190/9	J. Heavey: 45	R. Stanton: 4/65
Malahide (C)	Lost	159	220/7	S. Parkinson: 36	P. Coghlan: 3/43
The Hills	Tied	138	138	D. McKenna: 37	E. Lewis: 4/30
Malahide	Drawn	130/7	197/3	K. Allwright: 38	R. Stanton: 2/61
Carlisle	Lost	108	111/5	J. Heavey: 30	P. Neilsen: 2/18
Phoenix	Lost	181	184/5	P. Neilsen: 61	J. Heavey: 2/24
YMCA	Lost	91	93/2	E. Lewis: 37*	R. Clarke: 1/20
Wiggins Teape					
Malahide	Lost			No umpires.	Merrion refuse to play.
Railway Union	Won	145	123	E. Lewis: 38	R. Stanton: 6/50
The Hills	Lost	126	217/8	D. McKenna: 33	R. Stanton: 4/55
YMCA	Lost	163/8	165/2	J. O'Hagan: 66	R. Stanton: 1/38
Leinster	Lost	131	132/2	S. Parkinson: 36	D. McKenna: 1/2

Junior: Merrion 2nds finish 8/10 in the Senior 2 League, with 38 per cent, having played 16, won 2, lost 7, drawn 7. Stephen King's team lose a close match to Leinster 2nds in the first round of the Senior 2 Cup, 161/8 to 162/9. Merrion 3rds finish 10/10 in the Middle League, with 32.9 per cent, having played 16, won 1, lost 9, drawn 6. Brendan Dowling's team beats YMCA 3rds in the first round of the Middle Cup, but loses to Leinster 4ths in the next round, 150 to 154/6. Merrion 4ths finish 6/9 in Section B of the Intermediate League, with 48.3 per cent, having played 16, won 5, lost 8, drawn 3. Eamon Ryan's team runs completely out of energy in the Intermediate Cup, losing to Addinstown in the second round, 59 to 62/1. Eamonn communicates his resignation before the end of the season, citing pressure of studies, and Tommy McGeady takes over. Merrion 5ths win their last nine matches in a row to finish 3/7 in Section C of the Junior League, with 75 per cent, having played 12, won 9, lost 3. Frank Dolan's team beats Ring Commons 2nds in the first round of the Junior Cup, 104/8 to 103, but loses to YMCA 4ths in the third round. Merrion Schoolboys win the Under-13 Jeyes Cup.

CLUB NOTES

Legal advice recommends not pursuing the occupants of 63 Anglesea Road to rebuild the wall. Tommy McGeady volunteers to pursue the matter in a neighbourly fashion instead. Repairs to the ground after Bective have finished with it are now carried out by Merrion staff, but paid for by the rugby club. A new scorebox is built and extra seating is arranged around the ground. Denis McKenna agrees to pursue the matter of sawdust. A glass washer and bottle cooler are purchased for the bar. A letter from a Mrs Connolly alleges assault on her son after a party. The question of exemption from VAT on car-parking receipts is raised. A meeting reluctantly agrees to accept the LCU decision awarding a Wiggins Teape match to Malahide, as Merrion refuse to play without official umpires. A letter from the club's solicitor states that the Bective licence can be terminated on 30 September 1985, provided notice is served to the rugby club by 30 September 1984. A meeting agrees to do this as a matter of urgency. A delegate to the LCU meeting is charged with the club's vote against professionals playing in Senior cricket in 1985. A motion at a committee meeting that two women be granted a vote at the AGM is defeated. The Hon. Secretary comments favourably on the huge amount of work carried out during the season by John O'Hagan. A meeting of the new committee agrees to host the 1985 Senior Cup final. The club's condolences are sent to Clare, the widow of Jack (Geke) O'Donnell, Merrion's 1940 winning captain of both the Senior Cup and Senior League. Jack McConnell threatens to leave the club unless he can get more games, and a decision is made to enter a 6ths the follow-ing year. The galvanised sheeting from the new covers is stolen. Double yellow lines are painted outside the club entrance, on the Donnybrook side. A club tour to Wales is planned for 1985.

PROFILE: STEPHEN KING

R-H solid, powerful, middle-order batsman. Occasional bowler of accurate R-A slow swingers. Educated at St Andrew's College. Works as a senior business specialist with Zurich Insurance. Played rugby at school and for Old Wesley Under-19s until a back injury forced his retirement. He has also played hockey for Pembroke Wanderers and has been a crew member in a yacht racing team. A treasurer of Merrion and a founder member and treasurer of *The Syndicate*, who never let such a difficult job get in the way of his cricket, where he played 252 games from 1980 to 2005 (for more years than he cares to remember), scoring 3,549 runs @ 17.92, with a top score of 87*, and including 12*50s. He took 53 wickets @ 21.64, with 5 wick-ets in an innings on 1 occasion, and 70 catches. He was a member of the Whitney Moore & Keller B League winning teams in 1997 and 1999, and the Lewis Traub League winning team in 1999. *Sid* came up through the Schoolboy ranks and continues to feature on the Junior sides, until the call from the Avenue of Bird reaches his ears, at which stage he will probably ignore it and turn to ruining good walks.

1985: SENIOR CUP RUNNERS-UP; SENIOR 2 LEAGUE RUNNERS-UP; MIDDLE B LEAGUE WINNERS; TOUR OF WALES

Senior: fixtures 20, reported 20, won 3, lost 11, drawn 4, no result 2. President: S. Curley. Captain: S. Parkinson. Professionals are banned by the LCU from this year until 1990. Merrion lose to North Down in the second round (bye in the first) of the Schweppes Cup. Belvedere Bond regulation changes: if a match has not commenced two hours after the scheduled starting time due to weather, then the match shall be refixed; once play has commenced and is interrupted by weather, then if the total playing time lost exceeds two hours, and the pitch is then declared playable by the umpires, the match may continue to the appointed finishing time if either captain so wishes, but if a match is continued like this and no result is achieved, then the match shall be refixed. None of this matters a monkey's to Merrion, who finish last in the Belvedere Bond League, with 78 points and no money, having played 12, won 1, lost 7, drawn 4. The Wiggins Teape League now involves the top two teams of each section in semi-finals, followed by a final. A damp end to the summer (the wettest July, August and September in 100 years) means that Merrion play only three games and finish 6/6 in Section A, with 4 points, having lost all 3. The poor performances in the leagues are somewhat nullified by a good run in the Sportsgear Senior Cup, where they beat Clontarf (for the first time since 1962, with Kevin Allwright winning the Man of the Match award) in the second round (bye in the first). A win against The Hills in the semi-final follows, with John O'Hagan getting his first Man of the Match award. But they lose a seesaw final to Leinster on a quirky pitch at Anglesea Road. Merrion bat first and are 8/5 after thirty minutes. The game might be over by lunch, but hey, at least Stan didn't *put them in*. Then Kevin Allwright and John O'Hagan come together to see off the dangerous seam attack of Jones and Wills, which should probably have been bowled through for the full 12 overs. Once settled, they take the game by the scruff of the neck and raise the Merrion total to a respectable 149. Then the stout-hearted O'Hagan rocks the Leinster batting with 3/7 in 8 overs, before himself being taken off after 8 overs, when his bristling tail is up. Leinster climb to 101/7 and there's still a good chance that Merrion might lift this trophy for only the third time since 1935. But Philip Nartey and Tom McDonnell have other ideas, and they apply themselves in the Allwright/O'Hagan manner to bring Leinster over the line, with the help of a significant 27 from Ernie Extras. John O'Hagan wins a consolation prize in his second Man of the Match award this season.

Kevin Allwright's maiden ton comes against Pembroke in the Belvedere Bond League, in 171 minutes, with 4*6s and 12*4s. Eddie Lewis is absent for this season, working in London. And by the way, Merrion 1sts have now won fourteen games out of their last seventy-eight. A tour of Wales is undertaken, with predictable consequences for one unfortunate hotel, including more than just sausages for breakfast. At least they don't have to bear the burden of the £29 worth of reverse charge calls made to the clubhouse. Kevin Allwright hoicks 302 runs @ 30.20. Stan Parkinson drives and cuts his way to 233 runs @ 14.56. Ken McDonald swishes 124 runs @ 15.50. John Heavey squirts 188 runs @ 12.53. John O'Hagan pulls 250 runs @ 19.23 and swings 23 wickets @ 19.56. Robbie Stanton wafts 255 runs @ 15.93 and filches 22 wickets @ 16.72. Stephen King delivers 18 wickets @ 15.38. David Heavey takes out 22 batsmen @ 18.81:

Opponent	Result	Mer.	Opp.	Best Batting: Runs	Best Bowling: Wickets
YMCA	Lost	63	64/1	K. McDonald. 23	J. O'Hagan: 1/16
Old Belvedere	Drawn	170/9	37/2	S. Parkinson: 35	J. O'Hagan: 1/13
DU	Drawn	107/6	147	J. Heavey: 22	J. O'Hagan: 6/48
Pembroke	Drawn	200/9	144/8	K. Allwright: 108*	D. Heavey: 4/20

Leinster	Lost	119	181/7	J. Heavey: 23	S. King: 3/30
The Hills	Lost	122/9	123/6	K.J. O'Herlihy: 27*	R. Stanton: 3/37
Carlisle	Lost	149	151/7	J. O'Hagan: 23	R. Stanton: 6/38
Clontarf (C)	Won	138/7	137	K. Allwright: 59*	S. King: 3/26
Railway Union	Drawn	108/7	165/8	J. Walsh: 24*	D. Heavey: 3/43
Phoenix	Lost	121/9	123/1	S. Parkinson: 21	S. King: 1/21
The Hills (C)	Won	185/7	149	K. McDonald: 47	J. O'Hagan: 3/30
CYM	Won	78/0	74	R. Stanton: 53*	D. Heavey: 5/28
Leinster	Lost	149/9	152/7	J. O'Hagan: 65	J. O'Hagan: 3/27
Senior Cup final					
Clontarf	Lost	139	142/2	D. McKenna: 24	D. McKenna: 1/4
Malahide	Lost	96	97/1	D. McKenna: 25	D. Heavey: 1/29
Wiggins Teape					
Railway Union	Lost	205/7	206/7	R. Stanton: 54	S. King: 4/66
Phoenix	Lost	70	151/9	E. Extras: 18	J. Craven: 2/22
Pembroke	No Res.				
YMCA	Lost	89	126/3	R. Stanton: 31	J. O'Hagan: 2/51
Malahide	No Res.				

Junior: Merrion 2nds finish 2/10 in the Senior 2 League, with 59.1 per cent, having played 16, won 7, lost 3, drawn 6. Alan Little's team loses to Clontarf 2nds in the first round of the Senior 2 Cup. Merrion 3rds win the Middle B League, finishing 1/9, with 77 per cent, having played 12, won 9, lost 1, drawn 2, and gain promotion to Middle A. Jimmy O'Cleirigh's team, including Siva, Eamonn Ryan and Les Deacon, beat Phoenix 3rds in the second round of the Middle Cup, 184/6 to 183, but lose to Leinster 3rds in the next round. Merrion 4ths finish 5/9 in the Intermediate A League, with 53.1 per cent, having played 11, won 4, lost 4, drawn 3. In the Intermediate Cup, Mick Shortall's team loses to Balbriggan in the replay of a tied semi-final. Merrion 5ths finish 4/10 in the Junior A League, with 54.5 per cent, having played 11, won 6, lost 5. Frank Dolan's team beats Sandyford in the first round of the Junior Cup, 81/2 to 80, then Knockbrack 2nds by 63/5 to 61, before losing to Aer Lingus in the semi-final. A Merrion 6ths makes a first appearance in the Junior B League, but do not participate in the Minor Cup, as the draw is already made. Pat Hinkson's team finishes 8/9 in the league, with 31 per cent, having played 8, won 2, lost 5, drawn 1. Despite this new team, Jack McConnell leaves Merrion for a season at Cold-Blow Lane. Merrion Schoolboys lose the final of the Under-15 Yates Hale Cup to Phoenix.

CLUB NOTES

A letter from Mrs Connolly's solicitor threatens legal action for the assault on her son. The owner of 43 Anglesea Road, Mrs Molloy claims to have a right of way into her garden, now that there are gates at the club entrance, and Mr Molloy drives his van through the gates to prove it. The owners of No.63 promise to rebuild the wall after six months and at the same time ask if they can park some cars on the grounds when their new Bed & Breakfast opens. Merrion's solicitor is busy, busy, busy. Problems also arise with the new pump, when it is discovered that the well is blocked forty-five feet down. It is blown clear, the pump is installed (not that it's needed this year) and a manhole cover created. No credit is to be given at the bar. Noel Mahony is suggested as a coach. Mrs Kirrane, of 63 Anglesea Road, has her request for car-parking spaces turned down. It's agreed to vote again at the LCU meeting to ban professionals in 1986. A levelling programme on the outfield is commenced. In September, a meeting reports that no money has been received from the women for 1985. The Hon. Treasurer makes provision for money outstanding from John A. Stanton. A Cosec grant of £300 is received. The ongoing issue of late payment of subscriptions is raised yet again by the Hon. Secretary at the AGM. Members express their dissatisfaction at the lack of organisation of practices. It's worth noting that this year, a quarter of the club's revenue derives from bar profits. The meeting voices its appreciation of the achievements of the women at club and international level. The owners of 65 Anglesea Road request permission to bring in and remove skips from the club grounds.

PROFILE: ROBBIE STANTON

R-H awkward batsman. R-A gangling, medium-pace bowler of off-cutters. It has been written that Robbie has only one shot, a lofted cover drive between mid-off and extra cover that provides 90 per cent of his runs. This is a diabolical calumny. Robbie has two shots. The second shot is a delicate leg glance to a ball on or outside the leg stump. Actually he can block, too. Educated at St Michael's College. Operations Manager in a pharmaceutical company. Also plays pitch and putt and can often be found rolling a cricket ball around the boundary after he's out and when he should really be supporting his team. Brother to women's cricketers Alice and Marie, he is Merrion's most-capped Senior player, with 395 games for Merrion 1sts, 26 more than Simon Curley. Scored 4,637 runs @ 17.63, including 16*50s and with a top score of 91*. Snared 300 wickets @ 20.49, including 5 wickets in a match on seven occasions, with best bowling figures of 8/16 against Pembroke in 1988. Took 102 catches. Captain in 1990 and 1993. Played for the Irish Under-19s in 1981 against Denmark, and in representative cricket for Leinster in the Guinness Cup. Like so many Merrion men, he met and married his trouble and strife in Merrion – Arlene, herself a cricketer with at least twice as many strokes as he has. Robbie is currently travelling down the ranks in style, with runs galore on the 2nds and 3rds, in preparation for twenty years of mat cricket on the avenue of tweeting birds. At sixteen years of age, on the tour of London in 1979, Robbie was tempted to try a very hot curry for the first time. His reaction and near-death experience are still remembered with fondness by those present, who will always regard him as *The Vindaloo Kid*. He is fifth on the list of Merrion all-rounders.

1986: SENIOR 2 CUP RUNNERS-UP; INTERMEDIATE CUP RUNNERS-UP; JUNIOR CUP WINNERS; WHELAN CUP WINNERS; HURRICANE CHARLIE

Senior: fixtures 18, reported 18, won 4, lost 10, drawn 4. President: S. Curley. Captain: S. Parkinson. Merrion lose to Donemana in a bowl-out in the second round (bye in the first) of the Schweppes Cup, with only one player out of twenty-two hitting the stumps. Belvedere Bond regulation changes: matches to be of 110 overs duration, with the side batting first not to exceed 60 overs; after the first innings is over, the balance of overs is available to the side batting second; if a match has not commenced three hours after the scheduled start due to weather, it shall be refixed; once play has commenced and as a result of weather interruption less than 60 overs have been bowled, the match shall be refixed; if a match commences and is interrupted by the weather but at least 60 overs have been bowled, or the side batting first has been dismissed or declared, then the match shall not be refixed but shall continue on the next weeknight at 6.00p.m.; if no play is possible then the match is treated as a draw. After a good start, Merrion fall away badly to finish 9/13 in the Belvedere Bond League, with 137 points and no money, having played 12, won 4, lost 4, drawn 4. They lose the toss to YMCA on a foggy morning in the second round (bye in the first) of the Sportsgear Cup, and are knocked out.

In the Wiggins Teape, Merrion finish 5/5 in Section A, with no points, having played 5, lost 5. They have now won eighteen games out of their last ninety-six. More often than not, it's the batting that lets them down this year, despite Eddie Lewis's return from his sabbatical. He drives 311 runs @ 18.29. John Heavey grinds 196 runs @ 19.60. Stephen King thumps 194 runs @ 16.16 and poaches 16 wickets @ 18.25. Kevin Allwright hoicks 261 runs @ 21.75. Paul Nielsen grooves 397 runs @ 28.35 and 14 wickets @ 27.14. John O'Hagan hooks 176 runs @ 13.53 and filches 20 wickets @ 16.25. Stan Parkinson pummels 308 runs @ 18.11. John Craven procures 23 wickets @ 19.08. Kirby Tarrant joins Merrion from Old Belvedere midseason and snatches 11 wickets @ 20.54:

Opponent	Result	Mer.	Opp.	Best Batting: Runs	Best Bowling: Wickets
CYM	Won	135	64	E. Lewis: 30	J. O'Hagan: 5/16
Carlisle	Lost	140/8	141/3	P. Nielsen: 40	D. Heavey: 2/30
Malahide	Won	218	114	S. Parkinson: 84	J. O'Hagan: 3/23
Old Belvedere	Lost	150	151/6	J. Heavey: 53	D. Heavey: 2/35
DU	Drawn	231/6	182/7	P. Nielsen: 105*	J. O'Hagan: 4/50
The Hills	Drawn	141/8	155	E. Lewis: 41	J. Craven: 4/35
Phoenix	Won	221/7	209	P. Nielsen: 77	P. Neilsen: 3/46
Clontarf	Lost	108	112/3	J. Heavey: 35	R. Stanton: 2/0
YMCA (C)	Lost	145/9	148/2	J. O'Hagan: 65*	J. O'Hagan: 2/22
Railway Union	Won	156/8	137	K. Allwright: 40	S. King: 5/21
Pembroke	Lost	44	47/0	P. Neilsen: 13	
YMCA	Drawn	54/6	177/7	D. O'Herlihy: 19	J. Craven: 3/30
Leinster	Drawn	172/7	133/7	S. King: 71*	K. Tarrant: 3/32
Wiggins Teape					
Clontarf	Lost	134/5	138/1	E. Lewis: 59	K. Tarrant: 1/43
Malahide	Lost	82	192/5	A. Little: 18	S. King: 3/50
Old Belvedere	Lost	95	147/6	K. Allwright: 33	J. Craven: 3/56
Pembroke	Lost	89	103	S. King: 33	P. Coghlan: 5/56
Carlisle	Lost	75	170/7	E. Lewis: 33	J. Craven: 3/43

Junior: Merrion 2nds finish 5/11 in the Senior 2 League, with 51.5 per cent, having played 10, won 4, lost 5, drawn 1. Alan Little's team loses the final of the Senior 2 Cup to Railway Union, 147 to 188/8, despite Derek Kilpatrick's 37 runs of doughty obstruction. But hey, at least he didn't *put them in*. After a poor start, Merrion 3rds finish 4/9 in the Middle A League, with 63.5 per cent, having played 12, won 5, lost 3, drawn 3, tied 1. Jimmy O'Cleirigh's team beat Leinster 4ths in the first round of the Middle Cup, 202/9 to 159, but is knocked out of the competition by Clontarf 3rds in the semi-final. Merrion 4ths finish 3/9 in the Intermediate A League, with 59.6 per cent, having played 10, won 4, lost 3, drawn 3. They lose to Balbriggan in the final of the Intermediate Cup, 104 to 132. Mick Shortall's team beats Aer Lingus to win the 20 overs Whelan Cup. Merrion 5ths finish 3/10 in the Intermediate B League, with 63.3 per cent, having played 11, won 5, lost 3, drawn 3. Mark Rutledge's team beats Aer Lingus to win the Junior Cup in a low-scoring match, thanks to Brendan Whyte's 12* and 7 wickets. Merrion 6ths finish 9/9 in the Junior B league, with 30 per cent, having played 10, won 3, lost 7. They lose the semi-final of the Minor Cup to Clontarf 6ths, 174/6 to 175/7.

CLUB NOTES

Simon Curley is absent from meetings for part of the season through ill health. Games against two touring sides are arranged for Anglesea Road – University of East Anglia and the Northern Club, Liverpool. New roller shutters are purchased for the bar counter. A Nottingham artificial practice wicket is installed. A lock is placed on the entrance gate. A letter is written to Mrs Molloy of 43 Anglesea Road, denying her a right of way, but suggesting a compromise whereby she might be permitted to use the club's entrance to her rear garden. A meeting decides to take legal proceedings against the owners of 63 Anglesea Road to force them to rebuild their wall. It is planned to employ David Murray, Malahide's West Indian coach, for one day per week throughout the season, but this doesn't work out. Noel Mahony and John Lyon of Clontarf are appointed instead. A letter of sympathy is written to the widow of Merrion stalwart Tommy Burke. The solicitors of the owner of 65 Anglesea Road claim a right of way and demand a key to the gate on her behalf. A presentation is made to Conor Devery, the 1sts scorer, on his return to England. Problems with the women's committee and teas are ongoing throughout this year.

On Monday 25 August, Hurricane Charlie makes an unwelcome appearance, causing the flashy Dodder to flood its banks and turn the ground into a sizeable swimming pool, up to five feet deep in places, including the pavilion. Severe damage is caused to all furniture and domestic equipment, as well as tractor, scarifier, mowers, rollers, practice wickets, sightscreens, cage nets and covers. Mud is deposited everywhere. The club is not insured against floods and storms. This is the third flooding of Merrion in the twentieth century and as on previous occasions, the members band together to remove the silt from the outfield and carry out the reseeding. An emergency meeting is called to plan the recovery of the machinery and pavilion. To help pay for this, it is decided to fix subscriptions at £50 for Senior members, £25 for Junior, £15 for Schoolboy and pavilion members, and to charge a extra levy of £10 on all members in 1987. A cheque for £100 is received from YMCA as a contribution to help defray the costs of repair. Other clubs also help out. The outfield at Gonzaga needs clearing. Wyse Management (responsible for the Hazeldene flats) are contacted about the damage to the practice nets. A claim for a grant is lodged with Cosec. The AGM is taken up with discussions about how to get the club back to normal, and to prevent a similar disaster in the future. Cosec provide a grant of £550 towards the ground repairs. The LCU recommend that a further application be made in 1987. The club also applies for a Cospoir grant from their 1987 fund. A tree used by vandals to cross the Dodder from Herbert Park is removed by Dublin Corporation. Representatives of the women's committee attend the final meeting of the year, and it is agreed to increase their contribution to the club in return for practice facilities on two nights per week, and the use of St Columba's for home games, but alternative arrangements will have to be made regarding teas in future.

PROFILE: NORMAN REEVES

R–H batsman. R–A accurate, slow, medium swing bowler. Educated at High School. Insurance official. Also played soccer and was a second-row forward for Old Wesley. Played Schoolboy

Merrion 5ths, Junior Cup winners, 1986. Back row: C. Gleeson, P. McGeady, R. Paul, T. McGeady, A. McKenna, A. O'Keeffe. Front row: F. Dolan, G. Quinn, M. Rutledge (C), B. Whyte, P. Hourihane, M. Little.

cricket for one year at Pembroke, but most of his early cricket was with 3rd Old Boy's Union, who played at Serpentine Avenue until their disbandonment in 1966. Norman played twenty-one games for Merrion 1sts between 1967 and 1974, taking 13 wickets @ 21.84, including 5/55 against Railway Union in 1968. Played most of his cricket on the Junior sides, captaining the 2nds and 3rds several times. He was the Merrion groundsman from 1999 to 2007, during which time he could be found on many a morning rolling the wickets at 6a.m. Those wickets were so good that there might be one for the month of April, one for May, etc., and they could be played on as many times as necessary. By the end of August, half the square might still be in pristine condition, not having been played on yet. '*Just in case there are a few rearranged games in September.*' His obsession with the quality of the wickets at Anglesea Road has been of great interest to members of the Merrion bar on more than one occasion, and his tenure coincided with a period of great success for the club at all levels, due in no small part to his preparation of good batting tracks, with just enough in them for those bowlers who were good enough to exploit it. He is married to former Maid of the Mountain, Margaret, who also played cricket for Merrion in the early '80s.

1987: INTERMEDIATE A LEAGUE WINNERS; WHELAN CUP RUNNERS-UP; INTERMEDIATE B LEAGUE RUNNERS-UP; JUNIOR B LEAGUE WINNERS; MINOR CUP RUNNERS-UP; TOUR OF LONDON AND SUSSEX

Senior: fixtures 18, reported 18, won 5, lost 10, drawn 3. President: S. Curley. Captain: J. Walsh. Merrion beat Bready in the second round (bye in the first) of the Schweppes Cup in a bowl-out, with Stan Parkinson hitting the stumps with the last ball to give them a 2/1 victory. But they lose to Clontarf in the next round. Belvedere Bond regulation change: if a team bowls its overs at less than 17 overs per hour (or 55 overs in an uninterrupted session) then it shall be deducted 2 points for each over or part of an over by which the average falls short of 17 per hour. Under new captain, Jim Walsh, Merrion finish 8/13 in the Belvedere Bond League, with 150 points and no money, having played 12, won 4, lost 5, drawn 3. Yet the final position is deceptive, as it would have been second place, had one loss by a margin of 6 runs and two draws by margins of 6 runs and 1 wicket, been translated into wins. They *put* YMCA *in to bat* in the first round of the Sportsgear Cup, and lose by 123 runs as a consequence, with their opponents using 10 bowlers for a lark.

In the Wiggins Teape, Merrion finish 5/5 in Section A, with 10 points, having played 5 games, won 1 and lost 4. Merrion 1sts have now won 23 games out of their last 114. A tour of London and Sussex takes place, with games against Morden, Haywards Heath, Carnegie Exiles, Portslade and Camberley scheduled. Eddie Lewis is once again the only Merrion representative in the provincial batting statistics, with a significant 606 runs @ 33.66. Other runs come from Kevin Allwright, with 269 runs @ 29.88; John Heavey, with 270 @ 20.76; John O'Hagan (in his last full season on the 1sts), with 325 @ 32.50, and Stan Parkinson, with 288 @ 18.00. Almost half the season's wickets come from Kirby Tarrant, who is fifth in the provincial bowling table, with 48 wickets @ 19.41. Other wickets are gained by Paul Coghlan, with 15 @ 34.73, John Craven, with 12 @ 32.75, and Jim Walsh, with 10 @ 32.80:

Opponent	Result	Mer.	Opp.	Best Batting: Runs	Best Bowling: Wickets
Railway Union	Lost	195/8	196/3		
CYM	Won	183/6	182	E. Lewis: 45	J. Craven: 4/48
Carlisle	Won	195/4	192/8	S. Parkinson: 50	K. Tarrant: 3/40
DU	Drawn	183/7	189	P. Neilsen: 50	J. Craven: 3/51
Old Belvedere	Lost	135	141	J. Heavey: 29	K. Tarrant: 5/53
YMCA (C)	Lost	212/7	335/4	S. Parkinson: 36	J. Craven: 2/45
Phoenix	Lost	170	171/3	J. Heavey: 53	K. Tarrant: 2/75
Pembroke	Lost	196/7	199/5	K. Allwright: 50*	J. O'Hagan: 1/34
YMCA	Won	184/5	180/6	J. O'Hagan: 88*	P. Coghlan: 2/49
Leinster	Drawn	216/5	188/9	E. Lewis: 64	E. Lewis: 4/44
Malahide	Won	172/3	171/9	P. Meehan: 61*	K. Tarrant: 6/34
The Hills	Drawn	169/7	224/6	J. Dunn: 52	K. Tarrant: 3/47
Clontarf	Lost	120	121/0	K. Allwright: 22	
Wiggins Teape					
Leinster	Lost	170	218/7	E. Lewis: 43	E. Lewis: 3/56
Phoenix	Lost	138	139/3	S. Parkinson: 38	K. Tarrant: 2/48
YMCA	Lost	104	107/5	S. King: 36	K. Tarrant: 3/46
Carlisle	Lost	123	127/8	E. Lewis: 28	K. Tarrant: 6/51
CYM	Won	182/7	128	E. Lewis: 75	S. Buckley: 5/3

Junior: Merrion 2nds finish 4/11 in the Senior 2 League, with 53 per cent, having played 18, won 6, lost 6, drawn 6. Niall Morrissey's team loses to CYM 2nds in the second round of the Senior 2 Cup. The 2nds/3rds lose the final of the first Tillain Cup (Sandymount clubs only) by 2 runs. Merrion 3rds finish 4/9 in Section A of the Middle League, with 53.8 per cent, having played 13, won 5, lost 5, drawn 3. Declan Abrahams's team loses to Clontarf 4ths in the second round of the Middle Cup. Merrion 4ths win Section A of the Intermediate League, beating along the way: North County 3rds, 162/6 to 110; Addinstown, 133/9 to 94; Old Belvedere 4ths, 152 to 109, and Civil Service 2nds, 141/4 to 140. Mark Rutledge's team finishes 1/9, with 87 per cent, having played 14, won 12, lost 1, drawn 1, and are promoted to Middle B. L. Pettitt and Brendan Dowling score most runs, while Brian Lovell takes most wickets. They lose to North County 3rds in the second round of the Intermediate Cup. They lose the final of the Whelan Cup. Merrion 5ths finish 2/9 in Section B of the Intermediate League, with 68.7

per cent, having played 14, won 7, lost 3, drawn 4, and are promoted to Intermediate A. Frank Dolan's team loses to CYM 5ths in the first round of the Junior Cup. Merrion 6ths win the Junior B League, beating along the way: North County 5ths, 69/1 to 68; The Hills 4ths, 237/5 to 47; Railway Union 6ths, 256/6 to 60, and North Kildare 2nds, 115/7 to 112. They finish 1/10, with 87.5 per cent, having played 16, won 14, lost 2, and are promoted to Junior A. Frank Fennell's team loses a close Minor Cup Final to Leinster 6ths, 170/8 to 171/9, despite J. Joyce's 48 and J. Kingston's 59 and 3/47.

CLUB NOTES

An early meeting decides to charge the women £400 for the season, instead of the usual £100, to cover the cost of employing a tea lady. Danny Parkinson becomes manager of the 1sts. The Hazeldene Management Company are allowed to enter the car park area to fix their wall, as they agree verbally to meet the cost of repairing the practice facility. Subsequently, their solicitor refuses liability. An insurance inspector checks out the ground for flood cover, and is not satisfied with the club's security precautions, particularly with respect to public liability and rights of way. Old Belvedere send a cheque for £200 to help out with repairs. The door in the boundary wall at 63 Anglesea Road is repaired at last. Perhaps the owners have perceived an advantage to having a wall over five-feet high along the end of their garden. It is agreed that all applications from the Anglesea Road residents to have equipment brought in to clear up their houses and gardens should be made in writing, and that our reply should also be written, and a record kept of such communication. The owners of 43 Anglesea Road fence out the jutting corner originally granted verbally to the club for its use. A meeting decides to discuss their right to a key to the gate, but without granting them a right of way.

Merrion 4ths, Intermediate A League winners, 1987. Back row: C. Gleeson, K. Gunn, P. Hourihane, S. Buckley, B. Lovell, J. Morrissey Snr, J. Hancock. Front row: D. Abrahams, B. Howell, M. Shortall (C), D. Soraghan, B. Little.

Philip Herron is asked to find an insurance policy that will provide cover for the three perils – flood, tempest and storm. Merrion's solicitor advises that they have no claim on Hazeldene for the damage to the practice nets. It is God, and not they, who are responsible. As yet another court case looms, the club offers to buy the disputed corner of the garden in 43 Anglesea Road, to square off the wickets. Failing to find an insurance company that will provide cover for the three perils, the club decides to remain with Sun Alliance. At least they provide public liability cover, although none for burst pipes. Someone buys three floppy hats from Sportsgear, without permission. The court action against the owners of 43 Anglesea Road is withdrawn, at considerable cost in legal fees. It is reported at a meeting that the cost of the flood is about £5,000.

New club caps are ordered. A phased programme of levelling the outfield is planned. The girl who does the teas complains about not being given money in advance to buy the food. It is reported that 43 Anglesea Road is being sold as eight flats with no tenants, and the club is invited to tender. A meeting decides to oppose a total ban on professionals for 1988, presumably due to difficulties in getting a proper coach. At the AGM, a vote of thanks to the outgoing President, Simon Curley, is passed by acclamation. A sponsorship deal with Budweiser is signed. Cathal McAlinden is asked to establish contact with the purchaser of 43 Anglesea Road, with a view to buying the garden, the club not being able to afford the full property. The LCU maintains the ban on professionals for 1988. The year ends with the worrying possibility that both the Spring and Horse Shows may be moved from Ballsbridge.

PROFILE: JOHN CRAVEN

R-H batsman, who made a sterling number 11. R-A slow off-break spinner. Born in Brighton and educated at Queen's University and the Royal School of Mines in London. Geologist, oil executive and businessman, who still supports Brighton & Hove Albion Football Club. Having played for the Junior sides in Leinster Cricket Club, John moved to Merrion in 1985, did well on the 3rds and 2nds, and earned his place on the 1sts as the only slow bowler during the difficult years of the late 1980s. He played ninety-six games for Merrion between 1985 and 1991, scoring 153 runs @ 4.25, with a top score of 26. He took 114 wickets @ 25.35, with 5 wickets in an innings on 1 occasion, and 17 catches. Firsts captain in 1988 and 1989. Ambitious to play for a better team, he returned to Leinster in 1992, where his exploits for Merrion gained him swift entry onto the 1sts. Over the following decade, he helped Leinster to reach two Irish Senior Cup finals, both of which they lost, despite his best efforts. Famous for his half-time dressing-room exhortations to his team, that it was, indeed, a game of two halves – although what that meant was anybody's guess.

1988: SENIOR 2 LEAGUE RUNNERS-UP

Senior: fixtures 18, reported 18, won 4, lost 10, drawn 3, no result 1. President: B. Dowling. Captain: J. Craven. Merrion beat Coleraine by 3 wickets in the second round (bye in the firsts) of the Schweppes Cup. The good run continues with a victory over Pembroke in the next round. But then they lose to North Down in the quarter final, 146/7 to 149/2. Belvedere Bond regulation changes: if a team bowls less than 55 overs in the first 3¼ hours session, it shall be fined 1 point for each over by which the overs bowled fall short of 55; if either team is bowled out within 3¼ hours or the team batting second reaches the target within 3¼ hours then no penalty points apply. No matter, as Merrion finish 12/13 in the

Belvedere Bond, with 114 points and no money, having played 12, won 3, lost 6, drawn 3. They lose to Pembroke by 18 runs in the first round of the Sportsgear Senior Cup. In the Wiggins Teape, Merrion finish 5/6 in Section B, with 14 points, having played 5, won 1, lost 3, no result 1. Merrion 1sts have now won 27 games out of their last 132. Inconsistent batting and bowling result in another disappointing season, wherein John Dunn plays for South Leinster and John Hancock makes his debut for the 1sts as a wicket-keeper at the tender age of fifty. He stands up to all the bowlers, thereby reducing the degree of movement he has to make.

A new surname appears in the Senior ranks, which will have a profound impact on Merrion's success over the following two decades. The name is Joyce. Brothers Damian and Johnny are the first to appear from a family of seven cricketers, five of whom will kick on to play for Ireland, and one of whom will reach the pinnacle of success for an Irish club cricketer. Most of the runs this season are fired from the bats of Eddie Lewis (in his last full season on the 1sts), with 303 runs @ 23.30; Kevin Allwright, with 337 runs @ 33.70; John Dunn, with 369 runs @ 28.38; John Heavey, with 284 runs @ 17.75; Stephen King, with 163 runs @ 20.37, and Stan Parkinson (in his last full season on the 1sts), with 271 runs @ 22.58. Robbie Stanton poaches 31 wickets @ 13.16, including 8/16 against Pembroke. Kirby Tarrant takes 10 wickets @ 36.60. Stephen Buckley grabs a promising 25 wickets @ 19.60 and John Craven delivers 22 wickets @ 24.00:

Opponent	Result	Mer.	Opp.	Best Batting: Runs	Best Bowling: Wickets
Malahide	Lost	99	100/3	J. Dunn: 35	E. Ryan: 1/21
Old Belvedere	Lost	121	125/3	S. Parkinson: 50*	J. Craven: 1/10
Pembroke (C)	Lost	149	167	E. Lewis: 43	S. Buckley: 2/17
DU	Won	209/6	207/6	J. Dunn: 56	S. Buckley: 3/49
Carlisle	Lost	232/3	233/1	E. Lewis: 81*	
Railway Union	Drawn	150/7	189/9	J. Dunn: 63	P. Coghlan: 3/53
Pembroke	Won	153	114	J. Dunn: 55	S. Buckley: 4/22
Leinster	Lost	110	184/7	S. King: 28	S. Buckley: 4/54
YMCA	Drawn	184/7	183/9	J. Dunn: 58	R. Stanton: 5/72
The Hills	Lost	138	139/6	S. Parkinson: 55	E. Lewis: 2/35
Phoenix	Lost	154	174	J. Heavey: 55	K. Tarrant: 3/44
Clontarf	Won	205/7	203/4	K. Allwright: 76	J. Craven: 2/41
CYM	Drawn	163/9	227/6	E. Lewis: 90	J. Craven: 2/56
Wiggins Teape					
Clontarf	No Res.				
CYM	Lost	112	115/4	A. Nixon: 51	J. Dunn: 2/22
Pembroke	Won	76/4	74	J. Heavey: 29	R. Stanton: 8/16
YMCA	Lost	152	210	K. Allwright: 36	S. Buckley: 4/64
Old Belvedere	Lost	145/9	151	R. Stanton: 22	R. Stanton: 4/28

Junior: Merrion 2nds finish 2/11 in the Senior 2 League, with 64.1 per cent, having played 18, won 10, lost 6, drawn 2. Robbie Stanton's team beats Rush in the first round of the Senior 2 Cup, 113/6 to 111/9, but loses to Pembroke 2nds in the next round. Despite being unable to play in the last two matches, Denis McKenna wins the Oulton Cup for Senior 2 bowling, with 46 wickets @ 7.78. Merrion 3rds finish 6/10 in Section A of the Middle League, with 44 per cent, having played 15, won 4, lost 4, drawn 7. Jimmy O'Cleirigh's team beats Old Belvedere 3rds in the first round of the Middle Cup, 207/9 to 189, then Rush 2nds, 212 to 139, then Railway Union 3rds, 116/8 to 115, only to lose to North County 2nds in the semi-final. Merrion 4ths finish 6/9 in Section B of the Middle League, with 46 per cent, having played 14, won 4, lost 5, drawn 5. Dick Clarke's team loses to North Wicklow, 164 to 167/5, in the second round of the Intermediate Cup. Merrion 5ths finish 5/9 in Section A of the Intermediate League, with 48.7 per cent, having played 13, won 5, lost 4, drawn 4. Tom McGeady's team beats Old Belvedere 4ths in the second round of the Intermediate Cup, 91/5 to 90, then Phoenix 4ths, 160/5 to 159, only to lose to YMCA 4ths in the semi-final. Merrion 6ths finish 7/8 in Section A of the Junior League, with 42.8 per cent, having played 14, won 6, lost 8. The points for one game are forfeited, as an ineligible player is fielded. Frank Fennell's team beats Clontarf 6ths in the first round of the Minor Cup, 218 to 188/9, but loses to The Hills 4ths in the next round.

CLUB NOTES

The role of Club President is redefined by a new, energetic, hands-on officer, who also acts as Hon. Treasurer for part of his stint. This job is no longer a reward for services rendered, nor is it thrust upon the last man standing. An early meeting notes that it may be several years before a decision is made to relocate either the Spring or Horse Shows. Nevertheless it is felt that alternative forms of revenue must be explored, such as a five-year subscription pre-payment. A redevelopment programme is undertaken, including some fundamental improvements to the pavilion, a mobile net and another artificial wicket. A special general meeting is called to vote on the proposed expenditure, which is passed by a comfortable majority. It is agreed that the club should not be responsible for the cost of teas. The charge for teas is subsequently agreed at £2 for Senior and Junior members, and £1 for Schoolboys, with the captains to collect the money.

The new owner of 43 Anglesea Road, also called Molloy, is approached with an offer: use of the corner of their garden, in return for a key to the front gate. His reply is to rebuild the wall in its original position and plant a line of conifers inside. The status quo as it was prior to 1952 is restored. It is agreed to use the ground for car parking during concerts at the RDS. The Donnybrook Garda detain some people in connection with the theft of a keg of beer from the club. The parking facilities for caravans in the Horse Show are to be advertised more widely. A helmet is purchased. Plans are made to erect a fence to protect the windows and cars in the Hazeldene flats. This is a good year for social events, with many club nights. John Lyon is employed as coach. It is agreed that the women must improve their organisation and become pavilion members in 1989, and also pay £400 or £25 per member, whichever is the greater. Merrion's insurance cover now includes damage to Hazeldene flats and cars by cricket balls. Changes to the club rules are necessary due to the new Licensing Act.

PROFILE: ANGUS HANCOCK

R-H middle-order batsman, prone to scoring his runs on the leg side. Wicket-keeper. Educated at St Andrews College and Newpark Comprehensive School. Studied Sports Management at Waterford Institute of Technology. Managing Director of Packaging Components Ltd, manufacturers of corrugated sheeting. Also played schools rugby, tennis, basketball, squash, soccer and hockey. He worked in Australia for three years as a basketball coach. Angus, son of 1sts wicket-keeper John Hancock, came up through the Schoolboy and Junior ranks in Merrion and played sixty-six games for the 1sts between 1984 and 1994, scoring 878 runs @ 15.40, with a top score of 90, and including 4*50s. As a wicket-keeper, he took 28 catches and 8 stump-ings, and also held onto 7 catches in the field. He left Merrion to join Clontarf in 1994, after a fuss involving a member of *The Syndicate*, who insulted his then girlfriend, with no apology forthcoming. After a decade with the Northsiders, he moved to Wicklow County, where he now paddles his wares with a few other Merrion refugees.

1989: TOUR OF SHROPSHIRE; DEATH OF SIMON CURLEY

Senior: fixtures 17, reported 17, won 0, lost 12, drawn 5. President: B. Dowling. Captain: J. Craven. Merrion 1sts suffer this season by the partial absence of the captain on business, particu-larly during practice. Bangor beat Merrion in the second round (bye in the first) of the Schweppes Cup, 109 to 267/6. Merrion finish 13/13 in the Belvedere Bond, with 62 points and no money, having played 11, lost 6, drawn 5. They lose comfortably to The Hills in the second round (bye in the first) of the Sportsgear Senior Cup. In the Wiggins Teape, Merrion finish 5/5 in Section B, with no points, having played 5, lost 5. Another demoralising season, with no wins, and Merrion 1sts have now won 27 games out of their last 149. Nevertheless, an enjoyable tour of the Shropshire area is undertaken by a motley crew of stalwarts, only a few of whom have their rooms hosed down regularly. Dave Coolican's inflatable doll fields at mid-wicket when the touring side is short, and does better than most of the rest. John Heavey scores 54 wearing his green wellies. This season's runs emanate from John, with 313 @ 18.41; Stephen King, with 317 @ 35.22; Denis McKenna, with 219 @ 18.25, and Andrew Nixon, with 197 @ 16.41. In a year when the opposition is bowled out twice, and only 102 wickets are taken, Kirby Tarrant (in his last season for the 1sts, before returning to the Cabra puddings) is responsible for 25 @ 27.84. Denis McKenna fools 17 batsmen into missing a straight ball @ 25.23. Stephen Buckley swings out 12 of the opposition @ 38.25 and John Craven nips out another 10 batsmen @ 35.90. Simon Curley, Merrion's greatest player and most loyal servant, dies at the relatively young age of seventy-one:

Opponent	Result	Mer.	Opp.	Best Batting: Runs	Best Bowling: Wickets
Pembroke	Drawn	142	121/6	J. Heavey: 56	R. Stanton: 3/31
The Hills	Lost	47	50/1	R. Stanton: 17	K. Tarrant: 1/25
DU	Drawn	122/8	202/8	E. Lewis: 31	A. Little: 4/39
Old Belvedere	Lost	107	172/6	E. Lewis: 28	D. McKenna: 3/67
Leinster	Drawn	127/6	168/8	D. McKenna: 33*	K. Tarrant: 5/65
Railway Union	Drawn	196/6	151/8	R. Stanton: 77*	C. Collings: 4/26
Carlisle	Lost	190/6	191/1	R. Stanton: 57	K. Tarrant: 1/69
The Hills (C)	Lost	165	247	J. Heavey: 36	K. Tarrant: 3/48
YMCA	Lost	164	165/4	J. Heavey: 60	D. McKenna: 1/21
Malahide	Drawn	149/8	182/6	K. Allwright: 40	D. McKenna: 2/61
CYM	Lost	143	196/9	D. McKenna: 60*	K. Tarrant: 4/68
Phoenix	Lost	107	110/2	S. King: 50	D. McKenna: 2/27
Wiggins Teape					
Old Belvedere	Lost	53	195/6	E. Extras: 12	K. Tarrant: 4/78
Pembroke	Lost	159	187/4	S. King: 87*	D. McKenna: 1/20
YMCA	Lost	162	240/6	S. King: 60	S. Buckley: 2/89
Clontarf	Lost	174	195	R. Stanton: 55	S. Buckley: 4/89
Malahide	Lost	164/9	180/7	A. Nixon: 33	D. McKenna: 2/23

Junior: Merrion 2nds finish 5/10 in the Senior 2 League, with 51.9 per cent, having played 16, won 7, lost 6, drawn 3. They lose to Railway Union 2nds in the first round of the Senior 2 Cup, 159 to 160/4. Merrion 3rds finish 6/11 in Section A of the Middle League, with 44.8 per cent, having played 14, won 3, lost 6, drawn 5. They lose to Old Belvedere 3rds in the first round of the Middle Cup, 146 to 189. Paul Hourihane's 4ths are forced to withdraw from the Middle B League, due to lack of players. The new 4ths (formerly the 5ths) finish 3/9 in Section A of the Intermediate League, with 61.3 per cent, having played 15, won 7, lost 4, drawn 4. They beat Rush 3rds in the first round of the Intermediate Cup, 221/6 to 88, with Barry Little scoring a ton, but lose to North County 3rds in the next round, 157 to 158/8. Merrion 5ths (formerly the 6ths) finish 9/9 in Section A of the Junior League, with 33.9 per cent, having played 11, won 3, lost 8. They beat The Hills 5ths in the first round of the Minor Cup, 116/4 to 115, but lose the next round to Phoenix 5ths, 135 to 200. John Dunn plays for the Leinster Under-19s in an Oxford tournament. Gus Joyce plays for the Leinster Under-15s and scores over 1,000 runs for all teams this year. The Junior Cup final is played at Anglesea Road.

CLUB NOTES

Improvements to pavilion security are necessary after yet another break-in. John Lyon is employed for the 1989 season as Schoolboy coach. Arlene Horgan is invited to attend MCMs. Against the Merrion vote, the LCU allows overseas players again in 1989. A bowling machine is planned. The women's committee still owes £400 from 1988. A successful race night takes place. A fire extinguisher is discharged at a women's club night, but there's no fire. As the wickets have been poor this year, Andy Atkinson is invited to examine them and make recommendations. At the end of the year, Merrion votes in favour of professionals for the 1990 season. The pavilion roof starts to leak. The question of the poor organisation of practices is raised again at the AGM, as is the problem of getting teams out each week, in a year the club is forced to withdraw the 4ths from Middle B. A reorganisation of the club management is discussed. It is agreed to employ an experienced professional coach for the 1990 season. His remit is to include the organisation of all coaching and practice sessions. Improvements are planned in the areas of selection procedures and functional organisation, with different members of the management committee having responsibility for certain aspects of the club, such as ground, pavilion, cricket, schoolboys, fundraising, women, etc. The president reiterates the need for a greater level of enthusiasm and commitment from the members to achieve these goals. The new owner of 43 Anglesea Road applies formally for a key to the entrance gate. For security reasons, his request is formally turned down.

PROFILE: GERRY DUFFY

R-H batsman and R-A slow bowler of gentle floaters – which looked like leg breaks but usually turned the other way – who never played for Merrion. In fact, he was probably more responsible than any other single cricketer for depriving Merrion of leagues and cups during the 1950s, '60s and '70s, as a player for Leinster, for whom he scored a mere 10,264 runs @ 35.27, and took 944 wickets @ 13.88. He won the Marchant Cup for batting on five occasions, two more than Merrion's entire total. He played fifty-five times for Ireland, scoring 1,123 runs @ 18.11 and taking 82 wickets @ 19.23, and was on the side that beat the West Indies at Sion Mills in 1969. He refused terms with Glamorgan. Educated at St Mary's, Gerry worked as an insurance official (or pen pusher, as he calls it) during the few hours per week when he wasn't playing or practising cricket. He was also a Leinster trialist at rugby and is known to play the odd game of snooker. In 1991, Gerry decided that he couldn't live with the guilt of all those trophies he'd stolen from Merrion in the past and agreed to coach the 1sts. Over the next decade, together with others, he was instrumental in changing a losing (and drinking) culture into a winning (and drinking) one. Quite apart from the individual coaching that he gave, with an unassuming manner that belied a shrewd cricketing brain, Gerry taught Merrion that limited overs cricket is all about winning the toss, batting first, and strangling the game, regardless of the state of the wicket. If the toss is lost, then the game must be strangled sooner. Assuming, of course, that the opposition hasn't made the mistake of *putting Merrion in to bat*. A Leinster, Ireland and Merrion colossus.

1990: INTERMEDIATE A LEAGUE WINNERS

Senior: fixtures 20, reported 20, won 6, lost 11, drawn 3. President: B. Dowling. Captain: R. Stanton. Merrion beat Limerick by 6 wickets in the second round (bye in the first) of the Schweppes Cup, 158/4 to 155/8, only to lose to NICC by 9 wickets in the next round. Professionals are allowed back into Leinster cricket, provided they have acceptable coaching certificates. Merrion employ a West Indian fast bowler called Michael Thompson. North County are added to the mix of Leinster Senior clubs. Merrion finish 12/14 in the Belvedere Bond League, with 134 points, having played 13, won 4, lost 6, drawn 3. They beat Dublin University in the second round (bye in the first) of the Sportsgear Senior Cup, with Stephen King winning the Man of the Match award. They lose to YMCA in the semi-final. In the Wiggins Teape, they finish 4/5, with 10 points, having played 5, won 1, lost 4. Ho, hum. Merrion 1sts have now won 33 games out of their last 169. Michael Thompson may have all the necessary papers, but his haul of 19 wickets @ 31.05, combined with 4 catches and 120 runs @ 12.00, hardly justifies his salary as a player. But he's not far off the mark when he tips Damian Joyce as a future captain of Ireland. The real runs this year come from John Heavey, with 364 @ 22.75, Stephen King, with 419 @ 26.18, Damian Joyce, with 262 @ 20.15 and Andrew Nixon, with 400 @ 26.66. Robbie Stanton turns in a fine all-round performance in his first year as captain, with 451 runs @ 25.05 and 10 wickets @ 22.00. Denis McKenna mysteriously twirls out 27 batsmen @ 24.48 with his dibbley-dobbleys. John Craven scalps 18 enemies @ 26.00. A sixteen-year-old Philip Quinlan deceives 19 batsmen into sacrificing their wickets @ 23.36. During the winter, Merrion loses one of its brightest prospects when John Dunn is seriously injured playing a rugby match:

Opponent	Result	Mer.	Opp.	Best Batting: Runs	Best Bowling: Wickets
DU	Won	176/5	175/9	S. King: 64	J. Craven: 3/55
Carlisle	Drawn	172/8	214/3	Da. Joyce: 44*	
YMCA	Lost	72	208/3	D. McKenna: 17	Ph. Quinlan: 3/52
CYM	Drawn	242/7	205/6	A. Nixon: 76*	J. Craven: 3/61
Phoenix	Lost	141	143	J. Heavey: 30	Ph. Quinlan: 8/49
Leinster	Lost	186/7	187/3	R. Staunton: 68	M. Thompson: 1/38
DU (C)	Won	183/1	182	S. King: 80*	D. McKenna: 4/17
The Hills	Lost	94	217/7	S. King: 25	J. Craven: 3/68
YMCA (C)	Lost	137	141/4	S. King: 23	A. Little: 2/38
Railway Union	Lost	200/7	203/3	J. Heavey: 56	D. McKenna: 2/37
Pembroke	Drawn	119/8	231/3	S. King: 22	

North County	Won	147	73	Da. Joyce: 41	M. Thompson: 4/14
Clontarf	Won	206/5	202/9	A. Nixon: 74	M. Thompson: 4/55
Malahide	Won	118/8	117	A. Little: 26*	Ph. Quinlan: 4/11
Old Belvedere	Lost	153	156/5	R. Stanton: 45	S. King: 1/6
Wiggins Teape					
CYM	Lost	112/9	238	M. Thompson: 29	J. Craven: 3.42
Leinster	Won	188	131	R. Stanton: 64	R. Stanton: 4/48
Carlisle	Lost	206/9	238/7	J. Joyce: 53	D. McKenna: 3/48
YMCA	Lost	103/9	104/3	Da. Joyce: 30*	D. McKenna: 1/12
Malahide	Lost	122	220/9	J. Heavey: 67	S. King: 2/21

Junior: Merrion 2nds finish 7/9 in the Senior 2 League, with 38.3 per cent, having played 14, won 2, lost 5, drawn 7, and narrowly avoid relegation. Eddie Lewis grooves 93 against Clontarf 2nds. Johnny Joyce thumps 100* against Malahide 2nds. Ross Kyne's team includes Alan Little, Adam O'Keeffe, Denis McKenna, Gus Joyce, Dave Coolican, Stephen Donovan, John Craven and Dick Clarke. The team mascot is a very young Edmond Joyce, the captain of the Under-11s. They beat Carlisle 2nds in the first round of the Senior 2 Cup, 121/4 to 120, followed by Leinster 2nds, 53/1 to 52, but fold to The Hills 2nds in the semi-final. Merrion 3rds finish 4/9 in Section A of the Middle League, with 49.8 per cent, having played 14, won 5, lost 5, drawn 4. Bob Howell scores a ton and his team beats Rush 2nds in the first round of the Middle Cup, but loses to Clontarf 3rds in the next round, 108 to 140. Merrion 4ths win Section A of the Intermediate League. Roger Fox's team consists of Paul Quinlan, Jim Joyce, Angus Fleming, Barry Little, Tom McGeady, Mike Murphy, Alan Parkinson, Brendan Dowling, Frank Nugent and Joe Morrissey Snr. They finish 1/8 with 70.3 per cent, having played 13, won 8, lost 1, drawn 4, and gain promotion to Middle B. They lose to North County 3rds in the first round of the Intermediate Cup, 97 to 98/2. Merrion 5ths finish 6/8 in Section B of the Junior League, with 40.6 per cent, having played 11, won 4, lost 7. Paul Jackson's team loses to The Hills 4ths in the first round of the Junior Cup. There is no sign of a Merrion 6ths this year. Teams are fielded at Under-11, Under-13 and Under-15 level, with some success in terms of wins, but no trophies. Gus Joyce is the player of the Leinster Under-15s Interprovincial Tournament with scores of 102*, 76 and 107.

CLUB NOTES

Merrion votes against splitting the Senior League into two sections. A Merrion club draw is organised to gain revenue. Indoor nets are organised at St Andrew's College in Booterstown. The women's captain is invited to attend MCMs. The right of way issue for 43 Anglesea Road raises its ugly head again, as Mr Molloy hands the matter over to his solicitor. There are difficulties in engaging a South African coach. Gus Joyce is proposed for a coaching scholarship at Lord's. Peter O'Reilly offers to play for Merrion from mid-July onwards, but subsequently terms cannot be arranged. Gerry Duffy agrees to coach the 1sts squad for one evening a week, a decision of some significance for the future of the club. The Theatrical Cavaliers start playing cricket in Merrion. They can join as Senior members and play for other teams, or become pavilion members, and only play Taverners cricket. A President's reception, a race night and a six-a-side competition are organised. A drive for new members is initiated. Michael Thompson, of Harringay Cricket College, London, is employed as a player/coach. A bowling machine is hired from the LCU for two weeks, to evaluate its usefulness. There are complaints about the quality of teas this season. Tommy McGeady fulfills yet another role within the club by looking after the ground. The LCU ban professionals from playing in the 1991 and 1992 seasons. There are problems with members tapping the phone. *Tapping the phone*: a method whereby calls could be made for nothing by simply tapping out each number, with a brief pause between numbers. Those were the days.

PROFILE: JIM WALSH

R-H batsman. R-A slow off-break bowler; more illusion than reality. Educated at Gonzaga College and UCD. Jim trained to be a teacher, but gave that up to work for the Voluntary Services Overseas in Camaroon, where he contracted malaria. Returning home, he changed careers into accountancy and now runs his own auditing firm. He has audited the club's books over many years. Played rugby for Old Belvedere at wing forward and was the first captain on the Senior team that had not gone to Belvedere College. Jim also captained Merrion 1sts in 1987 and 1992. However, his profile is dictated by the seven trophies that he has brought back to Anglesea Road as a captain of the Junior sides: 1981 (Senior 3 League); 1995 (Senior 2 Cup); 2001 (Senior 2 Cup); 2002 (Senior 2 League and Cup, Tillain Cup), and 2010 (Middle Cup). He is the only captain in Merrion history to win more than five trophies at any level. Jim was responsible for running youth cricket in Merrion from 2003 to 2009, which enabled him to mentor his three sons, any one of whom may be destined to follow in his footsteps as a cleaner-up of rabbits and ferrets after the quickies have softened them up. Even a hip replacement couldn't keep *Squelch* out of the game of cricket for very long. He just goes on and on relentlessly, like the robotic gunslinger in the movie *Westworld*, captaining any team that will keep him playing in Anglesea Road. Hang on a minute. Don't the Taverners play there?

NB Other teams playing between 1981 and 1990: Camolin, Kilrane, Mount Juliet, Waterford.

Merrion 4ths, Intermediate A League winners, 1990. Back row: Pa. Quinlan, A. Fleming, B. Little, T. McGeady, M. Murphy, J. Morrissey Snr. Front row: B. Dowling, J. Joyce, R. Fox (C), F. Nugent, A. Parkinson.

4.4. THE NINETIES: 1991-2000

The early part of this decade continued in the losing vein of the eighties, until a threatened demotion to Junior status galvanised the club into concerted action that resulted in a significant improvement in performances on the field and in the club's organisation off the field. This coincided with the reintroduction of 'overseas players' into the game, with Merrion employing a succession of excellent young cricketers, including the remarkable Brad Spanner in 1999. The 1sts won the Alan Murray 20 Overs Cup in 1996, 1997, 1998 and 1999, the Senior B League in 1997, the Whitney Moore & Keller B League and the Lewis Traub League in 1999, and the Beckett Cup in 1996, 1999 and 2000. They were runners-up in the 1995 Senior Cup and Senior B League, the 1998 Lewis Traub League and, controversially, the 2000 Whitney Moore & Keller A League.

Junior Merrion also improved, and the number of men's teams had grown to seven by the end of the decade. The 2nds won the Senior 2 Cup in 1992, 1995 and 2000, and the Tillain 20 Overs Cup in 1996 and 2000. They were runners-up in the Senior 2 Cup in 1997 and in the Tillain 20 Overs Cup in 1997 and 1998. The 3rds won the YMCA 20 Overs Salver in 1992, the Middle Cup in 1993 and 1998, and the Middle A League in 1995. The 4ths won the Whelan 20 Overs Cup in 1993, the Intermediate Cup in 1995 and the Middle B League in 1997. They were runners-up in the 1993 Intermediate A League, the 1998 Middle A League and the 1999 YMCA Salver. The 5ths won the 1992 Minor Cup, the 1993 Junior B League and Junior Cup and the 1997 Junior A League (played 12, won 12). The 6ths won the Junior C League in 1995, the Junior Cup in 1998 and the Junior B League in 1999. The 7ths were runners-up in the Junior C League in 1997 and 2000, and in the Minor Cup in 1999. Merrion Schoolboys came along in leaps and bounds in the second half of the decade, with the Under-11s winning the Molins Cup in 1998; the Under-13s winning the Top 4 Cup in 1996 and the Jeyes Cup in 1996 and 2000; the Under-15s winning the Robertson Cup in 1998, the Yates Hale Cup in 1998 and 2000, and the All-Ireland Cup in 1998; the Under-18s winning the Amoroso Cup in 1996 and 2000, and the Sean McGrath Cup in 1996.

Off the field, it was a decade of two halves. During the first half, the club trundled along as usual, gradually improving the club facilities and employing non-playing coaches. The shock of possibly returning to Junior status in 1995 for the first time since 1925 led to a rapid investment in playing facilities and an improved coaching structure. A formal five-year plan was introduced and implemented, driven by the Hon. Secretary, Eddie Lewis. After several false starts, the club finally came around to the need for a more formal structure in its organisation, with the creation of cricket, finance and grounds committees, responsible to the management committee. The need to generate funds to pay for extra paid positions, a bowling machine, new practice and playing facilities and a major upgrade of the pavilion and dressing rooms, dominated the second half of the decade. Discipline issues led to the introduction of a code of conduct and an internal disciplinary committee. Newsletters and yearbooks were produced to document club activities. Several campaigns to recruit new playing members were undertaken. The decade ended with the very real tragedy of a promising young 1sts player being injured for life after an accident on the club's premises; the farcical tragedy of the club's treatment as the result of what will be forever known in the annals of Merrion lore as the *Poder Incident*; and a continually lurking tragedy in a landswap deal that could have threatened the club's very existence.

1991: TOUR OF THE ISLE OF MAN

Senior: fixtures 20, reported 20, won 2, lost 11, drawn 7. President: B. Dowling. Captain: J. Heavey Jnr. Merrion lose to Lisburn by 107 runs in the second round (bye in the first) of the Schweppes Cup. Belvedere Bond rule changes: Rush are allowed to play in the Senior Cup, as they won the Senior 2 Cup and League in 1990; no professional of any sort is allowed to play; this is the first of two years from which results will be used to set up two leagues of seven, based on merit, for the 1993 season. Merrion already look set for Division 2, as they finish 14/14, with 86 points, having played 13, won 1, lost 5, drawn 7. In the first game of this league, Alan Brophy takes all 10 wickets for Malahide. In the last game, Merrion bat 64 overs to score 54/7 in a bloody-minded and successful attempt to prevent YMCA from catching the eventual winners, Clontarf. YMCA thrash them in the second round (bye in the first) of the Sportsgear Cup, however. Merrion finish 7/7 in Section A of the Wiggins Teape, with 10 points, having played 6, won 1, lost 5. Merrion 1sts have now won 35 games out of their last 189.

They lose to CYM by 7 wickets in the preliminary round of the Alan Murray 20 Overs Cup. The poor batting displays match the bowling problems in a season when the opposition is bowled out on three occasions, although an Englishman called Maxwell and an Australian called Fardoulys do provide some firepower towards the end. A time-travel tour of the Isle of Man takes place, where the team enjoys the chairoplanes and dodgems of Douglas, a 1950s tourist resort. This year's runs come from Gus Joyce, with 345 @ 21.56; Colm Gleeson, with 206 @ 20.6; John Heavey, with 310 @ 18.23; Andrew Nixon, with 292 @ 18.25, and Robbie Stanton, with 401 @ 20.05. Robbie just qualifies for the Marchant Cup, even though he ends up in twenty-fifth place. Denis McKenna, in his last full season on the 1sts, turns in a good all-round performance, with 189 runs @ 13.50, and 23 wickets @ 32.21. John Craven, in his last season with Merrion before returning to Leinster (*'It's a career of 2 halves, know what I mean?'*), baffles 23 batsmen @ 22.56 each. Ross Kyne pilfers 10 wickets @ 26.30. Jim Fardoulys poaches 11 victims @ 23.54. Jim Maxwell snaffles 16 wickets @ 11.43 in his only season with Merrion:

Opponent	Result	Mer.	Opp.	Best Batting: Runs	Best Bowling: Wickets
Malahide	Lost	59	60/4	E. Extras: 19	J. Craven: 2/8
Old Belvedere	Drawn	169	152/8	A. Joyce: 44	J. Craven: 4/50
The Hills	Drawn	76/4	150	A. Joyce: 35*	D. McKenna: 4/45
CYM	Lost	204/8	205/8	R. Stanton: 63	J. Craven: 3/61
Pembroke	Lost	188/8	189/2	P. Neilsen: 75	
Leinster	Drawn	196/9	218/5	J. Heavey: 75	R. Kyne: 2/45
DU	Drawn	140/8	79/9	E. Lewis: 34	J. Craven: 6/27
Railway Union	Drawn	127/7	193/3	R. Stanton: 33	J. Craven: 1/35
YMCA (C)	Lost	83	251/5	A. Joyce: 19	R. Kyne: 2/49
Clontarf	Lost	54	186/6	J. Heavey: 16	D. McKenna: 3/47
North County	Lost	169/8	172/0	R. Stanton: 48	
Phoenix	Drawn	103/6	219/4	A. Joyce: 46	D. McKenna: 2/35
YMCA	Drawn	54/7	186/5	E. Extras: 16	D. McKenna: 2/49
Carlisle	Won	100/4	96	A. Nixon: 29	R. Clarke: 7/45
Wiggins Teape					
Carlisle	Lost	139	124	C. Gleeson: 40	J. Maxwell: 6/33
Phoenix	Lost	71/6	72/6	J. Heavey: 24*	J. Fardoulys: 4/40

Pembroke	Lost	118	129/9	R. Stanton: 25	J. Maxwell: 5/25
Malahide	Lost	212	246/6	R. Stanton: 64	A. Fleming: 2/43
The Hills	Lost	159	160/7	C. Gleeson: 49	J. Fardoulys: 3/34
North County	Won	188/4	185/7	A. Joyce: 65	J. Maxwell: 3/49

Junior: Merrion 2nds finish 7/9 in the Senior 2 League, with 41.0 per cent, having played 14, won 4, lost 7, drawn 3. Paul Nielsen is top scorer for this team with 230 runs. Dave Coolican's team loses to Clontarf 2nds in the first round of the Senior 2 Cup, 99 to 206/6. Merrion 3rds finish 3/9 in Middle A, with 64.8 per cent, having played 14, won 8, lost 3, drawn 3. Kevin Allwright and Marcus Kelly are this side's top performers. Les Deacon's team is drawn against Pembroke 3rds in the first round of the Middle Cup. Merrion 4ths finish joint 6/9 in Middle B, with 40.5 per cent, having played 14, won 4, lost 8, drawn 2. Colin Doolin takes 9/18 in one match and Joe Morrissey Snr, the captain, scores the only club century of the season, with 105*. His team is drawn against Balbriggan 2nds in the second round of the Intermediate Cup. Merrion 5ths finish 6/8 in Junior B, with 46.4 per cent, having played 13, won 3, lost 7, drawn 2, tied 1. Peter Dolan's team loses to North County 4ths in the first round of the Junior Cup, 104 to 105/3. The Under-11s narrowly lose the final of the Mini-Cricket competition. Ed Joyce and Joe Morrissey Jnr play for Leinster Under-13s. Joe scores 95* in an Under-13 20 Overs game.

CLUB NOTES

Early meetings discuss maintenance work that needs to be carried out before the season starts. New furniture is planned for the lounge area of the pavilion, and both inside and outside are to be painted. The club photographs are framed and hung. A self-financing tour of the Isle of Man is scheduled. The LCU refuse registration of a new Merrion player, Steve Alleyne. This decision is appealed, but to no avail. The Taverners team is revived by Jack McConnell, with a concomitant increase in bar profits. New charges for caravans, tents, horseboxes and trucks are agreed for the Horse Show. A joint shipment of Surrey loam for the square is arranged with Pembroke. The subscriptions for Senior playing members for 1992 are set at £75, Junior £35, Pavilion £25. A twice-weekly bridge club is permitted to use the pavilion during the winter. The cheque from the women for their membership remains in the post as at 25 September. Wyse Management, on behalf of the residents of the Hazeldene flats, write to complain about the level of noise at club events. At the AGM, the issue of getting captains for the Junior teams is raised, and it's agreed that the positions should always be filled by the time of the Club Dinner. A bowling machine and a mobile net are to be purchased. The women are granted one night per week, either Monday or Wednesday, for the following season, in which Chris Gibson is to be employed as Schoolboy coach.

PROFILE: GUS JOYCE

R-H stylish opening batsman and occasional wicket-keeper. Educated at Presentation College Bray, a non-cricket playing school, and at Nottingham Trent University, where he studied sports science. He now works as a software developer for EMAP Media, and is the creator of the current Merrion website. Also played soccer, chess (represented Leinster) and has unfortunately gone to ruining good walks. Augustin played 191 games for Merrion 1sts between 1990 and 2010, scoring 4,498 @ 26.15, including 4*100s and 25*50s, with a top score of 191*. He took

51 catches and 12 stumpings as wicket-keeper in 63 matches, winning the Hopkins Cup for wicket-keeping in 1999. Also took 56 catches in the outfield. He played for Dublin University, and at interprovincial level. Gained four international caps, scoring 49 runs, with a top score of 29 against Scotland. He was captain of Merrion 1sts in 1999, 2000 and 2003, when his team won the Lewis Traub League, the Whitney Moore & Keller B League, the Beckett Cup and the Alan Murray 20 Overs Cup. Gus coached youth members for twelve years and has played a season's cricket in Melbourne. He is a leading member of the ubiquitous Joyce dynasty. Along with Kevin Allwright and Richard Dowse, he played a significant role in improving the performances of the 1sts in the late 1990s and early 2000s, by focusing on the technical and strategic side of the game, before having to take the London work trail in 2004.

1992: SENIOR 2 CUP WINNERS; YMCA SALVER WINNERS; MINOR CUP WINNERS

Senior: fixtures 20, reported 20, won 1, lost 18, drawn 1. President: E. Lewis. Captain: J. Walsh. Donemana defeat Merrion in the first round of the Schweppes Cup, 150 to 151/3. Belvedere Bond rule changes: this is the second year of two, in preparation for setting up two leagues of seven each, based on merit for the 1993 season; there is to be one up, one down between the sections after 1993, with the bottom club in Section B possibly leaving Senior status altogether, to be replaced by a Junior Club if certain criteria are met. This is a distinctly worrying prospect for Merrion 1sts, who finish 13/14 in the Belvedere Bond League, with 81 points, having played 13, won 1, lost 11, drawn 1. At the end of the Belvedere Bond League, the new structure for 1993 is, **Section 1**: Clontarf, YMCA, Phoenix, Leinster, Pembroke, Malahide, CYM; **Section 2**: The Hills, Old Belvedere, Railway Union, Carlisle, Dublin University, Merrion, North County. Merrion lose by 1 run to Pembroke in the second round (bye in the first) of the Sportsgear Cup, having been 141/1 chasing 207. They finish 6/6 in Section A of the Wiggins Teape, with 0 points, having played 6, lost 6. Merrion 1sts have now won 36 games out of their last 209.

After a promising start to the season at College Park, Merrion fail to win another game in this unfortunate season, and lose eighteen games, with fourteen games on the trot, possibly setting two wrong kinds of club record. Nevertheless, there are some close results, and the captain brings on some good young bowlers in Philip Quinlan, Patrick O'Herlihy and Angus Fleming. Why he never bowls himself remains a Merrion mystery. Stephen King pummels 383 runs @ 23.93. Angus Hancock manages 351 @ 19.50. Robbie Stanton wafts 307 @ 17.05. A newcomer from Munster, Richie Waddell scores a valuable 310 runs @ 19.37 and takes 16 wickets @ 27.94. Jim Fardoulys is responsible for 10 wickets @ 33.10. Patrick O'Herlihy, son of Kevin, swings 17 victims back to the pavilion @ 17.17. John Stevenson delivers 25 wickets @ 23.00, and is picked to play for South Leinster. Philip Quinlan poaches 15 wickets @ 27.93:

Opponent	Result	Mer.	Opp.	Best Batting: Runs	Best Bowling: Wickets
DU	Won	164/8	120	S. King: 55	J. Fardoulys: 5/46
Old Belvedere	Lost	48	213/6	R. Waddell: 26	D. McKenna: 2/69
Railway Union	Lost	180	183	A. Nixon: 46	J. Stevenson: 4/40
Pembroke	Lost	118	121/5	J. Stevenson: 61	J. Stevenson: 3/44
Clontarf	Lost	190/7	192/2	R. Stanton: 48	R. Waddell: 1/21
Malahide	Drawn	172	142/8	R. Waddell: 43	Ph. Quinlan: 4/30
Phoenix	Lost	85	220/5	J. Stevenson: 24	R. Waddell: 3/32
Pembroke (C)	Lost	205/7	206/8	R. Stanton: 66	J. Stevenson: 3/54

Carlisle	Lost	239/5	242/5	A. Hancock: 90	R. Clarke: 4/66
CYM	Lost	115	203	S. King: 31	R. Clarke: 3/39
North County	Lost	118	119/6	J. Heavey: 34	A. Fleming: 2/14
Leinster	Lost	113	180/8	A. Nixon: 28	Ph. Quinlan: 3/52
The Hills	Lost	79	80/8	S. King: 38	M. Kelly: 3/25
YMCA	Lost	120	124/9	P. Quinlan: 48	P. O'Herlihy: 6/62
Wiggins Teape					
Old Belvedere	Lost	102	171/6	R. Waddell: 23	A. Fleming: 2/29
Leinster	Lost	175/9	178/6	A. Hancock: 71	A. Fleming: 2/30
Carlisle	Lost	128	147/5	R. Waddell: 28	P. O'Herlihy: 3/60
The Hills	Lost	123	124/6	M. Little: 32*	Ph. Quinlan: 3/32
Malahide	Lost	96/8	136/6	S. King: 23*	J. Stevenson: 3/59
CYM	Lost	244/4	245/7	S. King: 81*	P. O'Herlihy: 4/65

Junior: Merrion 2nds finish 3/9 in the Senior 2 League, with 54.2 per cent, having played 12, won 5, lost 2, drawn 5. Eddie Lewis's team beats Carlisle 2nds, 124/4 to 123 and Balbriggan, 203 to 93 to reach the semi-final of the Senior 2 Cup against Railway Union. The captain shrewdly holds back Alan Little until the opposition are 85/2, and then brings him on to bowl in the 40th over, after which the Wheeltappers and Shunters succumb to 106 all out and Little's 8/4. Merrion struggle to get to 107/6. Subsequently those same eight Railway Union players retire from cricket and take up golf in Edmonton. The 2nds go on to win the final against Clontarf, 179/8 to 140, despite Lewis holding back Little until the 41st over. This is the first time that Merrion have won the Senior 2 Cup. John O'Hagan wins yet another Man of the Match award to add to his collection.

Merrion 3rds finish 3/9 in the Middle A League, with 57.6 per cent, having played 14, won 7, lost 5, drawn 2. Damian Joyce thumps 81* against YMCA. Mark Rutledge's team beats YMCA 3rds 178/8 to 177 and Rush 2nds 166/2 to 165/7, only to lose to Phoenix 3rds in the semi-final of the Middle Cup. They beat Old Belvedere 3rds in the final of the YMCA 20-Overs Salver. Merrion 4ths finish 8/9 in Middle B, with 27.4 per cent, having played 12, won 2, lost 6, drawn 4, and are relegated to Intermediate A. Mick Keogh's team beats Knockbrack 155/4 to 154 in the second round of the Intermediate Cup, but loses to Clontarf 4ths, 228/9 to 246/5, in the next round, despite Adam O'Keeffe's aggressive 97*. Merrion 5ths finish 3/9 in the Junior B League, with 63.9 per cent, having played 12, won 7, lost 5. Jim Joyce scores the club's only century this year. Gerry Rafferty's team beats Balbriggan 3rds, 244/6 to 130, in the semi-final of the Minor Cup and then Old Belvedere 5ths in the final, 126 to 68, with Al McKenna whiffling 3/19, Roger Fox scoring 35 and Ed Joyce chipping in with 21. Ed and Joe Morrissey Jnr play for the Leinster Under-15s, and Joe goes on to play for the Irish Under-15s. The Under-18s tour Waterford and Cork.

CLUB NOTES

Women are allowed to participate in Chris Gibson's Schoolboy coaching sessions, while Merrion's old nemesis Gerry Duffy focuses on the Senior teams. Quotes for tarmacing the entrance area are solicited. The new bowling machine is delivered, and a battery and charger are ordered. It is agreed to open the bar for all matches. The idea of a Simon Curley Memorial Trophy for the player of the year is agreed. The tea charge for Senior members is increased to £3. Ex-captain John Craven resigns from the Merrion management committee, but retains his membership of the club, even though he starts playing his cricket for Leinster again. He is replaced on the committee by Ross Kyne. Crusaders Athletic Club are permitted to use the ground for training during the winter, under certain conditions. It is noted that the club's insurance policy does not cover storm and tempest damage, burst pipes, earthquake and aircraft damage.

Due to a misunderstanding about the reading of the electricity meters, the club owes £3,500 to the ESB for usage over the previous three years. Andy Atkinson is again consulted about the inadequate state of the wickets. The club sanctions its approval of professionals for 1993, provided they have adequate coaching qualifications. There are ongoing problems with the alarm system, which seems to have a life of its own. At the AGM, Jack McConnell climbs down as Taverners captain, to acclamation and tumbling bar profits. Denis McKenna is acknowledged for his work on the grounds and wickets. A wide-ranging discussion takes place about the necessity to change the rules to allow the new position of Club Captain, who will chair a cricket committee responsible to the management committee for all cricket matters. It is agreed to hold a Special General Meeting (SGM) the following year, to formalise the changes in the club organisation. Changes to the rules to allow family and five-year memberships are passed. The elected 1sts captain for 1993, John McGeady, has taken the entirely logical step of emigrating, and a decision about his replacement is deferred until early in the New Year. A proposal is agreed to bring Wilf Paish, the Yorkshire Coach, over for two sessions in 1993.

PROFILE: PATRICK O'HERLIHY

R-H late-order batsman. R-A fast opening swing bowler. Educated at Synge Street and the University of the Streets of the World. Worked in Dublin in advertising sales. Has gone to ruining good walks and is known to play an occasional game of cards. One of Kevin O'Herlihy's four sons, Patrick played eighty-two games for Merrion 1sts between 1992 and 1996, scoring 281 runs @ 6.53, with a top score of 31. He took 180 wickets @ 17.39, with 5 wickets in an innings on 5 occasions, and 15 catches. In 1995, he took 70 wickets, decided correctly that such a feat could never be equalled, and emigrated to Thailand in 1998, where he bought a bar in Koh Samui with ex-Leinster cricketer Paul Ryan and settled down to his memories of those 70 wickets. After a couple of years, he sold the bar and managed several other drinking establishments before moving up to Bangkok, where he now works for a finance company and is married with a three-year-old daughter.

Merrion 2nds, Senior 2 Cup winners, 1992. Back row: P. O'Herlihy, A. Nixon, R. Clarke, J. O'Hagan, J. Dunne, I. Noonan. Front row: Pa. Quinlan, D. McKenna, J. Morrissey Jnr, E. Lewis (C), T. Lewis (M), A. Little.

1993: MIDDLE CUP WINNERS; INTERMEDIATE A LEAGUE RUNNERS-UP; WHELAN CUP WINNERS; JUNIOR B LEAGUE WINNERS; JUNIOR CUP WINNERS

Senior: fixtures 18, reported 18, won 2, lost 11, drawn 5. President: E. Lewis. Captain: R. Stanton. Merrion beat Sion Mills by 33 runs in the second round (bye in the first) of the Schweppes Cup, with Angus Hancock winning the Man of the Match award for his 57. They lose to Lurgan by 4 wickets in the next round. Belvedere Bond rule changes: two sections, with one up, one down; no professionals are allowed to play; win=20 points, tie=10 points, rained-off draw=5 points each, other draws=2 points each if a team bats over 55 overs, else 8; bonus points, 1 point for every 30 runs scored, with a maximum of 7, 1 point for each wicket from 2 to 8. Despite such eccentricity, or perhaps because of it, Merrion finish 5/7 in Section B, with 170 points, having played 12, won 2, lost 5, drawn 5 (2 of which are not played at all). Old Belvedere beat them by 30 runs in the first round of the Sportsgear Cup. They finish 6/6 in the Wiggins Teape, with 0 points, having played 5, lost 5. Merrion 1sts have now won 38 of their last 227 games and it's beginning to look like the '60s/'70s merry-go-round all over again.

In this wet summer, Angus Hancock paddles 328 runs @ 20.50. Steve Morone, in his only season for Merrion 1sts, scores 216 runs @ 27.00. Mark Little, grandson of Cecil, skelps 171 runs @ 24.42. Andrew Nixon compiles 141 runs @ 14.10. Stephen King pulverises 167 runs @ 13.91. Robbie Stanton, in his last year as captain, wafts 248 runs @ 19.07 and manages 11 wickets @ 23.45. In a year in which only 83 wickets are taken, Richie Waddell works 368 runs @ 26.28 and wheedles 14 wickets @ 19.85. John Stevenson takes 15 scalps @ 20.80, before disappearing into the ether like so many others before him. Patrick O'Herlihy seizes 30 wickets @ 20.86. Angus Fleming accounts for 10 batsmen @ 27.80. Both batting and bowling seem equally inadequate this year, but things are about to change, despite a perilous year ahead:

Opponent	Result	Mer.	Opp.	Best Batting: Runs	Best Bowling: Wickets
North County	Drawn	116	106/7	A. Hancock: 28	P. O'Herlihy: 3/45
Carlisle	Lost	171/9	174/9	S. King: 46	J. Stevenson: 3/39
DU	Drawn	183/7	73/5	R. Waddell: 75*	M. Kelly: 2/19
Old Belvedere (C)	Lost	196	226/4	A. Hancock: 70	P. O'Herlihy: 2/52
Railway Union	Drawn	r.s.p.			
Carlisle	Lost	120	160/8	R. Stanton: 28	R. Waddell: 3/14
DU	Drawn	r.s.p.			
The Hills	Won	151	137	A. Nixon: 41	R. Stanton: 4/12
North County	Won	58/3	57		
Old Belvedere	Lost	139	141/1	M. Little: 55	R. Stanton: 2/29
The Hills	Drawn	85/4	r.s.p.	A. Hancock: 18	
Railway Union	Lost	138	139/4	R. Waddell: 31	J. Stevenson: 2/38
Old Belvedere	Lost	214	215/6	S. Morone: 71	A. Fleming: 2/12
Wiggins Teape					
Old Belvedere	Lost	199/8	200/4	M. Little: 72	R. Stanton: 2/29
Leinster	Lost	110/9	138/5	R. Stanton: 31*	P. O'Herlihy: 3/61
Carlisle	Lost	159/8	160/8	A. Hancock: 55	P. O'Herlihy: 5/40
Railway Union	Lost	74	78/0	R. Dowse: 20	
Clontarf	Lost	143	144/4	A. Hancock: 45	A. Fleming: 2/31

Junior: Merrion 2nds finish 5/9 in the Senior 2 League, with 42.4 per cent, having played 11, won 2, lost 2, drawn 7. Eddie Lewis's team beats Old Belvedere 2nds in the first round of the Senior 2 Cup, but loses the next round to The Hills 2nds, 110 to 245/9. Merrion 3rds finish 7/10 in the Middle A League, with 42.7 per cent, having played 11, won 3, lost 4, drawn 4. Denis McKenna scores a century against CYM. Ed Joyce also hits a ton in his first match on the 3rds. Michael O'Doherty's team beats Old Belvedere 3rds, 183/8 to 163/8 in the final, to win the Middle Cup, thanks to Ed Joyce's 53 and Les Deacon's 4/62. Merrion 4ths finish 2/9 in the Intermediate A League, with 70.0 per cent, having played 13, won 7, lost 4, drawn 2, and so gain promotion to Middle B. Oliver Rye's team includes Mark Rutledge, Ed Joyce, Michael O'Herlihy, Joe Morrissey Snr, Alan Parkinson, Peter Geoffroy, Mark Forbes and Kieran Fulcher, and is drawn against Carlisle 3rds in the second round of the Intermediate Cup. They win the Whelan 20 Overs Cup, beating Malahide 4ths 118/6 to 102/4, Michael O'Herlihy pummelling 54. Merrion 5ths win the Junior B League, finishing 1/7, with 88.5 per cent, having played 9, won 8, lost 1, and are promoted to Junior A. Ronan McCullough, Mick Keogh, Keith Noonan, Al McKenna, Niall Tempany and Simon Hederman feature on this side. Roger Fox's team also wins the Junior Cup, beating Bagnelstown in the final, 149 to 124, with Gerard Parkinson top scoring at 34 and Frank Nugent whiffling 4/50. Gus Joyce is selected for the Ireland Under-21s and Under-19s. Ed Joyce plays for Ireland Under-15s.

CLUB NOTES

Improvements to the alarm system are implemented. Stephen King resigns as vice-captain for work reasons. Subsequently, members of the squad elect Robbie Stanton to replace John McGeady and it is ratified at an SGM. The same meeting fails to pass the proposed changes to the rules concerning the new position of Club Captain, the idea of a cricket committee and the splitting of the selection committee between Senior and Junior. A minute's silence is held to note the death of fine *Irish Times* journalist and former Merrion cricketer, Sean Pender. Cricket and fundraising subcommittees are set up by the management committee. A quiz night is arranged. Barry Little – the last of the summer wine – bows to the inevitable and agrees to captain the Taverners. Merrion send a team to participate in the St Columba's Floodlit Charity Cup. At an LCU meeting, Senior clubs vote in favour of an All-Ireland League, 13 to 1, with Merrion voting against. Subscriptions for 1994 are fixed at £85 for Senior playing members and £30 for pavilion members. The showers are converted to provide instant heat and to run on natural gas. At the AGM it is noted that the finance subcommittee did not function as planned. This time, after two voting sessions, the rule changes for the formal setting up of finance and cricket committees are passed. A subsequent meeting notes that the departure of the Spring Show from the RDS to Ashbourne will significantly reduce the club's revenue from car parking. A tighter control on expenditure is introduced. The return of the 6ths is planned for 1994. Another helicopter is allowed to land on the outfield.

PROFILE: ANGUS FLEMING

R-H lower-order hard-hitting batsman; R-A seam bowler, very fast through the air. Educated at Gonzaga. One-time male model. Financial services salesman. Club manager and groundsman. Played rugby for Leinster Under-20s until injury forced an early retirement.

Also ruins good walks and considers himself one of the best darts players in Anglesea Road. Number 53, that is. Played 265 times for Merrion 1sts between 1991 and 2009, scoring 1,411 runs @ 10.61 and taking 360 wickets @ 19.74, an average of 19 wickets per season. Won the O'Grady Cup for bowling in 1998, with 46 wickets @ 17.74. Took 7 wickets on 2 occasions – 7/61 against Phoenix in 1996, and 7/22 against North County in 1994, in a cup match, at the end of which one of the authors of this book (the Life Member) gave the Man of the Match award to Kevin Allwright for his 54 runs. Angus took 64 catches, and featured in all seven Alan Murray Cup wins between 1996 and 2005, the LCU Team of the Year 1998, the Whitney Moore & Keller B League wins of 1997 and 1999, the Lewis Traub win in 1999 and the Whitney Moore & Keller A League win of 2001. Angus came up through the Schoolboy and Junior ranks with modest ability and worked at his game so hard (it's called going down to the nets twice a week for years and bowling, bowling, bowling) that he almost gained an international cap. As such, he is a model for all younger players, as well as being ninth on the list of Merrion all-rounders.

Merrion 3rds, Middle Cup winners, 1993. Back row: S. Buckley, R. Kyne, J. Morrissey Jnr, D. McKenna, Pa. Quinlan, D. Coolican, P. Broughan (S). Front row: A. Parkinson, P. Hourihane, E. Joyce, M. O'Doherty (C), L. Deacon, R. Murray.

Above left: Merrion 4ths, Whelan Cup winners, 1993. Back row: M. Rutledge, P. Hourihane, J. Morrissey Jnr, E. Lewis, K. Fulcher, M. Forbes, G. Parkinson. Front row: F. Nugent, M. O'Herlihy, O. Rye (C), P. Geoffroy, I. Noonan, A. Parkinson.

Above right: Merrion 5ths, Junior B League/Junior Cup winners, 1993. Back row: T. Fulcher, R. McCullough, A. McKenna Jnr, C. Fulcher, S. Hederman, N. Tempany, F. Crean. Front row: M. Keogh, K. Noonan, R. Fox (C), G. Parkinson, F. Nugent, T. McGeady.

1994: MERRION AVOIDS DEMOTION TO JUNIOR STATUS

Senior: fixtures 20, reported 20, won 6, lost 10, drawn 4. President: R. Clarke. Captain: K. Allwright. Brigade beat Merrion by 53 runs in the second round (bye in the first) of the All-Ireland Cup, 195 to 248/3, despite Angus Fleming's 52*. Belvedere Bond rule changes: no professionals are allowed to play, but young overseas players can play as amateurs. Despite the presence of a young South African, Riain Smit (who scores 98 runs and takes 6 wickets in 15 matches), Merrion finish 7/7 in Section B of the Belvedere Bond League, with 174 points, having played 12, won 2, lost 6, drawn 4. Having disposed easily of North County in the first round of the newly sponsored Conqueror Cup, Merrion fall to YMCA in the following round. They finish 4/7 in Section A of the Wiggins Teape, with 30 points, having played 6, won 3, lost 3. Although this is by no means the worst season in the history of the club, at its conclusion Merrion are threatened with demotion to Junior status. However, on the basis of arguments raised in favour of the club remaining Senior, not least by Aidan Dempsey of Pembroke, sanity prevails and a club with a modest record in Senior cricket, a club that has won a mere 44 of their last 247 Senior games, is reprieved, and the counting stops again.

Richie Waddell is the only Merrion batsman in the provincial batting averages this season, with 471 runs @ 24.78. Other runs come from Kevin Allwright, with 319 @ 29.00; Gus Joyce, with 263 @ 20.23; Mark Little, with 260 @ 18.57; Andrew Nixon, with 306 @ 23.53, including a chanceless ton against Dublin University, and Robbie Stanton, who turns in another excellent all-round performance, with 332 runs @ 18.44 and 16 wickets @ 18.31. Angus Fleming is third in the provincial bowling analysis, with 41 wickets @ 15.19. Richie Waddell whiffles 16 wickets @ 16.56 in his last season with Merrion, before following John Craven to Leinster. Patrick O'Herlihy scalps 33 victims @ 23.12. Joe Morrissey Jnr wheedles out 18 batsmen @ 13.38:

Opponent	Result	Mer.	Opp.	Best Batting: Runs	Best Bowling: Wickets
Old Belvedere	Drawn	196/8	151/7	K. Allwright: 43*	R. Smit: 3/34
North County	Drawn	139/7	167/9	R. Stanton: 37	A. Fleming: 4/42
DU	Lost	105	107/5	R. Stanton: 31	A. Fleming: 4/19
Leinster	Lost	169/9	171/5	R. Stanton: 43	P. O'Herlihy: 3/59
DU	Won	251/4	135	A. Nixon: 109*	R. Stanton: 4/23
North County (C)	Won	183	57	K. Allwright: 54	A. Fleming: 7/22
Old Belvedere	Lost	109	114/4	A. Nixon: 38	A. Fleming: 2/20
YMCA (C)	Lost	217	135	R. Waddell: 35	A. Fleming: 4/25
The Hills	Drawn	156	73/9	A. Joyce: 69	P. O'Herlihy: 5/24
North County	Won	161	119	R. Waddell: 39	P. O'Herlihy: 5/34
Leinster	Lost	168	170/5	K. Allwright: 80	J. Morrissey Jnr: 2/28
Railway Union	Drawn	203/8	177/9	R. Waddell: 53	P. O'Herlihy: 6/50
Railway Union	Lost	116	117/3	M. Little: 37	A. Fleming: 2/37
The Hills	Lost	90	144	A. Nixon: 29	R. Waddell: 4/23
Wiggins Teape					
Leinster	Lost	142/5	143/5	S. King: 56*	R. Waddell: 3/40
North County	Won	167/6	105	R. Waddell: 68*	R. Stanton: 4/25
Carlisle	Won	148	146	C. Gleeson: 33	R. Waddell: 3/27
Phoenix	Won	185	145	K. Allwright: 50	J. Morrissey Jnr: 4/22
YMCA	Lost	119	122/5	A. Joyce: 42	J. Morrissey Jnr: 3/21
Malahide	Lost	208/7	209/2	R. Waddell: 68	P. O'Herlihy: 1/68

Junior: Merrion 2nds finish 7/9 in the Senior 2 League, with 36.7 per cent, having played 13, won 2, lost 6, drawn 5. Eddie Lewis snaffles 7 Leinster wickets for 39 runs on a damp pitch. Alan Little's team beats YMCA 2nds 181 to 120 in the first round of the Senior 2 Cup, but loses to Clontarf 2nds in the next round, 103 to 216/9. Michael O'Doherty, Rashid Khan (Rico), Paul Nielsen, Joe Morrissey Jnr and Ed Joyce also feature on this side. Merrion 3rds finish 4/9 in the Middle A League, with 52.1 per cent, having played 14, won 6, lost 5, drawn 3. Les Deacon's team is drawn against Halverstown in the first round of the Middle Cup. Merrion 4ths finish 7/9 in the Middle B League, with 41.7 per cent, having played 12, won 2, lost 5, drawn 5. Mark Rutledge hoicks a score of 80 for Oliver Rye's team, which is drawn against Phoenix 4ths in the second round of the Intermediate Cup. Merrion 5ths finish 5/9 in the Junior A League, with 56.8 per cent, having played 14, won 7, lost 7. Peter Geoffroy takes 7/45 against North County 3rds and Frank Nugent's accuracy is too much for the Garda, 7 of whom just give themselves up for 47. Roger Fox's team loses to Leinster 5ths in the first round of the Junior Cup, 172 to 211/9. Merrion 6ths return for the first time in five years. Charlie Pollard's team finishes 5/9 in the Junior C League, with 55.9 per cent, having played 15, won 8, lost 7. They beat North Wicklow 3rds in the second round of the Minor Cup, 91/8 to 89, but lose in a subsequent round. Barry Fitzsimons, John Bristow, Dermot Cooney, Denis Brownlee, Nicky Kenny and Dominick Joyce are the stars of this side. The club withdraws from the Under-18 League and loses the final of the Under-11 Molins Cup to Railway Union.

CLUB NOTES

Gerry Duffy agrees to take a supervisory role in the preparation of the square, as well as managing the 1sts. The bowling machine goes missing and Donnybrook Garda are informed, but it turns up again, in the hands of the coach, Chris Gibson, who has just borrowed it for a while. Angus Hancock moves to Clontarf, setting a new trend for disaffected Merrion youngsters. The possible relegation of Merrion from Senior status is discussed at an LCU meeting. An MCM agrees to apply immediately for readmission to the Senior League in 1995, if that is necessary. The same meeting discusses the interpretation of club rule 12, whereby only Senior playing and pavilion members with ten years' consecutive membership are entitled to a share of the proceeds, should the club be dissolved and sold. Tommy McGeady and Eddie Lewis are charged with attending the meeting of the LCU that is considering Merrion's application for reinstatement as a Senior club. At the AGM in September, a letter to the LCU Hon. Secretary is read to the members, formally requesting the reinstallation of Merrion as a Senior club for 1995. Concern is expressed from the floor at the state of the club's finances, with a poor Horse Show and a bar that is not properly controlled throughout the year. It is felt that a deposit should be required in future for functions, to discourage cancellations at short notice. John Heavey Snr resigns from the position of Hon. Secretary and is elected a Life Member, to warm acclamation. It's agreed to set up a finance committee to help generate funds to pay for improvements.

PROFILE: RICHIE WADDELL

R-H middle-order batsman who grafted for his runs. R-A steady, medium pace seam bowler with a high action. Originally played for Waterford in Munster. He joined Merrion for three seasons, before taking the usual route to Rathmines and Leinster Cricket Club. For Merrion

1sts, Richie played fifty-two games from 1992 to 1994, scoring 1,149 runs @ 23.44, with a top score of 75* against Dublin University in 1993, and including 4*50s. He also took 46 wickets @ 21.52, and 9 catches.

1995: SENIOR CUP RUNNERS-UP; SENIOR B LEAGUE RUNNERS-UP; SENIOR 2 CUP WINNERS; MIDDLE A LEAGUE WINNERS; INTERMEDIATE CUP WINNERS; JUNIOR C LEAGUE WINNERS

Senior: fixtures 22, reported 22, won 14, lost 5, drawn 3. President: T. McGeady. Captain: K. Allwright. Merrion beat Ardmore by 1 wicket in the first round of the All-Ireland Cup, but lose to Bready by 4 wickets in the next round. Belvedere Bond rule changes: one 'overseas player' is allowed, as long as he's young and not first class; Merrion are demoted to Senior 2 after 1994, but gain a reprieve on appeal to the LCU Executive; Rush are promoted; Dublin University drop out of this League, as the season structure changes, with the Wiggins Teape League (no semi-finals, just the winner of each section going directly into the final) being played first and the Belvedere Bond League in the second half of the season. Merrion employ a young batting/wicket-keeping South African 'overseas player', Gerard Brophy. Brophy's parents hail from Carrickfergus, and in 2000 he will get three Irish caps while playing for Cliftonville, before moving to Northants and Yorkshire. In this important season, when Merrion turns a corner and begins to head towards the uplands, the club benefits hugely from the presence of an explosive opening batsman from a continent south-east of Asia called Brett Saxon, who usually scores most of his runs in the first couple of overs. Against North County, Merrion are 14/0 after 1 ball, with Saxon hitting 2*4s and 1*6, with 2 no balls. They finish 4/7 in Section A of the Wiggins Teape League, with 30 points, having played 6, won 3, lost 3. In the Conqueror Cup, the team is inserted by Old Belvedere and beats the Northsiders by 2 runs in the first round, with G. Brophy winning the Man of the Match award, although Robbie Stanton's 12 overs for 9 runs may have merited a nod. This is followed by a victory over Rush (who also *put them in*) by 130 runs in the next round, with Brett Saxon taking the award this time. Gus and Ed Joyce miss their brother Johnny's wedding to play in this game. The semi-final against YMCA produces a close win by 3 wickets, with K. Allwright and R. Stanton putting together a stand of 52 to win in the last over, and it's Kevin Allwright's turn to be Man of the Match. Unfortunately, Clontarf conquer the Anglesea Road team in the Rathmines final by batting them out of it, with Botha and Vincent each contributing centuries in a total of 363/9 – a record for the limited overs version of this competition. A lack of variety in the bowling may have contributed to this score.

Merrion finish 2/7 in Section B of the Belvedere Bond League, with 266 points, having played 12, won 8, drawn 3, lost 1. This is the best result in any league since 1960, and but for a bad loss against Rush away, would have resulted in the first Senior trophy in thirty-five years. Gus Joyce is ninth in the provincial batting averages, with 706 runs @ 37.15. Brett Saxon is tenth, with 729 runs @ 33.13 and takes 15 catches. Ed Joyce, at sixteen years of age, scores 468 runs @ 31.20 and takes 16 catches. Gerard Brophy grinds 583 runs @ 32.38, and is third in the provincial wicket-keeping statistics, with 26 catches and 4 stumpings. How Kevin Allwright succeeds in batting on fifteen occasions is anybody's guess, but he manages to hoick 159 runs @ 17.66 nevertheless. Andrew Nixon adds 214 runs @ 15.28, while yet another Australian refugee, Richard Dowse, chips 190 runs @ 15.83. Robbie Stanton wafts 188 runs @17.09 and poaches 34 wickets @ 13.26. But the bowling belongs to Patrick O'Herlihy this year. He snaffles a mighty 70 wickets @ 11.57, yet loses out to Charlesworth of Phoenix in the O'Grady Cup. Joe Morrissey Jnr has 13 wickets @ 19.30. Marcus Kelly nips out 18 batsmen @ 25.38. Angus Fleming fiddles 27 wickets @ 19.59:

Opponent	Result	Mer.	Opp.	Best Batting: Runs	Best Bowling: Wickets
Wiggins Teape					
North County	Won	183	46	G. Brophy: 26	P. O'Herlihy: 6/19
CYM	Won	73/2	72	R. Dowse: 33	P. O'Herlihy: 6/13
Railway Union	Won	218/7	103	G. Brophy: 66	P. O'Herlihy: 4/41
Phoenix	Lost	93	128	B. Saxon: 19	M. Kelly: 4/50
Pembroke	Lost	81	82/8	B. Saxon: 22	R. Stanton: 2/12
Old Belvedere (C)	Won	205/9	203/9	G. Brophy: 74	A. Fleming: 3/57
Carlisle	Lost	190/6	191/3	G. Brophy: 44	J. Morrissey Jnr: 2/38
Belvedere Bond					
Rush (C)	Won	287/7	157	B. Saxon: 137	P. O'Herlihy: 6/45
Leinster	Won	253/7	157	G. Brophy: 71	R. Stanton: 3/36
YMCA (C)	Won	201/7	197	A. Joyce: 50	R. Stanton: 3/21
North County	Won	222/3	126	E. Joyce: 83	R. Stanton: 4/8
Leinster	Drawn	88/1	r.s.p.	B. Saxon: 47	
Phoenix	Drawn	157/9	205	B. Saxon: 52	J. Morrissey Jnr: 4/53
Clontarf	Lost	248	363/9	E. Joyce: 55	P. O'Herlihy: 4/53
Senior Cup Final					
Old Belvedere	Won	178/7	88	B. Saxon: 53	R. Stanton: 6/8
The Hills	Drawn	238/7	177/6	A. Joyce: 89	R. Stanton: 4/36
North County	Won	134	84	R. Stanton: 33*	P. O'Herlihy: 4/34
Old Belvedere	Won	184/4	180	E. Joyce: 65*	P. O'Herlihy: 4/52
Rush	Lost	144	145/3	A. Joyce: 51	A. Fleming: 2/46
Phoenix	Won	170	79	B. Saxon: 37	A. Fleming: 4/28
The Hills	Won	196/7	130	A. Joyce: 60	P. O'Herlihy: 7/44
Rush	Won	217/8	202	A. Joyce: 111	P. O'Herlihy: 4/59

Junior: At this level, 1995 might be considered the most successful in the history of the club to date, with four trophies won. Merrion 2nds, under Jim Walsh, finish 4/9 in the Senior 2 League, with 51.2 per cent, having played 14, won 5, lost 7, drawn 2. Richard Dowse manages 104 runs against Old Belvedere 2nds and 7/57 against Clontarf 2nds. They beat Railway Union 2nds, Clontarf 2nds and Civil Service on the way to winning the Senior 2 Cup against Pembroke 2nds at Rush, 263 to 184, in a final that sees Stephen King hockeying 65, Adrian Goodrich scoring 62, Eddie Lewis grooving 42 and Mark Little whiffling 3 wickets for 39. Merrion 3rds win the Middle A League, finishing 1/8 with 83.9 per cent, having played 13, won 11, lost 2. Kevin O'Herlihy Jnr hoicks 110* to mid-wicket against Malahide 3rds, while C. Gummersall filches 7/52 against Phoenix 3rds. They lose to Rush 2nds in the first round of the Middle Cup. Ian Noonan, Jeff Short and Mark Forbes also feature strongly for this side.

Merrion 4ths finish 5/8 in the Middle B League, with 44.7 per cent, having played 10, won 2, lost 5, drawn 3. They beat YMCA 4ths, 240/7 to 160 in the first round of the Intermediate Cup, thanks to Les Deacon's 8/61. This is followed by County Wexford, 200/5 to 84, with Michael O'Herlihy chipping 93 and Deacon confusing another 4 batsmen for 12 runs with his donkey drops. Old Belvedere 4ths provide the semi-final fodder, 240/6 to 110/5, with O'Herlihy whacking 79 and Mark Forbes edging 58*. Then it's on to Leinster 4ths in the final, and the players respond to Mark Rutledge's exhortation of his M People to '*search for the hero inside themselves*'. The result is victory by 135/7 to 134, with Adam O'Keeffe hoicking 35, Tempo edging the winning runs (he searched, he found) and Michael O'Herlihy offing 4 batsmen for 25 runs. Conall Gibson also stars for this side. Merrion 5ths finish 6/9 in the Junior A League, with 52.8 per cent, having played 13, won 5, lost 8. Dominick Joyce takes 7/45 against Phoenix 5ths. They beat YMCA 5ths in the first round of the Junior Cup, 177/2 to 176, with D. Joyce driving 58* and N. Kerrall top scoring on 69. Leinster 5ths beat them in the next round. Merrion 6ths win the Junior C League, with 81.7 per cent, having played 12, won 10, lost 2. They beat the Central Bank in the first round of the Minor Cup, followed by Clontarf 6ths in the next round, 256 to 111, Henry Rhodes pummelling 167 and Barry Fitzsimons grabbing 7/50. North Wicklow 3rds spoil the party in the semi-final, 75 to 76/5. Merrion lose the final of the Under-18s Amoroso League to The Hills. Dominick Joyce plays for a successful Leinster side in the Under-13s Interprovincial Competition.

CLUB NOTES

A new artificial wicket is laid at the beginning of the season, which enables the club to protect the main square, and it is used on about ninety occasions throughout the year. A glass washer and ice maker are installed in the bar. A third-party claim is lodged against the club for an accident that happened in 1984, when a child was crossing the Dodder to supposedly enter the club grounds. It is passed over to the club's insurers, who are responsible for public liability claims. At the AGM in September, the Hon. Treasurer reports a turnaround in the club's finances, with a surplus being generated to bring the accounts back into balance. The Hon. Secretary reports on the most successful season in years, with six new trophies in the cabinet and an increased active membership, up to 136 from 107 in 1994.

A five-year development programme is adopted, with the following broad objectives: to replace ground maintenance equipment; secure more permanent ground-maintenance staff; improve the seating, retarmac and upgrade the club entrance; create a new 7th men's team and a 2nd women's team; grow pavilion membership; refurbish the kitchen and dressing rooms; provide central heating; purchase a third 'non-turf' practice surface; appoint a youth development officer and assist schools in the area; put the annual finances on a secure basis, and appoint more permanent staff to run the club. The meeting recommends implementing this plan as quickly as possible.

The issue of discipline within the club is raised from the floor and the new management committee is asked to examine the introduction of a code of conduct and a disciplinary committee. Subsequently sponsorship is secured for the position of youth development officer and a thorough job description is drawn up. AC Portobello request the use of the ground for practices throughout the winter and are prepared to join as pavilion members. CUS request a 'special relationship' with Merrion, which includes the use of the school's sports grounds during the summer months in return for expert coaching in the school. Work programmes for each functional area within the club are drawn up for the winter. The central weave carpet/mat is damaged by vandals exploding fireworks on it. Subscriptions are now £85 for a full playing member, £30 for a pavilion member, and £40 for a Junior member. John Byrne and Alan Parkinson are employed to look after the square. Tables go missing from the pavilion. Representatives of the Anglesea Residents' Association complain about the Rehab recycling bins at the entrance to the ground. A meeting agrees to ask Rehab to remove them. It is agreed that the club should keep VAT books from the beginning of 1996.

PROFILE: BRETT SAXON

R-H explosive opening batsman. R-A medium pace bowler. All-round excellent sportsman who played Australian football until an ankle injury curtailed that sport. Was also into golf, motor racing and water sports. From Euroa, North-East Victoria. Electronic security consultant. Brett played forty-seven games for Merrion 1sts between 1995 and 1999, scoring 1,472 runs @ 31.31, with a top score of 137, and taking 22 wickets @ 23.77, with 23 catches. He scored 2*100s and 9*50s. His wife Robyn played for Merrion women and helped them to win the Division 3 and 4 Leagues in 1995-1996. In 2005, weighing 105 kilos and feeling very unfit, like Forrest Gump, Brett started running. He ran so much that in 2008 he was ready for a gruelling Ultra Endurance Marathon of 162 kilometres in twenty-four hours, in aid of a charity called Canteen, for children living with cancer. That's four marathons in a day. And so, Merrion's extreme cricketer of 1995/96, who helped to turn the fortunes of the club around, has turned himself into an extreme athlete.

Merrion 1sts, Senior Cup runners-up, 1995. Back row: A. Fleming, E. Joyce, S. King, J. Morrissey Jnr, M. Kelly, R. Stanton. Front row: P. O'Herlihy, A. Joyce, K. Allwright (C), G. Brophy, B. Saxon, A. Nixon.

Above left: Merrion 2nds, Senior 2 Cup winners, 1995. Back row: A. Little, M. Little, A. Goodrich, E. Lewis, L. Casey, J. O'Hagan, S. King. Front row: A. Lynch, J. Short, J. Walsh (C), R. Dowse, K. O'Herlihy Jnr.

Above right: Merrion 3rds, Middle A League winners, 1995. Back row: D. McKenna, M. Forbes, K. O'Herlihy Jnr, J. Heavey Jnr, R. Cross, G. Parkinson. Front row: I. Noonan, J. Joyce, A. Parkinson (C), M. O'Herlihy, J. Short.

1996: BECKETT CUP WINNERS; ALAN MURRAY CUP WINNERS; TILLAIN CUP WINNERS; YMCA SALVER RUNNERS-UP; UNDER-13 TOP 4 CUP WINNERS; UNDER-13 JEYES CUP WINNERS; UNDER-18 AMOROSO CUP WINNERS; UNDER-18 SEAN MCGRATH CUP WINNERS

Senior: fixtures 20, reported 20, won 8, lost 7, drawn 5. President: T. McGeady. Captain: K. Allwright. Merrion beat Cork Harlequins 343/6 to 54 in the second round (bye in the first) of the Royal Liver Irish Senior Cup, with Gus Joyce slamming 141*, Kevin Allwright blocking and hoicking 54 and Angus Fleming fiddling 3 wickets for 17 runs. This victory by 289 runs is probably a record, not just for Merrion, but also possibly for Leinster cricket. They lose to Leinster in the next round, 185/8 to 186/8, despite Brett Saxon's 57 and Richard Dowse's 3/31. As Wiggins Teape have withdrawn their sponsorship, the limited overs league is now called 'The Limited Overs League', and there's a return to semi-finals. Merrion employ another young South African, Tristan McClaren, as their 'overseas player/ coach'. Gus Joyce is employed as youth development officer. Brett Saxon returns for another hectic summer of sixes by the Dodder. Merrion finish 3/8 in Section B of the 50-over league, with 40 points, having played 7, won 4, lost 3. They almost make it into the semis, but for some reason YMCA escape disqualification for playing an ineligible player. Leinster knock Merrion out of the Conqueror Cup in the first round.

There's a new sponsor for the Senior League, which is now called the River House League, after a hotel in Temple Bar. Rule changes: a win can now earn up to 30 points; if sent in, a team can bat 60 overs without penalty in a drawn match; for a match in which there is no play or play in which neither side gets at least 2 bonus points, the teams receive 12 points each. A good start to this competition sees Merrion top Section B by mid-August, but the batting falls away alarmingly towards the end, to see them finish 4/7, with 262 points, having played 12, won 4, lost 3, drawn 5. Merrion defeat Clontarf in the final of the Alan Murray 20 Overs Cup to bring home a rare trophy to Anglesea Road, Brett Saxon belting 58* and taking 3/23. Another one follows when the Beckett Cup final is played in late September. Merrion beat Strabane, 238/2 to 161, with Ed Joyce slashing 114* and Tristan McLaren skelping 51, while Stephen King pilfers 2/12 and Kevin Allwright fiddles a totally inexplicable 1/6. Brett Saxon is thirteenth in the provincial batting table, with 650 runs @ 34.21, and eleventh in the all-rounders' table, with 1,350 points, having pilfered 13 wickets @ 17.08. Tristan McClaren scores 477 runs @ 23.85 and is joint third in the provincial wicket-keeping table, with 28 catches and 1 stumping. Kevin Allwright hoicks 280 runs @ 20.00 in his last full season on the 1sts – it's obviously that captaincy thing again. Stephen King blasts 215 runs @ 17.92. Damian Joyce grooves 374 runs @ 26.71. Brother Ed spanks 392 runs @ 28.00 and also manages 11 wickets @ 21.55. Brother Gus has a lean season, with 204 runs @ 12.75. Joe Morrissey Jnr powers 188 runs @ 37.60. Richard Dowse paddles 300 runs @ 16.66 and filches 28 wickets @ 14.25 with his swinging off-cutters. Angus Fleming is seventh in the provincial bowling averages, with 42 wickets @ 16.86. Patrick O'Herlihy, unhappy with only another 30 wickets @ 21.33 to add to his career haul, disappears to run a bar in Phuket, Thailand:

Opponent	Result	Mer.	Opp.	Best Batting: Runs	Best Bowling: Wickets
Limited Overs					
Pembroke	Lost	162	163/6	T. McClaren: 43	R. Stanton: 2/29
Old Belvedere	Lost	175/8	178/6	B. Saxon: 61	P. O'Herlihy: 3/33
CYM	Won	202/7	201	T. McClaren: 44	R. Dowse: 4/42

TEAMS – 1

1: 1968 – 1sts.

2: 1973 – end of season match.

3: 1980 – 1sts.

4: 1984 – 2nds.

5: 1985 – 2nds at Senior 2 Cup Final in Rathmines.

6: 1984 – 3rds.

TEAMS – 2

1: 1988 – 1sts.

2: 1990 – 2nds.

3: 1991 – 1sts.

4: 1995 – 1sts.

5: 1995 – 6ths.

6: 1998 – 1sts.

TEAMS – 3

1: 2000 – 1sts.

2: 2000 – 3rds at Middle Cup Final.

3: Merrion President's XI v. Middlesex CCC.

4: 2005 – 3rds.

5: 2005 – 4ths.

6: 2010 – 1sts. Irish Senior Cup winners.

TOURS

1, 2: 1979 – London Tour.

3, 4, 5, 6: 1981 – Nottingham Tour.

7: 1989 – Shropshire Tour.

PAVILLION

1, 2: Old pavillion after fire.

3, 4, 5: 2000s – New pavillion.

6: 1987 – Painting of Merrion.

PERSONALITIES – 1

1: Kevin and Kieran O'Herlihy.

2: Ken McDonald.

3: Mark Rutledge, Merrion's Wellington.

4: Danny Parkinson calls it a day.

5: 1970s – Hugh Coleman, Cecil Little, Chris Mara.

6: Simon Curley, John Byrne.

PERSONALITIES – 2

1: Peter McWilliam, Raj Ramsaroop.

2: Kevin Allwright, Danny Parkinson.

3: Barry Little, Roger Fox.

4: Gerry Duffy.

5: Three generations of Parkinson, Danny Snr, Alan, Stanley.

6: Andy Irvine.

PERSONALITIES – 3

1: Barry Little.

2: Ann Short, Danny Parkinson.

3: Paul Coghlan, John O'Hagan, Jim Walsh, John McGeady, Dick Clarke.

4: John Heavey Snr.

5: Peter Quinlan, Mrs Quinlan, Tony Fleming, Brenna Clarke, Carmel Fleming.

6: Anne Lewis, Maureen Joyce, Kevin O'Herlihy, Ursula Lewis.

HURRICANE
CHARLIE

HURLERS ON THE DITCH

1: The Parkinson family.

2: Gerry Doyle, Cathal McAlinden, Chris Mara, Al McKenna, Danny Parkinson, Joe Morrissey Snr (inset).

3: Barry Little, Cathal McAlinden, Jimmy McAlinden.

4: Norman Reeves, Robbie Stanton, Declan Carty.

5: Adam O'Keeffe, Stephen King, Robbie Stanton, Kevin Allwright, Angus Fleming, Ann Short, Tony Fleming, Barry Little, Arthur Short.

6: The women.

THE JOYCES

1: Bray Cricket Club Arovan Bray Under 13s, 1983: Damian Joyce, Brian Marrimam, Bill Wright, Kevin Mcloughlan, Eoin Dargan, Tom Rice, Jonathan Raymond, Ed Joyce, Dom Joyce, Gary Joyce, Gus Joyce.

2: A young Ed Joyce.

3: Gus Joyce, Ed Joyce.

4: Ed Joyce.

5: Jim Joyce, Maureen Joyce.

6: Gus, Dom, Jim, Ed, Damian Joyce.

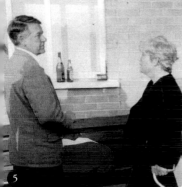

THE PROFESSIONALS

1: The professional of professionals: Brad Spanner.

2: Shawn Flegler.

3: Matt Petrie.

4: Gerry Brophy.

5: Jodi Myers.

6: Dean Waugh and Mrs Dean Waugh.

CENTENARY

1: John Hancock, Fergus O'Flynn.

2: Damian Poder, Kade Beasley.

3: Mrs Declan Abrahams, Dick Clarke.

4: Mr and Mrs Angus Fleming.

5: Alice Stanton, Peter Geoffroy, Joan Soraghan.

6: Denis McKenna, Tony Fleming.

7: Jim Walsh, Stephen King.

8: Michael and Philip Quinlan and friends.

GAMES – 1

1: Robbie Stanton's 2nd shot.

2: Mark Little and Denis McKenna await the inevitable.

3: Simon Morrissey, in full flight.

4: Ed Joyce.

5: Angus Fleming, following through.

6: Kevin Allwright takes evasive action.

7: World Cup qualifiers, 2005: Tony Fleming, Adam O'Keeffe.

GAMES – 2

1: Stephen King.

2: Liam Casey.

3: Rory Allwright.

4: Adam O'Keeffe.

5: Robbie Ensor.

6: Isobel Joyce.

7: Jill Whelan.

8: Cecilia Joyce.

YMCA	Won	180	145	B. Saxon: 47	A. Fleming: 5/46
Phoenix	Won	153	137	B. Saxon: 43	A. Fleming: 3/26
Leinster (C)	Lost	188	189/5	S. King: 43	P. O'Herlihy: 3/53
Cork Co.	Lost	128	166	Da. Joyce: 27*	P. O'Herlihy: 4/61
DU	Won	246	88	B. Saxon: 61	R. Dowse: 5/42
River House					
Rush	Lost	136	139/8	T. McClaren: 35	R. Dowse: 4/19
Phoenix	Won	221	138	F. Joyce: 102*	R. Dowse: 4/35
The Hills	Won	238/7	89	B. Saxon: 59	R. Dowse: 6/33
Old Belvedere	Drawn	254/5	141/7	Da. Joyce: 65*	P. O'Herlihy: 3/48
CYM	Drawn	237/8	139/8	B. Saxon: 45	P. O'Herlihy: 4/52
North County	Drawn	111/4	r.s.p.	Da. Joyce: 47*	
CYM	Won	265/6	99	J. Morrissey Jnr: 77*	A. Fleming: 6/29
The Hills	Lost	121	125/5	A. Joyce: 30	B. Saxon: 3/32
Old Belvedere	Drawn	178/8	174/7	R. Dowse: 41	A. Fleming: 3/38
Rush	Lost	142	145/3	K. Allwright: 51*	A. Fleming: 2/49
North County	Drawn	208	198/8	B. Saxon: 71	B. Saxon: 3/36
Phoenix	Won	270	144	B. Saxon: 117	A. Fleming: 7/61

Junior: Merrion 2nds finish 4/9 in the Senior 2 League, with 50.8 per cent, having played 12, won 4, lost 5, drawn 3. Robbie Stanton, Eddie Lewis, Michael O'Herlihy and Jeff Short star for Jim Walsh's team, which is drawn against Railway Union 2nds in the first round of the Senior 2 Cup. A 2nds/3rds combination beats Old Belvedere 2nds in the final of the Tillain Cup, 127/6 to 79, with Robbie Stanton wafting 41 runs and Jim Walsh diddling 4 batsmen for 11 runs. Merrion 3rds finish 8/9 in the Senior 3 League, with 42.0 per cent, having played 10, won 2, lost 5, drawn 3. Colm Gleeson hoicks a ton against Malahide 2nds, while Liam Casey, Kevin O'Herlihy Jnr and John Heavey provide support. Having disposed of North County 2nds in the first round of the Middle Cup, Mark Forbes's side loses narrowly to Old Belvedere 4ths in the next round, 234/6 to 235/9. They lose the final of the YMCA Salver 20 Overs competition to Old Belvedere 3rds, 101/8 to 103/2, despite Eddie Lewis's valiant 59 runs with a damaged hamstring in his last performance in a 20 Over match. It's rumoured that he walked off the field, grumbling to himself about bloody limited-overs cricket.

Merrion 4ths finish 7/8 in the Middle B League, with 36.7 per cent, having played 13, won 4, lost 6, drawn 3. They lose to YMCA 4ths in the second round (bye in the first) of the Intermediate Cup, 138/4 to 192/8. Merrion 5ths finish 3/9 in the Junior A League, with 67.2 per cent, having played 13, won 8, lost 5. Dick Clarke and Roger Fox are the backbone of Andy Irvine's team, which is drawn against CYM 4ths in the second round of the Junior Cup. Merrion 6ths finish 4/8 in the Junior B League, with 54.6 pe cent, having played 12, won 6, lost 6. Dermot Cooney's team loses to Malahide 5ths in the first round of the Junior Cup, 117 to 203. For the first time in the club's history, Merrion fields a 7ths, who finish 3/9 in the Junior C League, with 65.7 per cent, having played 15, won 9, lost 5, tied 1. Jack McConnell edges 54 runs against Aer Lingus. Jack Scott takes 8/35 against Knockbrack 3rds. Duncan Smythe and Barry Fitzsimons also feature on this new side, captained by Tony Gilmore, which loses to North Kildare 4ths in the second round of the Minor Cup, 161 to 162/2. Merrion Under-13s beat Railway Union twice, to win both the Top 4 Cup and the Jeyes Cup. Merrion Under-18s beat Old Belvedere to win the Amoroso League Cup, and Railway Union to secure the Sean McGrath Cup, and they are unbeaten.

CLUB NOTES

The five-year plan (1996-2000) is discussed in detail, with the following preamble: Merrion must remain a cricket club and control of the ground must remain in the hands of the members; the overriding consideration is the quality of the cricket that is played; a large membership and a strong youth section must be maintained; coaching must be improved to attract new members; Merrion must take its place at the forefront of Leinster cricket. Some concrete proposals are made: gradually replace aging ground equipment; refurbish the water pump; reseed the outfield; extend the sprinkler system; replace the seating around the ground; purchase a new 'non-turf' wicket; provide signage and lighting at the entrance; resurface the main driveway; upgrade the kitchen facilities; refurbish the dressing rooms; enter a 7ths in the Leinster League in 1996; actively recruit more Taverners and women cricketers; produce a quarterly newsletter; continue with the successful Summer Cricket School for children; maintain close contact with local schools; appoint a coaching co-ordinator for youth cricket, separate to the 1sts manager; consider the employment of people to run certain key functions within the club; review the club constitution; replace photos, and write a club history.

Agreement is reached with CUS for the use of their ground in Bird Avenue for some Junior matches. The LCU approves the proposal that the women's Irish squad be allowed to play in men's competitions in 1996. New sweaters, caps and ties are ordered, with the proper colour gold being reduced to a dull yellow. A court case for late drinking is thrown out because of a failure in the summons. The Anglesea Residents' Association call for the removal of the recycling bottle banks at the entrance to the club, and it is done. Will Robertson is appointed to look after the bar. Signboards for presidents, captains and internationals are planned. A distant relative of one of the authors of this book is suspended for the remainder of the season, after his behaviour in the 20 Overs Salver against YMCA. AC Portobello inquire about using the ground for soccer during the winter months. The possibility of using the club for bridge during the winter is also discussed.

An SGM is held in August to sanction an indenture between Borg Developments and Merrion Cricket Club for the laying of a permanent wayleave pipe from their property across the ground to the Dodder. Although this does generate considerable once-off income for the club and the septic tank is replaced by a direct connection to the public sewers on Anglesea Road, the subsequent ongoing problems with repairing the damage done to the outfield does bring into question the advisability of allowing such a fundamental undertaking ever again. Alex Burns resigns as club auditor. At the AGM in September, the Hon. Secretary points out that Merrion is now the largest cricket club in the country, in terms of registered players. An update to the five-year development plan is discussed at this meeting. Subsequently, a budget is drawn up for the work to be undertaken over the following year. A letter is written to the LCU requesting their support for Merrion's application for a Cospoir grant in 1997. Crusaders build a fourth floodlight on the ground. Glen Edwards, an Australian from Victoria, is scheduled to become the overseas player for 1997, but terms cannot be agreed. The club licence is renewed.

PROFILE: RICHARD DOWSE

R-H late-order batsman and R-A swing bowler. Born in Malaysia, but grew up in a continent south-east of Asia. Works as a schoolteacher. Also plays golf to an impressive handicap of around 4, give or take 3. Richard has close ancestry in Clonmel, so he's almost a part of the

Merrion 1sts, Alan Murray 20 Overs Cup winners, 1996. Back row: T. McLaren, C. Gleeson, R. Stanton, S. King, A. Fleming, P.J. O'Herlihy. Front row: R. Dowse, A. Joyce, K. Allwright (C), B. Saxon, Da. Joyce.

Irish diaspora. Like Damian Poder, he returned to Ireland to see what all the fuss was about and got lost by the Dodder off Anglesea Road. He played 152 games for Merrion 1sts between 1993 and 2003, scoring 991 runs @ 12.39, with a top score of 45. He was 1sts captain in 1997 and 1998 and took 214 wickets @ 16.66, including 5 wickets in an innings on 8 occasions, and 47 catches. He played in the 1997 and 1999 Whitney Moore & Keller B League wins, the 1999 Lewis Traub win and the 2001 Whitney Moore & Keller A League win, as well as five Alan Murray 20 Overs Cup wins. He is seventh in the list of all-time Merrion bowlers and played an important part in the turnaround of Merrion's fortunes that occurred in the second half of the 1990s. *Tazzie* went down the ranks for a relatively short while before returning to Oz with his Swiss wife, where he now lives in a place called Geraldstown, in North West Australia. Apparently they do an excellent battered shark and chips there.

1997: SENIOR B LEAGUE WINNERS; ALAN MURRAY CUP WINNERS; SENIOR 2 CUP RUNNERS-UP; TILLAIN CUP RUNNERS-UP; MIDDLE B LEAGUE WINNERS; JUNIOR A LEAGUE WINNERS; JUNIOR C LEAGUE RUNNERS-UP

Senior: fixtures 23, reported 23, won 16, lost 4, no result 3. President: T. McGeady. Captain: R. Dowse. Merrion beat Ardmore, 231/5 to 138 in the second round (bye in the first) of the Royal Liver Irish Senior Cup, thanks to Ed Joyce's 105* and 3/26. They lose to Strabane, 131 to 202/7, in the next round. This year's overseas player is Jodi Myers, another South African wicket-keeper. The first Leinster Senior competition is now called the Lewis Traub Insurance League. In an atrocious summer, eleven games are not started and a further six are badly affected by the weather. Merrion 1sts finish 2/8 in Section A, with 44 points, having played 7, won 4, lost

2, no result 1. In a semi-final reduced to 25 overs, Pembroke beat them by 9 runs. Merrion defeat CYM in the first round of the Conqueror Cup and Carlisle in the second round (with Damian Poder winning the Man of the Match award), but fail to defend 166 in the semi-final with The Hills, when wicket-keeper Jodi Myers takes 4 of the 5 wickets to fall.

The Leinster Senior League has no sponsor this year. Rule changes: 55 overs per innings, with the top score winning (an end to time draws); continuation is allowed on one night if at least half the match is played on the scheduled date; if there is no play or very little play in a match, there is no result and 5 points each are awarded; 30 yard fielding rings are introduced; at least six fielders plus bowler and wicket-keeper must be within this ring; bowlers are limited to a maximum of 15 overs. Merrion win Section B of this league and gain promotion to Section A. They are undefeated, with 296 points from 12 games, having won 10, drawn 2 (1 rain-affected, 1 washout). This is Merrion's first Senior trophy win since the 1960 Cup win.

They also win the Alan Murray Cup again, defeating Railway Union and Pembroke on the way to a final victory against The Hills, 113/7 to 95/8, when Damian Poder grabs 3 wickets for 23 runs. Poder, yet another Aussie refugee camping out in Anglesea Road, provides some much-needed variation in the bowling attack, and goes on to win the O'Grady Cup in his first season in Leinster Senior cricket, with 46 wickets @ 8.91. In typical Merrion fashion, where it's a flood or a fire, this is the first time a Merrion player has topped the provincial bowling averages since T. O'Niell Kiely in 1929, and they will win it twice more over the following two years. Ed Joyce plays seven times for Ireland in his debut season, scoring 50s against MCC, Scotland and the Earl Of Arundel's XI. Jodi Myers pummels 614 runs @ 38.38 and is tenth in the provincial batting table. He is also second in the provincial wicket-keepers' table, with 21 catches and 5 stumpings, and he is seventh in the Samuels all-rounders' table, with 1,314 points. All in all, a very satisfactory 'overseas player'. Other runs in this fantastic season come from Gus Joyce, with 298 @ 27.09; Ed Joyce, with 249 @ 19.15; Damian Joyce, with 175 @ 14.58; Robbie Stanton, with 324 @ 21.60, and Stephen King, with 235 @ 19.58. Ed Joyce also snaffles 26 wickets @ 13.58. Joe Morrissey Jnr snatches 26 wickets @ 14.81, Richard Dowse swings out 28 batsmen @ 12.39, and Angus Fleming earns 29 wickets @ 15.83:

Opponent	Result	Mer.	Opp.	Best Batting: Runs	Best Bowling: Wickets
Lewis Traub					
Old Belvedere	Lost	101	103/3	J. Myers: 32.	E. Joyce: 3/42
Phoenix	Lost	142	143/9	Da. Joyce: 31	E. Joyce: 4/29
Clontarf	No Res.				
Railway Union	Won	57/3	56	J. Myers: 40*	A. Fleming: 5/14
CYM	Won	137/3	134	J. Myers: 82*	D. Poder: 4/18
CYM (C)	Won	233/9	123	A. Joyce: 62	D. Poder: 5/32
Rush	Won	115/2	114	J. Myers: 56*	E. Joyce: 3/27
DU	Won	109/2	105	J. Myers: 39	E. Joyce: 4/25
Carlisle (C)	Won	94/5	93	A. Joyce: 21*	D. Poder: 4/22
Pembroke (S-F)	Lost	105/7	114/7	J. Myers: 38	A. Fleming: 5/48
Senior League					
Malahide	Won	62/0	61	J. Myers: 40*	D. Poder: 4/10
North County	Won	200/7	74	S. King: 56	D. Poder: 6/13
The Hills (C)	Lost	166	168/5	S. King: 41	J. Myers: 4/35
Malahide	Won	67/0	66	J. Myers: 29*	R. Dowse: 4/19
Phoenix	Won	176/8	172	A. Joyce: 43	J. Morrissey Jnr: 4/36

The Hills	Won	97/9	93	E. Joyce: 25	A. Fleming: 4/13
CYM	No Res.				
North County	Won	148/7	146/9	J. Morrissey Jnr: 30	S. King: 3/11
Phoenix	Won	196/8	155	J. Myers: 47	J. Morrissey Jnr: 4/29
Old Belvedere	No Res.	118/5	r.s.p.	J. Myers: 41	
CYM	Won	79/1	74	J. Myers: 34	D. Poder: 4/35
Old Belvedere	Won	159/7	139	D. Joyce: 45	E. Joyce: 3/27
The Hills	Won	139/8	125	J. Morrissey Jnr: 28*	D. Poder: 4/35

SENIOR LEAGUE FINAL GAME 1997, MERRION V. THE HILLS

Merrion			The Hills		
J. Myers	c. B. Archer b. L. Clinton	18	P. Mooney	c. E. Joyce b. A. Fleming	0
R. Stanton	c. & b. P. Mooney	15	J. Archer	run out	12
A. Joyce	c. J. Archer b. Matt Dwyer	26	B. Archer	c. J. Morrissey b. D. Poder	39
E. Joyce	c. & b. L. Clinton	8	M. Clinton	c. D. Poder b. E. Joyce	0
S. King	c. L. Clinton b. Matt Dwyer	5	D. Moore	l.b.w. b. D. Poder	3
D. Joyce	l.b.w. b. Matt Dwyer	0	J. Andrews	st. J. Myers b. S. King	25
D. Poder	c. J. Andrews b. P. Mooney	14	B. Moore	l.b.w. b. S. King	11
Da. Joyce	c. J. Archer b. Matt Dwyer	11	Matt Dwyer	l.b.w. b. D. Poder	0
J. Morrissey Jnr	not out	28	J. Clinton	c. & b. D. Poder	0
A. Fleming	d.n.b.		Mick Dwyer	run out	6
R. Dowse	d.n.b.		L. Clinton	not out	11
	Extras	14		Extras	18
	Total	**139**		**Total**	**125**

Junior: Merrion 2nds finish 5/9 in the Senior 2 League, with 62.5 per cent, having played 12, won 5, lost 6, no result 1. In the Senior 2 Cup, Jim Walsh's team beats Pembroke 2nds, 255/9 to 254/6, Malahide 2nds, 265/9 to 118, and Old Belvedere 2nds, 217/8 to 99, on their way to the final, which they lose to The Hills 2nds by 69 runs. A 2nds/3rds combination loses to Old Belvedere 2nds in the final of the Tillain Cup. Merrion 3rds finish 5/9 in the Senior 3 League, with 57.8 per cent, having played 11, won 4, lost 6, no result 1. Adam O'Keeffe's team loses to Balleighan in the first round of the Middle Cup, 50 to 130, on the side of a hill in County Offaly, where an off-break can mysteriously turn into a leg break, and vice versa. Like Gerry Duffy's bowling, really. Merrion 4ths win the Middle B league, finishing 1/9, with 78.6 per cent, having played 13, won 9, lost 3, drawn 1. Denis McKenna, John Blakeney, John O'Hagan, John Heavey, Dick Clarke, K. Black and Johnny Fennell feature for Niall Tempany's team, which beats North Kildare 2nds, Clontarf 4ths (Dick Clarke: 8/21), Pembroke 4ths (M. Rutledge: 40*), on the way to losing the semi-final of the Intermediate Cup to Knockbrack, 117 to 118/5. Merrion 5ths win the Junior A League, finishing 1/8, with 97.6 per cent, having played 12, won 12 – possibly the best league performance ever by a Merrion side. Andy Irvine's team includes John Bristow, Duncan Smythe, Nicky Kenny, Jimmy Robertson, Roger Fox, Simon Morrissey and Mark Willis. But they lose to North Wicklow in the second round of the Junior Cup. Merrion 6ths finish 6/8 in the Junior B League, with 53.2 per cent, having played 11, won 5, lost 6. Barry Fitzsimons, Brad Garnett and Michael Shanahan excel on Eoin Costello's Australian-heavy side. They beat Sandyford 3rds in the second round of the Junior Cup, 76/3 to 75 (Barry Little: 46*; Freddy Gilmore: 6/23), but are knocked out in a subsequent round. Merrion 7ths finish 2/8 in the Junior C league, with 86.5 per cent, having played 13, won 11, lost 2. Tony Gilmore's team beats North Kildare 3rds, 154/1 to 153, in the first round of the Minor Cup (Kevin O'Herlihy: 95*; Jack Scott: 53*), but lose to Clontarf 5ths, 101 to 102/1, in the next round. Ed Joyce, Michael O'Herlihy and Joe Morrissey Jnr are selected for the Irish Under-19 tour of Bermuda. Representative honours are also gained by Simon Morrissey at Leinster and Irish Under-13 level, Ian O'Herlihy and Mark Willis at Leinster Under-15 level, and Dan Clarke, Dominick Joyce and Nicky Kenny at Leinster Under-17 level.

CLUB NOTES

An SGM is held in February to discuss proposals for the redevelopment of the pavilion, the dressing rooms, the movement of the bar store and the creation of a new committee room. After some discussion about the relative merits of spending money on coaching versus such improvements, the motion is unanimously approved by the members. Cosgrave Bros agree to paint the sightscreens, build a fence in front of the pavilion and paint lines on the tarmac for parking. The phone is vandalised again. Jodi Myers is appointed club professional for the 1997 season. Ed Joyce and Kevin Black are to work on the ground together. There are further problems with the alarm system, but it transpires that it is not being reset properly after going off. Wyse Management write to the club, requesting that Merrion remove the Beer Keg Corral from the upper left-hand side of the ground, as it is an eyesore to the residents of Hazeldene. The selection committee is to be asked to take due note of the number of players not getting games, and the need for a link to the Taverners to accommodate them. Approval is given for the purchase of new covers and a water hog. There is a problem with Merrion's international Schoolboys playing for the club before an Irish match. A draft development plan is published, which proposes a reorganisation along functional lines, to take account of the growing size and complexity of the club. FÁS approve the employment of a caretaker and assistant groundsman for a period of one year. Concern is expressed about the quality of the wickets.

At the AGM, the main discussions focus on the need for more social functions, more pavilion members and a club manager. It is felt that CUS is not suitable as a second ground, and that the younger members want more games at Anglesea Road. The standard of umpiring and coaching also needs to be raised. The Hon. Secretary reports that the work carried out by Cosgrave Bros has been completed satisfactorily and that purely cricket matters should dominate the next few years. He points out that there were only eighteen new members in 1997. Trent Johnston inquires about the position of professional with Merrion in 1998. The scorebox is to be repaired. It is agreed that fresher and more varied teas are needed. The possibility of paid positions for bar manager, youth development officer and groundsman, as well as club professional/coach causes some concern for the Hon. Treasurer. A new groundsman is needed urgently and the options considered include a student of horticulture, a groundsman from a rugby club, a greenkeeper from a golf club, or someone from within Merrion. A budget is to be prepared for the 1998 season. Trent Johnston decides to join Carlisle. The Club Secretary reports that the pavilion cleaning arrangements are totally unsatisfactory.

PROFILE: DAMIAN JOYCE

R–H stroke-playing middle-order batsman. R–A medium-pace seam bowler, capable of throwing down an occasional rocket. Educated at Presentation College, Bray. A civil servant in the

Department of Foreign Affairs, he also plays recreational soccer. Damian played 147 games for Merrion 1sts between 1988 and 2005, scoring 1,872 runs @ 18.00, with a top score of 70 and including 3*50s. He also took 9 wickets @ 44.67, and 48 catches. He played in the 1997 and 1999 Whitney Moore & Keller B League wins, and in the 1999 Lewis Traub League win. He is the second of the redoubtable Joyce brothers, all of whom came up through the ranks of Schoolboy and Junior cricket in Merrion. Although he never attained the same degree of success as his three younger international siblings – Gus, Ed and Dom – they have credited a large part of their success to his early coaching in the back garden. Like the eldest brother Johnny, Damian left Merrion to play his cricket for Wicklow County, where he is now a part of one of the most successful Junior clubs in Ireland, with the serious risk of returning to the top flight within the coming years.

Above: Merrion 1sts, Alan Murray 20 Overs Cup/Section B League winners, 1997. Back row: G. Duffy (Ch), J. Morrissey Jnr, A. Fleming, D. Poder, S. King, J. Myers. Front row: R. Stanton, D. Joyce, R. Dowse (C), Da. Joyce, E. Joyce, A. Joyce.

Left: Merrion 5ths, Junior A League winners, 1997. Played 12, won 12. Back row: J. Bristow, B. Fitzsimons, M. Shanahan, J. Robertson, N. Kenny, R. Fox. Front row: D. Smythe, S. Morrissey, A. Irvine (C), R. Tracey, M. Willis, B. Garnett.

1998: LEWIS TRAUB LEAGUE RUNNERS-UP; ALAN MURRAY CUP WINNERS; TILLAIN CUP RUNNERS-UP; MIDDLE CUP WINNERS; MIDDLE A LEAGUE RUNNERS-UP; JUNIOR CUP WINNERS; UNDER-11 MOLINS CUP WINNERS; UNDER-15 ROBERTSON CUP WINNERS; UNDER-15 YATES HALE CUP WINNERS; ALL-IRELAND UNDER-15 CUP WINNERS

Senior: fixtures 24, reported 24, won 12, lost 12. President: J.P. Joyce. Captain: R. Dowse. Merrion beat Cliftonville in the second round of the Royal Liver Irish Senior Cup (bye in the first), 194/6 to 144, with Ed Joyce scoring 71 and brother Dominick 47, while Dowse and Fleming grab 6 wickets between them. The next round against Clontarf is abandoned due to bad light, with Merrion on 198/6 and Clontarf on 100/4. In a midweek replay, Clontarf bat first, score 224/4 and whiffle out Merrion (with only three of the regular 1sts) for 117. It's another wet summer, with ten matches not starting and Carlisle finishing up altogether, having lost the use of their ground. Merrion's overseas player is Bruce Hughes, another South African wicket-keeper.

Lewis Traub regulation changes: if there's a tie between two teams for first or second place in a section, the initial tiebreaker is the result between those two teams in the round robin section; likewise if three or more are tied, the tiebreak goes to the team that has beaten all the others; only if the above fails to break the tie will the run rate come into operation for that purpose. These rules work to Merrion's advantage, as they tie with Leinster in second place, and go into the semis having beaten the Rathmines side. Their final position in Section B is 2/8, with 50 points, having played 7, won 5, lost 2. They beat The Hills in the semi-final, but can't bowl out Malahide in the final, as the Village successfully chase down 212, managing 49 off the last 5 overs. Merrion have a good run in the Conqueror Cup, with victories over Dublin University and Clontarf, before losing again to Malahide in the semi-final, 190 to 234, despite Damian Joyce's 43.

The Senior League is now called the Whitney Moore & Keller League. Rule changes: there is no continuation on a weekday night; if the rain intervenes, the overs can be reduced to a minimum of 20 overs per match; if the scores are tied, the team which has lost fewer wickets wins; no bonus points awarded; slow over rates bring a penalty of receiving less overs; in the event of a tie, the first tiebreaker is the result of head-to-head matches between teams; if that does not break the tie, then a run rate applies; points: win=20, tie=10, no result=5; the Marchant Cup qualification is increased to 500 runs. A season that starts so well disintegrates inexplicably at the end, with seven straight losses and immediate demotion back to Section B. They finish 6/7 in Section A, with 80 points, having played 12, won 4, lost 8. But they prove again how good they are when they don't have to concentrate for more than 20 overs by winning the Alan Murray Cup for the third consecutive season, beating North County, The Hills, Clontarf and finally YMCA in the final, 154/2 to 127/9, with Poder notching 64* and D. Joyce capturing 3 wickets for 28 runs.

Angus Fleming wins the O'Grady Cup for bowling. He is the only player to qualify, with 46 wickets, among eligible bowlers (overseas players are ineligible). Apparently his average of 17.74 is the worst ever to win the Cup, or prior to its introduction, ever to top the averages. Angus also chips in with 185 runs @ 10.88 and features in the LCU Team of the Year. B. Hughes is eleventh in the provincial batting averages, with 600 runs @ 31.58. He's fourth in the wicket-keeper's table, with 15 catches and 10 stumpings, and eighth in the all-rounders' table, with 1,390 points. He scores 44* for the LCU Development XI against MCC. Ed

Joyce plays seventeen times for Ireland, scoring a 50 against Warwickshire. For Merrion, he spanks 157 @ 19.63 in only eight games, and nabs 13 wickets @ 16.00. Brother Augustin squirts 304 runs @ 25.33. Brother Damian tops the family tree, with 437 @ 21.85. Brother Dominick pulls 299 @ 16.61. Robbie Stanton wafts an impressive 520 runs @ 27.37, including 91* against Leinster, batting through the innings. Stephen King pummels 223 runs @ 18.58. Damian Poder swipes 321 runs @ 20.06 and confuses 33 batsmen into throwing their wicket away @ 18.79. Richard Dowse skittles 25 kingpins @ 23.68. Marcus Kelly manages 18 wickets @ 25.38. Joe Morrissey Jnr wheedles 11 victims @ 15.55, before heading to the USA for the summer:

Opponent	Result	Mer.	Opp.	Best Batting: Runs	Best Bowling: Wickets
Lewis Traub					
Leinster	Won	179	107	A. Joyce: 39	A. Fleming: 3/44
Carlisle	Won	168	70	R. Stanton: 65	A. Fleming: 4/16
Clontarf	Lost	171/9	217/8	Da. Joyce: 37	D. Poder: 2/36
DU (C)	Won	271/6	252	B. Hughes: 87	J. Morrissey Jnr: 4/38
Old Belvedere	Lost	128	129/6	B. Hughes: 37	A. Fleming: 5/37
Malahide	Won	51/2	50	R. Stanton: 25*	J. Morrissey Jnr: 5/22
Rush	Won	146/3	60	D. Poder: 48	Ph. Quinlan: 3/4
Phoenix	Won	255/8	155	B. Hughes: 106	A. Fleming: 6/27
The Hills (S-F)	Won	161/8	122	S. King: 31	A. Fleming: 4/28
Malahide	Lost	211/8	212/7	R. Stanton: 40	D. Poder: 3/36
League Final					
Whitney Moore & Keller					
Clontarf (C)	Won	232/4	203	B. Hughes: 75*	
Pembroke	Won	190/9	142/9	D. Poder: 43*	E. Joyce: 5/34
Malahide (C)	Lost	190	234/7	Da. Joyce: 43	M. Kelly: 2/52
The Hills	Won	168/9	159/6	A. Joyce: 39	D. Poder: 4/37
Rush	Lost	156	184/9	S. King: 32	A. Fleming: 4/41
YMCA	Won	121/3	109	B. Hughes: 54*	R. Dowse: 4/26
Leinster	Won	184/9	182/9	R. Stanton: 91*	E. Joyce: 2/37
Carlisle	Lost	155	156/2	E. Joyce: 64	R. Dowse: 1/18
YMCA	Lost	124	125/4	B. Hughes: 40	E. Joyce: 4/37
The Hills	Lost	180	241/7	B. Hughes: 39	R. Dowse: 3/52
Pembroke	Lost	190	352	D. Poder: 54	D. Poder: 4/87
Leinster	Lost	73	75/2	E. Joyce: 19	D. Joyce: 1/7
Carlisle	Lost	100/8	103/3	D. Joyce: 32	
Rush	Lost	174	177/3	D. Joyce: 41	

Junior: Merrion 2nds finish 3/9 in the Senior 2 League, with 69.5 per cent, having played 13, won 7, lost 5, tied 1. Jim Walsh's team beats Malahide 2nds in the first round of the Senior 2 Cup, but loses to Leinster 2nds in the next round, 126 to 127/5. Dominick Joyce and Philip Quinlan star for this side, with Philip missing out on the Oulton bowling cup by 0.09 of a run, and Dom playing just one game too few to win the Bookman Cup. Jim Walsh gets a hat-trick to tie the last game of the season against The Hills and John Blakeney scores a century. A 2nds/3rds combination just fails to beat The Hills 2nds in the final of the Tillain Cup. Merrion 3rds finish 6/9 in the Senior 3 League, with 56.0 per cent, having played 9, won 3, lost 6. Adam O'Keeffe's team wins the Middle Cup, beating Balleighan and Clontarf 3rds along the way

(Alan Parkinson, son of Stanley and grandson of Danny, scoring 116), before dealing with a strong Old Belvedere 3rds at Park Avenue in the final, 175 to 163, Denis McKenna baffling 4 Cabra men for 29 and Ian O'Herlihy striking 30 runs.

Merrion 4ths finish 2/9 in the Middle A League, with 72.8 per cent, having played 13, won 9, lost 3, no result 1, and might have won it but for the weather. Johnny Joyce's team beats Sandyford in the first round of the Middle Cup, but loses in a subsequent round. Merrion 5ths finish 3/9 in the Intermediate B League, with 59.8 per cent, having played 12, won 5, lost 7. Andy Irvine's team beats Athy in the second round of the Intermediate Cup but loses the semi-final against Portlaoise, despite Niall Tempany's doughty 80. Merrion 6ths finish 5/9 in the Junior B League, with 55.4 per cent, having played 10, won 4, lost 6. Eoin Costello's team beats Balbriggan 3rds, YMCA 4ths and North Kildare 2nds on the way to winning the Junior Cup Final against Bagnelstown, 123/4 to 122. Peter Geoffroy stars for this team, scoring his first 50 and topping the bowling averages. Merrion 7ths finish 3/9 in the Junior C League, with 69.0 per cent, having played 15, won 9, lost 6. Ray Clarke's team is drawn against North Wicklow 2nds in the first round of the Minor Cup. David Blackmore's 6/18 is the stand-out achievement for this side. Mark Willis, Ian O'Herlihy, John Blakeney and Duncan Smythe play for the Irish Under-15s. Simon Morrissey is picked for the Irish Under-14s. Merrion Schoolboys beat Donemana to win the All-Ireland Under-15 Cup. They also win the Under-15 Yates Hale Cup, the Under-15 Robertson League Cup and the Under-11 Molins Cup, 127 to 106. They are runners-up in the Under-13 Top 4 Cup and the Under-11 Mini-Cricket competition.

CLUB NOTES

An SGM is held in conjunction with a New Year's Party, to agree the execution of an indenture between the trustees of the club and Cosgrave Bros, in connection with the wayleave pipe they have laid across the ground. It is explained that maintenance will be at a minimum, as it is a 'sealed' system and that it will not be possible to build over it in the future. Once the motion is passed, it is suggested from the floor that combining an important subject with a party is trivialising the matter. At a subsequent meeting, Kevin O'Herlihy's proposal of a cricket committee that consists of the Chairman, Team Secretary, a captain to represent Senior teams, and a captain to represent Junior teams, a women's representative, a youth representative and the 1sts captain, is accepted.

Yet another drive to attract new members is undertaken, with schools and embassies being contacted, and an advertisement being placed in *The Irish Times*. A 1997 yearbook is produced, which documents the work that has been carried out over the previous two seasons: a storm water pipe has been laid; there are major renovations to the pavilion and ground; the pavilion has been repainted and replastered, with new timber floors, flooring and carpeting laid, showers and toilets tiled, an electric fire fitted and new cross doors in the main lounge; a third general changing room has been built; there is now a separate changing room for umpires and a new viewing area for matches; the roof has been repaired; new wicket-fencing has been introduced; there's now a play area for kids; the scoreboards, sightscreens and sheds have been fixed; a third 'no-turf' practice wicket has been laid; a new ground mower has been purchased, as well as new tarpaulin covers. The yearbook also makes certain proposals for 1998-2000: to improve the square and playing field; to relay the artificial practice and square wickets to ensure an even bounce; to prepare grass practice wickets; to employ a part-time groundsman and FÁS trainee; to improve the visual aspect and functionality of the Dodder bank; to have extra Schoolboy teams at Under-

11 and Under-13 levels; to improve the integration of youth members into the Senior ranks; to provide more coaching and to an older age for young cricketers; to actively recruit new playing members; to provide formal coaching for Junior members; to organise social activities more effectively; to consider entering an 8ths team in the Leinster leagues; to gain sponsorship of the 1sts for gear; to increase income levels; to plan for the commercial use of the pavilion during the winter, and to create a paid post of Club Manager.

The LCU produces a three-year plan for the development of cricket in Leinster, 'Plan 2000 … And Beyond', which sets out standards for wicket preparation, necessary ground equipment, practice facilities, coaching structure and youth development. A meeting advises the women's team not to accept promotion to the top league, but agrees to abide by whatever decision they make. In the end, they decide to remain where they are. Robbie Stanton agrees to act as temporary groundsman. Subsequently, Damian Joyce is employed for the season, both as coach and to look after the ground, with considerable success. A proposal is made to examine the hiring of a company to treat the outfield over a number of years (cutting, respraying, resodding). Kevin O'Herlihy mentions the broadleaf weed. A job description for a youth development officer is drawn up. Brenna Clarke, the Hon. Secretary, states that she has no intention of doing any more cleaning. It's agreed to support Alan Tuffery's vote at the next LCU meeting against the introduction of the Duckworth-Lewis method into Leinster cricket.

A South African wicket-keeper/batsman named Bruce Hughes is employed as professional for 1998. A job description for bar manager is drawn up. Kevin O'Herlihy plans to hold six coaching clinics for members of the lower men's teams throughout the season. A new sponsor for the sign at the entrance is needed. Barry Little agrees to look after the Taverners again. Merrion now has the largest number of teams in Leinster cricket, placed in the highest leagues. The matter of insurance for the Theatrical Cavaliers is raised, and it's agreed that a family membership should be obtained for the group. A 'No Dogs' sign is planned. The barman is assured that he is not responsible for members who drink and drive. The Hon. Treasurer agrees to harass members for subscriptions. Kevin O'Herlihy resigns as chairman of the cricket committee, citing ill health. It's reported that the 1sts are getting a bad reputation as 'sledgers' and for not socialising with the opposition after games.

Merrion 1sts, Alan Murray 20 Overs Cup winners, 1998. Back row: S. King, A. Fleming, R. Stanton, A. Thomas, D. Poder, K. Allwright, G. Duffy (Ch). Front row: Da. Joyce, D. Joyce, R. Dowse (C), B. Hughes, A. Joyce, J. Blakeney.

Merrion 6ths, Junior Cup winners, 1998. Back row: J. Robertson, J. Fennell, D. Carty, J. Bristow, B. Garnett, P. Blakeney (12th man), F. Gilmore. Front row: O. Rye, P. Jackson, E. Costello (C), G. Morris, P. Geoffroy.

Above left: Merrion Under-11s, Molins Cup Winners, 1998.

Above right: Merrion Under-15s, League, Cup and All-Ireland Cup winners, 1998.

Another SGM is held in July to ratify a resolution that permits Point Information Systems to use twenty-three car parking spaces at the entrance to the club from Monday to Friday, between 7a.m. and 6.30p.m., with an extension up to 10.00p.m. for ten spaces. The Australian Women's team use Anglesea Road to practise. Muckross College request the use of the ground every Tuesday evening. An LCU disciplinary meeting is held concerning the behaviour of Adam Thomas on the field of play. The right of way problem rises like Dracula from his grave, as the owner of No.61 (formerly the residence of staunch Merrion man Jack '*Who could be bluer than me*' Boland, uncle of ex-1sts player Michael Boyle), lodges a planning application to build a two-storey extension on a site around his garage. The club launches an objection and subsequently the application is refused. It's reported that the financial position of the club has now stabilised. Complaints are formally made about the way that nets have been organised during the season. The effectiveness, use and maintenance of CUS as an alternative ground for lower teams is discussed. It is suggested that Norman Reeves be approached in connection with the job of groundsman for the 1999 season. He responds that he is interested in working twenty hours a week.

1999: LEWIS TRAUB LEAGUE WINNERS; BECKETT CUP WINNERS; WHITNEY
MOORE & KELLER B LEAGUE WINNERS; ALAN MURRAY CUP WINNERS;
SENIOR 3 LEAGUE RUNNERS-UP; YMCA SALVER RUNNERS-UP; JUNIOR B
LEAGUE WINNERS; MINOR CUP RUNNERS-UP

Senior: fixtures 23, reported 23, won 20, lost 2, no result 1. President: G. Ormonde. Captain: A. Joyce. This season starts with a fine victory over Limavady in a delayed 1998 Beckett Cup final, 147/4 to 145/7, when Merrion recover from 7/3 to chase down the Northerners' total while losing only 1 more wicket. Merrion beat Ballymena in the first round of the Royal Liver Irish Senior Cup, 160 to 124, with Gus Joyce top scoring on 80, and Richard Dowse swinging out 3 Northeners for 18. They beat North County in a replayed game in the second round, 147/5 to 146, Ed Joyce pinging 56* and Damian Poder tweaking 3/19. For the first time in this competition, Merrion progress to the last four, by beating Glendermott 195/4 to 194/6. That's it, though, as Brigade whop them in the semi-final, 94 to 199/9.

Merrion's overseas player this year is an all-rounder from Toowoomba, Australia named Brad Spanner, while John Harmer is employed as youth development officer, with the specific remit of setting up a coaching system. In what is the most successful season in their history in terms of games won, Merrion finish top of Section A of the Lewis Traub League, with 60 points, having played 7, won 6, lost 1. In the semi-final they trounce Leinster, 130/0 to 126, with Joe Morrissey powering 71* and Damian Poder whiffling 3/34. A low-scoring but exciting final against Pembroke follows at Castle Avenue, with 8 wickets down and Robbie Stanton wafting 6 runs to long off from the last 2 balls to win the trophy, 136/8 to 135 (24 extras!), Dominick Joyce scoring a dour 51 in 120 balls (Man of the Match) and Joe Morrissey spoiling 3 Sydney Parade batsmen's day for a meagre 25 runs. They beat Dublin University in the first round of the Conqueror Cup, 288/6 to 117, with Stephen King (Man of the Match) pummeling 78* and Damian Poder nabbing 4 students for 38. In the next round, Railway Union inflict the second of only two defeats this year on Merrion 1sts by an inexplicable 10 wickets, 107 to 108/0, to a sustained slow attack. Whitney Moore & Keller League rule changes: there'll be a refix if there's no result in Section A matches; 5 bonus points are to be awarded per match – to be determined between teams by margin of victory. Merrion win Section B of this competition, with 268 points, having played 12, won 11, no result 1, and so gain promotion back to Section A.

As further proof of their lack of concentration, they win the Alan Murray Cup for the fourth year in a row, beating Dublin University, Clontarf (Merrion scoring 183/2) and The Hills along the way to a final that sees a resounding victory against North County, 97/1 to 96, with Joe Morrissey Jnr whacking 56* and Damian Poder fiddling another 3 wickets for 23 runs. Uniquely, Poder wins the O'Grady Cup for the second time in three years, with 43 wickets @ 12.02, the only eligible Merrion player ever to achieve this feat. Brad Spanner finishes second in the provincial batting statistics, with 1,014 runs @ 67.60, the first Merrion player to break the 1,000 mark. He also finishes fourth in the Leinster bowling statistics (one of four Merrion bowlers in the top eight), with 31 wickets @ 13.87, and takes 15 catches in the field. This is the best all-round performance by an overseas player in Merrion's history. And to the club's immeasurable benefit, Brad is about to marry an Irish girl, Gillian Daly from Cork, so he plans to remain in Ireland for some time, as an 'island-bound player', working as a journalist and youth development officer in Merrion.

Gus Joyce is sixth in the provincial batting averages, with 848 runs @ 49.88, including a Merrion record individual score of 191* against Rush, which broke Simon Curley's 1951 record of 175. He is also the first Merrion player to win the Hopkins Cup for wicket-keeping, although Billy Lindsay did top the provincial averages in 1940. Ed and Gus Joyce and Joe Morrissey Jnr feature in the LCU Team of the Year. Ed Joyce is eleventh in the provincial batting averages, after only 8 innings, with 332 runs @ 41.50. He plays seven times for Ireland this year, with a top score of 39* against Leicestershire. Brother Damian grinds 232 runs @ 17.85, while brother Dominick strikes 421 runs @ 26.31 and takes 17 catches in the field. Robbie Stanton wafts 382 runs @ 27.29. Joe Morrissey Jnr begins to fulfill his promise, with 301 runs @ 21.50, and tops the LCU catches table with 21. Stephen King thwacks 251 runs @ 22.82 in his last full season on Merrion 1sts. Richard Dowse is seventh in the O'Grady bowling analyses, with 47 wickets @ 14.89. Joe Morrissey Jnr is eighth, with 33 @ 15.33. Angus Fleming scalps 21 victims @ 18.52:

Opponent	Result	Mer.	Opp.	Best Batting: Runs	Best Bowling: Wickets
Lewis Traub					
North County	Won	153	66		R. Dowse: 6/18
Phoenix	Won	200/9	114	B. Spanner: 62	D. Poder: 4/13
Rush	Won	256/8	210	D. Joyce: 73	R. Dowse: 4/68
Malahide	Won	194/7	103	Da. Joyce: 40*	R. Dowse: 5/34
DU (C)	Won	288/6	117	S. King: 78*	D. Poder: 4/38
Clontarf	Won	241/5	136	B. Spanner: 101*	A. Fleming: 3/24
Old Belvedere	Won	227/7	64	B. Spanner: 85	R. Dowse: 5/12
CYM	Lost	142/9	148/4	B. Saxon: 31	D. Poder: 3/23
Railway Union (C)	Lost	107	108/0	D. Joyce: 27	
Leinster (S-F)	Won	126	130/0	J. Morrissey Jnr: 71*	D. Poder: 3/34
Pembroke	Won	136/8	135	D. Joyce: 51	J. Morrissey Jnr: 3/25
League final					
Whitney Moore & Keller					
Malahide	Won	150/4	146	E. Joyce: 68	
Rush	Won	318/6	238/7	B. Spanner: 130	R. Dowse: 3/63
Railway Union	Won	251/7	157	D. Joyce: 70*	D. Poder: 6/42
North County	Won	206/7	136	Da. Joyce: 44	B. Spanner: 5/41
Malahide	No Res.		148/5		
Old Belvedere	Won	266/4	84	B. Spanner: 110*	D. Poder: 3/20
CYM	Won	207/6	153/9	B. Spanner: 53	D. Poder: 3/42
CYM	Won	201/9	97	B. Spanner: 98	B. Spanner: 3/14
Railway Union	Won	165/2	160	A. Joyce: 70*	
Old Belvedere	Won	190/1	189/8	A. Joyce: 100*	J. Morrissey Jnr: 4/55
Rush	Won	315/6	127	A. Joyce: 191*	R. Dowse: 3/14
North County	Won	151/3	150	B. Spanner: 91*	B. Spanner: 3/42

LEWIS TRAUB LEAGUE FINAL 1999, MERRION V. PEMBROKE

Merrion			Pembroke		
A. Joyce	l.b.w. b. Hastie	11	L. Jackson	c. D. Joyce b. Morrissey	0
J. Morrissey Jnr	l.b.w. b. J. Davy	0	B. O'Rourke	b. Poder	5
D. Joyce	c. & b. Hastie	51	T. Dagg	c. Dowse b. Spanner	8
B. Spanner	c. Kavanagh b. O'Rourke	1	P. Davy	c. Quinlan b. Dowse	38
Da. Joyce	c. Smith b. Hastie	18	T. Williamson	b. Dowse	11

S. King	b. O'Rourke	10	J. Davy	c. & b. Poder	27
D. Poder	c. J. Davy b. O'Rourke	10	E. Whaley	c. & b. Morrissey	1
R. Dowse	b. O'Rourke	4	M. Butler	c. Stanton b. Morrissey	3
R. Stanton	not out	10	R. Hastie	run out	8
A. Fleming	not out	7	R. Smith	not out	8
Ph. Quinlan	d.n.b.		C. Kavanagh	c. A. Joyce b. Fleming	2
	Extras	14		Extras	24
	Total (for 8 wickets)	**136**		**Total**	**135**

WHITNEY MOORE & KELLER B LEAGUE FINAL GAME 1999, MERRION V. NORTH COUNTY

Merrion			North County		
A. Joyce	c. D. Armstrong b. C. Armstrong	9	C. Armstrong	l.b.w. b. Willis	18
B. Spanner	not out	91	D. Armstrong	c. Da. Joyce b. Spanner	14
D. Joyce	l.b.w. b. Paddy Martin	26	M. Murphy	b. Fleming	1
R. Stanton	c. Andrews b. Rooney	7	Paul Martin	c. Spanner b. Willis	0
S. King	not out	0	J. Andrews	c. A. Joyce b. Spanner	48
R. Dowse	d.n.b.		C. Fittler	c. Willis b. Fleming	2
Da. Joyce	d.n.b.		G. McNally	c. & b. Dowse	1
I. O'Herlihy	d.n.b.		T. Rooney	c. Smythe b. Fleming	7
R. Willis	d.n.b.		J. Mooney	not out	39
D. Smythe	d.n.b.		R. Gilsenan	c. Stanton b. Spanner	3
A. Fleming	d.n.b.		Paddy Martin	c. King b. Smythe	1
	Extras	18		Extras	16
	Total	**151**		Total	**150**

Junior: Merrion 2nds finish 7/9 in the Senior 2 League, with 56.5 per cent, having played 12, won 5, lost 6, no result 1. Jim Walsh's team beats Railway Union 2nds in the first round of the Senior 2 Cup, 203 to 187, but falls to the The Hills 2nds in the next round. Brett Saxon flashes through to blast 249 runs in 3 games, but apart from him, only Kevin Allwright and Eddie Lewis score 50s. Mike Townsend googles 29 wickets, while Jim Walsh manages another 21 softened-up rabbits. Merrion 3rds finish second in the Senior 3 League, with 73.6 per cent, having played 13, won 8, lost 3, no result 2. They miss winning this league by 0.9 per cent. John Blakeney, Niall Tempany, Dan Clarke and Graham Palmer feature for Alan Parkinson's side, which beats Railway Union 3rds, 91/9 to 89 and Portlaoise, before succumbing to Rush 2nds in the semi-final of the Middle Cup, 168 to 191/9.

Merrion 4ths prop up the Middle A League in tenth place, with 41.7 per cent, having played 12, won 2, lost 9, no result 1, despite Nicky Kenny's 334 runs @ 47.70. He belts 92 and Mark Forbes whiffles 4/23 against Rush 2nds. Joe McNabb's team loses to Old Belvedere 4ths in the first round of the Middle 2 Cup. Les Deacon and Garret Banahan try their best for this weak 4ths. In the YMCA Salver, they beat CYM 3rds and Pembroke 3rds/4ths, before losing to The Hills 3rds in the final, 120/9 to 148/6. Merrion 5ths finish 4/9 in the Intermediate B League, with 58.7 per cent, having played 14, won 7, lost 7. Andy Irvine's team loses to Bagnelstown in the first round of the Intermediate Cup. Oliver Rye, Bob Howell, Fiachra Crean, Fergus O'Flynn, Freddie Gilmore (hat-trick against Phoenix) and Roger Fox feature strongly for the 5ths this year.

Merrion 6ths win the Junior B League and gain promotion to Junior A. Peter Geoffroy's team finishes 1/8 with 79.1 per cent, having played 13, won 10, lost 3 and so gain promotion to Junior A. They lose to Portlaoise 2nds, 135 to 220/5, in the first round of the Junior Cup. Merrion 7ths finish 3/8 in the Junior C League, with 65.1 per cent, having played 14, won 7, lost 7. Jack Scott, Brett Woudstra, Tim Collier and Will Houston contribute most to Ray Clarke's team, which beats Rush 4ths and CYM 5ths to reach the Minor Cup final. They lose this to County Mayo, 71 to 72/6, Isobel Joyce top scoring with 20. Mike Kavanagh books 41 batsmen for the pavilion library @ 10.00. The presence of sisters Isobel and Cecelia Joyce on the men's 7ths throughout this record-breaking season marks another first in the club's history. Merrion Schoolboys are runners-up in the Under-11A Molins Cup, the Under-13A Jeyes Cup, the Under-15 Robertson League Cup and the Under-15 Yates Hale Cup. Ian O'Herlihy, Duncan Smythe and John Blakeney are selected for the Irish Under-17s. Dominick Joyce and Smythe play for Ireland Under-19s in Sri Lanka.

CLUB NOTES

A 1998/1999 yearbook is produced, which updates the five-year development plan with proposals for 1999/2000: to seek more playing members at the level of the top three teams; to develop a website to attract new members; to create a business plan for the use of the club during the winter months; to employ a full-time groundsman; to provide a higher profile to the selection process; to employ a full-time youth development officer and coach; to set up a coaching system; to enter B teams at the Under-11 and Under-13 age groups; to reduce weed growth and level the outfield; to install new showers for the home dressing room; to maximise the playing of cricket on the artificial mat, and to create a social committee responsible for organising events throughout the year.

Norman Reeves becomes the official groundsman. The Merrion website is soon up and running. Brad Spanner is appointed professional for the 1999 season, following a positive reference from Scotland. A letter is written to the Hon. Secretary from a group of women cricketers, complaining about their status within the club – the absence of women captains and internationals on the board, the lack of supporters at their matches, the bar not being open for those games (*a women's match in Merrion is like a funeral*), preference being given to Junior men's teams when there's a contention for dates. A mower is stolen and needs to be replaced. The question of paying bar workers is debated. It's reported that the outfield needs landscaping, rolling, fertilising, weedkilling and deworming. A detailed proposal for the organisation of youth cricket in Merrion is prepared by Eddie Lewis. The President reads a letter from CUS at a meeting, renewing their commitment to improving the ground at Bird Avenue. It is agreed that a letter asking for membership of the Irish Cricket Union be passed on to the members. There is a problem with finding a captain and manager of the women's teams, and it's agreed to approach Kate Dowling about captaining the 1sts. A social evening is planned to try to involve the women cricketers more in the club.

As part of a recruitment drive, the Hon. Secretary is to contact Earle St Aubin Scarlett from the American Embassy. There's a suggestion that a men's team be dropped, due to the difficulties in getting players to turn out. Sausage rolls are requested by players as a part of each tea. Several members of the 1sts are reported to the LCU by the umpires, due to their excessively vocal behaviour in a match against North County. Efforts are made to employ a FÁS worker to help Norman Reeves with the ground. A *blind date* function is held at Anglesea Road on 10 July, after an Irish Senior Cup game against Glendermott, and descends into chaos when the local residents complain so much about the noise that the Gardaí arrive at around

3a.m. and throw everybody out. There's a distinct possibility of half the club ending up in the Donnybrook nick, especially after an offensive remark is made to a Ban Garda, again by a distant relative of one of the authors of this book. But the premises are cleared and everyone is instructed to move on, even those awaiting taxis at the entrance.

Much more serious, and tragic, is an accident that occurs to a member of the 1sts, Philip Quinlan, who is returning through Hazeldene with some others to reclaim their property from the club. Attempting to climb over a fenced wall, he catches his foot on the tip of the fence and dives headfirst into the ground. He is left partially paralysed and requires constant care for life as a result. An emergency management committee meeting is held on Monday 12 July to establish the sequence of events. At this meeting, the question of insurance is discussed and further bar extensions for the remainder of the year are cancelled. As a result, changes are introduced into the running of the bar. This tragedy lingers on in the history of Merrion Cricket Club and casts a pall over its subsequent social life. A presentation is made to Gerry Duffy, in consideration of his contribution as coach over the previous years. A course in wicket-preparation is to be arranged for Norman Reeves. The telephone, toilet area and certain cars are vandalised, and the matter is handed over to the Gardaí. The owner of 51 Anglesea Road requests a private parking space, which will not be used by Point Information Systems, and a yellow box space is marked out for her. A meeting agrees that both Brad Spanner and John Harmon have done excellent work during the season. At the AGM, the Hon. Secretary commends Ray Clarke, nepotistically, for his excellent job as chairman of the cricket committee. She also recommends that the names of women internationals be added to the honours board. Bobby Blakeney is lauded for his work around the ground. A fundraising committee is to be formed to assist Philip Quinlan.

PROFILE: BRAD SPANNER

R-H hard-hitting batsman. R-A medium-pace seam bowler. Professional cricketer/coach, journalist and mortgage broker. Played one first-class match for Queensland in 1992, against the touring West Indies side, when his innings read, 'B. Spanner, caught Lara, bowled Hooper, 0'. But he was to last more than one ball at Anglesea Road, where he served as Merrion's overseas player in 1999. In that season, he scored 1,014 runs @ 67.60, including 3*100s and 8*50s, and took 31 wickets @ 13.87, helping Merrion to win the Lewis Traub and Whitney Moore & Keller B Leagues. From 2000 to 2002, he acted as youth development officer and scored 2,708 runs @ 57.61, including 9*100s and 10*50s, with a best score of 204*. He took 70 wickets @ 15.09 during this period, which saw another Alan Murray Cup win, and a Whitney Moore & Keller A League win. Captain in 2001. During his four years with Merrion, the 1sts won eight competitions, and were runners-up in four others. Brad tops the Merrion batting table for professionals and non-professionals with averages that will probably never be surpassed. In 2000, he scored 1,201 runs, another Merrion record that is unlikely to be beaten. He won the Samuels all-rounder cup in 2000 and 2002, and the Solomons Cup for catches in 2001. He featured in 5*200 runs partnerships, including 280 in 2001, which was a record for a Leinster club at the time. The success of the Merrion Schoolboy teams throughout the noughties owes much to his inspirational time as youth development officer. Brad is living proof that not all Aussies are addicted to the art of sledging, as he did his talking on the field of play with both bat and ball. The man from Toowoomba remains the yardstick by which all subsequent Merrion professionals have been, and will continue to be, measured.

Merrion 1sts, Lewis Traub League winners, 1999. Back row: B. Spanner, A. Fleming, D. Poder, J. Morrissey Jnr, S. King, P. Quinlan, G. Duffy (Ch). Front row: I. O'Herlihy, D. Joyce, A. Joyce (C), R. Dowse, R. Stanton, Da. Joyce.

Merrion 1sts, Alan Murray 20 Overs Cup winners, 1999. Back row: R. Stanton, A. Fleming, D. Poder, S. King, J. Morrissey Jnr, D. Joyce, D. Smythe, G. Duffy (Ch). Front row: I. O'Herlihy, R. Dowse, A. Joyce (C), B. Spanner, Da. Joyce.

2000: BECKETT CUP WINNERS; WHITNEY MOORE & KELLER A LEAGUE RUNNERS-UP; SENIOR 2 CUP WINNERS; TILLAIN CUP WINNERS; MIDDLE CUP RUNNERS-UP; JUNIOR C LEAGUE RUNNERS-UP; UNDER-13A JEYES CUP WINNERS; UNDER-15 YATES HALE CUP WINNERS; UNDER-17 AMOROSO CUP WINNERS

Senior: fixtures 21, reported 21, won 15, lost 4, no result 2. President: G. Ormonde. Captain: A. Joyce. Merrion beat Glendermott in the second round (bye in the first) of the Royal Liver Irish Senior Cup, 288/6 to 144, with Dominick Joyce scoring 80 and Damian Poder (Man of the Match) taking 5/14. They continue with a third round win against Strabane, 162/8 to 159/8, Brad Spanner belting 59 and Angus Fleming filching 3/33. Their run comes to an end in the fourth round, when North Down beat them in a rearranged match, 148 to 196/6, Robbie Stanton's 59 and Australian expatriate David Drane's 4/46 being in vain. Merrion's overseas player this year is yet another Aussie batsman, Chris Torrisi. Merrion win Section B of the Lewis Traub League, with 54 points, having played 6, won 5, no result 1. They lose to Phoenix by 6 runs in the semi-final, 234/7 to 240/7, despite Torrisi's 76, and miss out on the final at Anglesea Road. They trounce Rush in the first round of the Conqueror Cup, but fall to North County in the next, 42 to 45/3, on what must be assumed to have been a spaniel of a wicket. Merrion beat Drummond to win the Beckett Cup. As Gus Joyce is away with the Irish squad in North Wales, Julia Price, the Australian women's wicket-keeper, plays for the 1sts and does a good job behind the stumps, conceding no byes.

Whitney Moore & Keller League rule changes: Munster join Section B; there are now seven teams in each section, so no refixes in either. Merrion finish second in Section A, with 194 points, having played 12, won 9, lost 2, no result 1. This is their highest position in this league since 1960. They would have won it comfortably had not 24 points been deducted by the LCU for bad conduct during a match against Phoenix in June, when an anonymous Merrion player (See profile of Damian Poder) is caught urinating behind the sightscreen in the Phoenix Park, something that wouldn't have caused the batting of an eyelid back in the 1920s, when such behaviour was both physically advisable and necessary to encourage growth in the outfield. How times change. In the first instance, 12 points are deducted for excessive 'verbal action' by the team during Phoenix's innings and Poder is banned for two games, despite his written apology to the LCU, wherein he admits to having a few roos loose in the top paddock. Merrion lodge a passionate, coherent appeal and the LCU take the dubious step of doubling the penalty to 24 points, with Poder being banned for eight games. Merrion threaten legal action against the LCU because of the original points deduction, but after an EGM is held to consider the action, decide not to pursue it, as the gap between first and second place at the end of the season exceeds 12 points. So there's nothing to gain and over three grand is already down the urinal on the issue. Nevertheless, the members continue to believe that a grave injustice is done to the club this year.

Brad Spanner and Chris Torrisi share a partnership of 269 against Pembroke at Sydney Parade, a Leinster record. For the first time in five years, Merrion fail to win the Alan Murray Cup. Their concentration is obviously improving, even though their behaviour on the field is not. They lose to Railway Union in the first round, 98/8 to 99/4, despite Angus Fleming's 31* and 2/25. At the end of the season, Merrion are runners-up in a six-a-side competition over two weekends in the North West. This year, Merrion have three brothers on the Irish cricket team, with Ed Joyce playing five times, scoring 50s against Scotland and Zimbabwe A, brother Gus making his debut and playing three games, top scoring with 29 against Scotland, and brother Dominick also debuting against the Netherlands. This is the first time since 1929 that Merrion have three international players in the same year. How would Thornton, Loughery and O'Donnell compare to the three brothers from

Bray? Impossible question to answer, but they'd surely have enjoyed the billiard-table outfields and the weed-and-stone-free covered wickets, if not the pace of the bowling and the athletic fielding. Brad Spanner breaks the record he set the previous year by belting 1,201 runs @ 85.79, finishing second in the provincial batting averages and including a score of 204* against Railway Union, which remains a club record and is the seventh highest in the history of Leinster cricket. He wins the Samuels Cup for all-rounders, with 2,677 points. Chris Torrisi is one place behind him in the batting table with 965 @ 60.31. Gus Joyce fills out the batting honours with 380 runs @ 23.75, while brother Damian chips in with 209 @ 20.90. Brother Ed scores 51* in his last game for Merrion, before departing to a career in English county cricket. Robbie Stanton surpasses Simon Curley's record 369 appearances for Merrion 1sts, and is promptly dropped. Richard Dowse finishes eleventh in the provincial bowling statistics, with 31 wickets @ 17.68. Other wickets come from Brad Spanner, with 25 @ 14.76; Angus Fleming, with 22 @ 22.05; Joe Morrissey Jnr, with 21 @ 17.62; Damian Poder, with 23 @ 15.61, and Duncan Smythe (twelfth man for Ireland on one occasion), with 12 @ 12.25. John Blakeney is called into the Irish development squad:

Opponent	Result	Mer.	Opp.	Best Batting: Runs	Best Bowling: Wickets
Lewis Traub					
DU	No Res.				
Pembroke	Won	237/6	122	C. Torrisi: 84	D. Poder: 4/36
Railway Union	Won	186/7	143/8	C. Torrisi: 85	R. Dowse: 3/26
Old Belvedere	Won	287/4	169	C. Torrisi: 80	R. Willis: 3/42
Rush (C)	Won	308/5	135	A. Joyce: 82	J. Morrissey Jnr: 3/14
North County	Won	260	192	B. Spanner: 110	R. Dowse: 3/44
Malahide	Won	176/8	53	B. Spanner: 41	D. Poder: 5/11
Phoenix (S-F)	Lost	234/7	240/7	C. Torrisi: 76	
North County (C)	Lost	42	45/3		
Whitney Moore & Keller					
Phoenix	Won	182/2	179	C. Torrisi: 87*	R. Dowse: 5/25
YMCA	Lost	139	188/9	S. King: 39	B. Spanner: 3/29
Pembroke	Won	314/2	242/8	B. Spanner: 140*	B. Spanner: 3/41
The Hills	Won	200/2	198/9	C. Torrisi: 101*	D. Poder: 5/41
Phoenix (run rate)	Lost	179/9	141/4	B. Spanner: 90	
YMCA	Won	149/5	147	B. Spanner: 48*	B. Spanner: 4/32
Railway Union	Won	148/5	147/8	B. Spanner: 62*	D. Drane: 3/34
Clontarf	Won	171	161	B. Spanner: 76	J. Morrissey Jnr: 5/41
The Hills	Won	228/8	129	B. Spanner: 50	D. Smythe: 3/31
Clontarf	No Res.				
Railway Union	Won	353/5	133	B. Spanner: 204*	D. Clarke: 3/33
Pembroke	Won	148/3	146/9	E. Joyce: 51*	D. Smythe: 3/32

Junior: Merrion 2nds finish 4/9 in the Senior 2 League, with 65.3 per cent, having played 14, won 7, lost 6, tied 1. Alan Parkinson's Aussie-laden team beats Malahide 2nds in the first round of the Senior 2 Cup. They follow this with victory against The Hills 2nds and a remarkable chase of Pembroke 2nds' 277/5 in the semi-final, winning by 3 wickets, thanks largely to another lost Australian, Kade Beasley's 115*. The final against Clontarf produces a Man of the Match award for Robbie Stanton, who wafts 51 and snaffles 4 for 22, in a victory by 52 runs, 231/9 to 179. Jim Walsh and Andrew Nixon also star in this game. The Tillain Cup is also brought home this year by the 2nds/3rds, who beat Pembroke 2nds, Leinster 2nds/3rds, Railway Union 2nds and then Phoenix 2nds in the final, 90/5 to 87/8. Kade Beasley just misses out on the Bookman Cup, with 379 runs @ 47.40. Mark O'Donoghue and Jake Hanneman also feature in the Senior 2 batting table. Merrion 3rds finish 5/10 in the Senior 3 League, with 61.6 per cent, having played 12, won 6, lost 5, no result 1. Alan Little's team beats Old Belvedere 3rds in the first round of the Middle Cup. They follow this with victories over Clontarf 3rds and Malahide 3rds, before meeting Mullingar in the final at Malahide. In one of those games where both umpires seemed to suffer from St Vitus's dance of the right forefinger whenever the ball hits the pads, Merrion have Mullingar 2/3 after Jeff Short's 1st over. The midlanders recover to 122, and its Merrion's turn for the reflex action, with six early batsmen back in the pavilion for 18 runs, cursing the lack of a decision review system. Thanks to Michael Townsend's determination, and in spite of Simon Morrissey's efforts to run everybody out, Merrion manage to reach 108.

Merrion 4ths finish 5/9 in the Middle B League, with 64.0 per cent, having played 12, won 6, lost 6. They beat Sandyford and Knockbrack on the way to the Middle 2 Cup semi-final, where they fall to The Hills 3rds. Merrion 5ths finish 5/9 in the Intermediate B League, with 69.2 per cent, having played 11, won 7, lost 4. After beating Rush 3rds in the first round of the Intermediate Cup, they lose to North Wicklow in the next round. Merrion 6ths finish 5/8 in the Junior A League, with 62.3 per cent, having played 11, won 6, lost 5. Peter Geoffroy's team loses to CYM 4ths in the first round of the Junior Cup. Merrion 7ths finish second in Junior C, with 86.2 per cent, having played 13, won 12, lost 1 – missing out on winning their league by 1 per cent. They are, however, promoted to Junior B. The Hills 5ths, the winning side, play four fewer games. Ray Clarke's team beats CYM 5ths and Malahide 6ths on the way to a semi-final loss in the Minor Cup against North County 4ths. Merrion Schoolboys win the Under-13A Jeyes Cup, the Under-15 Yates Hale Cup and the Under-17 Amoroso Cup. They are runners-up in the All-Ireland Under-13 David Pigot Memorial Cup and the Under-15 All-Ireland Cup.

CLUB NOTES

A 2000 yearbook is produced with another update of the development plan: the key objectives of the five-year plan initiated in 1995, concerning ground improvements, expansion of membership, refurbishment of the pavilion, overhaul of the coaching structure, and stabilisation of the financial base, are met. It outlines further work for 2000: level the outfield; restore bounce to the artificial wicket; extra grass wickets for youth teams; more midweek matches; publish a Millenium Yearbook; improve the website; publish a club history; hold a major final at Anglesea Road, and draw up a new five-year plan for 2000-2005.

The LCU write to Merrion, inviting opinion on the prevailing restrictions on overseas players. The Leinster Grounds Committee makes a special commendation on the ground at Anglesea Road. Chris Torrisi is employed as the new professional. The Lewis Traub final is to be held at Anglesea Road. A discussion takes place about the cost of a youth development officer, and whether the club can afford it. A presentation is made to Robbie Stanton on the occasion of his breaking Simon Curley's record for most appearances on the 1sts. A meeting recommends that all captains should inform players who are dropped as to the reason for it, especially when young players are involved. The rules of the club are revised in August to reflect the changes in its organisation. Much time and energy is occupied this year in coping with the fallout of Damian Poder's unfortunate micturation behind the sightscreen in Phoenix, and the excessive vocal action on the field of play. The EGM agrees to send a letter to all the other clubs, outlining Merrion's side of the affair. At the AGM in September, the Hon. Secretary points out the fact that any player who has not paid his or her subscription is not insured. Gerry Ormond is thanked for all the medical assistance he has provided to players during the season.

The meeting is carried over to November, when Brad Spanner is elected 1sts captain, and a landswap deal with a certain Michael Roden is discussed. This involves the club moving out to Knockrabo, the former Bank of Ireland grounds off Roebuck Road, in return for a sum of money and the ground at Anglesea Road (part of which is not owned by Merrion Cricket Club, unknown to Mr Roden), and it is roundly rejected by the AGM. It is suggested that a list of all members of ten years' standing or more be drawn up. Eddie Lewis comments that there will be other similar proposals, and the club rules should be amended to protect Merrion against any further threats. Duncan Smythe is named Irish Schoolboy cricketer of the year. A letter from Wyse Management, responsible for the Hazeldene flats, seeks closer communication between Merrion and its management committee.

Above: Merrion 1sts, WMK A League runners-up, 2000. Back row: R. Dowse, J. Short, R. Stanton, D. Poder, A. Joyce (C), A. Fleming. Front row: B. Spanner, K. Beasley, C. Torrisi, D. Joyce, D. Drane.

Left: Merrion 2nds, Senior 2 Cup winners, 2000. Back row: J. Walsh, D. Verry, R. Stanton, A. Nixon, R. Willis. Front row: M. O'Donoghue, R. Sofra, I. O'Herlihy, A. Parkinson (C), G. Banahan, D. Clarke, J. Hanneman.

Left: Merrion 2nds, Tillain Cup winners, 2000. Back row: M. Tichband, T. Smith, D. Drane, A. Nixon, R. Stanton, J. Short. Front row: M. Townsend, A. Parkinson (C), R. Willis, I. O'Herlihy, D. Clarke.

Below left: Merrion Under-13As, Jeyes Cup winners, 2000.

Below right: Merrion Under-15s, Yates Hale Cup winners, 2000.

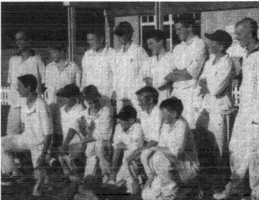

PROFILE: JOE MORRISSEY JNR

L-H aggressive, middle-order batsman. R-A accurate opening-seam bowler. Educated at Gonzaga College. Studied Economics at university. Financial analyst. Also played rugby as a forward for UCD and Blackrock, taking the number 8 jersey. Came up through the Schoolboy ranks in Merrion. Played 133 games for Merrion 1sts between 1993 and 2004, scoring 1,625 runs @ 20.06, including 8*50s and with a top score of 80. Also took 161 wickets @ 19.13, with 3*5 wickets in an innings, and 52 catches. Moved to Clontarf after the 2004 season, as he was living near the ground. Also played for Dublin University, the Irish Under-19s and was twelfth man for the full Irish side on several occasions, missing out on a full cap, perhaps because of his inability to control his volatile emotions on (and off) the field of play. Even so, his all-round abilities were a significant loss to Merrion, which is still felt today.

NB Other teams playing between 1991 and 2000: County Galway, Crusaders, Drogheda Ramblers.

4.5. THE NOUGHTIES: 2001-2010

The noughties continued the success of the late nineties for Merrion 1sts, with wins in the Whitney Moore & Keller A League in 2001 (first Senior League win since 1958), the 20/20 Alan Murray Cup in 2001, 2002 and 2005, the Dublin Grass Machinery 45 Overs League Cup in 2007, and the Bob Kerr Irish Senior Cup in 2010. They finished runners-up in the 2001 Lewis Traub League, the 2002 WMK A League, the 2002 and 2007 Senior Cups, the 2006 WM B League, the 2008 WM A League and Lewis Hohn Williams 20/20 Alan Murray Cup. Towards the end of the decade, they came close to winning the WM A League in 2009 and 2010. The return of Brad Spanner to Australia after the 2002 season left a gap that took about five years to fill, but his legacy was shown in the achievements of the Junior and Schoolboy teams.

This was the decade of the 6ths and the 2nds, who won the Senior 2 Cup in 2002, 2003, 2007 and the Senior League in 2002, 2004, 2007 and 2008. They were runners-up in this league in 2001 and 2003. A 2nds/3rds combination won the Tillain Cup in 2002 and were runners-up in 2009. The 3rds won the Middle Cup in 2006, 2009 and 2010, and were runners-up in 2004. They won the Senior 3 League in 2006. The 4ths won the Middle B League in 2001 and the Middle 2 Cup in 2004. They were runners-up in Division 6 in 2010. Merrion 5ths won the Intermediate B League in 2005 and were runners-up in the 2004 Intermediate Cup and the 2009 Intermediate A League. A 5ths/6ths/7ths/8ths combination won the Whelan Cup in 2004 and 2009, and were runners-up in 2003 and 2005. The 6ths just got better and better, winning the Junior Cup in 2002, 2004 and 2005; the Intermediate Cup in 2006; the Intermediate B League in 2009; and Division 9 in 2010. They were runners-up in the 2005 Junior A League and the 2008 Intermediate B League and Intermediate Cup. Merrion 7ths were runners-up in Division 12 in 2010. The 8ths were runners-up in the Junior C League in 2005, 2006 and 2009, and in the Minor Cup in 2007 and 2008. The Schoolboys brought home the Under-11 All-Ireland Cup in 2005; the Under-13 Jeyes Cup in 2001 and 2007; the Under-15 Yates Hale Cup in 2002 and 2009; the Under-15 Robertson Cup in 2001 and 2002; the Under-17 Amoroso Cup in 2003, 2004 and 2005, and the Under-19 Sean McGrath Cup in 2002 and 2005. All of which boded very well for the future.

It was a busy time for the club off the field, with the Philip Quinlan Trust Fund set up in 2001 and a successful invitation match held between a President's XI and Middlesex, including Ed Joyce, in 2002. An ICC World Cup qualifying match took place on the ground in 2005. There was a gradual improvement in the facilities of the clubhouse and the practice and playing areas throughout this period, together with new security gates and an electronic scoreboard. A three-year investment programme was initiated in 2003 to prepare for the club's centenary in 2006. A larger membership and more sponsorship were actively sought, and a growing number of functions were held to help finance the growth of the club. The driveway was fully tarmaced and income was generated from car parking there throughout the working week, all year round. Car parks were held for rugby matches and other RDS events. The centenary year passed off with a successful Summer Ball. An agreement was reached with Vodafone to erect a 3G mobile-phone mast on the right-hand side of the bank, where a floodlight used to be. Sky cameras invaded the club in 2009 for their 'Clublife' series, and there was no end to the showing off. Members of the 1sts were filmed doing physical training, which must have been a new experience for some of them, as well as illustrating how manifestly unfit they really were. The decade ended with the complete replacement of the square and plans for a new pavilion that was better suited to a more active social club and capable of hosting corporate events. The Irish Senior Cup brought the history to a timely end.

Merrion lost nearly an entire cricket team of players and supporters during this period: Al McKenna Snr, Chris Mara, Liam Keegan, Joe Burke, Joe Hopkins, John Heavey Snr, Cathal McAlinden, Peter Quinlan, Paddy Waldron, Roger Fox. *Requiescant in pace.*

2001: DEATH OF CHRIS MARA; WHITNEY MOORE & KELLER A LEAGUE WINNERS; LEWIS TRAUB LEAGUE RUNNERS-UP; ALAN MURRAY CUP WINNERS; SENIOR 2 LEAGUE RUNNERS-UP; MIDDLE B LEAGUE WINNERS; UNDER-13A JEYES CUP WINNERS; UNDER-15A ROBERTSON CUP WINNERS

Senior: fixtures 21, reported 21, won 12, lost 6, no result 3. President: G. Ormonde. Captain: B. Spanner. Merrion beat Instonians, 240/7 to 173, Phoenix, 260/5 to 220 and The Hills, 216/7 to 195/9, on the way to the semi-final of the Royal Liver Irish Senior Cup against North County. After a first attempt is abandoned, Merrion lose the replay, 247 to 262/6, despite Brad Spanner's 109 and Angus Fleming's demonic 40 in 23 balls. Chris Torrisi continues as Merrion's overseas player. Merrion finish the Lewis Traub B League in second place, with 44 points, having played 6, won 4, lost 1, no result 1. On equal points with North County, the Northsiders take the first place, having beaten Merrion in the league match. A narrow victory over Pembroke in the semi-final takes them to yet another match against the men of the Nevitt, in which the expatriate battle is won by Andre Botha, Chris Torrisi failing to fire for once. Merrion lose to YMCA in the second round (bye in the first) of the Conqueror Cup. They finally achieve glory with victory in the WMK Senior A League (for the first time since 1958), beating Clontarf into second place by 12 bonus points, gained largely by the batting of Spanner and Torrisi. They finish 1/7 with 192 points, having played 12, won 7, lost 3, no result 2. They lose three of the first seven games, then suffer two washouts, and the last three are won by comfortable, bonus-gaining margins.

Another competition win this season is the Alan Murray Cup (fifth in six years), in which Merrion beat YMCA, Leinster and Phoenix on the way to a final against Railway Union. A thrilling, tied match results, 114/6 to 114/7, with Merrion winning on the basis of losing fewer wickets. Brad Spanner is the top scorer with 35, and Richard Dowse filches 3 wickets for 28 runs. Two competitions won, yet no Merrion player features on the LCU Team of the Year. It must have been a great team effort. Chris Torrisi is fifth in the provincial batting table, with 917 runs @ 57.31. Brad Spanner is nineteenth on the same table, with 530 runs @ 31.18. Spanner also wins the Solomons Cup for fielding, with 14 catches, coming second to the ineligible Bryn Thomas of CYM. Spanner and Torrisi break the LCU record they set in 2000, by sharing 280 against The Hills at Anglesea Road, their third double-century partnership. Damian Poder chips 294 runs @ 22.62 and fiddles 22 wickets @ 19.73. Kade Beasley paddles 333 runs @ 30.27 and is third in the provincial wicket-keeping table, with 28 catches and 3 stumpings. Dominick Joyce drives 354 runs @ 29.50. He plays nineteen times for Ireland this year, with a top score of 67 against Wiltshire. Brother Gus manages 193 @ 32.17 in only 8 innings. Stephen King plunders 173 runs @ 28.83, also in only 8 innings. Richard Dowse is third in the provincial bowling table, with 37 wickets @ 14.32. Angus Fleming purloins 16 wickets @ 21.44. Justin Manville, late of the Yorkshire ground staff, makes a model appearance with the ball, for 16 wickets @ 12.88. Dan Clarke skittles 13 batsmen @ 25.38. David Drane lords it over 15 opposition batsmen @ 18.93. In November, the club says farewell to a staunch servant in the person of Chris Mara, just five days short of his ninetieth birthday:

Opponent	Result	Mer.	Opp.	Best Batting: Runs	Best Bowling: Wickets
Lewis Traub					
DU	No Res.	r.s.p.			
Leinster	Won	219/9	88	C. Torrisi: 84	D. Poder: 3/14
Old Belvedere	Won	356/3	97	C. Torrisi: 138	R. Dowse: 3/24
North County	Lost	203/9	246/9	K. Beasley: 72*	D. Joyce: 2/20
The Hills	Won	228/6	197	D. Joyce: 103	D. Clarke: 3/33
YMCA	Won	218/7	88	B. Spanner: 49	A. Fleming: 4/12
YMCA (C)	Lost	152	153/7	A. Joyce: 63	D. Drane: 3/23
Pembroke (S–F)	Won	215/7	190	K. Beasley: 55	B. Spanner: 3/28
North County	Lost	207	240/4	A. Fleming: 43	A. Fleming: 2/37
League Final					
Whitney, Moore & Keller					
The Hills	Won	81/2	79	C. Torrisi: 54*	D. Poder: 4/11
YMCA	Won	201	127	C. Torrisi: 60	S. Morrissey: 5/40
CYM	Lost	162/9	163/4	D. Poder: 58	S. Morrissey: 1/26
Clontarf	Lost	127	173	K. Beasley: 37	R. Dowse: 5/45
North County	Won	145	83	D. Smythe: 31	J. Manville: 5/36
Phoenix	Lost	254/6	258/5	C. Torrisi: 95	J. Manville: 3/60
YMCA	Won	236/9	175	K. Beasley: 96	R. Dowse: 4/43
Clontarf	No Res.	r.s.p.			
Phoenix	No Res.	r.s.p.			
CYM	Won	252/7	179	D. Smythe: 57	J. Manville: 4/37
North County	Won	233/6	122	C. Torrisi: 57	R. Dowse: 3/30
The Hills	Won	318/4	156	C. Torrisi: 157*	R. Dowse: 3/30

WHITNEY MOORE & KELLER A LEAGUE FINAL GAME 2001, MERRION V. THE HILLS

Merrion			The Hills		
A. Joyce	c. Archer b. J. Clinton	13	M.D. Dwyer	b. Spanner	1
D. Joyce	b. J. Clinton	3	P.J. Byrne	run out	54
C. Torrisi	not out	157	B.J. Archer	c. Spanner b. Dowse	44
B. Spanner	c. Hillary b. Akhtar	107	A. Raza	c. A. Joyce b. Dowse	4
A. Fleming	c. Raza b. Akhtar	0	B. Hillary	st. Beasley b. Poder	2
D. Poder	not out	7	N. Akhtar	b. Poder	0
K. Beasley	d.n.b.		D. Dundon	c. D. Joyce b. Blakeney	21
D. Smythe	d.n.b.		M. Clinton	st. Beasley b. Poder	9
D. Drane	d.n.b.		J. Bennett	c. D. Joyce b. Dowse	1
J. Blakeney	d.n.b.		L. Clinton	b. Smythe	6
R. Dowse	d.n.b.		J. Clinton	not out	0
	Extras	31		Extras	14
	Total (for 4 wickets)	**318**		**Total**	**156**

Junior: Rain deprives Merrion 2nds of victory in the Senior 2 League, and they finish 2/9, with 78.8 per cent, having played 15, won 10, lost 4, no result 1. Jim Walsh's team beats Pembroke 2nds and Clontarf 2nds in rounds one and two of the Senior 2 Cup, but loses to Malahide 2nds in the semi-final. A 2nds/3rds combination beats CYM 2nds and the Midland League in the Tillain Cup, only to lose to Leinster 2nds in the semi-final. Merrion 3rds finish

8/9 in the Senior 3 League, with 52.4 per cent, having played 12, won 4, tied 1, lost 7, and are relegated to Middle A. Portlaoise beat Alan Parkinson's team, 273/4 to 277/5, in the first round of the Middle Cup. Merrion 4ths win the Middle B League, finishing 1/9 with 81.1 per cent, having played 14, won 10, lost 2, no result 2. They cannot be promoted, due to the demise of the 3rds. Niall Tempany's band of brothers beats Wexford Wanderers and North County 3rds in the Middle 2 Cup, on the way to a semi-final defeat by Balleighan. They lose to Pembroke 3rds in the first round of the YMCA Salver. Merrion 5ths finish 3/10 in the Intermediate B League, with 68.5 per cent, having played 16, won 8, lost 7, drawn 1. John Bristow's team beats Pembroke 5ths in the first round of the Intermediate Cup, but loses to Bagnelstown in the next round. The 5ths/6ths/7ths combination loses to YMCA 4ths/5ths in the first round of the Whelan Cup. Merrion 6ths finish 5/9 in the Junior A League, with 54.9 per cent, having played 10, won 4, lost 6. Peter Geoffroy's team loses to Mullingar 2nds in the second round (bye in the first) of the Junior Cup. Merrion 7ths finish 5/8 in the Junior B League, with 54.8 per cent, having played 11, won 5, lost 6. Mike Kavanagh's team beats The Hills 5ths in the first round of the Minor Cup, but lose to Malahide 6ths in the next round. Merrion 8ths feature for the first time, but only in the Minor Cup, in which Maurice O'Donoghue's team beats The Hills 5ths in the first round, but loses to Malahide 6ths in the next. Merrion Schoolboys have another good year, winning the Under-13A Jeyes Cup and the Under-15A Robertson Cup, while coming runners-up to Lisburn in the All-Ireland David Pigot Memorial Cup.

CLUB NOTES

At the beginning of the year, a new sign at the entrance to the club is erected with sponsorship from Paddy Power. A new roller arrives and a meeting discusses the disposal of the old heavy roller, an important part of Merrion's history. There are new covers and the old covers also need to be dumped. Alan Parkinson is asked to investigate the problem of lack of pressure in the showers. Considerable maintenance work needs to be carried out on the nets, clubhouse and ground before the season can begin. There is a possibility of Simon Milton joining Merrion as wicket-keeper from Railway Union, but this does not materialise, as he cannot obtain a work permit. Chris Torrisi is re-employed as club professional for 2001. A letter is written to Dublin Corporation concerning the proximity of parking spaces on Anglesea Road to the club entrance. At the AGM in September, Alphonsus McKenna Snr is elected a Life Member. A report on youth cricket highlights the fact that almost 200 members played during the 2001 season. The problem of tea money collection is raised again. A motion is passed after some discussion that subscriptions be increased as follows: Senior playing member, €140; pavilion member, €50; Junior playing member, €70; playing family member, €200; pavilion family member, €100; schoolboy/girl member, €35. It is announced that a year-long Philip Quinlan trust fund is being launched with a target of €1 million. The meeting discusses various methods by which the club can contribute to this.

Subsequent MCMs agree to give the old covers to Wexford Wanderers and the heavy roller to North County. Work continues on levelling parts of the outfield. Fergus O'Flynn is to be responsible for the youth section and coaching in 2002. It is generally agreed that winter functions are not worth the hassle of organising. A quote for new security gates is obtained. A tour of Somerset is proposed for the following season. A letter of sympathy is written to the McKenna family on the recent death of their father, Alphonsus, and to Kitty Mara on the death of her brother, Chris. An 8ths team is entered into the 2002 Junior Cup. Changes to the club rules are discussed, in relation to selection committee responsibilities, the effect of a dissolution of the club and the rights of those who use the ground in winter, e.g. Crusaders. It is planned to move the shed from the entrance to free up more parking spaces.

PROFILE: ED JOYCE

L-H graceful, lazy, Goweresque stroke-player. R-A medium-pace seam bowler. Yet another member of the prodigious Joyce dynasty. Educated at Aravon, Presentation College, Bray and Trinity College. Also ruins good walks. Ed first played cricket for Bray at the age of four and debuted for the Bray Under-13s at the age of seven. He came up through the Merrion ranks and at fourteen he scored his first century for Merrion 3rds in the Middle Cup final. At sixteen he played for Merrion 1sts. Over the next six years, Ed creamed 1,448 runs @ 26.81 in eighty-four games for Merrion 1sts, with a highest score of 103* and 6*50s. He also whiffled out 56 batsmen for 15.64 and took 24 catches, and that was while playing for Trinity in the early part of the season. But his keen eye was on a career in county cricket, so in 2000 he left Merrion to join Middlesex for eight seasons before moving to Sussex in 2009. Ed has played fifty games for Ireland so far, spanking 1,637 runs @ 37.20, with 2*100s, 12*50s and a top score of 115*. His 7 wickets @ 51.43 are best not mentioned. In 2005, he qualified for England, and played seventeen ODIs for the old enemy, scoring 471 runs @ 27.70, with a century against Australia. In 2010, Ed switched his allegiances back to Ireland, having been ignored by those foolish England selectors for several years. Their loss is Ireland's gain, and whenever he gets fed up with Sussex, no doubt Merrion will also welcome him back with open arms. He is, after all, our pride and joy.

Merrion 1sts, WMK A League winner, 2001. Back row: B. Spanner (C), D. Verry, *A. Joyce*, A. Fleming, D. Poder, D. Drane, R. Dowse, G. Duffy (Ch), R. Stanton. Front row: S. King, C. Torrisi, D. Joyce, D. Smythe, K. Beasley, P. Blakeney, J. Blakeney, D. Clarke, S. Morrissey.

Merrion 1sts, Alan Murray 20 Overs Cup winners, 2001. Back row: G. Duffy (Ch), J. Manville, D. Joyce, J. Short, D. Clarke, D. Poder, A. Fleming. Front row: A. Joyce, B. Spanner (C), K. Beasley, C. Torrisi, R. Dowse.

2002: WHITNEY MOORE & KELLER A LEAGUE RUNNERS-UP; ALAN MURRAY CUP WINNERS; SENIOR CUP RUNNERS-UP; SENIOR 2 LEAGUE WINNERS; SENIOR 2 CUP WINNERS; TILLAIN CUP WINNERS; MIDDLE A LEAGUE RUNNERS-UP; JUNIOR CUP WINNERS; UNDER-15 ROBERTSON CUP WINNERS; UNDER-15 YATES HALE CUP WINNERS; UNDER-19 SEAN MCGRATH CUP WINNERS

Senior: fixtures 23, reported 23, won 15, lost 5, no result 3. President: P. Willis. Captain: K. Beasley. Merrion beat Lurgan, 250/9 to 165/7, on run rate, in the first round of the Royal Liver Irish Senior Cup. This is followed by victory over Pembroke, 197 to 155, but their run comes to an end in the third round, with a hammering from Rush, 245/7 to 142. This year's overseas player is Shawn Flegler, an Australian all-rounder. Merrion finish 2/7 in Section B of the Lewis Traub League, with 44 points, having played 6, won 4, lost 1, no result 1. In the semi-final against Railway Union, they fail by 2 runs to chase down 214. They reach the final of the Conqueror Senior Cup with victories over Leinster, The Hills and North County, but fail to chase YMCA's modest 173 by 59 runs. Captain Beasley wins the toss and makes the mistake of *putting them in* on a soggy wicket. Yet a score of 173 in a 60-over game at Rathmines is very chasable, provided the early batsmen show some patience. This doesn't happen. The rains come down and Merrion are 69/5 when stumps are drawn at 6.30p.m. on Saturday. The last 5 wickets fall for 45 runs when play resumes on Monday evening and another opportunity to lay the Senior cup bogey to rest disappears. The WMK Senior League provides a tighter finish, with Pembroke's superior bonus points beating Merrion into second place by a margin of 3, on the last day of the season. The two losses to North County make the difference and they end up with 194 points, having played 12, won 8, lost 2, no result 2. A sixth Alan Murray 20 Overs Cup is won by the reduced-overs specialists, with victories over Old Belvedere, Dublin University, CYM and, in another nail-biting final, Malahide, 119/6 to 115/5, wherein Joe Morrissey Jnr thumps 46 and takes 3/27.

Brad Spanner, in his last season with Merrion before returning to Australia, is second in the provincial batting table with 977 @ 61.06, including 171* against Clontarf in a 200 run partnership (his fifth) with Gus Joyce. He is also second in the provincial bowling table, with 38 @ 15.76, and wins the Samuels Cup for all-rounders for the second time, with 2,447 points. Shawn Flegler is fifth in the batting table with 749 @ 46.81 and eighth in the bowling table, with 44 @ 18.45. He is the leading wicket taker in Leinster this season and is third in the all-rounders' table, with 2,179 points, and fourth in the catches table with 10. Kade Beasley notches 446 runs @ 27.88 and wins the Hopkins provincial wicket-keeping trophy for the first time, with 27 catches and 4 stumpings. The other runs come mainly from Gus Joyce, with 311 @ 38.88, brother Dominick, with 212 @ 42.40, Damian Poder, with 184 @ 26.29 and Duncan Smythe, with 183 @ 20.33. Dominick plays eight times for Ireland, with a top score of 31 against Denmark. Apart from Flegler and Spanner, this year's wickets are contributed mainly by Justin Manville, with 17 @ 24.82, Dominick Joyce, with 12 @ 13.50, Joe Morrissey Jnr, with 11 @ 35.18, and Robin Willis, with 19 @ 25.63:

Opponent	Result	Mer.	Opp.	Best Batting: Runs	Best Bowling: Wickets
Lewis Traub					
North County	No Res.	r.s.p.			
Phoenix	Won	183/1	182/7	B. Spanner: 112*	S. Flegler: 3/19
YMCA	Won	234/7	133	K. Beasley: 71	D. Clarke: 5/20
The Hills	Won	240/6	216/8	B. Spanner: 140*	S. Flegler: 3/15
CYM	Won	159/4	158/9	B. Spanner: 56	B. Spanner: 5/26
Leinster (C)	Won	106	107/3	S. Flegler: 41*	R. Dowse: 5/27
Old Belvedere	Lost	121	155/8	S. Flegler: 32	S. Flegler: 2/26
The Hills (C)	Won	226/2	225/9	S. Flegler: 94*	B. Spanner: 4/40
Railway Union (S-F)	Lost	212/8	214	S. Flegler: 75	R. Willis: 3/37
North County (C)	Won	205/2	201/7	A. Joyce: 103*	B. Spanner: 2/20
Whitney, Moore & Keller					
Malahide	No Res.	35/0	130		
Phoenix (run rate)	Won	218	150	A. Fleming: 77	J. Manville: 5/41
North County	Lost	171	175/6	S. Flegler: 51	J. Manville: 3/67
CYM	Won	259/8	235	B. Spanner: 109	R. Willis: 4/58
Clontarf (run rate)	Won	130/7	155/7	J. Blakeney: 37	R. Dowse: 3/49
Pembroke	Won	209/6	208/6	B. Spanner: 45	J. Manville: 2/41
CYM	No Res.	77/4	206		
YMCA	Lost	114	173	J. Morrissey Jnr: 22	J. Manville: 3/47
Senior Cup Final					
Phoenix	Won	214/7	213/8	D. Joyce: 82*	D. Joyce: 3/37
Pembroke	Won	118/5	115	S. Flegler: 67*	B. Spanner: 3/22
Clontarf	Won	313/4	206	B. Spanner: 171*	D. Joyce: 5/40
Malahide	Won	187	182	D. Smythe: 53	S. Flegler: 4/34
North County	Lost	244/8	246/4	A. Joyce: 62	M. Kelly: 2/10

Junior: Merrion 2nds clean out the Leinster trophy stable comprehensively at this level, winning the Senior 2 League (for the first time in Merrion's history), the Senior 2 Cup and the Tillain Cup. Jim Walsh's team finishes 1/9 in the Senior 2 League, with 85.7 per cent, having played 12, won 10, lost 2. Stephen Tolputt, Robbie Stanton, Duncan Verry, David Drane, Richard Dowse, Jeff Short and Simon Morrissey are the stars of the most successful 2nds in Merrion history. In the Senior 2 Cup, they beat YMCA 2nds, Clontarf 2nds and The Hills 2nds on the way to a final against Malahide 2nds, which they win 260/9 to 204, thanks largely to Robbie Stanton's 90 runs. They beat Pembroke 2nds/3rds in the second round (bye in the first) of the Tillain Cup, and continue by beating Railway Union 2nds/3rds in the semi-final. They win the final against Phoenix 2nds, 158/5 to 103/9, thanks to another of Robbie Stanton's electrically wafted 90 runs and Richard Dowse's 3/16. Merrion 3rds finish 2/9 in Middle A and gain promotion back to Senior 3, with 78.2 per cent, having played 12, won 7, lost 2, no result 3. Alan Parkinson and David Rosenkowitz feature for Tim Ackland's team, which beats Malahide 3rds, 161 to 120, in the first round of the Middle Cup, but is forced to yield a walkover in the next round, to Pembroke 3rds. A 3rds/4ths team beats CYM 3rds in the first round of the YMCA Salver, but loses to Sandyford in the next round. Merrion 4ths finish 3/10 in the Middle B League, with 81.8 per cent, having played 12, won 9, lost 3, and so missing out on promotion by 0.2 per cent. Alistair Howell's team, starring Sum, Tim Collier, Denis McKenna, Eric Flanagan, Niall Tempany and Daniel Campion, is drawn against Wexford Wanderers in the first round of the Middle 2 Cup.

Merrion 5ths finish 5/9 in the Intermediate B League, with 59.5 per cent, having played 11, won 5, lost 5, no result 1. Oliver Rye and Roger Fox have personal best scores of 84 and 89 in the same match. John Bristow's team loses to Portlaoise 2nds, 161/7 to 162/5 in the first round of the Intermediate Cup. A 5ths/6ths/7ths combination beats Sandyford 2nds/3rds and the Garda in the Whelan Cup, before succumbing to Railway Union 4ths in round two. Merrion 6ths finish 4/9 in the Junior A League, with 62.1 per cent, having played 11, won 6, lost 5. They gain a walk-over in the first round of the Junior Cup, and continue to the final by beating Malahide 5ths in the next round, and North County 4ths in a replay after a tied match. The day after the replayed semi-final, Leinster 6ths provide the opposition in the final at Civil Service, and Merrion 6ths bring home yet another trophy. It's a triumph for Will Houston, the captain, and also for Barney Bulmer, Peter Geoffroy, Richard Keaveney, Daniel Campion, Dara O'Donoghue, Frank Nugent, J.P. Khan, G. Singh, F. Nazzem and S. Barr. Merrion 7ths finish 6/9 in the Junior B League, with 51.8 per cent, having played 10, won 4, lost 6. Mike Kavanagh's team loses to Portlaoise 3rds in the first round of the Minor Cup. Merrion 8ths beat North Kildare 3rds in the first round of the Minor Cup, but Barney Bulmer's boys lose to Leinster 7ths in the next.

The Schoolboys continue to thrive, with victories in the Under-15 Robertson Cup, the Under-15 Yates Hale Cup (Tim Lewis: 99*, against a Malahide team captained by Eoin Morgan) and the Under-19 Sean McGrath Cup. They are runners-up in the Under-13 Top 4 Cup and the Under-15 All-Ireland Masonic Cup.

CLUB NOTES

Donnybrook GAA's request for use of the ground to train is rejected. A meeting chooses Shawn Flegler as the new overseas player, with Chris Torrisi as the club coach from June to August and Brad Spanner as youth development officer and director of coaching. The subject of an All-Ireland League is raised, but few of the committee members are keen on the idea, and the club representative is mandated to vote against it. Subsequently, the idea is voted down by the

LCU, eight to three. Plans for the coming season include: a new central artificial wicket; new sightscreens; two replacement mats for practice nets; new bar furniture; the upgrading of three changing rooms, showers and toilets; restructuring the area behind the bar, and electronic security gates. It is agreed that teas should be €5 for adults, €3 for students and €2 for schoolgoers.

The highlight of this summer is a benefit match in aid of the Philip Quinlan Trust Fund on Sunday 23 June, between Middlesex (featuring Merrion's own Ed Joyce) and a President's XI, made up largely of Leinster pros and a few from Merrion's 1sts, including John Blakeney, Dominick Joyce and Shawn Flegler. Brad Spanner is captain. Also featuring is a young Eoin Morgan from Malahide, who is destined for greater things. The club is busy preparing the pavilion and grounds for this match, which is won easily by the President's XI, possibly because of the Middlesex team's sojourn in Temple Bar the previous night. The occasion is a resounding success. Merrion prove they are capable of hosting full internationals, and Middlesex enjoy themselves so much that they suggest making it an annual match, although this doesn't materialise. Donations towards the fund are received from many clubs around Ireland throughout the season, and other events are held during the summer.

Water is leaking under the new covers. The bar is not being managed properly and a new bar manager is appointed. The club writes to the LCU, objecting to the sharp increase in affiliation fees. The poor attitude and behaviour of a player on the 1sts, both on and off the field, is raised as a disciplinary issue. There are problems with the way the club's finances are being handled by the treasurer. At the AGM, the Hon. Secretary reports that the overall trust fund for Philip Quinlan has reached €1 million. A three-year investment plan is drawn up to bring Merrion's ground to international standard by 2006, the centenary year of the club's foundation. Suggestions include an electronic scoreboard, a water hog for the square, tarpaulin sheets for the run-ups, improved practice facilities, a boundary rope (it is suggested, somewhat facetiously, that this might solve the Senior player's 'white-line fever' problem), overhauling of the bowling machine, a slip cradle, further levelling of the outfield, etc. As Sean Flegler is unavailable for the 2003 season, an offer is made to Lachlan Stevens, a member of the Queensland squad.

Merrion 1sts, Alan Murray Cup winners, 2002. Back row: S. Morrissey, S. King, B. Spanner, R. Willis, J. Morrissey Jnr, J. Manville, A. Fleming, G. Duffy (Ch). Front row: P. Blakeney, S. Flegler, K. Beasley (C), D. Smythe, Da. Joyce.

Merrion 2nds, Senior 2 League/Cup/Tillain Cup winners, 2002. Back row: R. Stanton, D.Verry, S. Morrissey, J. Short, S. Tolputt, R. Dowse, F. Bronkhurst. Front row: A. Parkinson, G. Eden, J. Walsh (C), D. Dorgan, D. Drane.

Merrion 6ths, Junior Cup winners, 2002. Back row: F. Nugent, S. Barr, B. Bulmer, D. Campion, G. Singh, F. Nazzem, G. Dungan. Front row: D. O'Donoghue, J.P. Khan, W. Houston (C), R. Keaveney, P. Geoffroy.

Merrion Under-15s, Yates Hale Cup winners, 2002.

PROFILE: JOHN HEAVEY SNR

Born in County Louth in 1930 into a family of twelve, where there was no history of any interest in the game of cricket. Graduated in Economics from UCD in 1953 and won a Kellogg's scholarship to study at the University of California-Davis, where he gained an Economics Masters Degree in 1963. He continued to live in America until 1967 and returned to Ireland to work for An Foras Talúntais and Teagasc, where he rose to become Head of Farm Management, a position he held until he retired. Also played golf, with a handicap of 4. Although there were no cricketers in the family, he and his two sons would listen avidly to Test Match Special on the radio, probably in the days of John Arlott. Their interest was sufficiently peaked for all three to join Merrion in 1977. John Snr played a few Taverners games and became a respected Leinster umpire and a superb Hon. Secretary from 1981 to 1994, while both sons, John Jnr and David went on the play for Merrion 1sts. In addition, John Snr umpired several international matches and many interprovincials. Subsequently, he was President of the Leinster and Irish Cricket Umpires' Associations and a Life Member of Merrion. *Richie's* support for the 1sts from the sideline was passionate and vociferous, even to the extent of arousing threats of physical violence from the opposition. For the team, it must have been like having a twelfth player.

2003: SENIOR 2 LEAGUE RUNNERS-UP; SENIOR 2 CUP WINNERS; WHELAN CUP RUNNERS-UP; UNDER-17 AMOROSO CUP WINNERS

Senior: fixtures 19, reported 19, won 5, lost 13, no result 1. President: P. Willis. Captain: A. Joyce. Merrion beat Cork Harlequins and Glendermott (K. Beasley: 136) in the first two rounds of the Royal Liver Irish Senior Cup, but fall to North County in the third round, 104 to 191/8. Some of the players spend the early part of the season with Trinity, and this, combined with the absence of the Spanner '*get out of jail*' card, leads to a disappointing season. Their overseas player is another Australian all-rounder from Toowoomba, Lachlan Stevens, although he has to return early in the season for family reasons and is replaced by Shawn Willoughby. But neither player can prevent Merrion from finishing 5/7 in Section A of the Lewis Hohn Williams League (the same sponsor, despite the change of name, and with a final at Anglesea Road) with 24 points, having played 6, won 2, lost 3, no result 1, and from being bounced out of the Conqueror Cup in the first round by Clontarf, 206 to 209/4.

The season gets worse, as Merrion finish 6/7 in Section A of the WMK League with 86 points, having played 12, won 3, lost 9. Several of the Senior players go on holiday rather than play the last two battles, and so relegation to Section B follows. They are drawn against YMCA in the second round of the Alan Murray Cup, but generously decide to allow another team to win this competition for a change. Kade Beasley swipes 433 runs @ 25.47 and is sixth in the provincial wicket-keeper's table, with 19 catches and 2 stumpings. Lachlan Stevens pummels 131 runs in his 6 games, @ 26.20, and buys 10 wickets @ 12.40. His replacement, Sean Willoughby manages 232 runs @ 23.20. David Drane whacks 189 runs @ 47.25. Gus Joyce, in his last year as captain before departing to work in England, drives 335 runs @ 23.93. John Blakeney spanks 252 runs @ 28.00. Dominick Joyce plays seven times for Ireland, with a top score of 29 against Zimbabwe. Stephen Tolputt slams 204 runs @ 12.75. Joe Morrissey Jnr strikes 271 runs @ 33.88 and bowls 91 overs at a miserly 2.32 per over. Damian Poder has 148 runs @ 29.60 and 19 wickets @ 23.32. In a year that the opposition is bowled out on only five occasions, no one takes 20 wickets. As usual, Angus Fleming has a tidy 16 @ 19.69 and Robin Willis captures 19 @ 20.16. Leinster Cricket and Merrion mourns the loss of a dedicated umpire and eccentric friend with the passing of Liam Keegan:

Opponent	Result	Mer.	Opp.	Best Batting: Runs	Best Bowling: Wickets
Lewis Hohn Williams					
Rush	Lost	93	94/1	D. Drane: 17*	R. Willis: 1/17
CYM	Won	147/3	144	D. Drane: 58*	L. Stevens: 4/26
North County	Lost	118	119/3	K. Beasley: 32	D. Poder: 2/43
The Hills (run rate)	Won	75/4	148	S. Tolputt: 21	D. Poder: 3/25
Old Belvedere	No Res.	39/2	160/9	r.s.p.	
Malahide	Lost	162/9	185	R. Stanton: 34*	R. Willis: 3/19
Clontarf (C)	Lost	206	209/4	K. Beasley: 81	D. Poder: 2/50
Whitney, Moore & Keller					
Pembroke	Won	220	173	A. Joyce: 53	A. Fleming: 4/25
Munster Reds	Lost	183/7	184/3	S. Willoughby: 51*	J. Morrissey Jnr: 1/4
Phoenix (run rate)	Won	188/7	199/7	D. Drane: 41	D. Poder: 3/26
Malahide	Lost	222/6	223/6	S. Willoughby: 56	J. Blakeney: 2/19
Munster Reds (run rate)	Lost	216/9	155/6	J. Blakeney: 52	A. Fleming: 3/48
North County	Lost	197	198/9	A. Joyce: 96	D. Verry: 3/18
Pembroke	Won	165	151	J. Blakeney: 42	D. Poder: 4/33
Phoenix	Lost	146/9	147/4	D. Verry: 35	D. Verry: 1/3
Malahide	Lost	215/5	219/3	J. Morrissey Jnr: 79*	S. Willoughby: 1/21
North County	Lost	160	209/7	J. Morrissey Jnr: 65	A. Fleming: 4/64
Railway Union	Lost	189	190/4	K. Beasley: 49	R. Willis: 2/22
Railway Union	Lost	197	259/5	K. Beasley: 67	D. Verry: 1/33

Junior: Merrion 2nds finish 2/9 in the Senior 2 League, with 85.7 per cent, having played 12, won 9, lost 2, no result 1. Chris Small narrowly misses out on the Oulton Cup, taking 25 wickets at 15.88. Stephen King wins the Sean Pender Cup for outstanding contribution on the field of play. The youngest player on Robbie Stanton's team is twenty-seven, but they beat Civil Service, YMCA 2nds, CYM 2nds on the way to a Senior 2 Cup final against North County 2nds, which they win easily, 225/9 to 99. Stephen King's tally for the four matches of 45, 116, 54* and 61 is almost as good as Stephen Tolputt's 57*, 104, 95 and 62. But Richard Dowse wins the Man of the Match award in the final. A 2nds/3rds combination beats CYM 2nds and Civil Service in the first two rounds of the Tillian Cup, but loses to Railway Union 2nds in the semi-final. Merrion 3rds finish 3/9 in the Senior 3 League, with 75.5 per cent, having played 13, won 7, lost 4, no result 2. Michael Tichband's team beats Leinster 3rds and Wexford Wanderers, before losing to Sandyford in the semi-final of the Middle Cup.

Merrion 4ths finish 7/9 in the Middle A League, with 56.3 per cent, having played 9, won 4, lost 5. Dan Clarke scores a maiden 100 against Wexford. Bob Howell's team beats Railway Union 4ths in the second round (bye in the first) of the Middle 2 Cup, but lose to The Hills 3rds in the semi-final. Railway Union beat them in the second round (bye in the first) of the YMCA Salver. Merrion 5ths finish 3/10 in the Intermediate B League, with 73.7 per cent, having played 16, won 11, lost 5. Oliver Rye's team loses to Pembroke 5ths in the first round of the Intermediate Cup. A 5ths/6ths/7ths combination beats the Garda, North Wicklow and Pembroke 5ths/6ths on the way to the final of the Whelan Cup, which they lose to Civil

Merrion 2nds, Senior 2 Cup winners, 2003. Back row: R. Dowse, C. Small, G. Eden, J. Short, R. Allwright, K. Allwright. Front row: S. King, J. Walsh, R. Stanton (C), F. Bronkhurst, M. Tichband, A. Parkinson.

Service 2nds/3rds. Merrion 6ths finish 4/8 in the Junior A League, with 69.6 per cent, having played 12, won 7, lost 5. In the Junior Cup, J.P. Khan's team beats The Hills 4ths and Laois 3rds on the way to a semi-final defeat by Old Belvedere 3rds/4ths. Merrion 7ths finish 6/8 in the Junior B League, with 52.5 per cent, having played 12, won 5, lost 7. Denis Brownlee's team beats Swagelok Tavs and North Kildare 4ths on the way to a semi-final defeat by Civil Service 4ths in the Minor Cup. Merrion 8ths again compete only in the Minor Cup, beating North Wicklow 3rds and Rush 4ths on the way to the other semi-final, which results in a loss to Clontarf 5ths. Ben Ackland, Peter Blakeney, Kyle Tonetti and Eoghan Furlong gain representative honours. Merrion Schoolboys are runners-up in the Under-13B League, the Under-15A League and the Under-19 Sean McGrath Cup. They win the Under-17 Amoroso Cup.

CLUB NOTES

A solicitor for Philip Quinlan serves notice that he is suing the trustees of the club for negligence concerning his accident in July 1999. The matter is passed to the club's insurance brokers, Alexander Forbes. A subsequent meeting decides to express more strongly the disappointment of the committee members at this course of action by the Quinlan family.

Stuart Kenny agrees to sponsor the sign at the club entrance. Ongoing problems caused by the inadequacy of the Hon. Treasurer are discussed, and Niall Tempany is forced to resign. Poor lad. The rumour is that he has discovered sex and gone to pieces altogether. The finance committee is active this year in encouraging companies to hold functions in the club. Yet again the toilets are continually blocked up. The club's plans for a youth development officer come to nothing this year, due to a last-minute withdrawal, the best kind.

Philip Quinlan writes to the MCM, informing them that he has no intention of proceeding with an action against the club. As recognition of her contribution to Irish Women's Cricket, Ursula Lewis wins a global ICC award for Best Women's Cricket Initiative. Complaints are registered about the lack of pace and bounce in the Merrion wickets, and the state of the outfield at the CUS ground in Bird Avenue, on which the 5ths-7ths play most of their home games. Much of the AGM is taken up with finding ways of improving the club facilities and performances after a poor season. An update to the development plan is produced by the cricket committee, highlighting problems with the way younger members are integrated into the Senior teams, and issues of discipline and commitment on the 1sts. An 8ths is to be entered into the league in 2004.

The new committee recommends to the LCU that the number of players being paid by other clubs could be controlled by a *'once a pro, always a pro'* rule. A discussion is held about how to persuade the reluctant groundsman that the wickets need to be improved, as Merrion are now ranked in the bottom three in Leinster, with only Old Belvedere and Pembroke below them. A suggestion is made to scrap the Taverners, to reduce fixture congestion on the ground. A communications strategy is presented to the MCM by Eddie Lewis for discussion, recommending a revamped website and options for members to receive all Merrion data electronically. The vigorous and active new President agrees to introduce himself to the vicar of Donnybrook and Irishtown. *'More tea, vicar?'*

2004: SENIOR 2 LEAGUE WINNERS; MIDDLE CUP RUNNERS-UP; MIDDLE 2 CUP WINNERS; INTERMEDIATE CUP RUNNERS-UP; WHELAN CUP WINNERS; JUNIOR CUP WINNERS; UNDER-17 AMOROSO CUP WINNERS

Senior: fixtures 21, reported 21, won 9, lost 11, no result 1. President: A.B. Fleming. Captain: D. Poder. Merrion lose to Bangor in the first round of the Royal Liver Irish Senior Cup, 174 to 177/1, despite David Drane's fighting 61. Merrion's overseas player this year is Dave Celep from Sydney, Australia, capable of bowling at least two gorgeous sixes every over. Apparently V.V.S. Laxman, Tyron Henderson, Steve Tikolo and Murali Kartick are in the agent's frame for this job, but Celep prevails, as he is not a first-class player. What Laxman (who scores a double century against Australia a week before his agent's offer) would have thought of the Merrion wickets is not recorded. John Brenton is also employed as a non-playing coach. Merrion finish 5/7 in Section A of the Lewis Hohn Williams League, with 20 points, having played 6, won 2, lost 4. Again, the absence of Trinity players tells in this result, which could easily have been much better, as there are several close finishes. They have a good run in the Conqueror Cup, beating Dublin University and Clontarf in the first two rounds (D. Poder winning both Man of the Match awards), before losing to Clontarf in the semi-final, 219 to 277/7.

The WMK League starts promisingly enough, with three wins, but the season falls apart after that, with six losses out of the last nine matches, and a dreadful batting display against Pembroke in the final encounter. Merrion finish 5/7 in Section B, with 145 points, having played 12, won 5, lost 6, no result 1. Their generosity continues in the Alan Murray Cup, when they lose to Railway Union in the second round (bye in the first), 128 to 203/4. The main factor in this year's poor results is the absence of a second-string pace attack to back up Morrissey Jnr and Fleming, and an over-reliance on some weak slow bowling, especially from the club professional. Good news arrives in the shape of Titiksh Patel from Dublin University, a tidy, left-arm, slow-medium bowler. Dominick Joyce plays six times for Ireland, with a top score of 66 against the MCC. Uniquely, Kade Beasley wins the Hopkins Cup for wicket-keeping again, with 26 catches and 14 stumpings. Merrion batting honours go to Beasley (sixteenth in the provincial batting table), with 586 runs @ 32.56; Dominick Joyce (eleventh in the batting table), with 369 @ 52.71; Damian Poder, with 479 @ 34.21; Joe Morrissey Jnr, with 368 @ 26.29 (before moving to Clontarf, where they have a boundary rope); David Celep, with 385 @ 25.67, and Grant Eden, yet another runaway from the southern hemisphere, with 170 @ 15.45. Eden also tweaks out 15 batsmen @ 16.27. Celep manages just 14 @ 23.64. Joyce twirls out 10 @ 19.10. Fleming beats

27 batsmen through the air @ 18.11. Poder buys 24 @ 23.79. Morrissey Jnr scalps 21 victims @ 19.10. Titiksh Patel bewilders 14 batsmen @ 15.43:

Opponent	Result	Mer.	Opp.	Best Batting: Runs	Best Bowling: Wickets
Lewis Hohn Williams					
Rush	Won	274/7	160	K. Beasley: 79	A. Fleming: 3/30
Pembroke	Lost	194/9	197/9	J. Morrissey Jnr: 67	J. Morrissey Jnr: 3/30
Railway Union	Lost	153	161	G. Eden: 62	D. Poder: 2/14
Clontarf	Lost	187/7	188/5	D. Poder: 50*	A. Fleming: 2/21
Malahide	Lost	201	229/9	D. Poder: 38	G. Eden: 4/56
DU (C)	Won	177/4	175	D. Poder: 80*	G. Eden: 3/27
Old Belvedere	Won	177/7	176/8	R. Stanton: 48	D. Poder: 3/41
Malahide (C)	Won	192/3	191	D. Poder: 60*	J. Morrissey Jnr: 5/35
Whitney, Moore & Keller					
CYM	Won	181/1	179	D. Celep: 76*	J. Short: 3/14
Clontarf (C)	Lost	219	277/7	J. Morrissey Jnr: 80	A. Fleming: 3/54
Old Belvedere	Won	209	203/9	D. Poder: 93	J. Morrissey Jnr: 3/25
Leinster	Won	127/3	123	K. Beasley: 75*	D. Celep: 2/0
YMCA	Lost	196	217	K. Beasley: 84	A. Fleming: 2/21
Pembroke	Lost	258	265/5	D. Joyce: 74	K. Tonetti: 2/34
Rush	Lost	138	139/7	K. Beasley: 40	D. Joyce: 3/24
YMCA	Lost	179	211/9	J. Morrissey Jnr: 49	T. Patel: 3/29
Old Belvedere	Won	220	116	K. Beasley: 68	T. Patel: 3/12
CYM	No Res.	41/1	r.s.p.		
Leinster	Won	163/9	100	G. Eden: 47	T. Patel: 3/33
Rush	Lost	222/8	226/5	D. Joyce: 87*	D. Joyce: 2/46
Pembroke	Lost	41	163	J. Blakeney: 29*	D. Poder: 3/19

Junior: Merrion 2nds finish 1/9 in the Senior 2 League, with 83.2 per cent, having played 13, won 10, lost 3. Stephen King blasts over 400 runs and Robbie Stanton wafts 380, including an undefeated century against Phoenix. Stanton's team loses to Phoenix in the first round of the Senior 2 Cup, 218 to 309/7. A 2nds/3rds combination beats CYM 2nds in the first round of the Tillain Cup, but loses to the Midland League in the next. Merrion 3rds finish 6/9 in the Senior 3 League, with 52.3 per cent, having played 11, won 2, lost 7, tied 1, no result 1. Dermot Dorgan's team, including John Heavey, John Souter, Kevin and Rory Allwright, Ronny Barker, Thushara Wijesundera (Sum) and Darragh O'Flynn, beats YMCA 2nds, 207/8 to 189 in the second round (bye in the first) of the Middle Cup. The semi-final against Pembroke 3rds is also won, 142 to 118, but that's it, as Phoenix 3rds beat them in the final.

Merrion 4ths finish 9/10 in the Middle A League, with 36.4 per cent, having played 15, won 3, lost 11, no result 1. Points are deducted for a failure to return the result cards, and they are relegated to Middle B. Liam Casey's team have a clear run in the Middle 2 Cup, in which they beat Phoenix 3rds, The Hills 4ths and Mullingar on the way to a final against Laois 2nds at Rush. They chase down 212/8, losing only 4 wickets in the process, and bring home another trophy, Cillian O'Donoghue featuring with 88* and Adam O'Keeffe contributing 50. Railway Union 3rds beat them in the second round of the YMCA Salver. Merrion 5ths finish 3/9 in the Intermediate B League, with 70.0 per cent, having played 13, won 8, lost 5. Oliver Rye's/Roger Fox's/Gupreet Singh's team beats Old Belvedere 4ths, Civil Service 2nds and Leinster 5ths to reach the final of

Above left: Merrion 2nds, Senior 2 League winners, 2004. Back row: A. O'Keeffe, S. King, T. Lewis, S. Tolputt, P. Blakeney, R. Flannery. Front row: R. Keaveney, T. Patel, R. Stanton (C), J. Short, J. Walsh.

Above right: Merrion 4ths, Middle 2 Cup winners, 2004. Back row: A.J. Da Silva, Sum, J. Heavey Jnr, K. O'Flynn, A. Howell, C. O'Donoghue. Front row: Ishfaq, N. Tempany, L. Casey (C), R. Keaveney, K. Tonetti. Missing: A. O'Keeffe, A. Kay.

Left: Merrion 6ths, Junior Cup winners, 2004. Back row: S. Furlong, J. Wilson, A. Skelton, N. Kenny, G. Rogers, J.P. Khan. Front row: F. Nugent, G. Dungan, W. Houston (C), F. Crean, P. Geoffroy.

the Intermediate Cup, which they lose to Clontarf 4ths, 108 to 192/6. Andreas Gilmore, Mark Rutledge, Rodney Smythe, Wasif Hussein, Gary Morris and A.J. De Silva star for this team. A 5ths/6ths/7ths/8ths mixture wins the Whelan Cup, beating YMCA 4ths, North Wicklow, Leinster 5ths/6ths/7ths and then Civil Service 2nds/3rds/4ths in the final. Merrion 6ths finish 7/9 in the Junior A League, with 48.4 per cent, having played 9, won 3, lost 6. Will Houston's team beats Laois 3rds, the Garda and Rush 4ths to reach the Junior Cup final, which they win, beating The Hills 4ths, 136/4 to 132. Mark Kelly scores a 100 and a 50. Merrion 7ths finish 3/9 in the Junior B League, with 63.5 per cent, having played 13, won 8, lost 5. They lose to Clontarf 5ths, 179 to 206 in the preliminary round of the Minor Cup. Merrion 8ths, in their first year in league cricket, finish 7/11 in the Junior C League, with 47.3 per cent, having played 8, won 3, lost 5. Barney Bulmer's boys beat Rush 5ths in the first round of the Minor Cup, but lose to Malahide 5ths in the next round. Merrion Schoolboys win the Under-17 Amoroso Cup and finish runners-up in the Under-15A Robertson Cup and the Under-19 Sean McGrath Cup.

CLUB NOTES

The first meeting confirms that Merrion will be awarded at least a single match in the 2005 ICC World Cup qualifying tournament. The committee agrees that the wickets were insufficiently rolled, and not early enough, the previous season. An application for a Department Of Sports, Arts & Tourism grant is made, to prepare for the ICC tournament. The money is to be spent on: relaying the artificial wicket and practice wickets; a new practice pitch; a slip cradle; boundary rope; new seating; electronic scoreboard; improving the mobility of the sightscreens; a fourth cover and layflat covers; more efficient showers, and a new changing room. A tramp has been sleeping rough outside the clubhouse during the winter. Donnybrook GAA apply again to use the ground for light training and the committee proposes an eight-week period in February and March. Yoga classes also take place. Quotes for a new security gate at the front entrance are discussed. There are problems getting out the 3rds and 4ths teams in the early part of the season.

It is suggested by the President and Hon. Secretary that there should be a specific annual budget for maintenance of the clubhouse. There are complaints about the opening hours of the bar, which some feel are too late in the afternoon. It is agreed to direct the selection committee to no longer consider players whose subs remain unpaid. There are problems with the behaviour of the club coach and a member of the 1sts, the latter being suspended by the LCU for two matches. The need for an internal disciplinary committee is agreed. Subscriptions are to be increased in 2005 to: €180 for Senior playing members; €250 for family playing; €125 for family pavilion; €70 for pavilion, and €40 for youth. The electronic security gates are purchased. Plans commence for the centenary of the club in 2006. An umpire reports that £7,000 sterling is stolen from the glove compartment of his car. And who said they were overpaid? By the end of the season, thanks to a better watering plan and more rolling, Merrion have reached fifth in the table for pitch standard. As 49 Anglesea Road is up for sale and the owners are claiming a right of way for vehicles into their back garden, it's time to call in the solicitors again. The old shed is finally demolished and two new lockups are installed beside the practice wickets. Arrangements are made to have the old shed base tarmaced, as well as the area to the right of the entrance lane. At the AGM, a local resident raises the issue of a helicopter landing in Merrion in the middle of the night on two occasions within the last year. Most members figure this is a drugs-for-money swap, but are afraid to say it.

PROFILE: DAMIAN PODER

R-H opening/middle-order batsman. R-A slow bowler of wristy, looping off-breaks. Highly energetic and vocal fielder. Educated at the Crow's Nest Boys' School in Sydney. He works as a physical fitness instructor, pilates teacher and personal trainer, and has also played rugby union, rugby league, netball and baseball. *Podes* was born in Sydney, but his mother was the former Dervla Brennan from Ballina, County Mayo, who emigrated to Australia in 1970. He came back to Ireland in 1997, searching for his roots, only to find Anglesea Road instead. He spent some time on the 3rds and 2nds, pretending to be a fast bowler and wicket-keeper, thereby establishing his credentials as a Senior Merrion player, incipient insanity being one of the main qualifications. Once he had come clean and admitted to being a slow bowler, he proceeded to win the O'Grady Cup for bowling in 1997 and 1999, a unique achievement in Merrion's history. Firsts captain in 2004, 2005 and 2006, he played 210 games between 1997 and 2010, scoring 2,929 runs @ 22.02, with a top score of 93, and including 10*50s. He also took 278 wickets @ 18.68, with 5 wickets in an innings on six occasions and best figures of 6/13. He has won three Man of the Match awards, and played in the Whitney Moore & Keller B League wins of 1997 and 1999, the Lewis Traub League win of 1999, the Whitney Moore & Keller A League win of 2001, the Dublin Grass Machinery League win of 2007 and the Irish Senior Cup win of 2010, as well as several Alan Murray 20 Overs Cup wins. But it might have been more if he had been able to control his bladder. Damian is tenth on the list of Merrion all-rounders.

2005: DEATH OF JOE BURKE; ALAN MURRAY CUP WINNERS; SENIOR 2 LEAGUE RUNNERS-UP; MIDDLE B LEAGUE RUNNERS-UP; INTERMEDIATE B LEAGUE WINNERS; WHELAN CUP RUNNERS-UP; JUNIOR A LEAGUE RUNNERS-UP; JUNIOR CUP WINNERS; JUNIOR C LEAGUE RUNNERS-UP; UNDER-11 ALL-IRELAND CUP WINNERS; UNDER-17 AMOROSO CUP WINNERS; UNDER-19 SEAN MCGRATH CUP WINNERS

Senior: fixtures 16, reported 16, won 5, lost 11. President: A.B. Fleming. Captain: D. Poder. Merrion beat Old Belvedere in the preliminary round of the Royal Liver Irish Senior Cup, 64/0 to 62. This is followed by victories over Ardmore, 231 to 215 (D. Poder: 93), Pembroke, 270/9 to 166 (D. Joyce: 127) and Rush, 231/7 to 155 (K. Beasley: 75). North County bring them down to earth in the semi-final, 163 to 167/5 (R. Allwright: 50, 3/30). This year's overseas player is Daniel Payne, an opening batsman from Queensland. Pat Carty, a friendly giant who also hails from the land of the queen, is employed as club coach. The structure of the early short league is changed. Unsponsored this year, it is now 45 overs and the teams are split into four sets of four, with Munster and the buffalo soldiers of Laois invited to make up the sixteen. Merrion finish 3/4 in Section A, with 10 points, having played 3, won 1, lost 2, and don't progress to the semi-finals, despite *being put in to bat* by the Laois captain, ex-Merrion fast bowler and underwater bomb-disposal expert, Will Gibbs. They lose to Leinster in the second round (bye in the first) of the Conqueror Cup, 203 to 204/7, despite Danny Payne's 90. They finish 5/7 in Section B of the WMK League, with 119 points, having played 12, won 4, lost 8. It's an unlucky season for them, as four of the eight losses are by margins of 2, 5 and 6 runs and a tie on wickets lost. They gain more bonus points than any other team. Overall, the batting depends too much on Payne, and Morrissey Jnr's absence reduces the already weak bowling strike force by a factor of 50 per cent.

The Alan Murray Cup is now sponsored by LHW and it's all white balls, black screens, bouncy castles, music and pyjamas for the first time. Merrion win this 20-overs competition for the seventh time in ten seasons. There are five groups of fifteen in the first round, in which Merrion beat Pembroke, 147 to 137/7, and lose to North County, 138/9 to 141/5. The next round sees off Phoenix, 204/5 to 101, and North County, 144/8 to 129/7. Then it's on to finals day in Rathmines, with Merrion beating Malahide in their semi-final, 161/9 to 150/7, in which Robin Willis bowls tightly for his 2/18 in 4 overs. Clontarf are beaten in the final, 147/9 to 126, with Damian Poder belting 60, Angus Fleming taking 4/23 and Willis again as mean as a snake with 2/19 from his 4 overs. Dominick Joyce plays thirteen times for Ireland, with a top score of 61 against Scotland. He scores 291 runs @ 36.38 for Merrion (including 197 against Pembroke) and also takes 10 wickets @ a very tidy 8.30. Danny Payne has 705 runs @ 50.36 (eighth in the provincial batting table) and 19 wickets @ 28.53, more than anyone else. Damian Poder spanks 209 runs @ 19.00 and pouches 15 wickets @ 33.07. Kade Beasley paddles 531 @ 35.40 and is third in the provincial wicket-keeping table, with 16 catches and 5 stumpings. Angus Fleming blasts 180 runs @ 20.00 and purloins 16 wickets @ 25.50. John Blakeney skelps 258 runs @ 28.67, including 94* against Old Belvedere, while his brother Peter has 178 @ 22.25. In a year that the opposition are bowled out on only three occasions, Titiksh Patel has 12 wickets @ 16.75:

Opponent	Result	Mer.	Opp.	Best Batting: Runs	Best Bowling: Wickets
45 Overs League					
Clontarf	Lost	110/5	111/5	D. Payne: 33	R. Keaveney: 1/19
Rush	Lost	115	119/4	K. Tonetti: 35	A. Fleming: 2/25
Laois	Won	236	198/6	K. Beasley: 79	T. Wijesundera: 3/25
Leinster (C)	Lost	203	204/7	D. Payne: 90	D. Poder: 3/35
Whitney, Moore & Keller					
Leinster	Lost	298/8	300/8	D. Joyce: 44	D. Payne: 3/55
Pembroke	Lost	251/8	255/1	D. Payne: 67	D. Poder: 1/50
Leinster	Lost	184	185/3	D. Payne: 61	D. Poder: 1/28
Railway Union (wkts)	Lost	215	215/5	D. Payne: 75	D. Payne: 2/53
Old Belvedere	Won	120/5	119/9	D. Poder: 36*	T. Patel: 3/14
Old Belvedere	Won	292/1	115	K. Beasley: 125*	A. Fleming: 5/29
Railway Union	Lost	179	185/8	D. Payne: 124	T. Patel: 3/24
YMCA (run rate)	Won	141/4	173/9	D. Payne: 67*	T. Wijesundera: 2/27
YMCA	Lost	164	166/2	D. Poder: 42*	T. Patel: 1/33
The Hills	Lost	260	265/8	D. Payne: 94	T. Patel: 2/36
Pembroke	Won	350/3	154	D. Joyce: 197	D. Joyce: 4/17
The Hills	Lost	239/9	139	A. Fleming: 63	D. Joyce: 5/58

Junior: Merrion 2nds finish 2/9 in the Senior 2 League, with 76.8 per cent, having played 15, won 10, lost 5. Jim Walsh's team beats Laois, 256/6 to 207 in the first round of the Senior 2 Cup, but lose to Clontarf 2nds in the next round. Rory Allwright wins the Webster Trophy for best all-rounder at this level. Sum takes 50 wickets between the 1sts, 2nds, 3rds. A 2nds/3rds combination beats Leinster 2nds/3rds and YMCA 2nds in the Tillain Cup, but loses to Pembroke 2nds in the semi-final. Merrion 3rds finish 6/9 in the Senior 3 League, with 58.9 per cent, having played 15, won 6, lost 9. Adam O'Keeffe's team loses to Phoenix 3rds in the first round of the Middle Cup, 139 to 196/9. Merrion 4ths finish 2/10 in the Middle B League, with 78.2 per cent, having played 13, won 9, lost 4, and are promoted back to Middle A. Niall Tempany's team loses to Rush 3rds in the first round of the Middle 2 Cup, 210 to 211/4. They beat Leinster 4ths in the first round of the YMCA Salver, but lose to Pembroke 3rds in the next round.

Merrion 5ths finish 1/10 in the Intermediate B League, with 90.5 per cent, having played 14, won 13, lost 1. Rodney Smythe's team beats Railway Union 4ths and Wexford Wanderers 2nds in the first two rounds of the Intermediate Cup, but loses to North County 4ths in the semi-final. Freddie Gilmore scores over 250 runs at an average of 61 and takes 19 wickets. Vijay Gill takes 44 wickets. A 5ths/6ths/7ths/8ths combination beats Leinster 5ths/6ths/7ths and Pembroke 5ths/6ths/7ths in the first two rounds of the Whelan Cup, followed by Sandyford 2nds/3rds in the semi-final. But they lose to Civil Service 2nds/3rds in the final. Merrion 6ths finish 2/10 in the Junior A League, with 76.8 per cent, having played 14, won 10, lost 4. Gary Morris/Andrew Skelton's team wins the Junior Cup. CYM 4ths concede the first round, then they beat Leinster 7ths, 185/3 to 182/7 in the next round, Sandyford 2nds in the semi-final, 115/8 to 114 and North Wicklow 2nds in a low-scoring final, 34/6 to 33 (N. Kenny: 18*). Merrion 7ths finish 4/9 in the Junior B League, with 61.1 per cent, having played 12, won 6, lost 6. Jack Scott's team loses to Phoenix 5ths, 130 to 155/9, in the first round of the Junior Cup. Arvind Chamala scores 124 and Bobby Blakeney gets 71 for the 7ths this year.

Merrion 8ths finish 2/9 in the Junior C League, with 75.3 per cent, having played 12, won 8, lost 3, no result 1. But they cannot be promoted. Barney's boys gain a concession from Sandyford 3rds in the first round of the Minor Cup, beat North Kildare 4ths 228 to 118 in the next round, but lose to Clontarf 5ths, 138 to 139/6 in the semi-final. The club wins sixty-two out of ninety-five Junior games this year. Ben Ackland captains the Ireland Under-15s and Richard Keaveney represents Ireland at Under-17 and Under-19 levels. In what is certainly the most successful season ever for Merrion Schoolboys, they win the Under-11A Molins Cup, the Under 11A Tolan Cup, the Under-11 Fingal Cup, the Under-11 All-Ireland Cup, the Under-17 Amoroso Cup and the Under-19 Sean McGrath Cup (Rory Allwright: 146 in the final). They share the Under-13B Caprani Cup with Malahide and Pembroke.

CLUB NOTES

The cables to the electronic scoreboard are laid. New gear is ordered for the 20/20 competition. The committee agrees to write to the owner of 63 Anglesea Road, confirming that he has pedestrian access via his rear gate. Merrion have been allocated a 7th/8th place playoff in the ICC Trophy on 9 July. Paddy Power agree to sponsor the 1sts in the 20/20. The water tank contains a wasps' nest. A new TV is purchased and a quote from NTL for Sky Sports is solicited. One side of the sightscreens must be painted black for the 20/20 games. A practice game for the ICC Trophy is arranged between Oman and a Leinster Development XI, for the third week in June. Gerry Ormond offers to arrange the MCC sign on the bank in flowers. The work on the changing rooms and showers is progressed as a matter of urgency. There are problems with the electronic scoreboard and a second, backup scoreboard is purchased. Weeks of frantic cleaning, tidying and painting ensue. An incentive scheme for the 1sts is proposed, but rejected. There's a rumour that the RDS has applied for planning permission for a multistorey car park. As Stephenson's property has been bought by a builder, it is felt that a 'triple lock' should be incorporated into the club rules against selling the grounds. The rules are updated accordingly.

Merrion 1sts, Alan Murray 20/20 Cup winners, 2005. Back row: B. Harrington, R. Flannery, D. Poder (C), J. Short, R. Willis, K. Tonetti, A. Fleming. Front row: D. Payne, R. Keaveney, B. Ackland, K. Beasley, D. Campion.

Merrion Under-11As, All-Ireland Cup winners, 2005. Back row: J. Walsh (Ch), R. Walsh, T. Kane, H. Kennedy, R. McGrath, A. Neary, R. Shimmins. Front row: E. McKeever, M. Kerr, S. Pigot, K. Shimmins, D. O'Tuama, M. O'Driscoll. Missing: S. Hanlon, M. McCann, M. Loughrey, C. Allwright.

The ICC match comes off without a hitch and feedback is positive, although the standard of the game isn't up to much. Joe Burke, former Merrion all-rounder and Irish international, dies in Ballyhaunis, County Mayo. A distant relative of one of the authors of this book (the Life Member) is banned for three weeks due to his behaviour on the 4ths in a YMCA Salver match. Priorities for the following year are agreed: revamp the practice area; drain the square; maintain the well; purchase a new roller, mower and coaching equipment; renovate the kitchen area; landscape the bank; improve the facilities at Bird Avenue, and move the sewage pump. A club manager is employed, in addition to a new bar manager. The owners of 49 Anglesea Road refuse to negotiate about a right of way and prepare for legal action. At the AGM, Ann Short is commended by the Hon. Secretary for supporting the 1sts in every game. The club writes to the owners of No. 51 to ask them to close up their double gates and make good the boundary wall. It's planned to overhaul the website. A social committee is set up to prepare for the club centenary in 2006. A summer ball is to be the highlight of the celebrations.

PROFILE: DOMINICK JOYCE

R-H opening/middle-order batsman. R-A medium-pace bowler of inswinging seamers. Educated at St Patrick's School, St Cronan's, Presentation College in Bray and Trinity College. The youngest male member of the sprawling Joyce family. Works as an account-ant, but hopefully not for much longer. Played schools rugby, gaelic football, and soccer in the United Churches Football Premier League. Currently spoils good walks, but only recreationally. Played cricket for Trinity and Ireland, in conjunction with Merrion. Came up through the Merrion Schoolboy and Junior ranks and played 180 games for Merrion 1sts, scoring 3,870 runs @ 26.33, with a top score of 197, and including 3*100s and 19*50s. Also took 72 wickets @ 21.17, with 5 wickets in an innings on two occasions. Dom was captain in 2007 and 2008, when the 1sts won one competition and were runners-up in three others. He played in the Lewis Traub League win of 1999, the Whitney Moore & Keller B League wins of 1997 and 1999, the Whitney Moore & Keller A League win of 2001, the Dublin Grass Machinery win of 2007, and was crucial in the Irish Senior Cup win of 2010. So far he has played for Ireland on sixty-nine occasions, which is thirteen times more often than the total of all the other Merrion internationals, apart from brother Ed. Between 2000 and 2007 he scored 1,518 runs @ 23.00 and took 1 wicket for 64 runs and 15 catches for his country. It is to be hoped that Ireland's memory of Dom is not as delinquent as England's memory of Ed. He is known for his quiet demeanour on and off the field of play, but don't be fooled. When it comes to the game of cricket there's plenty of noise going on inside.

2006: CENTENARY YEAR; WHITNEY MOORE B LEAGUE RUNNERS-UP; SENIOR 3 LEAGUE WINNERS; MIDDLE CUP WINNERS; INTERMEDIATE CUP WINNERS; JUNIOR C LEAGUE RUNNERS-UP

Senior: fixtures 17, reported 17, won 11, lost 6. President: A.B. Fleming. Captain: D. Poder. Merrion beat Leinster in the first round of the Irish Senior Cup, 326/7 to 210 (D. Joyce: 105), but lose to Bready in the next round, 160 to 161/6. The rules for overseas players are adjusted and now anyone who is qualified to play for Ireland can play. After a doppleganger called Jason Smith from Barbados in the West Indies is sent packing, Dean Parma Waugh arrives from New South Wales. He is the younger brother of the more famous Mark and Steve. Pat Carty returns as club coach. The early 45 overs league is now sponsored by Dublin Grass Machinery, and starts off again as four sets of four teams, Civil Service replacing Laois, who have been demoted to Senior 3, having had their year in the sun. Merrion finish 2/4 in Section A of the Group Stage, with 20 points, having played 3, won 2, lost 1. Railway Union beat them comfortably at the quarter-final stage, 69 to 162/7. Railway Union also knock them out of the Antalis Senior Cup in the first round, chasing down 221 for the loss of 6 wickets, despite Marthinus Jacobus Fourie's 68 runs and 3 wickets for 37 runs. The Hills beat North County in the final, which is played at Anglesea Road.

The good news is that Merrion finish 2/7 in Section B of the Whitney Moore League, with 216 points, having played 12, won 9, lost 3, and are promoted back to Section A. Merrion beat North County in the first round of the LHW Alan Murray 20 Overs competition, 74/0 to 69/6, (D. Joyce: 45*), but lose to Railway Union, 47/8 to 82/5 in an 8-over match in the same round. Nevertheless, they go through to round two, where they lose to Clontarf, 122 to 154/6, and beat Railway Union, 189/2 to 182/5 (M. Fourie: 62*). But it's Clontarf that go through to finals day, on run rate. There's a definite improvement in the bowling department this year, with Fourie and Keaveney joining Willis and Fleming. Dean Waugh shows why his nickname is Korea (the forgotten Waugh, gettit?) by scoring a modest 333 runs @ 25.62. Thinus Fourie has 468 runs @ 36.00 and just misses out on the O'Grady Cup, as he is 1 wicket short of the requirement, with 34 @ 11.21. He comes fifth in the provincial all-rounders' table, with 1,518 points. Kade Beasley has 317 runs @ 22.64 and takes 11 catches and 2 stumpings behind the wicket. D. Joyce plays ten times for Ireland, with a top score of 45 against Middlesex at Lords. For Merrion, he drives 227 runs @ 18.92. John Blakeney blasts 189 runs @ 47.25, including a majestic ton against Munster Reds, before disappearing to Japan to learn another useful language. Damian Poder, in his last year as captain, thwacks 239 runs @ 18.38 and tweaks out 15 victims @ 27.60. Jeff Short hoicks 201 runs @ 20.10 and blasts Railway Union's middle order away in August. Robin Willis filches 12 wickets @ 16.50 before following Gus Joyce to London. Titiksh Patel bewilders 19 batsmen @ 12.79. Richard Keaveney manages 11 wickets @ 24.55, while Angus Fleming secures his usual decent haul of 21 wickets @ 16.62:

Opponent	Result	Mer.	Opp.	Best Batting: Runs	Best Bowling: Wickets
Dublin Grass Machinery					
North County	Lost	171	174/2	E. Extras: 50	D. Poder: 2/41
Civil Service	Won	134/6	133	K. Beasley: 24	D. Poder: 5/28
DU	Won	93/1	92	M. Fourie: 50	A. Fleming: 4/21
Railway Union (Q-F)	Lost	69	162/7	M. Fourie: 16	A. Fleming: 2/29
Railway Union (C)	Lost	221/7	224/6	M. Fourie: 68	M. Fourie: 3/37
Whitney Moore					
Pembroke	Won	148/2	147	M. Fourie: 71*	M. Fourie: 3/8
CYM	Won	188/7	138	D. Poder: 54	M. Fourie: 5/53
Old Belvedere	Won	176/2	172	D. Waugh: 71*	R. Willis: 3/30
Munster Reds	Won	237/9	153	J. Blakeney: 100	R. Keaveney: 5/18
Railway Union	Lost	170/9	172/5	M. Fourie: 81*	R. Willis: 2/41
Munster Reds	Won	236/7	115	D. Poder: 61*	T. Patel: 5/37
Leinster	Won	130/7	128	R. Allwright: 36*	T. Patel: 4/24
Leinster (run rate)	Lost	106	94/4	K. Beasley: 32	A. Fleming: 2/17
Railway Union	Lost	98	101/6	J. Short: 28	J. Short: 4/26
Old Belvedere	Won	75/8	74	E. Extras: 13	T. Patel: 3/10
CYM	Won	301/6	141	K. Beasley: 104*	M. Fourie: 4/16
Pembroke	Won	218/9	122	D. Joyce: 61	M. Fourie: 3/26

Junior: Merrion 2nds finish 5/9 in the Senior 2 League, with 65.1 per cent, having played 10, won 5, lost 5. Sum's team suffers from a mid-season washout of five consecutive games. David Rosenkowitz scores 147 against Pembroke. Pat Carty is second in the Senior 2 bowling analysis, with 16 wickets @ 12.69. They beat CYM 2nds 187/4 (R. Stanton: 100+) to 186 in the first round of the Senior 2 Cup, but lose to Balbriggan in the next round, 125 to 126/8. A 2nds/3rds combination loses to Pembroke 2nds/3rds in the first round of the Tillain Cup. Merrion 3rds win the Senior 3 League, finishing 1/9 with 78.6 per cent, having played 14, won 10, lost 4. Adam O'Keeffe's team, including R. Barker, D. Drane, J. Souter, M. Tichband, S. Morrissey, E. Furlong, A. Khan, L. Casey and A. Rehman also wins the Middle Cup, beating North Wicklow, 174 to 122, Bagnelstown, 265/9 to 250/7 (R. Barker: 114), and Old Belvedere 2nds on the way to a final against Clontarf 3rds, which they win, 214 to 134. Amir Rehman wins the Man of the Match award, with 4/36 and 30 very quick runs, batting at number 11. Eoghan Furlong plays an important innings to steady the ship in this match.

Merrion 4ths finish 8/10 in Middle A, with 49.7 per cent, having played 13, won 5, lost 8. Alan Parkinson is the pick of the batsmen with 4*50s and an average over 30. Killian O'Flynn, Gareth Banahan and Mark Kelly also do well. Andrew Kay's team beats Civil Service 2nds in the first round of the Middle 2 Cup, 176/6 to 175/8, and Laois 2nds in the next round, 307/8 to 295, but loses to Knockharley, 218 to 227/6 in the semi-final. In the YMCA Salver, they beat Railway Union 3rds and YMCA 3rds before losing to North Wicklow in the semi-final. Merrion 5ths finish 5/10 in the Intermediate A League, with 61.7 per cent, having played 15, won 8, lost 7. Fred Gilmore's team beats Leinster 6ths, 102/5 to 99 in the first round of the Intermediate Cup, but loses to Old Belvedere 4ths, 121 to 151 in the next round. A 5ths/6ths/7ths/8ths combination loses to CYM 3rds in the second round (bye in the first) of the Whelan Cup.

Merrion 6ths finish 8/10 in the Intermediate B League, with 40.8 per cent, having played 14, won 5, lost 9. Geoff Dungan's team outshines the 5ths by winning the Intermediate Cup for the first time (their fourth Cup win in five years), highlighting some possible inconsistencies in the Merrion starring list. They beat Wexford Wanderers (254 to 128), Mullingar 2nds (287/8 to 79) and Clontarf 4ths (261/6 to 215) to face Old Belvedere 4ths in the final, which they win, 312/7 to 274. That's a total of 1,114 runs over the four rounds. Stephen McGrath gets a hat-trick and Will Houston a century. Jimmy Robertson, Peter Geoffroy and Frank Nugent also perform consistently for this team. Merrion 7ths finish 4/9 in the Junior B League, with 62.8 per cent, having played 10, won 6, lost 4. Having received a concession from Malahide 5ths in the first round of the Junior Cup, Jack Scott's team loses to Balbriggan 2nds, 132 to 182, in the next round. Mike Kavanagh, Sazza Hemchana, Andrew O'Tuama, Ray Clarke, Tony Gilmore, Roger Fox and Bobby Blakeney are the stars of this team.

Merrion 8ths emulate their achievement of the previous year, by finishing 2/10 in the Junior C League, but are forced to remain there. Barney Bulmer is learning on the job, and the mistake of fielding a player starred on the 5ths may have cost him the title. He and his cohorts lose comfortably to YMCA 5ths in the first round of the Minor Cup, 190 to 317/4. The club wins fifty-one out of ninety-three Junior games this year. Alex O'Brien makes the Irish Under-13 squad. Merrion Schoolboys win no competition outright, but they share the Under-9 Mini-Cricket with Malahide; the Under-11 Molins Cup with CYM and Pembroke; the Under-11A Tolan Cup with YMCA; the Under 13A Jeyes Cup with Leinster and North County; the Under-13 Watkins Cup with North County; the Under-13 All-Ireland Cup with Waringstown; the Under-13B Caprani Cup with Malahide, and the Under-19 Sean McGrath Cup with North County.

CLUB NOTES

A young West Indian all-rounder named Jason Smith is chosen as Merrion's overseas player for the 2006 season. A sum of money is offered for a vehicular right of way by the solicitors acting for 49 Anglesea Road, but an independent valuation is twenty times higher. Jim Walsh agrees to act as youth co-ordinator. Much of the committee's time is taken up with plans for celebrating the club's centenary. A maintenance contract is negotiated for the security gate. No.45 Anglesea Road now also feels entitled to a vehicular right of way. A serious problem arises when the Jason Smith who arrives to play cricket for Merrion this year appears to be an altogether different Jason Smith than the person expected, and not good enough for the 3rds, let alone the 1sts, although he may actually be a cousin of the real Jason Smith. Anyway, he is relieved of his duties and a replacement is found quickly, in the shape of Dean Waugh, from New South Wales.

A complaint is made to the LCU about the behaviour of a North County player in a 4ths game. The practice netting is upgraded. A third tool/machine shed is acquired. Concerns are expressed by the committee members about a perceived lack of application by the 1sts in certain matches. A Centenary Yearbook is produced and the Centenary Ball comes off smoothly, with an attendance of around 250 happy penguins. Preparations are made for the Senior Cup Final. A formal complaint is made to Pembroke after one of their players physically threatens a Merrion supporter. The box for the electronic gate is vandalised and there are a number of thefts from the dressing rooms. The committee expresses its general dissatisfaction with the performance of the bar manager. Crusaders Athletic Club terminate their arrangements for the use of the grounds during the winter. At the AGM, it is recommended that an agency be used to select overseas players in future. The groundsman complains about the leftovers of dog walkers around the ground. It's reported that the women have played twenty-two fixtures at Anglesea Road, that they refuse to play at Bird Avenue and that a total of seven subscriptions have been received from them this year. A large tree falls onto the nets from Hazeldene. Fortunately it's a practice night, and there's nobody there.

PROFILE: KADE BEASLEY

R-H solid, opening/middle-order batsman, with a penchant for square cutting and paddling the ball to leg. Wicket-keeper. Educated at Assumption College, Kilmore, Victoria. Also studied Computer Applications & Support at the National College Of Ireland. Head of Portfolio Administration at Merrion Investment Managers. Also played Australian Rules Football. *Beezo* played 169 games for Merrion 1sts between 2000 and 2010, scoring 3,580 runs @ 26.32, with a top score of 125*, including 2*100s and 19*50s. As wicket-keeper, he took 170 catches and 41 stumpings, many more than any other keeper in Merrion's history. Uniquely, he won the Hopkins Cup for wicket-keeping in 2002 and 2004. He played in the 2001 Whitney Moore & Keller A League win, several 20/20 wins, the 2007 Dublin Grass Machinery win and the 2010 Irish Senior Cup win. Kade belongs to a very small and private club of Merrion captains who have won the toss in a Leinster Senior Cup final, put the opposition in to bat, and lost. Welcome. One of his first games for Merrion was for the 4ths against Pembroke, and when he arrived at Sydney Parade he discovered he had also been named on the Pembroke 3rds side, having inquired about playing there. Pembroke's loss was to be Merrion's gain, as he is eighth on the list of Merrion all-rounders.

Merrion 3rds, Senior 3 League/Middle Cup winners, 2006. Back row: A. Rehman, R. Barker, J. Souter, D. Drane, M. Tichband, E. Furlong. Front row: A. Parkinson, L. Casey, A. O'Keeffe (C), S. Morrissey, A. Khan.

Merrion 6ths, Intermediate Cup winners, 2006. Back row: G. Dungan (C), W. Houston, N. Kenny, P. Johnstone, S. Katta (Sub). Front row: A. Haider, F. Nugent, S. McGrath, J. Robertson, M. Keaveney, P. Geoffroy, A. Moosani.

2007: DUBLIN GRASS MACHINERY LEAGUE WINNERS; ANTALIS CUP RUNNERS-UP; SENIOR 2 LEAGUE WINNERS; SENIOR 2 CUP WINNERS; MINOR CUP RUNNERS-UP; UNDER-13 JEYES CUP WINNERS

Senior: fixtures 21, reported 21, won 12, lost 4, no result 5. President: A. B. Fleming. Captain: D. Joyce. Brigade beat Merrion in the first round of the Irish Senior Cup, 167 to 168/8 (P. Lavang: 55; R. Ensor: 4/19). Merrion's overseas player this year is Matt Petrie, a very fast bowler from Western Australia. Pat Carty returns for a third season as club coach. Merrion finish 1/4 in Section C of the Group Stages of the DGM League, with 30 points, having played 3, won 3. They beat North County, Dublin University and Civil Service on the way to an easy victory over YMCA in the quarter-final. A Duckworth-Lewis semi-final win against Malahide follows, in which Merrion chase down 114 in 24 overs. The final against Phoenix at the park provides a more comfortable win, with Phoenix succumbing 90 runs short of their target to the pace of Petrie, Fourie and Keaveney. Kade Beasley wins the Man of the Match award.

They also have a good run in the Antalis Cup, beating Leinster in the second round (bye in the first) and Malahide in the semi-final, before carrying on the good old Merrion tradition (this is the eleventh) of losing the final, this time to Clontarf. Bemused onlookers wonder why Titiksh Patel is not bowled. Apparently the captain decides not to bowl him, as Hokin has taken a liking to him in the past and a fairly modest 254 chase at Rathmines in 60 overs isn't going to be that difficult. They finish 4/7 in Section A of the Whitney Moore League, with 138 points, having played 12, won 4, lost 3, no result 5. The first of several wet summers leads to almost half this league being washed out and the Duckworth-Lewis software in steady use. The team beats Phoenix 143/8 to 136/9 (M. Petrie: 33*), and Pembroke, 157/6 to 119, in round one of the LHW Alan Murray 20 Overs competition. Round two produces another couple of victories against Leinster, 98/0 to 94/9 (M. Fourie: 44*), and North County, 126/7 to 85. Unfortunately, Messrs Duckworth and Lewis deprive Merrion of a win in the semi-final against The Hills (127 to 110/6).

The pace bowling this year is the best in Leinster, as witnessed by the provincial table finishing positions of Matt Petrie, first with 36 wickets @ 9.36, and Richard Keaveney, second with 31 @ 13.54. As Petrie is ineligible, the seventeen-year-old Keaveney wins the O'Grady Cup, the first schoolboy ever to do so. He also wins the Whitney Moore Young Player of the Year award. Dominick Joyce plays three times for Ireland and finishes fifth in the Leinster batting table with 453 runs @ 37.75. He also hurtles down 13 wickets @ 20.00 and takes 10 catches. Alex Morison totals 315 runs @ 39.38, including a debut ton against North County. Kade Beasley whacks 278 runs @ 25.27 and takes 15 catches and 1 stumping behind the wicket. Thinus Fourie belts 244 runs @ 24.40 and scalps 23 batsmen @ 17.13. He plays eight times for Ireland, with a top score of 14* against Scotland. Rory Allwright biffs 215 runs @ 30.71 and takes 10 catches and 2 stumpings as wicket-keeper. Matt Petrie contributes 186 runs @ 16.91. Damian Poder has 191 runs @ 23.88 and 14 wickets @ 20.14:

Opponent	Result	Mer.	Opp.	Best Batting: Runs	Best Bowling: Wickets
Dublin Grass Machinery					
North County	Won	268/1	225	A. Morison: 108*	S. Morrissey: 3/41
DU	Won	115/0	111	M. Fourie: 54*	D. Poder: 4/24
Civil Service	Won	295/8	131/9	D. Poder: 87	M. Petrie: 4/33
YMCA (Q–F)	Won	81/5	78	M. Fourie: 21	M. Petrie: 5/21
Malahide (S–F) (D–L)	Won	114/8	155/9	R. Allwright: 34	R. Keaveney: 5/39
Phoenix	Won	190/6	100	D. Joyce: 47	M. Fourie: 3/27
DGM Cup Final					
Leinster (C)	Won	263	143	A. Morison: 58	M. Petrie: 4/14
Malahide (C)	Won	153/1	151	D. Joyce: 68*	M. Fourie: 4/29
Clontarf	Lost	127	253/8	S. Morrissey: 33	R. Keaveney: 4/55
Senior Cup Final					
Whitney Moore					
YMCA	Won	100/2	99	A. Morison: 28*	M. Petrie: 6/22
Rush	No Res.	r.s.p.			
North County	No Res.	r.s.p.			
Railway Union	No Res.	r.s.p.			
Clontarf	Lost	143	144/6	R. Allwright: 36	T. Patel: 5/21
North County	No Res.	r.s.p.			
Rush	No Res.	r.s.p.			
YMCA	Won	247/9	45	K. Beasley: 61	R. Keaveney: 6/24
Railway Union (D–L)	Won	177/8	156/9	D. Joyce: 71	D. Joyce: 3/53
The Hills	Lost	92	95/5	R. Barker: 32	M. Petrie: 3/22
The Hills	Won	217/9	216	M. Fourie: 40	D. Poder: 3/55
Clontarf (D–L)	Lost	154	177	D. Joyce: 53	M. Fourie: 3/20

DUBLIN GRASS MACHINERY LEAGUE FINAL 2007, MERRION V. PHOENIX

Merrion			Phoenix		
D. Joyce	c. Conliffe b. R. Flanagan	47	R. Flanagan	c. Beasley b. Keaveney	36
A. Morison	b. R. Flanagan	10	R. Mitchell	b. Fourie	5
M. Fourie	b. McDonald	38	R. Nandi	c. Beasley b. Petrie	0
K. Beasley	l.b.w. b. Meth	37	K. Meth	c. Poder b. Petrie	0
M. Petrie	c. McDonald b. Meth	17	M. Ward	l.b.w. b. Lavang	5
P. Lavang	l.b.w. b. Meth	1	D. Langford-Smith	l.b.w. b. Poder	16
S. Morrissey	not out	9	C. Dickieson	l.b.w. b. Lavang	0
D. Poder	not out	14	P. Conliffe	not out	14

R. Keaveney	d.n.b.			G. Flanagan	c. Keaveney b. Fourie	1
R. Flannery	d.n.b.			M. Kumar	c. Poder b. Fourie	1
J. Short	d.n.b.			R. McDonald	b. Keaveney	0
	Extras		17	Extras		22
	Total		190	Total		100

Junior: Merrion 2nds win the Senior 2 League, with 80.1 per cent, having played 9, won 7, lost 1, no result 1. The success continues in the Senior 2 Cup, as Sum's team beats CYM 2nds 180/7 to 176 in the first round, Balbriggan (A. Fleming: 6/36) in the second round, Civil Service, 83/1 to 82 (R. Flannery: 7/33) in the semi-final, and North County, 246/8 to 245/9 in a close encounter of the 2nds kind of final (sixth win in the sixteen years between 1992 and 2007, having never won it before). The squad includes Robbie Stanton, Stephen King, Ronnie Barker, Ronan Flannery, Pat Carty, Alan Parkinson, Angus Fleming, Michael Tichband, Titiksh Patel, Jim Walsh, Robbie Ensor, Daniel Campion and David Drane, who wins the Sean Pender Cup for outstanding contribution on the field of play. A 2nds/3rds combination beats Pembroke 2nds in the first round of the Tillain Cup, but loses to Railway Union 2nds in the next round.

Merrion 3rds finish 6/9 in Senior 3, with 42.7 per cent, having played 10, won 4, lost 6. Ronnie Barker scores 100* against North Wicklow. They beat Pembroke 3rds, 220/4 to 217/5 in the first round of the Middle Cup, but lose to Laois, 108 to 164, in the next round. Merrion 4ths finish 9/10 in the Middle A League, with 35.6 per cent, having played 11, won 2, lost 9, but are not demoted. Andrew Kay, Alex O'Brien and Killian and Darragh O'Flynn star for this team. They beat Phoenix 4ths and Mullingar in the first two rounds of the Middle 2 Cup, but fall to Dundrum in the semi-final, 198/9 to 288. They lose to Railway Union 3rds in the first round of the YMCA Salver. Merrion 5ths finish 6/10 in the Intermediate A League, with 57.8 per cent, having played 9, won 4, lost 5. They beat Pembroke 4ths, 173 to 103, in the first round of the Intermediate Cup, CYM 3rds in the next round, 166/8 to 165, but lose to Malahide 4ths in the semi-final. A 5ths/6ths/7ths/8ths combination beats Dundrum, followed by Pembroke 4ths/5ths/6ths before losing to Sandyford 2nds/3rds in the semi-final of the Whelan Cup. Merrion 6ths finish 6/9 in the Intermediate B League, with 54.0 per cent, having played 8, won 4, lost 4. They beat Laois 2nds in a bowlout in the first round of the Intermediate Cup, but lose to Leinster 6ths in the next round.

Merrion 7ths finish 3/10 in the Junior B League, with 71.9 per cent, having played 12, won 7, lost 4, no result 1. They lose to Railway Union 4ths, 107 to 108/5 in the first round of the Junior Cup. Merrion 8ths finish 6/9 in the Junior C League, with 40.3 per cent, having played 8, won 3, lost 5. After a concession from YMCA 5ths in the second round (bye in the first) of the Minor Cup, they beat Railway Union 5ths and Ballyeighan to get to a final against Laois 3rds at Anglesea Road. The Midlanders bat first and score 175, which is 32 runs too many for Barney's boys. In another excellent year for Merrion Schoolboys, they win the Under-13A Jeyes Cup, the Under-13 Watkins Cup, the Under-13 Top 4 Beamers Cup and the Under-13B Caprani Cup, as well as finishing runners-up in the Under-11 Fingal Cup and the Under-13 All-Ireland Cup.

CLUB NOTES

After the excitements of the previous two seasons, this is a quiet year. Early on, Vodafone approach Merrion with a plan to site a 3G mobile-phone mast on the bank. An EGM is called for March to hear their proposal and it votes almost unanimously in favour of going ahead. As a result, the mast is located on the site of the corner floodlight, and is less obtrusive than originally proposed. Several applications for overseas players are turned down by the LCU before Matt Petrie is employed. A planning application is lodged to tear down the new structure in Stephenson's and build an apartment block. The committee decides to raise an objection. Norman Reeves, the groundsman, is retiring and the club must find a replacement. A new club manager and bar manager are appointed. The mat at Bird Avenue needs to be repaired.

Merrion loses its staunchest supporter with the untimely death of John Heavey Snr, for many years a prominent umpire and Hon. Secretary to the club. A new deal is arranged with Irish Distillers for the use of car parking, Monday to Friday, on the driveway all year round. There is significant damage to the outfield after the Horse Show in this year of torrential rain. The bowling machine is not working properly. There are problems with the collection of tea money, and an annual match levy is proposed, to cover the cost of teas. A meeting discusses whether Merrion can continue to field eight men's teams. At the AGM, a minute's silence is observed in memory of Joe Hopkins, John Heavey Snr and Peter Quinlan.

The subject of overhauling the website is raised again. The rules are amended to allow electronic communication to willing members and to create a three-member audit committee to review the Hon. Treasurer's accounts in advance of each AGM. A group is set up, consisting of Roger Fox and the captains of the 5ths, 6ths, 7ths and 8ths, to help prepare and maintain the second ground at Bird Avenue. It's agreed to use Merrion for car parking during Leinster rugby matches over the winter. Planning permission for the redevelopment of Stephenson's house on the Bailey site is refused.

Merrion 1sts, DGM League winners, 2007. Back row: C. O'Donoghue, R. Flannery, T. Fourie, J. Short, R. Keaveney, D. Poder, S. Morrissey. Front row: D. Joyce (C), M. Petrie, K. Beasley, A. Morison, P. Lavang.

Merrion 2nds,
Senior 2 League/
Cup winners, 2007.
Back row: P. Carty, A.
Fleming, R. Stanton,
S. King, D. Campion,
R. Flannery. Front
row: M. Tichband, A.
Parkinson, R. Barker,
Sum (C), T. Patel, J.
Walsh, R. Ensor.

PROFILE: JOHN BLAKENEY

R-H middle-order batsman. R-A medium-pace seam bowler. Educated at Wesley College and Trinity College Dublin. Currently having a prolonged break from cricket by studying for a Masters Degree in Japanese in the Land of the Rising Sun. Also played hockey and cricket for Dublin University. He played sixty-five games for Merrion 1sts from 1998 to 2006, scoring 1,009 runs @ 22.93, with a top score of 100 against Munster Reds in 2006 (one of the finest ever scored by a Merrion batsman, according to those present), and including 4*50s. He took 15 wickets @ 15.47 and as wicket-keeper caught 5 batsmen, in addition to 16 catches in the outfield. He played on the 2001 Whitney Moore & Keller A League-winning team and was a part of the Irish Development Squad. It is to be hoped that he does not study too deeply the writings of Yukio Mishima, and that when he returns to Ireland, he will be able to stop bowling for long enough to play some serious cricket again.

2008: DEATH OF PADDY WALDRON; WHITNEY MOORE A LEAGUE RUNNERS-UP; LEWIS HOHN WILLIAMS ALAN MURRAY CUP RUNNERS-UP; SENIOR 2 LEAGUE WINNERS; INTERMEDIATE B LEAGUE RUNNERS-UP; INTERMEDIATE CUP RUNNERS-UP; MINOR CUP RUNNERS-UP

Senior: fixtures 17, reported 17, won 8, lost 6, no result 3. President: J. P. Joyce. Captain: D. Joyce. Merrion have a good run in the Irish Senior Cup, beating Glendermott in the first round, 79/7 to 77, YMCA in the second round, 251/7 to 247/8 (K. Beasley: 45; M. Petrie: 5/28), Limavady in the third round, 142/7 to 152 (D-L, R. Barker: 60), before losing to Donemana in the semi-final, 166 to 203/9 (R. Barker: 66). Matt Petrie returns for another season as Merrion's overseas player and Pat Carty for his fourth as club coach. The 1sts finish 2/4 in Section B of the Group Stages of the DGM League, with 14 points, and do not progress. The first game against Railway Union is a washout, the second is a 4-run defeat by YMCA, 131 to 135, and the third is a victory over The Hills, 69/2 to 65. In the Antalis Cup,

Merrion beat Malahide by 2 runs in the first round, and lose to The Hills by 5 runs in the second round.

The season ends well with a second placement (for the seventh time in the Senior League) in Section A of the Whitney Moore League, with 166 points, having played 12, won 6, lost 4, no result 2. The team beats YMCA, 135 to 117/7, and Dublin University, 129/4 to 128/7 (J. Anderson: 40) in round one, Section 4 of the LHW Alan Murray 20 Overs. This is followed by a win over Phoenix, 134/7 to 131, in the semi-final, and a loss to Pembroke, 76 to 78/3, in the final. Matt Petrie thwacks 178 runs @ 22.25 and tops the provincial bowling table with 35 wickets @ 7.03, but is not eligible for the O'Grady Cup. However, Titiksh Patel is eligible, and consequently he wins it with 25 wickets @ 13.16. Dominick Joyce is injured for part of the season and Jeff Short takes over as captain. Joyce still manages 369 runs @ 41.00, while Short pouches 10 wickets @ 18.20. Damian Poder swipes 258 runs @ 25.80. Rory Allwright belts 175 runs in only 5 innings, @ 43.75. New recruit John Anderson tops the batting honours with 421 @ 35.08, including a match-winning century against Malahide, and filches 16 wickets @ 24.56. Kade Beasley paddles 293 runs @ 22.54 and scoops 13 catches and 5 stumpings behind the wicket. Alex Morison contributes 209 runs @ 23.22:

Opponent	Result	Mer.	Opp.	Best Batting: Runs	Best Bowling: Wickets
Dublin Grass Machinery					
Railway Union	No Res.	r.s.p.			
YMCA	Lost	131	135	D. Poder: 44	J. Anderson: 4/30
The Hills	Won	69/2	65	J. Anderson: 27*	M. Petrie: 4/19
Malahide (C)	Won	230/7	228	R. Allwright: 56*	T. Patel: 4/56
The Hills (C)	Lost	250/9	245	D. Poder: 55	S. Morrissey: 4/54
Whitney Moore					
Clontarf	Won	287/7	236	A. Morison: 97	J. Short: 2/2
Rush	Won	238/6	39	R. Allwright: 59	M. Petrie: 5/6
Leinster	Won	183/9	150	D. Joyce: 78	M. Petrie: 4/32
The Hills	Lost	164	168/5	A. Morison: 48	N. Curran: 2/35
Malahide	Won	211/5	27	K. Beasley: 72	M. Petrie: 8/15
The Hills	No Res.	r.s.p.			
North County	Lost	112/3	122/8	D. Joyce: 45*	J. Short: 2/31
Leinster	Won	213/9	69	D. Joyce: 52	J. Anderson: 3/11
Clontarf	Lost	143	144/3	M. Petrie: 36*	J. Short: 1/10
Rush	No Res.	r.s.p.			
Malahide	Won	183/7	118	J. Anderson: 102*	M. Petrie: 4/8
North County	Lost	218/8	223/4	D. Joyce: 96	P. Lavang: 1/29

Junior: Merrion 2nds finish 1/8 in the Senior 2 League, with 63.1 per cent, having played 9, won 6, lost 3. Sum's team beats Civil Service 145/7 to 141 in the first round of the Senior 2 Cup, but loses to Laois, 68 to 72/4, in the next round. David Drane scores over 250 runs @ 51.00, and wins the Sean Pender award again for his contribution on the field of play. Sum snaffles 24 wickets. A 2nds/3rds combination gains a walkover from CYM 2nds in the second round of the Tillain Cup, but loses to Leinster 2nds in the semi-final. Merrion 3rds finish 5/10 in the Senior 3 League, with 49.6 per cent, having played 10, won 5, lost 5. Adam O'Keeffe's team beats Malahide 3rds 238/8 to 236/8 in the first round of the Middle Cup and Leinster 3rds in the next round, before succumbing to Old Belvedere 2nds on a mongrel of a wicket at Cabra in the semi-final, 87 to 90/4. Alex O'Brien is the outstanding bowler on this side.

Merrion 4ths finish 5/10 in the Middle A League, with 57.2 per cent, having played 13, won 6, lost 7. They lose to Sandyford, 177 to 228/9 in the first round of the Middle 2 Cup. K.P. Singh's team beats Pembroke 3rds in the first round of the YMCA Salver, but loses to Dundrum in the next round. K.P. scores 459 runs and takes 22 wickets. Merrion 5ths finish 8/10 in the Intermediate A League, with 49.7 per cent, having played 9, won 3, lost 6. Nicky Kenny's team beats Rush 3rds in the first round of the Intermediate Cup, but loses to Pembroke 4ths, 139 to 140/2, in the next round. Tim Lewis scores a century at Rush. A 5ths/6ths/7ths/8ths combination loses to CYM 2nds in the first round of the Whelan Cup. Merrion 6ths finish 2/9 in the Intermediate B League, with 73.1 per cent, having played 12, won 8, lost 4, but cannot be promoted. Will Houston's team fares better than the 5ths in the Intermediate Cup, beating Phoenix 4ths, 128/5 to 127, Laois 2nds, 135/7 to 134, and CYM 2nds 246/9 to 144 on the way to a final in which they are beaten by Pembroke 4ths, 92 to 112. Geoff Dungan and Will Houston score centuries.

Merrion 7ths finish 6/10 in the Junior B League, with 56.0 per cent, having played 11, won 5, lost 5, no result 1. Tony Gilmore's team beats Wexford Wanderers 2nds, 110/5 to 109/9 in the first round of the Junior Cup, but loses to Pembroke 5ths in the next round, 130 to 133/6. Frank Nugent celebrates his seventieth birthday in a rain-drenched match at Marlay Park. Jeremy Dunleavy, Karra Rao and Imran Khan also star for Tony's side. Merrion 8ths finish 6/10 in the Junior C League, with 62.9 per cent, having played 13, won 8, lost 5. Barney Bulmer's team has another good run in the Minor Cup, beating North County 5ths, 244 to 180, the Garda, 26/4 to 24 and Civil Service 4ths, before repeating the previous year's experience of losing the final to Laois 3rds, 145 to 188/8. Merrion Schoolboys have a quiet year, winning the Under-13 Top Four Cup and finishing runners-up in the Under-11A Molins Cup, the Under-13A Cecily Vincent Cup, the Under-15 20/20 Gerry Duffy Cup and the Under-15A Robertson Cup.

CLUB NOTES

There are yet more problems with the residents of 49 and 51 Anglesea Road and the right of way issue. A break-in occurs and money is stolen from the bar till, which needs to be repaired, as do the security gates. A meeting decides to limit heavy vehicles to the tarmac driveway for future Horse Shows, due to the ground damage in 2007. An ECC international match between Denmark and Italy is planned for Anglesea Road. The bowling machine needs to be repaired again, and a new cable laid. Preliminary discussions concerning the replacement of the square and the installation of a drainage system are held. Matt Petrie, Robbie Ensor and Rory Allwright are involved with coaching at the national schools: Sandford, Taney and Belmont. The alarm system needs to be upgraded. The LCU reject a proposal that a club can have more than one professional receiving payment for playing. A four-day Under-15s tour to Warwickshire is planned. Another wet Horse Show means considerable damage to the ground. It's agreed to close the bar from 8 September, as so few people use it during the winter rugby matches. This decision is overturned at a subsequent meeting. The lack of a manager for the 1sts is noted. At the end of the playing season, the square is completely relaid. At the AGM, the subscription for pavilion members is increased to €100. Norman Reeves is elected a Life Member, to acclamation. A local resident expresses the view that there is a definite risk of cancer from the Vodafone mast, and requests that a short lease be taken. On 26 December, Merrion legend Paddy Waldron dies, aged ninety-one.

PROFILE: JEFF SHORT

R-H late-order batsman, always good for a quickfire 20-30 runs in the final overs of a game. L-A fast-opening/shock bowler, capable of either a feast or a famine where going for runs and taking wickets are concerned. Educated at CUS and the Dublin Business School, he works as a financial advisor in the life, pensions and investments fields. Also played rugby, soccer, chess and the piano, at which he achieved Level 3 through the Royal Academy of Music. The son of Taverners stalwart Arthur, Jeff came up through the Merrion Schoolboy and Junior sides before playing 123 games for Merrion 1sts between 1997 and 2010, scoring 877 runs @ 11.85, with a top score of 48. He also took 42 wickets @ 28.71 and 35 catches. He featured in many of the Alan Murray 20 Overs Cup wins, the 2007 Dublin Grass Machinery win, and was a member of the 2010 Irish Senior Cup-winning squad. Jeff was captain of the 1sts in 2009, when Sky television captured the team's efforts at training and playing. His natural performances in front of the cameras led to jealous rumours of a contract with Sky, and the possibility of his replacing Daniel Craig as the next James Bond. Fortunately for all Bond fans, the audition includes a test. Each candidate must be capable of running across a single width of Merrion's cricket ground without collapsing.

2009: TILLAIN CUP RUNNERS-UP; MIDDLE CUP WINNERS; INTERMEDIATE A LEAGUE RUNNERS-UP; INTERMEDIATE B LEAGUE WINNERS; WHELAN CUP WINNERS; JUNIOR C LEAGUE RUNNERS-UP; UNDER-15 YATES HALE CUP WINNERS

Senior: fixtures 16, reported 16, won 7, lost 7, no result 2. President: J.P. Joyce. Captain: J. Short. Merrion beat Ballymena, 112/0 to 111 (D. Joyce: 61*) in the second round (bye in the first) of the Bob Kerr Irish Senior Cup, followed by North Down in the next round, 227/3 to 226/6 (D. Joyce: 112). That's it for this year, as Messrs Duckworth and Lewis join Limavady to deprive them of victory in the next round, 147 (29.3 overs) to 225/7. The DGM League is a weather lottery in its last year, with Merrion finishing 2/4 in Section A of the Group Stages, on 18 points, having played 3, won 1, no result 2. Despite trouncing Clontarf in the one game they played, Merrion have to watch as Railway Union win two out of three and go through to the semi-final. The Senior Cup is now sponsored by Lewis Hohn Williams, but this matters not a whit to Merrion, who lose to Clontarf, 226/9 to 227/6 in the second round (bye in the first). They finish 4/7 in Section A of the Senior League (no sponsorship this year), with 171 points, having played 12, won 7, lost 5. Thanks to North County (***) playing an unregistered player, Merrion are awarded the points and they are still in with a shout of winning this league, before a brace of losses to Railway Union at the end of the season.

There are some polite complaints from the Merrion players about the standard of umpiring in these games, which leads to disciplinary action against a few of them and a depleted team at the beginning of the 2010 season. The Alan Murray Cup is now sponsored by 4FM. Merrion beat Dublin University, 109/2 to 108, before losing narrowly to Railway Union, 120/9 to 129/6 (K. Beasley: 50), and to Pembroke by 3 runs. This is another season where the dictum '*so near and yet so far*' prevails. But for a little luck, better weather and different umpires, Merrion might have brought home three trophies. Instead, *nada*. Jeff Short is the only player to appear in the provincial tables, with 13 catches and third place in the catches list. Ben

Ackland plays for the Irish Under-19s team in Canada. Dominick Joyce notches 384 runs @ 32.00. Kade Beasley cuts 188 @ 17.09 and takes 10 catches and 4 stumpings behind the stumps. John Anderson compiles 270 runs @ 24.55 and bewilders 12 batsmen @ 23.67. A slightly injured Matt Petrie has a good all-round year, with 194 runs @ 21.56 and 24 wickets @ 15.04. Pradeep Lavang strikes 264 runs @ 26.40. Ben Ackland strokes 198 runs @ 28.29. Titiksh Patel wheedles out 14 victims @ 20.29. Richard Keaveney purloins 17 wickets @ 19.12:

Opponent	Result	Mer.	Opp.	Best Batting: Runs	Best Bowling: Wickets
Dublin Grass Machinery					
Rush	No Res.	r.s.p.			
Clontarf	Won	81/2	80	D. Joyce: 35*	R. Keaveney: 6/39
Railway Union	No Res.				
Clontarf (C)	Lost	226/9	227/6	E. Extras: 44	B. Ackland: 2/44
Senior League					
The Hills	Lost	78	179/9	E. Extras: 15	J. Anderson: 3/36
North County ***	Lost	236/7	237/4	P. Blakeney: 98*	M. Petrie: 2/36
The Hills	Lost	183	214/8	P. Lavang: 59	R. Keaveney: 4/22
Leinster	Won	244/8	199/7	D. Joyce: 103	M. Petrie: 3/14
Clontarf (D-L)	Won	152/3	181/9	D. Joyce: 64*	M. Petrie: 2/20
North County	Won	113/4	112	K. Beasley: 38*	T. Patel: 4/15
Pembroke (D-L)	Won	195	172	K. Beasley: 66	S. Morrissey: 3/26
Pembroke	Lost	191	194/8	D. Joyce: 72	M. Petrie: 2/41
Clontarf	Won	149/3	148	P. Lavang: 60	J. Anderson: 3/9
Leinster	Won	125/6	123	J. Anderson: 47*	M. Petrie: 5/18
Railway Union	Lost	221	240/6	M. Petrie: 54	J. Anderson: 2/69
Railway Union	Lost	106	107/5	P. Lavang: 34	D. Poder: 2/26

Junior: Having won the Senior 2 League on three occasions and been runners-up once over the previous five seasons, Merrion 2nds explore the other end of the table for a change, using thirty-eight players, and are demoted. They finish 9/10, with 34.6 per cent, having played 15, won 4, lost 10, no result 1. This means they will start 2010 in Division 4 of the new league structure. Simon Morrissey flagellates the Railway Union 2nds bowling attack for 179 runs. They lose to North Wicklow in the first round of the Senior 2 Cup, 234 to 236/1, due to poor seam bowling on a batting track in Kilbride. A 2nds/3rds combination beats Leinster 2nds, Pembroke 2nds and Railway Union 2nds on the way to the final of the Tillain Cup against North County 2nds, which they lose, 104/9 to 105/5. Merrion 3rds emulate them in the Senior 3 League, by finishing 9/10, with 31.4 per cent, having played 13, won 4, lost 9. But Adam O'Keeffe's team makes amends by winning the Middle Cup, beating Pembroke 3rds, 177 to 142, Railway Union 3rds, 158 to 131, and Malahide 3rds, 103/4 to 102, to reach the final against North County 3rds, which they win comfortably, 69/1 to 68 (Amir: 5/9).

Merrion 4ths finish 8/10 in the Middle A League, with 52.1 per cent, having played 14, won 4, lost 10. Nicky Kenny scores a century and there are 50s from Kevin and Philip Allwright, Shane Cullen, Jeremy Dunleavy and Andrew Kay. Pat Carty's team loses to Knockharley, 191/8 to 194/7 in the first round of the Middle 2 Cup, and to Dundrum in the first round of the YMCA Salver. Merrion 5ths finish 2/10 in the Intermediate A League, with 72.3 per cent, having played 13, won 8, lost 3, no result 2. Gerald Rogers's team beats Halverstown in the first round of the Intermediate Cup, 189/9 to 123, but lose to North Wicklow 2nds, 152 to 167/7, in the next round. Steve McGrath whacks a 59-ball 150, and takes 2*5 wicket hauls. Dylan Souter, Killian O'Flynn and Will Houston also fare well. A 5ths/6ths/7ths/8ths combination wins the Whelan 20 Overs Cup, beating Railway Union 4ths/5ths, YMCA 3rds and Sandyford 2nds/3rds/4ths on the way to a final victory against North County 4ths/5ths, 96 to 68. Merrion 6ths win the Intermediate B League with 85.8 per cent, having played 16, won 13, lost 3. Chandra Aramalla's team loses to North County 4ths, 179 to 190, in the first round of the Intermediate Cup.

Merrion 7ths finish 7/10 in Junior B, with 44.5 per cent, having played 12, won 5, lost 7. Tony Gilmore's team loses to Laois 3rds, 114 to 115/5, in the first round of the Junior Cup. Oliver Rye, Nick Staveley and Imran Khan star for this side. Merrion 8ths are back to their almost-winning ways again, with 2/9 in the Junior C League. They gain 62.7 per cent of the points, playing 12, winning 7, losing 5. They beat Bells Academy, 179 to 122, in the first round of the Minor Cup, but lose to Dundrum 2nds in the next round, 107 to 108/6. Merrion Schoolboys win the Under-15 Yates Hale Cup and are runners-up to Donemana in the All-Ireland Under-15 final.

CLUB NOTES

There's more vandalism this year, as the tractor shed is broken into and a fire is lit on the ground in front of the pavilion. The clubhouse roof needs to be repaired, but it's decided to perform emergency short-term maintenance only, and to employ an architect to propose an entirely new development. As Dominick Joyce has had an operation during the off-season, he is forced to resign from his elected position of captain. His elected vice-captain Jeff Short takes over, with John Anderson as the new vice-captain. It's agreed to proceed with swipe cards for the security gates. The edges of the new square are reseeded. The Vodafone mast is installed. A new artificial wicket is laid at Bird Avenue.

Throughout the summer, in their Clublife series, the Sky cameras capture Merrion's efforts on and (in the case of the captain) off the field of play. Ian '*Beefy*' Botham manages the barbecue at one event, and is interviewed by Paddy Willis, whose light-hearted demeanour brings him instant, intergalactic stardom. Despite Botham's claim that Merrion is a drinking club, the players perform well for the cameras and show the club in an extremely positive light, before retiring to the bar. At the end of the season, the 1sts are invited by Sky to play against Hagley and Cairns Fudge clubs at Stratford-upon-Avon, who the team of Hamlets defeat, strangely appropriately.

A new club manager is appointed. A '*clamping of cars*' sign is organised to prevent unauthorised parking on the driveway. The new wickets play low and slow, due to poor drainage. The clubhouse is broken into again, with till money and cheques stolen. Some bushes are removed from the extended driveway to make space for more car parking. Gerry Doyle and Brendan Curley are elected Life Members at the AGM. A ring-in only phone is to be organised for the 2010 season. Concern is expressed at the state of the outfield due to heavy parking in bad weather. The LCU disciplinary committee has imposed bans on certain players, including the club professional, for the beginning of the 2010 season, and the players are advised by the new MCM to appeal these decisions. Yet another new website is planned. A club development subcommittee is set up. Pat Carty is appointed youth development officer for the 2010 season, with more input to coaching to come from qualified club members. Matt Petrie is expected to return as playing professional. Baileys receive planning permission for a building on Stephenson's old site, which is one storey lower than originally requested. A meeting agrees to appeal this decision.

Above left: Merrion 5ths/6ths/7ths/8ths, Whelan Cup winners, 2009. Back row: P. Allwright, G. Dungan, J. Dunleavy, S. MacKenzie, K. O'Flynn, W. Houston, N. Tempany, S. McGrath, D. Campion. Front row: Murali R.R., G. Rogers (C), C. Allwright, M. O'Driscoll.

Above right: Merrion 3rds, Middle Cup winners, 2009. Back row: W. Dassanayaka, H. Barla, Q. Roux, P. Carty (Ch), L. Casey, N. Brown, S. King. Front row: A. Rehman, A. Morison, A. O'Keeffe (C), D. Watkins, A. O'Brien.

Merrion 6ths, Intermediate B League winners, 2009. Back row: Ramu A., Raghu J., Rajesh M., Sreedhar P., Chandra A. (C), Ramana Y., Ravi D., J. Dunleavy. Front row: Deepak T., R. Walsh, J. Ryan, D. Souter.

PROFILE: TITIKSH PATEL

R-H late-order batsman, who claims to be an opener. L-A slow bowler of leg breaks, with subtle variation of pace and flight, who is difficult to get away. Graduated from the University of Jodhpur in India, where he gained a degree in Civil Engineering. Indian born, he came to Dublin in December 2003 to work for a PhD in Trinity College. He played cricket for Trinity with Dominick Joyce, who persuaded him to join Merrion on graduation. Works now as a civil engineer in a consulting company. Also plays chess and table tennis. T.P. played seventy games for Merrion 1sts between 2004 and 2010, scoring 201 runs @ 9.57, with a top score of 35*. He took 101 wickets @ 15.99, with best figures of 5/21 and 5 wickets in an innings on two occasions. He won the O'Grady Cup for bowling in 2008, with 25 wickets @ 13.16. Yet another bowler who wants to be a batsman.

2010: BOB KERR IRISH SENIOR CUP WINNERS; MIDDLE CUP WINNERS; DIVISION 6 RUNNERS-UP; DIVISION 9 WINNERS; DIVISION 12 RUNNERS-UP

Senior: fixtures 14, reported 14, won 7, lost 7. President: K. Allwright. Captain: J. Anderson. Merrion beat Strabane, 261/4 to 203 (G. Clarence: 103), in the second round (bye in the first) of the Bob Kerr Irish Senior Cup. Round three sees off CIYMS, 251/8 to 131 (G. Clarence: 41). Round four says farewell to North County, 274/9 to 269/7 (J. Anderson: 62). And so up to Waringstown for the semi-final, which is won easily, 202/9 to 121 (J. Anderson: 101). The final is at Inch and the weather is bad, but not so bad that the game can't be finished according to the rules of the competition. These state that the game must finish by a certain time, and if 20 overs have been bowled in the second innings, then Messrs Duckworth and Lewis are sent for. If fewer than 20 overs, the game must continue the next day. On a day when play is bound to be interrupted by rain, Railway Union win the toss and strangely decide to bat, when *putting them in* would seem to be the only way of controlling the outcome. In retrospect, their score of 317/3 might be considered about 50 runs short on a good, bouncy track at the tiny ground of Inch, and their two internationals may have changed gear a little too late. Fortunately, Merrion have a strategy, which is based upon the knowledge that the match might probably last about 25 overs if the rain holds off, and their D-L target might be anything between 120 and 160, depending on wickets lost. See off the main bowler and score the runs at the other end. The strategy falters early on, as Merrion's opening batsman falls to a brilliant return catch by Johnston. But there is a special providence in the fall of a wicket, and the next batsman is Merrion's overseas player, Greg Clarence, ex-captain of the Australian Under-19s, from Sydney, who already has over 800 runs under his belt in Irish cricket, despite playing with a chronic knee problem. And so, the readiness is all. Fortunately, Railway Union do not play the two bowlers who are mainly responsible for Merrion's total of 86 at Park Avenue, two weeks earlier. While Joyce nullifies Johnston at one end, Clarence, thoroughly at home on the bouncy track, unleashes a ferocious assault on the rest of the wheeltappers at the other end. After 26 overs, the game is finished, Merrion having scored 164/1, to win by 36 runs. Joyce, with 72*, almost catches Clarence, 80* and the celebrations begin immediately. During this successful season, the new captain, John Anderson deserves full credit for his field-placing and refusal to stick to a conservative, pre-ordained bowling plan. He manages a limited bowling attack well and reacts quickly to changing situations out in the middle. For the first time in several years, there is a forward short leg up the nose of new batsmen.

This is the first season of the new Leinster League structure. Gone are the short 45-overs league and the old distinctions of Senior, Junior, Intermediate, Middle, Minor. There are now thirteen divisions of eight teams each, with promotion and relegation between divisions, of the top and bottom two teams, provided that no two teams from the same club are in the same division. Each team plays each other twice. Abandoned matches do not count for any points nor are they rearranged, but there is a provision in the league that each pair of teams must meet at least once. All leagues are determined on a percentage basis, which is calculated by what percentage the team's actual points bear to the number of matches they play, multiplied by twenty-five. Exceptions to this are Dublin University and Cork County, whose actual points are calculated by reference to twenty-nine points, as they only play seven matches. Merrion finish 4/8 in Division 1, with 51.38 per cent, having played 13, won 7, lost 6, including the last match of the season against North County the day after winning the Irish Senior Cup and a 1-run defeat by Leinster. They lose to Malahide in the first round of the Lewis

Hohn Williams Senior Cup, mainly due to two batsmen having to return to England after the wet weekend and before the completion of the Merrion innings on the Monday evening. They lose to North County, 147/7 to 180/5 (G. Clarence: 51), and Leinster, 137/8 to 141/6, but beat Old Belvedere, 150/6 to 149/4 to finish 3/4 in Section I of the Alan Murray 20 Overs Cup, and do not progress. Quite apart from his heroics in the Irish Senior Cup and his 20/20 scores, Greg Clarence flays 639 runs @ 53.25, including tons against YMCA and Clontarf, and finishes second in the provincial batting table. He adds 13 wickets @ 23.08. John Anderson grooves 448 runs @ 40.73 and filches 23 wickets @ 10.74. He's just 2 wickets away from winning the O'Grady Cup, and comes sixth in the list of provincial all-rounders, with 908 points. Kade Beasley paddles 175 runs @ 21.88. Dominick Joyce has 214 runs @ 16.46 and 11 wickets @ 32.18. Most of the remaining wickets come from Simon Morrissey, with 17 @ 23.05, and Ronan McDonald, with 13 @ 25.23:

Opponent	Result	Mer.	Opp.	Best Batting: Runs	Best Bowling: Wickets
League Division I					
North County	Lost	143/9	144/3	K. Beasley: 42*	A. Chetkovich: 2/35
Leinster	Lost	233/5	234/8	B. Ackland: 56*	R. Keaveney: 2/29
Malahide (C.)	Lost	173	236	J. Anderson: 49	D. Poder: 4/16
Leinster	Won	188/2	132	G. Clarence: 86*	S. Morrissey: 4/26
YMCA (D-L)	Won	268/6	269	G. Clarence: 110	J. Anderson: 3/25
YMCA	Won	156/5	155	G. Clarence: 55*	J. Anderson: 2/0
Clontarf	Won	251/5	250/8	G. Clarence: 115	S. Morrissey: 3/61
The Hills	Lost	162	168/6	K. Beasley: 50	J. Anderson: 4/21
Malahide	Lost	239/8	240/7	G. Clarence: 71	D. Joyce: 2/40
Railway Union	Lost	86	139	G. Clarence: 29	J. Anderson: 4/12
Railway Union	Won	167/3	166	G. Clarence: 69	J. Anderson: 3/31
Malahide	Won	168/6	124/8	B. Ackland: 42	S. Morrissey: 2/18
Clontarf (D-L)	Won	168/9	146/7	J. Anderson: 93	D. Poder: 2/23
North County	Lost	85	87/2	J. Anderson: 24	K. Beasley: 1/12

BOB KERR IRISH SENIOR CUP FINAL 2010, MERRION V. RAILWAY UNION

Merrion			**Railway Union**		
B. Ackland	c. & b. T. Johnston	1	K. Carroll	l.b.w. b. S. Morrissey	46
D. Joyce	not out	72	T. Fisher	c. S. Morrissey b. J. Anderson	69
G. Clarence	not out	80	G. McDonnell	c. R. Allwright b. T. Patel	34
P. Blakeney	d.n.b.		K. O'Brien	not out	76
J. Anderson	d.n.b.		T. Johnston	not out	71
K. Beasley	d.n.b.		C. Mullen	d.n.b.	
D. Poder	d.n.b.		T. Townend	d.n.b.	
A. Chetkovich	d.n.b.		M. Tariq	d.n.b.	
S. Morrissey	d.n.b.		P. Conliffe	d.n.b.	
R. Allwright	d.n.b.		S. Farthing	d.n.b.	
T. Patel	d.n.b.		S. Ullah	d.n.b.	
	Extras	11	Extras		21
	Total (for I wicket)	164	Total	(for 3 wickets)	317

Junior: Merrion 2nds finish 3/8 in League Division 4, with 56.0 per cent, having played 9, won 5, lost 4. Alan Parkinson's team beats North Kildare, 154/3 to 153 (Sum: 5/23), in the first round of the Senior 2 Cup, but loses to Clontarf 2nds, 145 to 148/4 in the next round. They beat YMCA 2nds 182/6 to 140 in the first round of the Tillain Cup, and Railway Union 2nds in the next round, only to lose to Pembroke 2nds, 130/8 to 191/2, in the semi-final. Merrion 3rds also miss promotion narrowly, finishing 3/8 in League Division 5, with 59.27 per cent, having played 11, won 7, lost 4. Jim Walsh's team, including A. O'Keeffe, A. Raghavan, S. McGrath, R. Ensor, P. Carty, R. Stanton, D. Watkins, A. O'Brien, D. O'Tuoma, R. Walsh and C. Allwright, take home the Middle Cup, beating Railway Union 3rds in a bowlout, Leinster 3rds, 163/5 to 162, Mullingar, 107 to 90, and The Hills 3rds in the final, 238/8 to 182 (S. McGrath: 68; A. O'Keeffe: 50). A 3rds/4ths/5ths combination beats Wicklow County 2nds, 156/7 to 75, in the first round of the YMCA Salver, but loses to YMCA 3rds, 114 to 121/6, in the next round.

Left: Merrion 1sts, Irish Senior Cup winners, 2010. Back row: J. Short, M. McGee (S), P. Blakeney, R. Allwright, G. Clarence, D. Poder, A. Chetkovich, T. Patel, D. Joyce. Front row: R. Keaveney, S. Morrissey, J. Anderson (C), K. Beasley, B. Ackland.

Below: Merrion 3rd XI, Middle Cup winners, 2010. Back row: A. Raghavan, S. McGrath, A. O'Keefe, M. McGee (S), R. Ensor, P. Carty, R. Stanton. Front row: D. O'Tuama, D. Watkins, A. O'Brien, J. Walsh (C), R. Walsh, C. Allwright, T. Stanton. Sitting: S. Stanton.

Merrion 6ths, Division 9 League winners, 2010. Back row: N. Staveley, Venkat C., Venkat K., Raghu K., Raghu J. Front row: M. Ryan, Rajesh M., Chandra A. (C), Vikas D., Sreedhar P. Sitting: Deepak T., Ramu A.

Merrion 4ths finish 2/8 in League Division 6, with 60.0 per cent, having played 12, won 7, lost 4, no result 1, but cannot be promoted. Andrew Kay's team loses to Clontarf 3rds, 97 to 112/7 in the first round of the Middle Cup. Merrion 5ths finish 4/8 in League Division 7, with 40.4 per cent, having played 10, won 4, lost 5, tied 1. Dylan Soutar's team loses to Civil Service 2nds, 120 to 173, in the second round (bye in the first) of the Middle 2 Cup. Merrion 6ths win League Division 9, with 76.73 per cent, having played 10, won 8, lost 1, no result 1. Chandra Aramalla's team loses to Pembroke 4ths, 143 to 206, in the first round of the Intermediate Cup. A 6ths/7ths/8ths combination beats Pembroke 4ths/5ths/6ths, 113/2 to 111/8 in the first round of the Whelan Cup, but loses to Dundrum 2nds, 104/8 to 106/3 in the semi-final. The 7ths, captained by Oliver Rye, finish 2/8 in Division 12, with 67.6 per cent, having played 10, won 7, lost 3. They beat North Kildare 3rds, 151/6 to 150, in the first round of the Junior Cup, but lose to Knockharley 2nds, 87 to 140, in the next round. Merrion 8ths finish 6/8 in League Division 13, with 39.0 per cent, having played 12, won 5, lost 7. Barney's boys lose to Civil Service 5ths in the first round of the Minor Cup, 150/9 to 151/6.

CLUB NOTES

A suggestion is made to offer life membership and access rights to certain residents in return for a contribution towards the clubhouse renovation. Matt Petrie is not available for the 2010 season, and a new professional is needed. The club manager takes on the extra duty of grounds-man. An appeal is lodged against the proposed development of twenty-nine apartments on the old Stephenson's site, on the basis that such a block would expose Merrion's ground to greater danger from flooding. Selection committee meetings are to be split between Tuesdays for 1sts-3rds and Wednesdays for 4ths-8ths. A new type of bowling/fielding machine is purchased. Swipe cards are introduced for the security gates, and the code changed. Greg Clarence is employed as the new club professional. A young international player is also expected. Nicky Kenny and Isobel Joyce are confirmed as club coaches. New playing gear is ordered for the 1sts.

An information night is held in April, when a presentation of the architect's drawings for a new two-storey clubhouse is made. At over €1 million, it is felt that the ambitious plan is too costly and that new drawings for a choice of two smaller types of pavilion, one modern, one traditional, be made later on in the year. The use of CCTV to improve security is to be investigated. The new website is ready in time for the 2010 season. It is confirmed that the residents of 51 Anglesea Road have no parking rights in the Merrion driveway. The new club manager is proving a success and the ground is looking at its best during this season. A meeting notes the untimely passing of Roger Fox, and proposes planting a tree in his memory on the Dodder bank that he tended so carefully. Eddie Lewis is acclaimed for his elevation to the presidency of the Leinster Cricket Union. The AGM congratulates the 1sts on winning the Irish Senior Cup and discusses the proposed new clubhouse development in some detail, with many of the older members feeling that such a venture might compromise the very nature and purpose of the club.

PROFILE: JOHN ANDERSON

R-H correct opening/middle-order batsman. R-A slow bowler of big wristy leg breaks, pushed through at speed. Educated at Merchiston Preparatory and Maritzburg High School, Pietermaritzburg, KwaZulu-Natal, South Africa. After school, he studied through UNISA and qualified in chartered accountancy (BCOMPT) in 2007. He currently works as an accountant and auditor with Carney Walsh. Also plays hockey (Under-16 and Under-18 Onterprovincial for Natal Midlands), tennis (Under-15 interprovincial for Natal Midlands), recreational golf, and is interested in canoeing. He played for Railway Union before moving through Sandymount to Anglesea Road. He has played forty-two games for Merrion 1sts between 2008 and 2010, scoring 1,139 runs @ 33.50, with a top score of 102*, and including 4*50s. John is already second in the all-time Merrion batting averages, behind Brad Spanner. He took 51 wickets @ 18.12, and 9 catches. In 2010, his astute captaincy of the 1sts helped Merrion to win the Irish Senior Cup.

5

WOMEN'S CRICKET

Women's cricket in Merrion began in **1975** with some young local girls copying their brothers and knocking a ball around the ground – Joan Soraghan and Alice and Marie Stanton, along with a few of the men's wives, such as Ann O'Herlihy and Sandie Geoffroy. Kevin O'Herlihy offered to coach them, under the watchful eye of his wife. Then, in **1976**, the Leinster Women's Cricket Union was reformed after a hiatus of five years, and Merrion managed to find eleven players and entered a team in the League. It came third and won the Pernod six-a-side competition in Clontarf, to considerable enthusiasm and excitement. And that was just the men.

In **1977** they went one better and came 2/5 in Section A, with 18 points. Marie Stanton scored 247 runs @ 30.90 and was third in the provincial batting averages. The captain, Ann O'Herlihy took 32 wickets @ 5.40 and was third in the equivalent bowling table. And they won the Pernod six-a-side again, as they were to do several more times in the years to come. In **1978** they came 4/6 in Division 1, with 12 points. Alice Stanton led the provincial batting table, with 255 runs @ 85.00, while sister Marie was second, with 235 @ 33.57. Alice, Marie and Mary Delaney played representative cricket for Ireland against Scotland this year. The following year, **1979**, saw another 4/6 placing for Merrion A in Division 1 of the League, with 10 points, having played 10, won 5, lost 5. They beat Clontarf in a nail-biting final of the Tyler Cup, with Marie Stanton, the captain, scoring a 4 off the second last ball. Merrion B finished 7/7 in Division 2, with 2 points, having played 11, won 1, lost 10.

In **1980** there was a temporary slump, with Merrion A finishing 5/6 in Division 1 of the League, with 4 points, having played 10, won 2, lost 8, including a 10-wicket victory over Phoenix, where Marie Stanton thumped 64* and Alice Stanton 37*. They lost to Phoenix in the first round of the Tyler Cup. Merrion B finished 8/8 in Division 2 of the League, with no points, having played 12 and lost the lot. In **1981**, the Irish Women's Cricket Union was formed, and Merrion A finished 3/7 in Division 1 of the League, with 16 points, having played 12, won 8, lost 4. Marie Stanton won the Division 1 batting cup. Alice Stanton scored 72 and took 4/2 for Leinster against Munster. In **1982**, Merrion A won Division 1 of the League for the first time, strengthened by the arrival of six talented Maids of the Mountain hockey players, such as Margarets Reeves and O'Brien. The 2nds were also strengthened by the arrival of six slightly disgruntled ex-1sts players. They had another Tyler Cup final win over Clontarf, in **1983**, but no leagues won. Alice Stanton gained the first of her fourteen international caps against Holland, while Rachel Hardiman gained the first of her seventeen caps, also against Holland.

Over the next five years – **1984-1988** – there were no competition wins, but some good individual performances from Karen Smith, who gained her two international caps in 1984 and 1985, and won the Tetra Pak Senior Interprovincial Cup in 1984; Rachel Hardiman, who won the Division 1 fielding award in 1985, and the Tetra-Pak Senior Interprovincial Cup in 1985 and 1986, and E. Roe, who won the Division 3 wicket-keeping award in 1987. In 1986, Alice, Rachel and Karen represented Merrion on the Irish squad that toured Trinidad and Tobago. But the period ended with relegation to Division 2, and the departure of some of the Senior players to Division 1 teams – Karen Smith to Pembroke, and Sandra Sawson and Rachel Hardiman to YMCA. Merrion continued to play in lower divisions over the next couple of years, but without winning anything other than Alice Stanton's Division 2 batting award in 1989.

In 1993 and 1994, Merrion pulled teams from all leagues, and it looked as though the experiment that started twenty years earlier had come to a premature end. Ex-Merrion wicket-keeper Sandra Dawson made her debut for Ireland in 1993 as a YMCA player. In 1995, thanks to the enthusiasm of Ursula Lewis, a visiting Australian called Robyn Saxon and a handful of Senior players, a team was relaunched in Division 4. Even though half this team consisted of Under-13 schoolgirls (including yet another two members of the Joyce dynasty), and the captaincy was shared between Deirdre Courtney and Robyn Saxon, they won the Windmill Leisure Minor Cup and the Division 4 League in their first year back, with Robyn Saxon winning the Division 4 batting and bowling awards and the Howard Cup for all-rounders. Julianne Morrissey was selected for the South Leinster Junior team.

In 1996, Merrion women continued on their winning ways with victory in the Division 3 League for the 1sts, and the Division 4 League for the 2nds. The captain, Robyn Saxon won the Division 3 batting award, Mags O'Cleary the Division 3 wicket-keeping award and Edwina O'Malley the Division 4 batting award. There was more success in 1997, even though a few of the older players had decided to hang up their boots and the team was now mainly schoolgirls. Margaret Downes's 1sts won the Division 2 League, with 9 wins and 2 losses. Una Budd averaged an impressive 68.33 with the bat and took 10 wickets @ 11.50, winning the Division 1 batting award for her stint with Dublin University and the Division 2 batting award for her time with Merrion. Isobel Joyce took 16 wickets @ 8.56 for the 1sts and 11 @ 10.90 for the 2nds. But the team decided to wait for a few more inches of growth in their players and chose not to go up to Division 1 in 1998. They agreed to share the 40 Overs Cup with Pembroke. The 2nds played 9 and won 6 games in the Division 3 League. There were thirty-four women players in the season that Merrion hosted the women's Minor Cup final and Una Budd was chosen to play for the Irish Development XI against New South Wales at Anglesea Road, with Aoife Budd as twelfth 'man'. Ursula Lewis was elected Hon. Secretary of the Irish Women's Cricket Union.

Pernod six-a-side winners: D. Dowling, A. O'Herlihy, A. Stanton, M. Stanton, M. Soraghan, J. Soraghan.

In **1998**, the 1sts were runners-up in Division 2, with 79.05 per cent, having played 6, won 5, lost 1. Cecelia Joyce won the Division 2 fielding award and made her debut for the Irish Development team. The 2nds won Division 3, with 64.86 per cent, having played 10, won 7, lost 3, but lost the final of the Cup to a more experienced YMCA side. This was the year that both Lisa Banahan and Cecelia Joyce got hat-tricks, Kate Dowling blasted 95 runs against Leinster (including 34 in a single over), and Gillian Lewis won the Division 3 wicket-keeping award. Merrion joined with Pembroke in the Division 1 Senior 40 Overs League, only to share the wooden spoon. Una Budd played a friendly match for Ireland before leaving to teach English in Japan. The Australian Women played Ireland at Anglesea Road.

In **1999**, Merrion 1sts were Division 2 winners, with 72 per cent, having played 7, won 6, lost 1, and they decided to accept promotion into Division 1. The team played in the 40 Overs League against Senior teams this year, with Arlene Stanton making a temporary return. They beat the eventual winners, YMCA, but didn't progress past the early rounds. Cecelia Joyce won the award for the most improved player and secured her place in the Irish squad, while twin sister Isobel Joyce gained her first international cap, against India. Isobel played four times for Ireland this year, with a top score of 7^* and best bowling figures of 3/15. The 2nds finished 3/5 in Division 3, with 45 per cent, having played 5, won 2, lost 3, and Lisa Banahan won the Division 3 batting award. A women's Taverners team played several games, under the watchful eye of Arlene Stanton.

In **2000**, the 1sts finished 3/6 in the Leinster Senior 40 Overs League, with 61.71 per cent, having played 5, won 3, lost 2. They finished 3/8 in the Senior 20 Overs League, with 63.93 per cent, having played 8, won 6, lost 2. Julia Price, the prevailing Australian wicket-keeper, who was working in Merrion as a coach that summer, won the Division 1 batting award. Isobel Joyce became the first Merrion player to feature in a World Cup, in New Zealand. Isobel played twelve times for Ireland this year, with a top score of 29 against Pakistan, and best figures of 6/21 in Ireland's only test match to date, also against Pakistan, which Ireland won by an innings and 54 runs. Aoife Budd scored a century for Merrion Under-19s. Cecelia Joyce and Lisa Banahan played for the Irish Under-21 side against Holland. The 2nds finished 4/6 in the Division 3 League, with 53.57 per cent, having played 8, won 4, lost 4.

In **2001**, Merrion won no leagues, cups or awards of any kind. Aoife Budd played three times for Ireland. In the year that Cecelia Joyce made her debut for the full Irish team, against Australia, Isobel Joyce played in six international games. The teams fared little better in **2002**, winning no leagues, and the 1sts being beaten by Malahide in the first round of the Senior Cup. Jillian Smythe won the Division 2 batting award and Isobel Joyce played three games for Ireland.

In **2003**, the 1sts won the Division 1 League and were runners-up in the 40-overs competition. Ursula Lewis won the ICC Development Program award for Best Women's Cricket Initiative. Cecelia Joyce won the most improved player award. Isobel Joyce was named captain of the Irish Under-21 team. This year, Merrion had four internationals in Holland at the World Cup qualifiers: Isobel and Cecelia Joyce, Emma Beamish and Una Budd. Later, Aoife Budd and Jillian Smythe were added to the squad. Emma Beamish scored 40 against Holland. Lisa Banahan and Gillian Lewis were picked on the Irish Development Squad. But Merrion 2nds had to pull out of the Division 3 league, due to insufficient players.

In **2004**, Gillian Lewis won the Division 1 wicket-keeping award, and Cecelia Joyce the Howard Cup for all-rounders. Merrion hosted 2 matches between the Irish women and New Zealand. Isobel Joyce scored 67^* in the first of these games, while Cecelia scored 33 in the second. In **2005**, Merrion 1sts finished 3/7 in Division 1, with 50.61 per cent, having played 7, won 4, lost 3. They won the 40 Overs Pilkington Plate for the first time, but lost the Senior Cup final to YMCA, 84/6 to 92/5. Cecelia Joyce won the Division 1 batting award, and the Howard Cup for all-rounders again. The 2nds finished 3/7 in Division 3, with 47.43 per cent, having played 10, won 5, lost 5. In March and April, the World Cup took place in South Africa, and Merrion had five representatives in the Irish squad: Una Budd, Jillian Smythe, Emma Beamish, Jill Whelan and Cecelia Joyce, who was vice-captain on this trip and scored 37 against the West Indies.

In **2006**, Cecelia Joyce won the Howard Cup yet again, and played four times for Ireland, scoring 33 against the Netherlands. Jill Whelan also played four times and took 3/20 against the Netherlands. Merrion 2nds won Division 3. In **2007**, the 1sts came 2/8 in Division 1, with 72.65 per cent, having played 7, won 6, lost 1. Cecelia Joyce played three times for Ireland, scoring 50* against Scotland. Isobel Joyce played three times for Ireland, scoring 46 against the Netherlands and 44* against Scotland. Jill Whelan played three times for Ireland and scored 39* against the Netherlands. The 2nds finished 4/7 in Division 2, with 44.29 per cent, having played 2, won 1, lost 1. In **2008**, Merrion 1sts won Division 1 again, with 89.58 per cent, having played 6, won 6. The World Cup qualifiers were held in South Africa, where Cecelia Joyce scored 65 against the Netherlands, 43 against South Africa and 36 against Pakistan. Isobel Joyce scored 70 and took 5/17 against Zimbabwe, 45* against Scotland and 29 against Pakistan. Merrion 2nds, co-captained by Lisa Banahan and Silean Flinter, won the Minor Cup, Lisa Banahan scoring 40* in the final. They also won the Division 3 League, with 87.5 per cent, having played 6, won 6, and were promoted to Division 2. Julianne Morrissey won the Division 3 batting award.

Merrion Women's 1sts, Division 1 League winners, 2003.

Above left: World Cup Qualifiers, 2003: Emma Beamish, Cecelia Joyce, Isobel Joyce, Una Budd.

Above right: Merrion Women's 1sts, Pilkington Plate winners, 2010.

In **2009**, with Emma Beamish as captain, the 1sts lost the final of the Senior Cup, but won the 50 Overs Pilkington Plate final, when Cecelia Joyce was Player of the Match with 76. They finished 2/5 in the Division 1 50-Overs League, with 85.63 per cent, having played 4, won 3, lost 1, and 2/5 in the Division 1 20-Overs league, with 69.50 per cent, having played 5, won 4, lost 1. Heather Whelan won the Division 1 bowling award. Heather and Jill Whelan and Isobel and Cecelia Joyce were selected for a European XI. Cecelia Joyce played eight times for Ireland, scoring 41* against Scotland. Isobel played nine times for Ireland, with a top score of 56* (in 32 balls) against Pakistan. Jill Whelan played nine times for Ireland, taking 3/33 against Nottinghamshire. After moving to Merrion, Heather Whelan played nine times for Ireland, taking 3/11 against Pakistan. The 2nds, led again by Lisa Banahan and Silean Flinter, finished 5/6 in Division 2, with 40.63 per cent, having played 8, won 3, lost 5.

In **2010**, Merrion 1sts won the 20 Overs Senior Cup and the 50 Overs Pilkington Plate, in which match Cecelia Joyce scored 49 and Jill Whelan got the Player of the Match award. Isobel Joyce won the Division 1 batting cup, while Heather Whelan won the Division 1 bowling cup. Cecelia Joyce played nine times for Ireland, scoring 78* against the Netherlands. Isobel Joyce played thirteen times for Ireland, scoring 63 against the Netherlands and 59 against the MCC. Jill Whelan played sixteen times for Ireland, scoring 53 against Leicestershire and 51 against Cumbria and taking 3/19 against Northumberland. Hannah De Burgh White played twice for Ireland A. Merrion 2nds finished 5/6 in Division 2 and lost to The Hills in the semi-final of the cup.

PROFILE: ISOBEL JOYCE

R-H Batsman. L-A medium-pace bowler. Educated at Loreto College, Bray. Daughter of ex-scorer and fixtures secretary Maureen Joyce and Jim Joyce, former Merrion President. Twin to fellow Ireland and Merrion cricketer Cecelia. Sister of Ed, Dominick, Gus, Damian and Johnny. Works as a sub-editor. Also plays hockey for Railway Union. Captain of Merrion 1sts over several years, including 2010, when the team won the 20 Overs Senior Cup and the 50 Overs Pilkington Plate. At the time of writing, from 1987 onwards, Isobel is the top Irish wicket-taker of the modern era, with 79 wickets @ 23.81 from seventy-six games. She has the best individual bowling analysis of any Irish player, with 6/21, and is the only Irish player to have taken 5 wickets in an innings on two occasions. She has most catches for Ireland, with 28, and most run outs, with 19. She is ranked as the top Irish all-round woman cricketer, with 79 wickets and 1,011 runs, and has captained Ireland.

6

APPENDICES

A. MAIN PROVISIONS OF THE CHURCH ACT OF 1869

1. The granting of compensation to all persons, lay and clerical, who were deprived of their income by the operation of the Act.

2. The undertaking of the charges on the public revenue in respect of the Regium Donum (the annual endowment granted to the non-conformist clergy by Charles II) and the college of Maynooth.

3. The commutation of the annuities which had been awarded to persons deprived of income.

4. The granting of compensation of private endowments which had been vested in the Commissioners.

5. The granting of compensation to lay patrons for loss of advowsons (clerical incomes).

6. The disposal of churches, school-houses, burial grounds, ecclesiastical residences and the mensal lands (home-farms) attached to these.

7. The disposal of national monuments of church lands.

8. The management and sale of tithe rent charges, church lands and the creation of a body of small proprietors. A tithe rent charge was defined as 'any annual sum payable to the Church Temporalities body under the 1869 Act'.

B. SENIOR RECORDS – PROFESSIONAL STATISTICS, 1926-2010

PROFESSIONALS RANKED BY BATTING AVERAGE

Name	Year	No.	Inns	Not Out	Most	Runs	Ave.	100s	50s
B. Spanner	1999	23	20	5	130	1014	**67.60**	3	8
C. Torrisi	2000	20	20	4	126*	965	**60.31**	3	7
C. Torrisi	2001	18	18	2	157*	917	**57.31**	2	6
G. Clarence	2010	14	14	2	115	639	**53.25**	2	4
D. Payne	2005	16	15	1	124	705	**50.36**	1	6
S. Flegler	2002	23	21	5	94*	749	**46.81**	0	6
C. Brockway	1942	4	4	1	84*	131	**43.66**	0	1
D. Robinson	1981	21	21	2	117*	746	**39.26**	2	4
D. Robinson	1980	20	20	0	133	776	**38.80**	1	6
J. Myers (W)	1997	21	21	5	82*	614	**38.38**	0	2
S. Uddin	1978	20	20	0	87	667	**33.35**	0	7
G. Brophy (W)	1995	21	21	2	74	583	**32.38**	0	4
B. Hughes (W)	1998	21	21	2	106	600	**31.58**	1	3
L. Stevens	2003	6	6	1	44	131	**26.20**	0	0
D. Celep	2004	18	18	3	76*	385	**25.67**	0	1
D. Waugh	2006	15	15	2	71*	333	**25.62**	0	3
S. Uddin	1979	20	20	0	81	503	**25.15**	0	4
T. MacLaren (W)	1996	20	20	0	49	477	**23.85**	0	0
S. Willoughby	2003	11	11	1	56	232	**23.20**	0	2
M. Petrie	2008	14	10	2	44	178	**22.25**	0	0
M. Petrie	2009	14	12	3	54	194	**21.56**	0	1
M. Petrie	2007	15	12	1	53	186	**16.91**	0	1
M. Thompson	1990	16	13	3	29	120	**12.00**	0	0
J. Smith	2006	1	1	0	4	4	**04.00**	0	0

PROFESSIONALS RANKED BY BOWLING AVERAGE

Name	Year	No.	Wkts	Runs	Ave.	Best	5+s	Ct.	St.
G. Brophy (W)	1995	21	0	0	**00.00**	0	0	26	4
T. MacLaren (W)	1996	20	0	0	**00.00**	0	0	28	1
J. Smith	2006	1	0	19	**00.00**	0/19	0	0	0

M. Petrie	2008	14	35	246	**07.03**	8/15	2	7	0
J. Myers (W)	1997	21	4	35	**08.75**	4/35	0	21	5
B. Hughes (W)	1998	21	2	18	**09.00**	2/18	0	15	10
M. Petrie	2007	15	36	337	**09.36**	6/22	2	5	0
L. Stevens	2003	6	10	124	**12.40**	4/26	0	3	0
C. Brockway	1942	4	5	66	**13.20**	2/7	0	0	0
B. Spanner	1999	23	31	430	**13.87**	5/41	2	15	0
D. Robinson	1981	21	45	663	**14.73**	6/27	3	4	0
D. Robinson	1980	20	41	613	**14.95**	7/24	2	6	0
C. Torrisi	2000	20	1	15	**15.00**	1/15	0	7	0
M. Petric	2009	14	24	361	**15.04**	5/18	1	1	0
C. Torrisi	2001	18	1	17	**17.00**	1/17	0	7	0
S. Flegler	2002	23	44	812	**18.45**	5/48	1	10	0
S. Uddin	1979	20	19	409	**21.52**	3/27	0	16	0
S. Uddin	1978	20	13	294	**22.61**	3/34	0	4	0
D. Celep	2004	18	14	331	**23.64**	2/0	0	8	0
G. Clarence	2010	14	14	355	**25.36**	3/44	0	7	0
D. Payne	2005	16	19	542	**28.53**	3/40	0	8	0
M. Thompson	1990	16	19	590	**31.05**	4/14	0	4	0
D. Waugh	2006	15	1	40	**40.00**	1/40	0	9	0
S. Willoughby	2003	11	6	315	**52.50**	2/37	0	2	0

C. SENIOR RECORDS – BATTING STATISTICS, 1926-2010, EXCLUDING PROFESSIONALS

Qualification = 1,000 runs.

SENIOR BATSMEN RANKED BY BATTING AVERAGE

Name	Playing	No.	Inns	Not Out	Runs	Average	Highest	100s	50s
Spanner, Brad	2000–2002	60	58	11	2708	**57.61**	204*	9	10
Anderson, John	2008–2010	42	41	7	1139	**33.50**	102*	1	4
Saxon, Brett	1995–1999	47	47	0	1472	**31.31**	137	2	9
Curley, Simon	1934–1966	369	353	29	9510	**29.35**	175	8	59
Waldron, Paddy	1936–1953	216	206	26	4994	**27.74**	111	4	32
Joyce, Ed	1995–2000	64	61	7	1448	**26.81**	103*	1	6
Joyce, Dominick	1996–2010	180	166	19	3870	**26.33**	197	3	19

Beasley, Kade	2000–2010	169	155	19	3580	**26.32**	125*	2	19
Joyce, Gus	1990–2010	198	190	18	4498	**26.15**	191*	4	25
Waddell, Richie	1992–1994	52	52	3	1149	**23.44**	75*	0	4
Lewis, Eddie	1967–1994	351	341	33	7183	**23.32**	90	0	32
Blakeney, John	1998–2006	65	54	10	1009	**22.93**	100	1	4
Delaney, Joe	1928–1936	81	75	2	1636	**22.41**	95*	0	5
Burke, Joe	1941–1962	208	187	25	3626	**22.38**	89*	0	16
Little, Cecil	1926–1958	260	233	33	4421	**22.10**	108	4	20
Poder, Damian	1997–2010	210	169	36	2929	**22.02**	93	0	10
Holloway, Vinny	1949–1966	96	87	11	1603	**21.09**	112*	1	8
Ramsaroop, Raj	1972–1983	103	99	3	1999	**20.82**	125	1	8
Dempsey, Kevin	1932–1940	88	86	3	1692	**20.38**	79*	0	11
Allwright, Kevin	1972–1998	199	174	30	2913	**20.22**	108*	1	14
Morrissey Jnr, Joe	1993–2004	133	103	22	1625	**20.06**	80	0	8
Parkinson, Stan	1963–1989	179	170	15	2871	**18.52**	86	0	11
Curley, Brendan	1952–1979	362	346	40	5665	**18.51**	87*	0	21
D'Arcy, Joe	1937–1961	106	94	18	1406	**18.50**	72*	0	4
O'Connor, Des	1929–1955	219	198	23	3182	**18.18**	115*	2	12
Kilpatrick, Derek	1970–1981	78	76	4	1299	**18.04**	74*	0	3
Joyce, Damian	1988–2005	147	125	21	1872	**18.00**	70	0	3
King, Stephen	1980–2005	252	222	24	3549	**17.92**	87*	0	12
Stanton, Robbie	1979–2006	394	340	77	4637	**17.63**	91*	0	16
Hopkins, Joe	1956–1964	104	99	8	1527	**16.78**	70	0	7
Heavey Jnr, John	1980–1994	204	198	9	3146	**16.65**	90	0	13
Nixon, Andrew	1982–2001	148	138	17	2004	**16.56**	109*	1	3
Warren, Paul	1940–1955	128	104	18	1400	**16.27**	76	0	4
O'Donnell, Jack	1926–1947	222	197	20	2868	**16.20**	86	0	10
O'Hagan, John	1966–1992	276	257	32	3721	**15.83**	88*	0	13
Lindsay, Billy	1938–1955	203	181	16	2539	**15.38**	91	0	6
McGeady, John	1978–1992	89	81	7	1129	**15.25**	83	0	6
Little, Alan	1963–1994	221	203	25	2621	**14.72**	77	0	3
Hayden, Noel	1961–1971	102	95	7	1269	**14.42**	78*	0	7
Burke, Tommy	1940–1969	247	207	23	2514	**13.66**	90	0	4
Parkinson, Danny	1955–1979	204	195	7	2497	**13.28**	64	0	3
McKenna, Denis	1977–1992	184	176	18	2088	**13.21**	60*	0	6
Bernstein, Rodney	1958–1966	102	89	6	1089	**13.12**	53	0	3

McDonald, Ken	1974-1987	178	160	23	1783	13.01	132*	1	2
Mara, Chris	1935-1960	313	230	48	2104	11.56	60	0	2
Coghlan, Paul	1976-1988	136	124	21	1151	11.17	54	0	2
Fleming, Angus	1991-2009	265	182	49	1411	10.61	77	0	3
Noble, Dennis	1960-1977	249	228	22	1835	08.90	56	0	2

D. SENIOR RECORDS – BOWLING STATISTICS, 1926-2010, EXCLUDING PROFESSIONALS

Qualification = 100 wickets.

SENIOR BOWLERS RANKED BY BOWLING AVERAGE

Name	Playing	No.	Wickets	Runs	Average	5 wkts	Best
Bernstein, Rodney	1958-1966	102	271	3206	11.83	19	8/22
Shortt, Rollie	1926-1956	270	701	9602	13.69	55	8/18
Mara, Chris	1935-1960	313	699	10245	14.65	42	9/52
Burke, Joe	1941-1962	208	280	4192	14.97	11	7/28
Little, Cecil	1926-1958	260	516	7897	15.30	29	8/33
Patel, Titiksh	2004-2010	70	101	1615	15.99	2	5/37
Dowse, Richard	1993-2003	152	214	3566	16.66	8	6/18
O'Herlihy, Patrick	1992-1996	82	180	3131	17.39	10	7/44
Hayden, Derek	1953-1963	96	144	2571	17.85	6	6/25
Noble, Dennis	1960-1977	249	417	7685	18.42	14	8/61
Curley, Simon	1934-1966	369	356	6623	18.60	11	7/59
Poder, Damian	1997-2010	210	278	5192	18.68	6	6/13
Ramsaroop, Raj	1972-1983	103	156	2930	18.78	7	7/61
Morrissey Jnr, Joe	1993-2004	133	161	3080	19.13	3	5/22
Fleming, Angus	1991-2009	265	360	7108	19.74	9	7/22
O'Herlihy, Kevin	1971-1981	155	208	4172	20.05	8	7/42
Stanton, Robbie	1979-2006	394	300	6147	20.49	7	8/16
Willis, Paddy	1959-1976	102	148	3317	22.41	6	7/35
Lewis, Eddie	1967-1994	351	186	4404	23.67	3	5/24
Keogh, Joe	1972-1978	98	119	2886	24.25	5	8/59
O'Hagan, John	1966-1992	276	159	4002	25.16	5	6/48
Craven, John	1985-1991	96	114	2890	25.35	1	6/27
Coghlan, Paul	1976-1988	136	100	2628	26.28	4	5/24

E. SENIOR RECORDS – WICKET-KEEPING STATISTICS, 1926-2010, EXCLUDING PROFESSIONALS

Qualification = 25 victims.

SENIOR WICKET-KEEPERS RANKED BY VICTIMS

Name	Playing	No.	Catches	Stumpings	Total
Beasley, Kade	2000–2010	169	170	41	211
Lindsay, Billy	1938–1955	203	120	60	180
McDonald, Ken	1974–1987	178	127	36	163
Hopkins, Joe	1956–1964	104	61	19	80
Joyce, Gus	1990–2010	198	51	12	63
Delaney, John	1931–1937	60	27	12	39
Hancock, Angus	1984–1994	66	28	8	36
Rumney, Bill	1926–1933	72	28	8	36
Burke, Tommy	1940–1969	247	21	8	29
Gaynor, Maurice	1943–1955	50	15	11	26

F. SENIOR RECORDS – FIELDING STATISTICS, 1926-2010, EXCLUDING PROFESSIONALS

Qualification = 50 catches.

SENIOR FIELDERS RANKED BY CATCHES

Name	Playing	No.	Catches
Curley, Simon	1934–1966	369	138
Curley, Brendan	1952–1979	362	112
O'Hagan, John	1966–1992	276	108
Lewis, Eddie	1967–1994	351	105
Stanton, Robbie	1979–2006	394	102
Poder, Damian	1997–2010	210	90
Little, Cecil	1926–1958	260	88
Burke, Joe	1941–1962	208	81
Little, Alan	1963–1994	221	81
O'Connor, Des	1929–1955	219	73
King, Stephen	1980–2005	252	70
Joyce, Dominick	1996–2010	180	69
Allwright, Kevin	1972–1998	199	69
Fleming, Angus	1991–2009	265	64
McKenna, Denis	1977–1992	184	61

O'Herlihy, Kevin	1971–1981	155	**56**
Joyce, Gus	1990–2010	198	**56**
Waldron, Paddy	1936–1953	216	**55**
O'Donnell, Jack	1926–1947	222	**53**
Morrissey Jnr, Joe	1993–2004	133	**52**
Shortt, Rollie	1926–1956	270	**52**
Burke, Tommy	1940–1969	247	**51**

G. SENIOR RECORDS – ALL-ROUNDER RATINGS, 1926-2010, EXCLUDING PROFESSIONALS

One point per run scored, 20 per wicket, 20 per w/k catch, 20 per stumping.
Qualification = 1,000 runs + (100 wickets or 25 w/k catches/stumpings).

Name	Playing	No.	Runs	Wickets	W/k Catches	Stumpings	Points
Curley, Simon	1934–1966	369	9510	356			**16630**
Mara, Chris	1935–1960	313	2104	699			**16084**
Little, Cecil	1926–1958	260	4421	516			**14741**
Lewis, Eddie	1967–1994	351	7183	186			**10903**
Stanton, Robbie	1979–2006	394	4637	300			**10637**
Noble, Dennis	1960–1977	249	1835	417			**10175**
Burke, Joe	1941–1962	208	3626	280			**9226**
Beasley, Kade	2000–2010	169	3580		170	41	**8710**
Fleming, Angus	1991–2009	265	1411	360			**8611**
Poder, Damian	1997–2010	210	2929	278			**8489**
O'Hagan, John	1966–1992	276	3721	159		1	**6921**
Bernstein, Rodney	1958–1966	102	1089	271			**6509**
Lindsay, Billy	1938–1955	203	2539		120	60	**6139**
Joyce, Gus	1990–2010	198	4498		51	12	**5758**
Ramsaroop, Raj	1972–1983	103	1999	156			**5119**
McDonald, Ken	1974–1987	178	1783		127	36	**5043**
Morrissey Jnr, Joe	1993–2004	133	1625	161			**4845**
Burke, Tommy	1940–1969	247	2514	29	21	8	**3674**
Coghlan, Paul	1976–1988	136	1151	100			**3151**
Hopkins, Joe	1956–1964	104	1527		61	19	**3127**

H. SENIOR RECORDS – INTERNATIONAL PLAYER STATISTICS, 1926 TO 30 SEPTEMBER 2010

Name	Years	No.	Inns	Most	Runs	Ave.	Wkts	Runs	Ave.	Ct.	St.
Thornton, Patrick	1927–1929	6	10	37	120	13.33	14	217	15.50	3	0
Loughery, Bill	1929–1933	6	12	29	134	12.18	0	4	–	3	0
O'Donnell, Jack	1929–1930	2	3	4	6	02.00	–	–	–	1	0
Shortt, Rollie	1934	1	2	0	0	00.00	3	66	22.00	0	0
Bex, Edgar	1937	1	1	1	1	01.00	–	–	–	0	0
Waldron, Paddy	1946–1947	5	9	32	100	11.11	–	–	–	0	0
Curley, Simon	1948–1951	8	15	43	208	14.86	–	–	–	8	0
Burke, Joe	1953–1958	6	8	19*	62	08.86	5	198	39.60	2	0
Bernstein, Rodney	1960–1962	8	14	18	96	07.38	21	538	25.62	1	0
Hopkins, Joe	1961	1	2	7	13	06.50	–	–	–	2	1
Joyce, Ed	1997–2005	50	51	115*	1637	37.20	7	360	51.43	19	0
Joyce, Gus	2000	4	4	29	49	12.25	–	–	–	3	0
Joyce, Dominick	2000–2007	69	70	67	1518	23.00	1	64	64.00	15	0
Fourie, Thinus	2007	8	7	14*	39	09.75	7	263	37.57	2	0

I. SENIOR RECORDS – MERRION'S GREATEST 1STS, 1926-2010, EXCLUDING PROFESSIONALS

(In batting order)

1. Paddy Waldron, batsman
2. Eddie Lewis, batsman
3. Ed Joyce, batsman
4. Brad Spanner, all-rounder
5. Simon Curley, captain and all-rounder
6. Dominick Joyce, batsman
7. Kade Beasley, wicket-keeper
8. Cecil Little, all-rounder
9. Rodney Bernstein, fast bowler
10. Chris Mara, fast bowler
11. Rollie Shortt, fast bowler
12th man: Joe Burke, all-rounder

J. SENIOR RECORDS – FASTEST BATTING & BOWLING, 1926-2010, EXCLUDING PROFESSIONALS

Fastest Batting		Fastest Bowling	
Fastest to 1,000 Runs		**Fastest to 100 Wickets**	
Player	**Games**	**Player**	**Games**
Brad Spanner (2000-2002)	19	Rollie Shortt	26
Brett Saxon	31	Rodney Bernstein	39
John Anderson	41	Patrick O'Herlihy	47
Joe Delaney	43	Damian Poder	50
Cecil Little	45	Cecil Little/Chris Mara	56
Fastest to 2,000 Runs		**Fastest to 200 Wickets**	
Brad Spanner (2000-2002)	41	Rollie Shortt	61
Kade Beasley	80	Rodney Bernstein	72
Simon Curley	91	Chris Mara	92
Paddy Waldron	92	Cecil Little	95
Cecil Little	94	Damian Poder	123
Fastest to 3,000 Runs		**Fastest to 300 Wickets**	
Kade Beasley	122	Rollie Shortt	93
Dominick Joyce	131	Chris Mara	125
Cecil Little	133	Cecil Little	147
Gus Joyce	134	Dennis Noble	190
Paddy Waldron	135	Angus Fleming	218
Fastest to 4,000 Runs		**Fastest to 400 Wickets**	
Simon Curley	163	Rollie Shortt	138
Gus Joyce	169	Chris Mara	156
Paddy Waldron	170	Cecil Little	201
Eddie Lewis	190	Dennis Noble	237
Cecil Little	192		
Fastest to 5,000 Runs		**Fastest to 500 Wickets**	
Simon Curley	186	Rollie Shortt	184
Eddie Lewis	240	Chris Mara	208
Brendan Curley	290	Cecil Little	249
Fastest to 6,000 Runs		**Fastest to 600 Wickets**	
Simon Curley	227	Rollie Shortt	219
Eddie Lewis	294	Chris Mara	257
Fastest to 7,000 Runs		**Fastest to 700 Wickets**	
Simon Curley	256	Rollie Shortt	268
Eddie Lewis	331		
Fastest to 8,000 Runs			
Simon Curley	290		
Fastest to 9,000 Runs			
Simon Curley	326		

K. SENIOR RECORDS – CENTURIONS, 1926-2010, EXCLUDING PROFESSIONALS

Scorers of 100+ in a single league/cup match.

Centurions Ranked By Number				
Name	Playing	No.	100s	Details
Spanner, Brad	2000–2002	60	9	110 v. North County, 2000; 140* v. Pembroke, 2000; **204* v. Railway Union, 2000;** 100 v. Old Belvedere, 2001; 107 v. The Hills, 2001; 112* v. Phoenix, 2002; 140* v. The Hills, 2002; 109 v. CYM, 2002; 171* v. Clontarf, 2002
Curley, Simon	1934–1966	369	8	112* v. YMCA, 1940; 100* v. YMCA, 1941; 107 v. Dublin University, 1951; 175 v. Leinster, 1951; 123* v. Phoenix, 1952; 155* v. Railway Union, 1955; 121* v. Leinster, 1960; 112 v. YMCA, 1961
Little, Cecil	1926–1958	260	4	102* v. Civil Service, 1928; 105 v. Phoenix, 1934; 108 v. Phoenix, 1935; 100 v. Clontarf, 1937
Joyce, Gus	1990–2010	198	4	111 v. Rush, 1995; 100* v. Old Belvedere, 1999; 191* v. Rush, 1999; 103* v. North County, 2002
Waldron, Paddy	1936–1953	216	4	101* v. Pembroke, 1943; 111 v. Civil Service, 1943; 100* v. YMCA, 1945; 108* v. YMCA, 1951
Joyce, Dominick	1996–2010	180	3	103 v. The Hills, 2001; 197 v. Pembroke, 2005; 103 v. Leinster, 2009
Beasley, Kade	2000–2010	169	2	125* v. Old Belvedere, 2005; 104* v. CYM, 2006
O'Connor, Des	1929–1955	219	2	103* v. Civil Service, 1941; 115* v. YMCA, 1944
Saxon, Brett	1995–1999	47	2	137 v. Rush, 1995; 117 v. Phoenix, 1996
Allwright, Kevin	1972–1998	199	1	108* v. Pembroke, 1985

Anderson, John	2008–2010	42	1	102* v. Malahide, 2008
Barber, Des	1929–1933	17	1	101* v. Civil Service, 1930
Blakeney, John	1998–2006	65	1	100 v. Munster Reds, 2006
Holloway, Vinny	1949–1966	96	1	112* v. Leinster, 1949
Joyce, Ed	1995–2000	64	1	103* v. Phoenix, 1996
McDonald, Ken	1974–1987	178	1	132* v. Carlisle, 1980
Morison, Alex	2007–2008	20	1	108* v. North County, 2007
Nielsen, Paul	1983–1992	81	1	105* v. Dublin University, 1986
Nixon, Andrew	1982–2001	148	1	109* v. Dublin University, 1994
Ramsaroop, Raj	1972–1983	103	1	125 v. Carlisle, 1976
Rumney, Bill	1926–1933	72	1	103* v. Railway Union, 1929

L. SENIOR RECORDS – GLADIATORS, 1926-2010, EXCLUDING PROFESSIONALS

Takers of 7+ wickets in a single league/cup match.

Name	Playing	No.	7+s	Details
Shortt, Rollie	1926–1956	270	16	7/35 v. Phoenix, 1926; 7/35 v. Clontarf, 1926; 7/13 v. Railway Union, 1927; 8/22 v. Civil Service, 1927; 8/47 v. Clontarf, 1928; 7/57 v. Pembroke, 1929; 7/14 v. Clontarf, 1930; 7/35 v. Civil Service, 1930; 7/26 v. Phoenix, 1931; 7/28 v. Pembroke, 1931; 8/56 v. DU, 1934; 8/22 v. Civil Service, 1935; 7/47 v. Clontarf, 1935; 8/18 v. Civil Service, 1936; 7/14 v. DU, 1940; 7/39 v. YMCA, 1944
Mara, Chris	1935–1960	313	9	7/61 v. Phoenix, 1940; **9/52 v. Phoenix, 1940;** 8/35 v. Pembroke, 1941; 7/75 v. DU, 1942; 7/29 v. Pembroke, 1942; 7/34 v. DU, 1944; 8/20 v. Civil Service, 1944; 7/48 v. Railway Union, 1955; 7/31 v. Phoenix, 1957
Bernstein, Rodney	1958–1966	102	6	7/22 v. Railway Union, 1959; 7/23 v. Phoenix, 1959; 7/41 v. Clontarf, 1960; 7/40 v. Pembroke, 1961; 8/22 v. DU, 1962; 8/26 v. YMCA, 1963
Little, Cecil	1926–1958	260	5	7/21 v. Pembroke, 1930; 7/33 v. Civil Service, 1931; 8/33 v. Clontarf, 1934; 7/41 v. Clontarf, 1938; 7/70 v. Phoenix, 1945
Curley, Simon	1934–1966	369	3	7/91 v. YMCA, 1939; 7/59 v. Malahide, 1954; 7/81 v. Pembroke, 1956

Noble, Denis	1960–1977	249	3	7/28 v. Pembroke, 1964; 8/61 v. Old Belvedere, 1973; 7/45 v. Clontarf, 1974
Gibbs, Will	1978–1982	36	2	7/54 v. DU, 1980; 8/41 v. Old Belvedere, 1980
Fleming, Angus	1991–2009	265	2	7/22 v. North County, 1994; 7/61 v. Phoenix, 1996
Fryer, Fred	1926–1928	16	2	7/27 v. Civil Service, 1926; 7/18 v. Civil Service, 1928
Keogh, Joe	1972–1978	98	2	8/59 v. Railway Union, 1974; 7/26 v. YMCA, 1975
O'Herlihy, Kevin	1971–1981	155	2	7/71 v. Old Belvedere, 1976; 7/42 v. Leinster, 1976
Stanton, Robbie	1979–2006	394	2	7/49 v. Pembroke, 1984; 8/16 v. Pembroke, 1988
Kiely, T. O'Neill	1929–1934	21	1	8/18 v. Railway Union, 1929
Burke, Joe	1941–1962	208	1	7/28 v. Railway Union, 1945
Clarke, Richard	1975–1992	24	1	7/45 v. Carlisle, 1991
Gunn, Ken	1959–1970	27	1	7/48 v. Clontarf, 1959
O'Herlihy, Patrick	1992–1996	82	1	7/44 v. The Hills, 1995
Quinlan, Philip	1988–1999	59	1	8/49 v. Phoenix, 1990
Ramsaroop, Raj	1972–1983	103	1	7/61 v. YMCA, 1976
Willis, Paddy	1959–1976	102	1	7/35 v. Phoenix, 1974

M. SENIOR RECORDS – THE CAPTAIN'S TABLE, 1926-2010, FROM MOST TO LEAST SUCCESSFUL

10 points/win; 3 points/tie or draw; 0 points/no result; 10 points trophy bonus; 20 points per year penalty for using a professional; average = points/games

Name	Captain	No.	Wins	Draws	Losses	Tro.Bon.	Pro.Red.	Points	Average
S. Curley	1948–49, 52, 60–61	79	43	17	19	2*10=20	0	501	6.3418
A. Joyce	1999–2000, 03	59	40	0	19	2*10=20	3*20=60	360	6.1017
C. Little	1931, 37	23	12	6	5	0	0	138	6.0000
K. Beasley	2002	23	15	3*n.r.	5	0	1*20=20	130	5.6522
J.A. Delaney	1935	14	7	2	5	0	0	76	5.4286
J. O'Donnell	1926, 28–30, 34, 36, 38, 40–42	124	58	30	36	2*10=20	1*20=20	670	5.4032
R. Dowse	1997–98	47	28	3*n.r.	16	1*10=10	2*20=40	250	5.3191
B. Spanner	2001	21	12	3*n.r.	6	1*10=10	1*20=20	110	5.2381

C.G. Mara	1944–45, 53–54	59	24	15	20	1*10=10	0	295	**5.0000**
R.H. Shortt	1933, 46	26	9	9	8	0	0	117	**4.5000**
D. Joyce	2007–08	38	20	8*n.r.	10	1*10=10	2*20=40	170	**4.4737**
K. Allwright	1994–96	62	28	12	22	0	2*20=40	276	**4.4516**
W. Lindsay	1943	16	5	5	6	0	0	65	**4.0625**
T. Burke	1957–59, 64, 67	81	21	34	26	1*10=10	0	322	**3.9753**
E.D. Hayden	1963	18	5	7	6	0	0	71	**3.9444**
J.K. Hopkins	1962	18	4	9	5	0	0	67	**3.7222**
P.B. Kenny	1932	13	3	6	4	0	0	48	**3.6923**
J. Anderson	2010	14	7	0	7	0	1*20=20	50	**3.5714**
D. Poder	2004–06	54	25	1*n.r.	28	0	3*20=60	190	**3.5185**
K. McDonald	1980	20	8	3	9	0	1*20=20	69	**3.4500**
K. O'Herlihy	1981	22	8	5	9	0	1*20=20	75	**3.4090**
W. Rumney	1927	13	2	8	3	0	0	44	**3.3846**
E. Lewis	1976–77, 82	61	18	8	35	0	0	204	**3.3443**
A. Little	1978–79	42	16	6	20	0	2*20=40	138	**3.2857**
J. Burke	1951, 55	26	6	8	12	0	0	84	**3.2308**
J. Short	2009	16	7	2*n.r.	7		1*20–20	50	**3.1250**
J. O'Hagan	1983	19	4	5	10	0	0	55	**2.8947**
P. Waldron	1947	8	2	1	5	0	0	23	**2.8750**
D. O'Connor	1939, 50	25	5	7	13	0	0	71	**2.8400**
D. Kilpatrick	1973 74	36	6	13/1*	16	0	0	99	**2.7500**
S. Parkinson	1985–86	36	7	8	21	0	0	94	**2.6111**
R. Stanton	1990, 93	38	8	8	22	0	1*20=20	84	**2.2105**
E. Bohane	1972	18	2	6	10	0	0	38	**2.1111**
A. Burns	1970–71	37	4	12	21	0	0	76	**2.0541**
J. Heavey	1991	20	2	7	11	0	0	41	**2.0500**
B. Curley	1956	14	1	6	7	0	0	28	**2.0000**
D. McKenna	1984	18	2	5	11	0	0	35	**1.9444**
J. Walsh	1987, 92	38	6	4	28	0	0	72	**1.8947**
J. Craven	1988–89	34	4	8	22	0	0	64	**1.8824**
D. Parkinson	1968–69	34	3	7	24	0	0	51	**1.5000**
D. Noble	1965–66, 75	53	2	13	38	0	0	59	**1.1132**

N. SENIOR RECORDS – MERRION 1STS, 1926-2010

(p: played, w: won, t: tied, d: drawn, l: lost, ps: position,
n: number of teams, nr: no result, pl: players used.)

Performances by Year																		
Leinster Senior League							Cup			League Cup							pl	Highlights
Year	p	w	T	d	l	ps	n	p	w	l	p	w	t	nr	l	ps	n		
1926	12	4		2	6	5	8											18	1st year in Senior Lge
1927	13	2	1	7	3	6	8											27	
1928	7	2		1	4	6	8											16	
1929	6	2		2	2	3	4											19	
1930	11	5		4	5	3	7											27	
1931	10	6		3	1	2	7											20	2nd in Table
1932	13	3		6	4	4	7											23	
1933	12	3		4	5	5	7											24	
1934	14	10		1	3	2	8											20	Lge Runners-up
1935	13	7		1	5	5	8	1		1								21	
1936	14	4		3	7	6	8	3	2	1								23	Cup Runners-up
1937	13	6		3	4	5	8	2	1	1								19	
1938	9	1		6	2	4	6	3	2	1								16	
1939	10	1		4	5	6	6	1		1								23	
1940	12	7		5	0	1	7	4	4									15	Lge & Cup Winners
1941	14	9		3	2	2	8	1		1								16	Lge Runners-up
1942	14	6		3	5	5	8	1		1								17	
1943	14	4		5	5	5	8	2	1	1								24	
1944	14	5		4	5	6	8	3	2	1								22	Cup Runners-up
1945	14	8		4	2	1	8	2	1	1								17	Lge Winners
1946	11	4	1	4	2	3	8	3	2	1								15	Cup Runners-up
1947	7	2		1	4	6	8	1		1								18	
1948	11	5		2	4	4	8	3	2	1								18	Cup Runners-up
1949	14	9		3	2	2	8	1		1								21	Lge Runners-up
1950	13	4		3	6	7	8	1		1								24	
1951	9	1		4	4	7	8	3	2	1								23	Cup Runners-up
1952	12	9		1	2	1	8	1		1								24	Lge Winners
1953	13	6		4	3	4	9	1		1								22	
1954	11	2		3	6	8	9	1		1								22	

Year																		Total	Notes
1955	12	2		4	6	8	9	2	1	1								26	
1956	13	1		6	6	9	9	1		1								30	
1957	15	4		6	5	6	10	1		1								30	
1958	12	5		6	1	1	10	3	2	1								21	Lge Winners
1959	16	6		5	5	3	10	2	1	1								23	
1960	15	7		5	3	2	10	4	4									27	Cup Winners; Lge Runners-up
1961	16	6		6	4	5	10	3	2	1								29	
1962	16	3		9	4	7	10	2	1	1								27	
1963	15	3		7	5	7	10	3	2	1								27	Cup Runners-Up
1964	16	1		5	10	10	10	1		1								24	
1965	17	1		3	13	10	10	1		1								31	
1966	14	0		6	8	10	10	1		1								28	
1967	14	2		1	11	9	9	1		1								25	
1968	16	3		3	10	8	10	1		1								28	
1969	16	0		4	12	10	10	1		1								23	
1970	19	2		5	12	11	11	1		1								29	
1971	16	2		7	7	10	11	1		1								28	
1972	17	2		6	9	10	11	1		1								24	
1973	16	3		8	5	7	11	1		1								22	
1974	9	1		5	3	9	11	1		1	9	2		1	6	9	10	24	
1975	9	0		4	5	11	11	1		1	9	1			8	10	10	25	
1976	10	4		2	4	6	11	1		1	9	4			5	5	10	24	
1977	10	2		4	4	7	11	1		1	9	3			6	8	10	25	
1978	10	4		3	3	5	11	3	2	1	9	3			6	8	10	19	Cup Runners-up
1979	10	3		3	4	6	11	1		1	9	4			5	6	10	24	
1980	10	2		3	5	11	12	1		1	9	6			3	3	10	21	
1981	10	5		3	2	4	11	2	1	1	10	2	1	1	6	11	11	21	
1982	10	2		2	6	11	12	1		1	10	3			7	11	11	20	
1983	6	0		4	2	6	7	2	1	1	11	3	1		7	9	12	24	
1984	12	1	1	4	6	11	13	1		1	5	1			4	6	6	20	
1985	12	1		4	7	13	13	3	2	1	5	0		2	3	6	6	22	Cup Runners-up
1986	12	4		4	4	9	13	1		1	5	0			5	6	6	24	
1987	12	4		3	5	8	13	1		1	5	1			4	6	6	18	
1988	12	3		3	6	12	13	1		1	5	1		1	3	5	6	27	
1989	11	0		5	6	13	13	1		1	5	0			5	6	6	23	
1990	13	4		3	6	12	14	2	1	1	5	1			4	5	6	24	

Year																		
1991	13	1		7	5	14	14	1		1	6	1			5	7	7	25	
1992	13	1		1	11	13	14	1		1	6	0			6	7	7	32	
1993	12	2		5	5	5	7	1		1	5	0			5	6	6	25	
1994	12	2		4	6	7	7	2	1	1	6	3			3	4	7	24	Junior Status Averted
1995	12	8		3	1	2	7	4	3	1	6	3			3	4	7	17	Lge & Cup Runners-up
1996	12	4		4	4	4	7	1		1	7	4			3	3	8	16	
1997	12	10		2	0	1	7	3	2	1	8	4	1		3	2	8	21	Senior B Lge Winners
1998	12	4		0	8	6	7	3	2	1	9	6			3	2	8	22	Lewis Traub Lge Runners-up
1999	12	11		0	1	1	7	2	1	1	9	8			1	1	8	22	Lewis Traub, WMK B Lge Winners
2000	12	9		1	2	2	7	2	1	1	7	5	1		1	1	6	22	Lewis Traub B Lge Winners; WMK A Lge Runners-up
2001	12	7		2	3	1	7	1		1	8	5	1		2	2	7	22	Lewis Traub Lge Runners-up; WMK A Lge Winners
2002	12	8		2	2	2	7	4	3	1	7	4	1		2	2	7	26	WMK A Lge Runners-up; Cup Runners-up
2003	12	3			9	6	7	1		1	6	2	1		3	5	7	31	
2004	12	5		1	6	5	7	3	2	1	6	2			4	5	7	28	
2005	12	4			8	5	7	1		1	3	1			2	3	4	29	
2006	12	9			3	2	7	1		1	4	2			2	2	4	27	WMK B Lge Runners-up
2007	12	4		5	4	4	7	3	2	1	6	6				1	4	21	DGM Lge Winners; Antalis Cup Runners-up
2008	12	4		5	3	2	7	2	1	1	3	1	1		1	2	4	20	WM A Lge Runners-up
2009	12	7			5	4	7	1		1	3	1	1		1	2	4	21	
2010	13	7			6	4	8	1		1								23	

O. SENIOR & JUNIOR RECORDS – OTHER NOTABLE COMPETITION PERFORMANCES, 1906-2010

Year	Team	Competition	Result
1914	1sts	Junior League, Div. 2	Winners
1916	1sts	Junior League, Div. B	Runners-up
1918	1sts	Junior League, Div. 1	Runners-up
1920	2nds	Junior League	Winners
1921	1sts	Intermediate League, Div. B	Runners-up
1923	1sts	Intermediate League	Runners-up
1924	1sts	Intermediate League	Winners
1925	1sts	Intermediate League	Winners; **Promoted**

1928	2nds	Intermediate Cup	Runners up
1929	2nds	Intermediate Cup	Winners
1936	3rds	Junior League, Div. D	Runners-up
1939	2nds	Intermediate Cup	Runners-up
1942	2nds	Intermediate League, Div. 3	Winners
1942	3rds	Junior League, Div. 1	Runners-up
1942	Under-18s	Vacation League	Winners
1943	2nds	Intermediate League	Winners
1943	3rds	Junior League	Winners
1943	4ths	Minor Cup	Runners-up
1943	Under-18s	Vacation League	Runners-up
1944	4ths	Minor League	Winners
1945	2nds	Senior 2 League	Winners
1945	3rds	Junior Cup	Runners-up
1952	4ths	Minor Cup	Runners-up
1953	4ths	Minor Cup	Winners
1954	2nds	Senior 2 League, Div. B	Runners-up
1955	2nds	Senior 2 League	Runners-up
1956	3rds	Intermediate League	Runners-up
1957	2nds	Senior 2 League	Runners-up
1958	4ths	Junior League	Winners
1959	4ths	Junior League	Runners-up
1960	3rds	Intermediate League	Winners
1961	4ths	Junior League	Winners
1962	3rds	Intermediate Cup	Runners-up
1968	Under-18s	Vacation League	Winners
1971	3rds	Intermediate Cup	Runners-up
1974	3rds	Intermediate Cup	Winners
1976	Under-13s	Mini-Cricket Cup	Winners
1976	Under-13As	Under-13A League	Winners
1976	Under-13Bs	Under-13B League	Runners-up
1976	Under-15s	League	Runners-up
1977	3rds	Intermediate League, Div. A	Runners-up
1977	3rds	Intermediate Cup	Runners-up
1978	4ths	Intermediate League, Div. C	Winners
1978	Under-15s	Robertson Cup	Winners
1978	Under-15s	Yates Hale Cup	Runners-up
1978	Under-13s	Jeyes Cup (Southern Section)	Winners
1978	Under-11s	Mini-Cricket Competition	Winners
1979	3rds	Middle League	Winners

1980	Under-18s	Amoroso Cup	Winners
1981	2nds	Senior 3 League	Winners
1981	2nds	Senior 2/3 Cup	Runners-up
1982	3rds	Middle Cup	Winners
1983	5ths	Junior League, Div. C	Runners-up
1984	Under-13s	Jeyes Cup	Winners
1985	2nds	Senior 2 League	Runners-up
1985	3rds	Middle B League	Winners
1986	2nds	Senior 2 Cup	Runners-up
1986	4ths	Intermediate Cup	Runners-up
1986	5ths	Junior Cup	Winners
1986	4ths/5ths/6ths	Whelan 20 Overs Cup	Winners
1987	2nds/3rds	Tillain 20 Overs Cup	Runners-up
1987	4ths	Intermediate League, Div. A	Winners
1987	4ths/5ths	Whelan 20 Overs Cup	Runners-up
1987	5ths	Intermediate League, Div. B	Runners-up
1987	6ths	Junior League, Div. B	Winners
1987	6ths	Minor Cup	Runners-up
1988	2nds	Senior 2 League	Runners-up
1990	4ths	Intermediate League, Div. A	Winners
1992	2nds	Senior 2 Cup	Winners
1992	3rds	YMCA 20 Overs Salver	Winners
1992	5ths	Minor Cup	Winners
1993	3rds	Middle Cup	Winners
1993	4ths	Intermediate League, Div. A	Runners-up
1993	4ths/5ths	Whelan 20 Overs Cup	Winners
1993	5ths	Junior B League	Winners
1993	5ths	Junior Cup	Winners
1995	2nds	Senior 2 Cup	Winners
1995	3rds	Middle A League	Winners
1995	4ths	Intermediate Cup	Winners
1995	6ths	Junior League, Div. C	Winners
1996	1sts	Beckett Cup	Winners
1996	1sts	Alan Murray 20 Overs Cup	Winners
1996	2nds/3rds	Tillain 20 Overs Cup	Winners
1996	4ths	YMCA 20 Overs Salver	Runners-up
1996	Under-13s	Top Four & Jeyes Cups	Winners
1996	Under-18s	Amoroso Cup	Winners
1996	Under-18s	Sean McGrath Cup	Winners
1997	1sts	Alan Murray 20 Overs Cup	Winners

1997	2nds	Senior 2 Cup	Runners-up
1997	2nds/3rds	Tillain 20 Overs Cup	Runners-up
1997	4ths	Middle League, Div. B	Winners
1997	5ths	Junior League, Div. A	Winners
1997	7ths	Junior League, Div. C	Runners-up
1998	1sts	Beckett Cup Winners	Winners
1998	1sts	Alan Murray 20 Overs Cup	Winners
1998	2nds/3rds	Tillain 20 Overs Cup	Runners-up
1998	3rds	Middle Cup	Winners
1998	4ths	Middle League, Div. A	Runners-up
1998	6ths	Junior Cup	Winners
1999	1sts	Alan Murray 20 Overs Cup	Winners
1999	3rds	Senior 3 League	Runners-up
1999	4ths	YMCA 20 Overs Salver	Runners-up
1999	6ths	Junior League, Div. B	Winners
1999	7ths	Minor Cup	Runners-up
2000	1sts	Beckett Cup	Winners
2000	2nds	Senior 2 Cup	Winners
2000	2nds/3rds	Tillain 20 Overs Cup	Winners
2000	3rds	Middle Cup	Runners-up
2000	7ths	Junior League, Div. C	Runners-up
2000	Under-13s	Jeyes Cup	Winners
2000	Under-15s	Yates Hale Cup	Winners
2000	Under-17s	Amoroso Cup	Runners-up
2001	1sts	Alan Murray 20 Overs Cup	Winners
2001	4ths	Middle B League	Winners
2002	1sts	Alan Murray 20 Overs Cup	Winners
2002	2nds	Senior 2 Cup	Winners
2002	2nds	Senior 2 League	Winners
2002	2nds/3rds	Tillian 20 Overs Cup	Winners
2002	3rds	Middle A League	Runners-up
2002	6ths	Junior Cup	Winners
2002	Under-15s	Yates Hale Cup	Winners
2002	Under-15s	Robertson Cup	Winners
2002	Under-19s	Sean McGrath Cup	Winners
2003	2nds	Senior 2 League	Runners-up
2003	2nds	Senior 2 Cup	Winners
2003	5ths/6ths/7ths	Whelan 20 Overs Cup	Runners-up
2003	Under-17s	Amoroso Cup	Winners
2004	2nds	Senior 2 League	Winners

2004	3rds	Middle Cup	Runners-up
2004	4ths	Middle 2 Cup	Winners
2004	5ths	Intermediate Cup	Runners-up
2004	5ths/6ths/7ths/8ths	Whelan 20 Overs Cup	Winners
2004	6ths	Junior Cup	Winners
2004	Under-17s	Amoroso Cup	Winners
2005	1sts	Alan Murray 20 Overs Cup	Winners
2005	2nds	Senior 2 League	Runners-up
2005	4ths	Middle B Leaugue	Runners-up
2005	5ths	Intermediate B League	Winners
2005	5ths/6ths/7ths/8ths	Whelan 20 Overs Cup	Runners-up
2005	6ths	Junior A League	Runners-up
2005	6ths	Junior Cup	Winners
2005	8ths	Junior C League	Runners-up
2005	Under-11s	All-Ireland Cup	Winners
2005	Under-13Bs	Caprani Cup	Winners (Shared)
2005	Under-17s	Amoroso Cup	Winners
2005	Under-19s	Sean McGrath Cup	Winners
2006	3rds	Senior 3 League	Winners
2006	3rds	Middle Cup	Winners
2006	6ths	Intermediate Cup	Winners
2006	8ths	Junior C League	Runners-up
2006	Under-9s	Mini-Cricket Cup	Winners (shared)
2006	Under-11s	Molins Cup	Winners (shared)
2006	Under-11As	Tolan Cup	Winners (shared)
2006	Under-13As	Jeyes Cup	Winners (shared)
2006	Under-13s	Watkins Cup	Winners (shared)
2006	Under-13	All-Ireland Cup	Winners (shared)
2006	Under-13Bs	Caprani Cup	Winners (shared)
2006	Under-19s	Sean McGrath Cup	Winners (shared)
2007	2nds	Senior 2 League	Winners
2007	2nds	Senior 2 Cup	Winners
2007	8ths	Minor Cup	Runners-up
2007	Under-11s	Fingal Cup	Runners-up
2007	Under-13s	All-Ireland Cup	Runners-up
2007	Under-13As	Jeyes Cup	Winners
2007	Under-13s	Watkins Cup	Winners
2007	Under-13s	Top 4 Beamers Cup	Winners
2007	Under-13Bs	Caprani Cup	Winners
2008	1sts	LHW 20 Overs Cup	Runners-up

2008	2nds	Senior 2 League	Winners
2008	6ths	Intermediate B League	Runners-up
2008	6ths	Intermediate Cup	Runners-up
2008	8ths	Minor Cup	Runners-up
2009	2nds/3rds	Tillain Cup	Runners-up
2009	3rds	Middle Cup	Winners
2009	5ths	Intermediate A League	Runners-up
2009	6ths	Intermediate B League	Winners
2009	5ths/6ths/7ths/8ths	Whelan Cup	Winners
2009	8ths	Junior C League	Runners-up
2009	Under-15s	Yates Hale Cup	Winners
2010	1sts	Irish Senior Cup	Winners
2010	3rds	Middle Cup	Winners
2010	4ths	Division 6	Runners-up
2010	6ths	Division 9	Winners
2010	7ths	Division 12	Runners-up

P. SENIOR & JUNIOR RECORDS – PROVINCIAL AWARDS, 1906-2010, EXCLUDING PROFESSIONALS

Year	Level	Player	Award Details
1929	1sts	T. O'Neill Kiely	Bowling: 16 @ 5.68 in 4 games
1929	1sts	C.J. Little	Catches: 6 in 6 games
1937	1sts	C.J. Little	All-rounders: 246 @ 30.75; 32 @ 33.37
1940	1sts	C.J. Little	All-rounders: 346 @ 31.45; 29 @ 16.86
1940	1sts	W.L. Lindsay	W/K: ct 16; st 8; total 24
1943	1sts	P.H. Waldron	Marchant Batting Cup: 487 @ 40.58 (League only)
1947	2nds	J.A. O'Donnell	Bookman Batting Cup: average of 42.87
1949	1sts	S.A. Curley	Catches: 14 in 12 games
1950	1sts	S.A. Curley	Catches: 13 in 13 games
1951	1sts	S.A. Curley	Marchant Batting Cup: 536 @ 59.55
1952	1sts	S.A. Curley	All-rounders: 343 @ 42.87; 24 @ 16.20
1957	2nds	T.F. MacMahon	Bookman Batting Cup: average of 42.87
1958	1sts	S.A. Curley	Marchant Batting Cup: 652 @ 59.27 (2=Unique)
1958	1sts	J.P. Burke	All-rounders: 278 @ 23.16; 34 @ 9.14
1976	2nds	K. Allwright	Bookman Batting Cup: 304 @ 76.00 in 5 games
1981	1sts	D.B. Robinson	Samuels All-rounders Cup: 746 @ 39.26; 45 @ 14.73
1983	1sts	J. O'Hagan	Catches: 15 in 18 games

1988	2nds	D. McKenna	Oulton Cup for bowling: 46 @ 7.78 (1=Unique)
1997	1sts	D. Poder	O'Grady Bowling Cup: 46 @ 8.91
1998	1sts	A. Fleming	O'Grady Bowling Cup: 46 @ 17.74
1999	1sts	D. Poder	O'Grady Bowling Cup: 43 @ 12.02 (2=Unique)
1999	1sts	A. Joyce	Hopkins W/K Cup: ct 26; st 5; total 31
1999	1sts	J. Morrissey Jnr.	Catches: 21 in 20 games (NB Scott–12; website–21)
2000	1sts	B. Spanner	Samuels All-rounders Cup: 1201 @ 85.79; 25 @ 14.76
2001	1sts	B. Spanner	Solomons Catching Cup: 14 in 18 games
2002	1sts	B. Spanner	Samuels All-rounders Cup: 977 @ 61.06; 38 @ 15.76
2002	1sts	K. Beasley	Hopkins W/K Cup: ct 27; st 4; total 31
2003	2nds	S. King	Sean Pender Memorial Award
2004	1sts	K. Beasley	Hopkins W/K Cup: ct 26; st 14; total 40 (2=Unique)
2005	2nds	R. Allwright	Webster All-rounders Cup (1=Unique)
2007	1sts	R. Keaveney	O'Grady Bowling Cup: 31 @ 13.54 (Aged 17)
2007	2nds	D. Drane	Sean Pender Memorial Award.
2008	1sts	T. Patel	O'Grady Bowling Cup: 25 @ 13.16
2008	2nds	D. Drane	Sean Pender Memorial Award

Q. MERRION RECORDS – SCHOOLS ATTENDED, 1906-2010

Based on profiles.

No. & Percentage of Players by School		
School	No.	Percentage
CUS	14	16.47
Blackrock	13	15.29
Presentation College, Bray	4	4.71
St Andrew's	3	3.53
Gonzaga	3	3.53
Mountjoy	3	3.53
Wesley	2	2.35
High School	2	2.35
Synge Street	2	2.35
Others	39	45.89
Total	**85**	**100.00**